D0390573

Cyprus

Vesna Maric

To Alanya
(Turkey; 150km)

To Taşucu
(Turkey; 60km)

33° E

MEDITERRANEAN
SEA

BELLAPAIS (p193)
Fabulous views, an enchanting
Augustinian monastery and former
home of writer Lawrence Durell

KYRENIA (p185)
A beautiful crescent-shaped harbour
sheltered by a burly Byzantine fort

ST HILARION CASTLE (p196)
A dreamy, ruined castle that inspired fairy
tales sits high in the mountains near Kyrenia

AKAMAS PENINSULA (p131)
This is nature's realm, where
the Mediterranean is untamed

Koruçam
Burnu
(Cape
Kormakitis)

Lapta
(Lapithos)

KYRENIA
(Girne)

KORUÇAM
(KORMAKITIS)
PENINSULA

Geçitköy
(Panagra)

St Hilarion
Castle

Bellap
(Beylerbe

BYZANTINE CHURCHES (p100)
Adore the images of the divine
at the Unesco-protected frescoed
churches of the Troödos Massif

BEŞPARMAK
(PENTADACTYLOS)
RANGE

Yilmazköy
(Skylloura)

Morfou
Bay

Agios Don
Crossir

UN Buffer Zone

MORFOU
(Güzelyurt)

LEFKO
NOR
NICO

Kokkina
(Erenköy)

Ancient
Vouni

Zodhia
Crossing

Pomos

Yeşilirmak
(Limnitis)

Peristerona

Ancient
Soloi

Orounda

Cape
Arnaoutis

Chrysochou
Bay

TYLLIRIA

SOLEA

MESAOR

B7

PAFOS FOREST

B9

ADELFI
FOREST

Ancient
Tamassos

AKAMAS
PENINSULA

Latsi

Polis

MARATHASA

Stavros tou
Agiasmati

Monastery of
Agios Irakleidios

Neo Horio

AKAMAS
HEIGHTS

Kakopetria

Mt Tripylos
(1362m)

CEDAR
VALLEY

PITSYLIA

MAHERA
FOREST

Terra Kritou

Kykkos
Monastery

TROÖDOS
MASSIF

Lara Beach

Ano Arodes

Mt Olympus
(1952m)

Troödos

Maheras
Monastery

REPUBLIC

Troöditissa
Monastery

Makria
Kontarka
(1680m)

Mt Papoutsa
(1554m)

Pano
Lefkara

OF

Mt Kionia
(1423m)

Ka
Lef

Coral
Bay

CYPRUS

B7

B8

Choirokoitia

PAFOS

A6

A1

Zy

Kouklia

Pafos
International
Airport

A6

Sanctuary of
Apollon Ylatis

Episkopi

Kolossi
Castle

LEMESOS
(Limassol)

Ancient
Kourion

Akrotiri
Bay

Petra tou Romiou
(Aphrodite's Rock
& Beach)

Cape
Aspro

Episkopi
Bay

Akrotiri

AKROTIRI
PENINSULA

KYKKOS MONASTERY (p110)
Cyprus' most important
religious site bigs it up with
wealth on display

Akrotiri Sovereign Base
Area (Great Britain)

TROÖDOS MASSIF (p98)
Trekking trails and cool mountain
refuges draw hikers and nature-love

PAFOS (p118)
Mosaics display Greek myths,
and morbidity and mystery
surround the Tombs of the Kings

ANCIENT KOURION (p94)
Cyprus' most stunning
archaeological site overlooks
the vast Mediterranean

33° E

(Cruise Ship Route Only)

To Rhodes (Greece; 400km);
Piraeus (Greece; 800km)

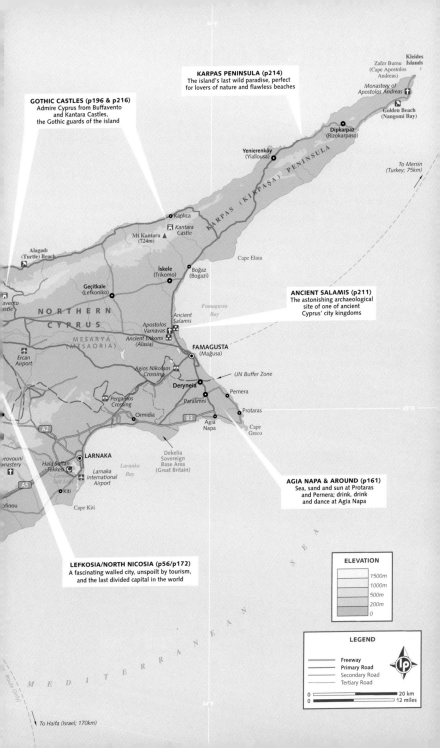

GOTHIC CASTLES (p196 & p216)
Admire Cyprus from Buffavento
and Kantara Castles,
the Gothic guards of the island

KARPAS PENINSULA (p214)
The island's last wild paradise, perfect
for lovers of nature and flawless beaches

Kleides
Islands
Zafer Burnu
(Cape Apostolos
Andreas)
Monastery of
Apostolos Andreas

Golden Beach
(Nangomi Bay)

Dipkarpaz
(Rizokarpaso)

Yenierenköy
(Yiallousa)

To Mersin
(Turkey; 75km)

Kaplica

Kantara
Castle

Mt Kantara
(724m)

Alagadı
(Turtle) Beach

İskele
(Trikomo)

Boğaz
(Bogazi)

Cape Elaia

Geçitkale
(Lefkoniko)

ANCIENT SALAMIS (p211)
The astonishing archaeological
site of one of ancient
Cyprus' city kingdoms

N O R T H E R N

C Y P R U S

Famagusta
Bay

avento
astle

M E S A R Y A
(M E S A O R I A)

Ancient
Salamis

Apostolos
Varnavas

Ercan
Airport

Ancient Enkomi
(Alasia)

FAMAGUSTA
(Mağusa)

Agios Nikolaos
Crossing

UN Buffer Zone

Deryneia

Pernera

Pergamos
Crossing

Paralimni

Ormidia

Protaras

Agia
Napa

Cape
Greco

rovouni
nastery

LARNAKA

Halá Sultan
Tekkes

B3

A2

Dekelia
Sovereign
Base Area
(Great Britain)

Larnaka
Bay

Larnaka
International
Airport

A5

AGIA NAPA & AROUND (p161)
Sea, sand and sun at Protaras
and Pernera; drink, drink
and dance at Agia Napa

Kiti

ofinou

Cape Kiti

LEFKOSIA/NORTH NICOSIA (p56/p172)
A fascinating walled city, unspoilt by tourism,
and the last divided capital in the world

M E D I T E R R A N E A N

S E A

Route Only)

To Haifa (Israel; 170km)

ELEVATION

1500m
1000m
500m
200m
0

LEGEND

Freeway
Primary Road
Secondary Road
Tertiary Road

0 ————— 20 km
0 ————— 12 miles

Destination Cyprus

Floating on the waters of the European Mediterranean, but pointing longingly towards the shores of Syria, Turkey and Lebanon, Cyprus is an odd mixture. It is a kaleidoscopic blend: its cultural influences are dominated by Western Europe, but its geographic proximity to Asia and Africa gives it more than just a hint of the East. Long coveted by mainland Greece and Turkey, this small island has its own definite and beguiling character.

Whether you know it as the 'island of sin' (or 'fun') thanks to wild stories from Agia Napa; the country that entered the EU only as a half; or, as the tourist brochures love to point out, 'the island of Aphrodite', Cyprus both confirms and confounds the stereotype.

Parts of Cyprus have been overrun by keen developers who (depending on who you're talking to) have either 'sold the country's soul' or 'are bringing great wealth to the island'. Whatever the truth, in places like Pafos, Agia Napa or Lemesos' tourist centre you might feel as if you've entered a sunny, scorching Essex suburb with lobster-red Brits letting it all hang loose with a lukewarm can of Foster's in tow.

But if curiosity draws you out of the cities, you'll discover the small villages of the Akamas Peninsula and the heavenly golden beaches of the Karpas (Kırpaşa) Peninsula. Walk the gorgeous Troödos and Kyrenia (Girne) mountain ranges and inhale the scent of the citrus groves of Morfou (Güzelyurt), or climb to the medieval castles with their shimmering island views. Wander through the sea of wildflowers covering the island in spring, and Cyprus will take your breath away. With good walking shoes, a swimsuit and some sunscreen in your bag, you can have a trip you'll remember for years.

Highlights

Stroll through the history-infused streets of Lefkosia (South Nicosia; p56)

Be awed by Petra tou Romiou
(Aphrodite's Rock & Beach; p93)

OTHER HIGHLIGHTS

- Get back to nature in Cedar Valley (p139), home of the unusual Cypriot cedar
- Visit Ancient Kourion (p94), one of the island's most impressive archaeological sites

Explore the fairytale ruins of
St Hilarion Castle (p196)

Hit the dance floor in Agia Napa (p161)

Travel back in time at the Pafos mosaics (p121)

OTHER HIGHLIGHTS

- Stretch out on Lara Beach (p131), the most spectacular beach in the South
- Don't miss enchanting Golden Beach (Nangomi Bay; p215), with sea so calm and clear, you may never want to leave

Wander through the Büyük Han (Great Inn; p176), once a medieval caravanserai, in the heart of North Nicosia (Lefkoşa)

JON DAVISON

Pay a visit to Kykkos Monastery (p110), Cyprus' richest and most famous religious institution

PAUL DAVID HELLANDER

Admire the columns at the
Sanctuary of Apollon Ylatis (p96)

Discover the countryside around Pafos (p116) and you might catch
a glimpse of the endangered moufflon

CHRIS CHRISTO

Experience traditional Cypriot life in
the Troödos Massif (p98)

Marvel at frescoed Byzantine churches such
as Agios Nikolaos tis Stegis (p112)

Contemplate the ruins of Ancient Salamis (p211)

OTHER HIGHLIGHTS

- Embrace the unique beauty of the Karpas
  (Kırpaşa) Peninsula (p214), far from the urban
  and tourist bustle
- Visit the Lala Mustafa Paşa Mosque (p207),
  Cyprus' finest example of Lusignan Gothic
  architecture
- Climb up to the heights of the island's ruined
  Gothic castles, Buffavento Castle (p196) and
  Kantara Castle (p216)

Contents

Regional Map Contents

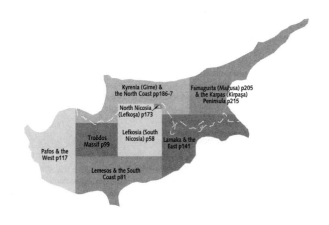

Kyrenia (Girne) &
the North Coast pp186-7

Famagusta (Mağusa) p205
& the Karpas (Kırpaşa)
Peninsula p215

North Nicosia
(Lefkoşa) p173

Lefkosia (South
Nicosia) p58

Troödos
Massif p99

Lamaka & the
East p141

Pafos & the
West p117

Lemesos & the South
Coast p81

The Author

VESNA MARIC

Vesna had her first taste of Cyprus when she visited a friend in the small village of Dhrousia on the Akamas Peninsula. Visiting Cyprus is always a different experience, as the country's changes are so rapid, and Vesna's curiosity about the island has never ceased. Cyprus' political troubles remind Vesna of the problems in her native Bosnia and Hercegovina, and she has always felt an affinity with the Cypriots from both sides of the Green Line. The landscape, beaches, fresh figs and haloumi (helimi) all lure her back for more.

My Favourite Trip

Starting from the crazy streets of North Nicosia (Lefkoşa; p172), I love the drive down to Kyrenia (Girne; p185), where a peek at the harbour is always a joy, before driving along the quiet north coast. Stopping off at beautiful Bellapais (Beylerbeyi) village (p193), and clambering up to St Hilarion and Buffavento Castles (p196) is a must. Further east Kantara Castle (p216) awaits, from where you can sigh over the beautiful views. It's Famagusta (Mağusa; p204) and Ancient Salamis (p211) next, and then relaxing at Golden Beach (Nangomi Bay; p215) on the Karpas (Kırpaşa) Peninsula, Cyprus' natural treasure.

From Lefkosia (South Nicosia; p56), I travel across the Troödos Massif (p99), visiting the area's frescoed Byzantine churches (p100), and then pay a visit to Lemesos (p82). I drive down the old B6 road to Pafos (p118) where I have some meze, and then it's up to Polis and the Akamas Peninsula (p131), with its beautiful villages. Finally, I settle down in the sun, at the amazing Lara Beach (p131).

Getting Started

Travelling to and through Cyprus is pretty effortless. Most people visit the island on package tours; it's also easy to get an independent flight, although these tend to get sold out and pricey in the peak summer months of June to September. Once there, you'll find everything that you can find at home and, particularly for Brits, there is a strange air of familiarity: apart from the fact that the island caters for swarms of British tourists, there are a number of colonial leftovers, like driving on the left. There is plenty of accommodation and, although package tours prevail, Cyprus works well for those who want to seek out lesser-known, quieter places. Getting yourself around this small island is easy by public transport or with your own wheels. Read up on Cyprus' history, pick up a couple phrases in Greek and Turkish, and your trip will be a fantastic treat that will stay with you for years.

WHEN TO GO

The best time to go to Cyprus depends on the kind of experience you wish to have. With its intense Mediterranean climate, the island's weather is easy to predict. The summer months of June to September are hot and action-packed. August in particular is the peak of Cyprus' tourist season, when the locals squeeze up next to the tourists on beaches and restaurant benches. Kids are on school holidays and things can get a bit raucous. Accommodation prices go up quite a lot during these months, so if you're on a budget, avoid the height of summer.

See Climate Charts (p224) for more information.

October to May are the quiet months of autumn, winter and spring, when the landscape is covered with wildflowers that seem to encompass every colour in the rainbow. Walking either the Troödos Massif or the Akamas Peninsula, or cycling the Karpas (Kırpaşa) Peninsula in the North is most enjoyable in the autumn and spring months. Autumn in October and spring in April and May are short and the transition between winter and summer is rapid. Rain falls mainly in autumn and winter, and outside these months precipitation is rare. Water shortages can be a real problem in Cyprus.

Winters are changeable, with cold and warmer weather alternating. Conditions also vary with elevation. The Troödos Massif usually gets some snow in winter and you can ski on Mt Olympus in the South from early January to mid-March.

DON'T LEAVE HOME WITHOUT...

- Clothes made from light-coloured and lightweight fabrics – you won't need heavier clothing or footwear unless you come in winter, or you plan to do some bushbashing in the Troödos Massif or Kyrenia (Girne) Range.
- A warm jacket if you plan to visit in winter. It can still get chilly, despite the country's Mediterranean climate.
- A good sunscreen, hat, sunglasses and mosquito repellent for the summer.
- The latest information on visas and travel between the Republic and the North (see the boxed text, p235).
- Your passport (which you'll have to flash if you intend to cross between the South and the North).
- Alka-Seltzers, if you're planning on partying in Agia Napa, that is.

Average daily summer temperatures in Lefkosia/North Nicosia are between 22°C and 37°C but often reach 40°C or more. From December to March the night temperature in the Troödos Massif is often below freezing.

COSTS & MONEY

Prices in Cyprus are reasonable in comparison to most Western European countries. The cost of tourist commodities in the North and the South tends to be similar, though the North is better value when it comes to eating out and also at the budget end of accommodation options. Items in supermarkets are probably more expensive than you will be used to paying. However, fruit and vegetables in local markets can be considerably cheaper than at home.

Accommodation in agrotourism houses in the South is usually around CY£30 for a double, and a meal with wine or beer in a local restaurant is around CY£12 to CY£15. In the North, bank on around UK£20 for a double room in a budget hotel and around 15YTL for a filling meal. Accommodation and general tourist services on both sides of the Green Line increase in price in July and August.

Prices quoted in this book are for the high season, unless otherwise stated.

In the South, costs for public transport – bus and service taxis – are low, though taxis are not such a bargain. Access to museums and archaeological sites never exceeds CY£1.50. However, entrance to such sites in the North is comparatively more expensive, with the average museum admission fee ranging from 4YTL to 6YTL.

Cyprus, in both the North and the South, has a 15% value-added tax (VAT), which is automatically added to the cost of more or less all services. An additional tax rate of between 2% and 10% is added to goods and services in Northern Cyprus. This tax and the VAT are not refundable to travellers upon departure.

TRAVEL LITERATURE

Lawrence Durrell's *Bitter Lemons of Cyprus* is a charming, funny and touching account of a Greek-speaking Englishman coming to live in Cyprus in the mid-1950s. The political tensions of the time serve as a backdrop to this classic of travel writing on Cyprus. Durrell lived in the village of Bellapais (Beylerbeyi) in Northern Cyprus and describes, in his inimitable style, life in Cyprus from the local point of view and from that of a willing expat colonial administrator.

Colin Thubron's *Journey Into Cyprus* was the last significant travelogue of the unified Cyprus, written following an amazing, almost 1000km walk undertaken in the spring and summer of 1972. Sprinkled with stories from the road and historical insight, this book is a must for anyone contemplating an extended visit to Cyprus.

Seamus MacHugh's *Cyprus: An Island Apart* is a modern travel memoir designed to give the short-term visitor a concise background to the island's history and culture, its archaeological treasures and its two religious contexts, together with the divisive politics of the island. Amusing anecdotes fill the pages and describe the quirkiness and foibles of Cyprus today.

If you want to know more about colonial Cyprus, read *My Old Acquaintance: Yesterday in Cyprus* by Barbara Cornwall. Cornwall recounts the customs of this bygone era drawn from the experiences and impressions of colonisers, pilgrims, churchmen, adventurers, military men, travellers and scholars who have visited the island over the centuries.

HOW MUCH?

Republic of Cyprus

Frappé CY£2

A feast of meze CY£6 to CY£10

Internet CY£1 per hour

Small-car hire CY£25

Museum ticket CY£0.50 to CY£1.50

Northern Cyprus

Two strong black Turkish coffees 5YTL

A meal 12YTL to 15YTL

Internet 1YTL per hour

Small-car hire UK£25

Museum ticket 4YTL to 6YTL

See also Lonely Planet Index, inside front cover.

TOP FIVES

Festivals & Events

Cyprus has some diverse and fun festivals all year round, with the locals gathering to drink, dance and have a good time. Religious festivals are important, particularly in the South. For more information on festivals and events in Cyprus, see p226.

- Carnival in Lemesos (February/March; p87)
- Easter Celebrations (March/April; p226)
- Bellapais Music Festival (May & June; p195)
- Lemesos Wine Festival (30 August– 11 September; p87)
- Pafos Aphrodite Festival (2–4 September; p124)

Beaches

Whether you like it hot and crowded or hot and deserted, Cyprus has plenty of pebbles and sand to stretch out on.

- Golden Beach (Nangomi Bay; p215)
- The beach at Agios Filon (p215)
- Lara Beach (p131)
- Petra tou Romiou (Aphrodite's Rock & Beach; p93)
- Konnos Beach (p170)

Ancient Sites

With a history like this, the island of Cyprus has more ancient sites than you can shake an archaeology buff at.

- Ancient Kourion (p94), west of Lemesos
- Ancient Salamis (p211), northwest of Famagusta (Mağusa)
- Pafos mosaics (p121), Pafos
- Tombs of the Kings (p120), Pafos
- Choirokoitia (p152), northeast of Lemesos

INTERNET RESOURCES

Cypnet (www.cypnet.com) One of the more useful sites on the North with information on history, accommodation, restaurants and more.

Cyprus Mail (www.cyprus-mail.com) An English-language daily, excellent for keeping up with news and features about the Republic of Cyprus.

Cyprus Tourism Organisation (www.visitcyprus.org.cy) The official website of the Republic's Cyprus Tourism Organisation (CTO), useful for general tourist information and basic government data.

GoNorthCyprus (www.gonorthcyprus.com) This site is handy for finding your flights, hotels and package holidays online, and offers 'email deals'.

Lonely Planet (www.lonelyplanet.com) Succinct summaries on travelling to most places on earth; the Thorn Tree bulletin board is great for exchanging up-to-date information with other travellers.

Ministry of Economy & Tourism (www.holidayinnorthcyprus.com) Good for updates on events and festivals in Northern Cyprus.

Itineraries

CLASSIC ROUTES

GEMS OF THE REPUBLIC OF CYPRUS   10 to 14 Days

Fly into **Larnaka** (p142) and dip your feet into the Mediterranean at the beaches around the nightlife centre of **Agia Napa** (p161) for a day, before taking a bus or taxi for the short trip to the capital, **Lefkosia** (South Nicosia; p56). Spend a couple of days exploring the city's walled old section and the modern streets that spill out from the ancient confines. From the capital, head up into the mountains for some trekking and cycling at **Troödos** (p100), and admire the divine images at the many **Byzantine churches** (p100). If hiking's not your thing, you can explore the mountain villages, and get tipsy on wine from the region's **krasohoria** (wine villages; p107).

From the Troödos Massif, roll down to **Lemesos** (p82) and enjoy the city's crazy nightlife and sample its varied cuisine, but spend most of your time exploring **Ancient Kourion** (p94), outside the city. Don't miss the excellent beaches, and make sure you bathe at the divine **Petra tou Romiou** (Aphrodite's Rock & Beach; p93), and perhaps catch some of the goddess' amorous powers.

Head west to **Pafos** (p118), where you can enjoy more ancient remains by viewing the **Pafos mosaics** (p121) and the mysterious **Tombs of the Kings** (p120). Base yourself in any one of the wonderful traditional restored houses in the **Akamas Peninsula** (p131), from where you can enjoy days of trekking and swimming at some of the most wonderful beaches in the South, such as **Lara Beach** (p131). The Akamas Peninsula is also the best place to glimpse traditional Cypriot life. Fly home either from Larnaka or Pafos.

Explore the beauties of the coast and inland terrains of the Republic of Cyprus. Experience ancient sights, mountain trekking and the life of exciting cities and traditional villages, before cooling off in the waters of the Mediterranean.

NORTHERN LIGHTS:
A JOURNEY THROUGH NORTHERN CYPRUS   10 to 14 Days

Providing you fly into Ercan airport, your first port of call will be **Famagusta** (Mağusa; p204). And a wonderful first stop it is, with its **Venetian walls** (p206) and the gorgeous **Lala Mustafa Paşa Mosque** (p207), originally a Lusignan Gothic church. From Famagusta, head straight to **Ancient Salamis** (p211), the island's most spectacular ancient site, with elaborate remains from the 6th century BC city kingdom.

Follow the highway to the capital, **North Nicosia** (Lefkoşa; **p172**), and spend a day or two exploring its **Old City** (p174), the **Büyük Han** (Great Inn; p176) and the **Selimiye Mosque** (p176). For all this, base yourself in **Kyrenia** (Girne; p185), only a short drive away from the capital. In Kyrenia, visit the dark caves of **Kyrenia Castle** (p187) and see the oldest shipwreck in Cyprus. Head up to **Bellapais** (Beylerbeyi; p193), and admire the ruins of **Bellapais Abbey** (p193), founded by Augustinian priests in the 12th century. Nearby, visit the dreamy **St Hilarion Castle** (p196), the place that is supposed to have inspired Disney's *Snow White*.

Head west to **Ancient Soloi** (p202) and **Ancient Vouni** (p202). Return to Kyrenia and drive east, following the spectacular road along the **north coast** (p197), forgotten by time and untouched by tourist development. Hike up to **Buffavento Castle** (p196), one of the three Lusignan castles perched on top of the Kyrenia Range, and then drive further east down the coast. Take the windy road up to **Kantara Castle** (p216) from where you can see Cyprus in its entirety. Drive down to the most beautiful part of the island, the **Karpas (Kırpaşa) Peninsula** (p214), ideal for lovers of nature, and for untouched landscapes. This area has the island's best beaches, such as **Golden Beach** (Nangomi Bay; p215) where turtles come to hatch. Fly home from Ercan airport.

A journey through Northern Cyprus, the island's lesser-known part, is a dizzying mix of Lusignan, Gothic and Islamic architecture, half-forgotten ancient sites and wild, unexplored nature. Take your time, indulge yourself and relax on golden beaches.

TAILORED TRIPS

ANCIENT TOURISM

Cyprus is a delight for travellers with a penchant for ancient sites and remains from the numerous empires that once ruled the island.

Ancient Kourion (p94) is regarded by many as one of the most spectacular ancient sites in the Republic, and it's certainly the most important.

Ancient Salamis (p211), the North's archaeological treasure, dates back to the 7th century BC, and bears the title of being one of the first cities in Cyprus.

Choirokoitia (p152), a Unesco World Heritage site since 1998, is the oldest archaeological site in the country. It dates from 6800 BC, when it housed more than 2000 people in the characteristic round houses that the inhabitants usually built over the graves of their dead.

The large **Pafos Archaeological Site** (Nea Pafos; p120) has been a Unesco World Heritage site since 1980. It holds the fascinating **Pafos mosaics** (p121), the most impressive being the House of Dionysus, a rich man's mansion with floors covered in intricate mosaics based on Greek mythology. Also part of the archaeological site, the morbid **Tombs of The Kings** (p120) has 100 tombs that were used to bury the town's wealthy population in the 3rd century BC.

The **Sanctuary of Apollon Ylatis** (p96) was a gathering place for pilgrims in 8th century BC, but was destroyed by an earthquake. Subsequently rebuilt, the present ruins date back to AD 365.

The North's two sites of **Ancient Soloi** (p202) and **Ancient Vouni** (p202) played a major role in the island's struggle against the Persians, in the 5th century BC. Soloi, a city loyal to the Greeks, struggled against the Persians, and Vouni was built by a Persian-supporting king from Marion (now Polis).

The frescoed **Byzantine churches** (p100) at Troödos are not to be missed, with their vivid images of scenes from the Bible. Ten of the churches are listed as Unesco World Heritage sites.

Lala Mustafa Paşa Mosque (p207) in Famagusta, is an exquisite piece of Gothic architecture.

Bellapais Abbey (p193), founded by exiled Augustinian monks in the 12th century, was an important spiritual centre for 300 years.

CYPRUS, NATURALLY

The island, although small and largely overbuilt, still has some stunning untouched nature.

The deserted and protected **Karpas Peninsula** (p214) will linger in your memory for years to come. This 'tail end' of the island positively has the best beaches, deserted and clean, with soft golden sand. Turtles hatch at **Golden Beach** (p215), where there is an official turtle-hatching protection programme. Wild donkeys, once Cyprus' equivalent of a lorry and even a currency, roam the endless fields undisturbed and none too friendly.

The **Akamas Peninsula** (p131) is the South's answer to the Karpas Peninsula. The Akamas Peninsula is ideal for trekking, swimming and getting to know the island's traditional villages. The rocky Mediterranean landscape has the region's typical juniper bushes and low pines, and the South's best beach, **Lara Beach** (p131), is a turtle-hatching zone. The **Tyllirian wilderness** (p136) has the lovely **Cedar Valley** (p139), bearing thousands of *Cedrus brevifolia,* an aromatic cedar type indigenous to Cyprus.

The **Troödos Massif** (p101) offers some of the island's best hiking opportunities, with four marked trails: the Artemis Trail, beneath Mt Olympus, the Troödos' tallest peak; the Atalanti Trail, leading you to a clear spring; the Caledonia Trail, where you follow the song of the nightingales; and the Persephone Trail, with nothing but amazing scenery.

Larnaka's salt lake (p151) is a magnet for migrant birds, including flamingos.

Snapshot

Since the one-legged entry into the EU in May 2004 of the internationally recognised Greek part of Cyprus, and the victory of moderate leader Mehmet Ali Talat in the Turkish Cypriot North the following year, the state of Cyprus' bi-communal relations is the hottest topic on the country's news agenda.

A month before the EU entry, Kofi Annan's reunification plan was rejected by nearly 76% of the Greek Cypriot population and, in contrast, endorsed by 65% of Turkish Cypriots. The 'Annan plan' envisaged a loose federal structure for the island, where many Greek Cypriots could return and recover some of the land they lost in the 1974 partition. Greek Cypriots were unhappy that the plan limited their right to return, while allowing tens of thousands of Turkish settlers, introduced since 1974, to remain.

Feelings ran high during this period as both the Greek Cypriot president Tassos Papadopoulos and the then Turkish Cypriot leader Rauf Denktaş urged a 'no' vote. (For more on Denktaş, see the boxed text, p29.) With the spectacular failure to reach agreement, the Republic of Cyprus entered the EU on its own, and Turkish Cypriots, much congratulated on their positive vote for the plan, were promised financial rewards by the EU.

The second most important change in the country is the present-day ease of crossing the once-menacing Green Line (part of the Attila Line) that divides Cyprus.

In the past, crossing the border was permitted only for diplomats, and under extreme circumstances (such as medical emergencies) for Greek and Turkish Cypriots. However, following a sudden and controversial decision by Denktaş in April 2003, it has become possible to cross to either side by car or on foot and to stay on the other side for up to three months.

When the Green Line first opened, hundreds of Cypriots, both Turkish and Greek, made the emotionally charged trip to the opposing side to visit their former homes, friends and, for some, family they hadn't seen for more than three decades. (For more background on the situation, see the boxed text, p30; for border-crossing information for travellers, see the boxed text, p235.)

April 2005 saw a historic change in the leadership of Northern Cyprus. Rauf Denktaş, who had lead the Turkish Cypriots since the 1974 partition, was replaced by the more moderate Mehmet Ali Talat, who had served as prime minister under Denktaş and was openly supportive of the 'Annan plan'.

Perhaps Turkey's EU entry talks, which are predicted to last until 2015, and its agreement to recognise the government of the Republic of Cyprus for the duration of the talks, will set the wheels in motion for resolution.

Meanwhile, the checkpoints continue to open across the island. Many tourists visiting the North fly directly to Larnaka in the Republic of Cyprus, and catch a taxi across the border. Crossing the border is easier for locals too. Turkish Cypriots have applied for Republic of Cyprus passports in their thousands, and many go to work on the other side of the border every day. In turn, Greek Cypriots drive to the North to gamble in the ubiquitous casinos.

FAST FACTS

Population: 780,133

GDP per capita: Republic of Cyprus US$20,300; Northern Cyprus US$7135

Inflation: Republic of Cyprus 2.4%; Northern Cyprus 12.6%

Unemployment: Republic of Cyprus 3.2%; Northern Cyprus 5.6%

Alleged number of eating and drinking spots: 4000 (that's roughly one for every five people)

Number of appearances at the Eurovision Song Contest: 25 (including one last place)

Third most important industry: cement production and export (after tourism, and food and beverage production). Could this explain the detrimental building frenzy across the island?

The accession of the Republic of Cyprus' to the EU means that the Cyprus pound (CY£) will be no more by 2007 to 2008; instead there will be the euro to spend.

The tragic events of 14 August 2005 saw Cyprus' biggest peacetime death toll, when a Helios Airways aeroplane plunged into a hill near Athens, killing all of its 121 passengers, most of them Greek Cypriots.

History

Situated at the maritime crossroads of the eastern Mediterranean basin, Cyprus has a rich and varied history. Many invaders, settlers and immigrants have come here over the centuries, and the island has seen Greeks, Romans, Byzantines, Lusignans, Genoese, Venetians, Ottomans, British and Turks seek to take a part of Cyprus for themselves.

Cypriots, whether Greek or Turkish, are proud of their nation and feel a strong sense of national identity. The division of their island in 1974 is viewed by many as a temporary setback, and Cypriots look to the day when Cyprus will be a united island once again.

www.ancientcyprus.ac.uk is the best site for dabbling in archaeology. Amateur or expert, you'll find plenty of resources here to aid your research of Cyprus' ancient history.

NEOLITHIC & CHALCOLITHIC CYPRUS

The first evidence of human habitation in Cyprus can be traced back to the Aceramic Neolithic period around 10,000 BC, with the discovery of manmade artefacts at the site of Akrotiri Aetokremnou, on the Akrotiri Peninsula on Cyprus' southern coast. These people may have brought about the extinction of the Pleistocene-era pygmy hippopotamus and dwarf elephant. By 8000 BC, domesticated animals such as cattle, pigs, sheep and goats had been introduced to Cyprus by agropasturalists from the Levantine mainland. This group laid the foundations for the development of the distinctively Cypriot culture best represented at the Aceramic Neolithic settlement of Choirokoitia (p152). Choirokoitia was an enclosed village built on the side of a hill in the southern part of the island in the 6th millennium BC. Its inhabitants lived in well-built round houses made of stone, and produced stone tools and containers. Other settlements from this period have been found scattered throughout Cyprus and show evidence of contact outside the island, such as the import of obsidian from Anatolia (in modern Turkey). There is a gap in the archaeological record dating from when Choirokoitia was abandoned; the next signs of activity on the site are vases made from clay, which date from the 5th millennium BC.

The Ceramic Neolithic period saw a new pattern of settlement emerge; its material culture was typified by the site of Sotira Teppes near the south coast, which has yielded abstractly painted ceramic artefacts. Copper began to be used in the 4th millennium BC and ushered in the Chalcolithic period. Among this era's most noteworthy artistic achievements was the production of cross-shaped human figurines made from picrolite, a local Cypriot stone. Around 2500 BC, a new wave of immigrants, believed to be from Anatolia, brought with them new technologies and styles, and started the island's transition to the Bronze Age.

THE BRONZE AGE

Implements of copper progressively replaced the old stone repertory and led to the development of the abundant copper deposits in the Troödos Massif. At the end of the Early Bronze Age (2300 BC to 1950 BC), bronze objects were cast using imported tin. Contacts with the outside world were otherwise few, but imaginative pottery designs flourished,

TIMELINE	10,000–3800 BC	3800–1200 BC
	First settlements in Cyprus, including Choirokoitia	Chalcolithic period and Bronze Age settlers

drawing conspicuously on the human and animal life in and around the villages.

The Middle Bronze Age (1950 BC to 1650 BC) marked an essential continuation of the material culture of the preceding period, with the reintroduction of painted pottery on a regional basis. Settlements tended to keep to the foothills and plains, and archaeological records suggest a largely agrarian community. The first evidence of sustained copper mining comes from the start of this period; by its end, Cyprus had already begun its trading relationships with the Aegean, western Asia and Egypt, as attested by the island's pottery exports.

The Late Bronze Age (1650 BC to 1050 BC) is considered to be one of the most important periods in Cyprus' cultural and historical development. Extensive foreign trade with Egypt and islands in the Aegean Sea characterised the era. Most importantly, writing in the form of a linear script known as Cypro-Minoan was adapted from Crete. Fine jewellery, ivory carvings and delicate pottery were produced during this time and, from around 1400 BC, there was a notable increase in the amount of Mycenaean pottery imported from mainland Greece.

During the Late Bronze Age, new towns were established around the coast, and overseas trade in pottery containers and, later, copper ingots, expanded. Cyprus enjoyed an unprecedented level of prosperity that was accompanied by the movement of foreign goods and people into the island. Around 1200 BC, the first Greek-speaking settlers arrived as part of the Sea Peoples (aggressive seafarers), causing the disruption of existing Cypriot communities. This led to the emergence of the city kingdoms of the Iron Age.

ARCHAIC & CLASSICAL CYPRUS

The first Greek settlers established a series of city kingdoms at Kourion, Pafos, Marion (now Polis), Soloi, Lapithos, Tamassos and Salamis. Two more were later established at Kition and Amathous. These kingdoms enjoyed a period of advancement and increasing prosperity from 750 BC to 475 BC, spectacularly demonstrated by finds at the Royal Tombs near Salamis (p213). These extensive tombs contained sumptuous examples of wealth, and closely matched Homer's description of Mycenaean burials in *The Iliad*.

During this time, Cyprus was ruled in turn by Assyrians, Egyptians and Persians as the fortunes of these various empires waxed and waned.

Cyprus' Classical Age coincides with that of mainland Greece (475–325 BC), and during this period Cypriot art came under strong Attic influence. Zenon of Kition, the founder of the Stoic philosophy movement, was born during this time in Cyprus. Evagoras, king of Salamis, maintained strong links with the Hellenic mainland and extended Greek influence over most of the island, despite Persian hegemony. However, he was finally overcome by the Persians in 381 BC and assassinated seven years later. His death effectively ended the Classical Age.

HELLENISTIC & ROMAN CYPRUS

After his victory over the last Persian ruler, Darius III, at Issus in 333 BC, Alexander the Great took control of the city kingdoms of Cyprus and

If you love ancient Cypriot pottery and sculpture, such as you will see displayed in museums and copied by artists, get more info at www.the britishmuseum.ac.uk.

For a thorough list of Cyprus' archaeological digs past and present, go to www.ancientneareast .net/cyprus.html.

1200–1000 BC	850–750 BC
Salamis, Kourion and Pafos flourish	Phoenician renaissance; the Assyrians, the first of a series of conquerors, control Cyprus

LOST ATLANTIS DISCOVERED?

The Utopian civilisation of Atlantis was described by Plato in 400 BC as 'an island larger than Libya and Asia put together'. The myth describes a powerful nation, destroyed by Zeus for its corruption, which disappeared in a flood some 11,600 years ago. The puzzle of whether Atlantis ever existed, and if it did, how it really perished, has never been resolved. But whatever the answer, Atlantis has bewitched the minds of philosophers and scientists for centuries, and has been 'rediscovered' no less than 47 times.

Over the years, Atlantis has been placed on the edge of a Bolivian volcano, under the Arabian desert sands, in the fourth dimension, or in the Bermuda Triangle. And the last time it showed up was off the coast of Cyprus.

An American researcher, Robert Sarmast, has claimed with certainty that this time, Atlantis has been found for real. His team spent six days surveying an area off the east coast of Cyprus using the latest sonar technologies to create images of the sea bed a mile underwater. He is convinced that he has found evidence of manmade structures submerged in the sea. The findings are said to match 60 specific points mentioned by Plato, such as the city's temples, represented on the site by two mile-long straight walls, and two stream beds.

Sarmast has been obsessed with Atlantis from a young age but has no academic qualifications to substantiate his claims; after ten years spent studying the various accounts of the lost city, he believes that his knowledge is enough. Scientists and philosophers dispute his theories, pointing out that Cyprus is not mentioned in any of the stories relating to Atlantis. However, no-one is sure.

Many other claims have been put forward over the years: in the 1970s, a Soviet Institute of Oceanography decided it had discovered the lost city near Gibraltar; in 1998, a British team claimed that Atlantis lay off the Cornish coast; in 2004, Gibraltar was a candidate for the second time; and in 2005, a Swedish geographer tried to convince the world that Ireland was Atlantis. And those are just a few of the theories – many more are surely still to come.

ushered in a new era. While essentially giving the kingdoms autonomy, he refuted their right to make coins. When Alexander died in 323 BC, Cyprus was ceded to Ptolemy I of Egypt who further suppressed the city kingdoms, eventually causing the last king of Salamis, Nikokreon, to commit suicide. For 250 years Cyprus remained a Ptolemaic colony, languishing under the rule of an appointed governor general.

Cyprus was annexed by the expanding Roman Empire in 58 BC. Orator and writer Cicero was one of Cyprus' first proconsuls. Despite being briefly given to Cleopatra VII of Egypt and subsequently handed back to Roman control, Cyprus enjoyed some 600 years of relative peace and prosperity under Roman rule. Many public buildings and roads date from this time; noteworthy among them were the theatre at Kourion, the colonnaded gymnasium at Salamis and the Sanctuary of Apollon Ylatis.

It was during this period, in around AD 45, that Christianity made its early appearance on the island. Barnabas (later to become St Barnabas; Agios Varnavas in Greek), a native of Salamis, accompanied the apostle Paul and preached on Cyprus. Among his first converts was Sergius Paulus, the Roman proconsul.

Christianity flourished on the island and, by the time of Constantine the Great, paganism had almost completely been supplanted in Cyprus by Christianity.

568–525 BC

Egyptian emperor Amasis rules Cyprus

525–333 BC

Persians occupy the island under King Cyrus

THE BYZANTINE EMPIRE

In 395, the Roman Empire was divided. Its eastern variant, the Byzantine Empire, was based in Constantinople and retained hegemony over Cyprus. However, Cyprus kept a considerable degree of ecclesiastical autonomy from Constantinople; in 488, the archbishop was granted the right to carry a sceptre instead of an archbishop's crosier, as well as the authority to write his signature in imperial purple ink. The practice continues to this day.

The expansion of Islam in the 7th century had profound effects on Cyprus, with a series of disastrous Arab raids starting in 647 causing great depredation and suffering. Salamis was sacked and never recovered, Kourion declined, and coastal settlers moved inland to escape the repeated warring and pillaging. In 688, a sort of truce was called when Justinian II and the Arab caliph Abd-al-Malik signed an agreement for the joint rule of Cyprus. This agreement lasted until 965 when Emperor Nikiforos Fokas regained Cyprus completely for the Byzantines.

Aphrodite Cypris: Goddess of Love – The Mythology of Cyprus by Stass Paraskos examines the legacy of the island's patron goddess through a variety of themes, such as Aphrodite's birth, children and husband, and the Trojan war.

LUSIGNAN, GENOESE & VENETIAN CYPRUS

Byzantine rule might well have continued had renegade governor Isaak Komninos not decided to proclaim himself emperor of Cyprus, and in 1191 take on the might of the crusader king Richard the Lionheart of England. Richard took possession of Cyprus and subsequently sold it to the Knights Templar. They were unable to afford the upkeep and in turn sold it to the dispossessed king of Jerusalem, Guy de Lusignan.

The new French-speaking lord of Cyprus established a lengthy dynasty that brought mixed fortunes to the island. He invited Christian families who had lost property in the Holy Land to settle in Cyprus, and for some time these settlers involved themselves in the affairs of the diminished territories that still belonged to the kingdom of Jerusalem. This proved an economic strain on Cyprus until the neighbouring kingdom finally collapsed with the fall of Acre (Akko) in 1291.

For a hundred years or so thereafter, Cyprus enjoyed a period of immense wealth and prosperity, with current-day Famagusta (Mağusa) the centre of unrivalled commercial activity and trade. Many fine buildings and churches were completed during this period, some of which are still visible in North Nicosia (Lefkoşa), Bellapais (Beylerbeyi) and Famagusta. Cyprus' prosperity reached its zenith under King Peter I (r 1359–69), who mounted an unsuccessful crusade in 1365 that only managed to achieve the sacking of Alexandria.

The citizens of Famagusta (Mağusa) were once so rich and so debauched that one merchant ground up a diamond to season a dish, in front of all his guests.

In the meantime, Orthodox Greeks, while nominally free to practise their religion independently, were becoming more and more restless at their obligation to pay homage to a Latin (Roman Catholic) ecclesiastical administration. Many Greek clerics retreated to the mountains and quietly and unobtrusively built simple churches and monasteries. They decorated their buildings with some of the finest frescoes ever painted in the Orthodox world (p100).

The fortunes of the Lusignans were to take a turn for the worse after the accession to power of Peter I's son and heir, Peter II. Eyeing Cyprus' wealth and strategic position as entrepôt, Genoa and Venice jostled for control. This led to Genoa seizing Famagusta, which it held for the next

| Hellenistic rule; Greek national dress and architecture are adopted | The Romans take over from the Greeks and build amphitheatres, baths and temples |

100 years. The fortunes of both Famagusta and Cyprus itself declined as a result. The last Lusignan king was James II (r 1460–73). He managed to expel the Genoese from Famagusta and married a Venetian noblewoman, Caterina Cornaro, who succeeded James, and became Queen of Cyprus and the last royal personage of the Lusignan dynasty. Under pressure, she ceded Cyprus to Venice.

The Venetians ruled Cyprus from 1489 to 1571, but their control was characterised by indifference and torpor. Corruption and inefficiency marked the administration, and the Greek peasantry fared no better under their new overlords than under the previous regime. In the meantime, the Ottoman Empire was expanding. In anticipation of attack from the north, the Venetians fortified Lefkosia with immense circular walls and built massive fortifications around Famagusta. Neither measures held back the Ottoman onslaught and, in 1570, Lefkosia was conquered. Almost a year later, after a long siege, Famagusta was taken by the Ottomans.

THE OTTOMAN EMPIRE

The newly arrived Ottomans suppressed the Latin Church and restored the Orthodox hierarchy. The peasantry, who had suffered under a feudal tenancy system, were given land. Taxes were initially reduced but later increased, often arbitrarily, with the Orthodox archbishop responsible for their collection. Some 20,000 Turks were settled on Cyprus following its capture, but the island was not high in the priorities of the ruling sultans.

Indolence, corruption and sloth marked the Ottoman rule, and dissent was frequently put down by oppression. In 1821, the Orthodox archbishop was hanged on suspicion of supporting the growing Greek revolution in mainland Greece.

The French poet Arthur Rimbaud visited Cyprus in 1878 and worked at a quarry in Larnaka for six months.

BRITISH RULE

Ottoman rule lasted 300 years, until another foreign power sought influence in the region. In 1878, Turkey and Britain signed an agreement whereby Turkey would retain sovereignty of the languishing colony, while Britain would shoulder the responsibility for administering the island. Britain's aim was to secure a strategic outpost in the Middle East from where it could monitor military and commercial movements in the Levant and the Caucasus. As part of the agreement, Britain would protect the sultan's Asian territories from threat by Russia.

However, in 1914, the parties were at war so Britain assumed outright sovereignty of Cyprus. Turkey's recognition of the annexation of its territory was not ratified until the 1923 Treaty of Lausanne, under which it also regularised territorial claims with the newly independent Greece.

British control of Cyprus was initially welcomed by its mostly Greek population, since it was assumed that Britain would ultimately work with the Greeks to achieve enosis, or union with Greece. Turkish Cypriots, though, were less than enthusiastic at the prospect. The British had offered to unite Cyprus with Greece as early as 1915 on condition that Greece fulfilled its treaty obligations towards Serbia when it was attacked by Bulgaria. The Greek government refused and the offer was never repeated again.

395–647
Cyprus comes under Byzantine rule after the split in the Roman Empire

647–965
Arab raids cause great depredation and suffering

Pro-enosis riots broke out in 1931, but it wasn't until the 1950s that the enosis movement really began to gather steam. Energy was generated by a Cypriot lieutenant colonel, Georgos 'Digenis' Grivas, who founded the Ethniki Organosi tou Kypriakou Agona (EOKA; National Organisation for the Cypriot Struggle). Between 1955 and 1958, EOKA launched a series of covert attacks on the British administration and military, and on anyone else who was seen as being against enosis. The British came up with various proposals for limited home rule, but all were rejected. The 17% minority Turkish Cypriots became increasingly alarmed at the prospect of being forcibly incorporated into Greece.

The respective governments in Greece and Turkey began to take an active interest in developments in Cyprus and, as Greek Cypriots called for enosis, the Turkish Cypriots demanded either retrocession to Turkey, or *taksim* (partition). In 1959, Greek Cypriot ethnarch and religious leader Archbishop Makarios III and Turkish Cypriot leader Faisal Küçük met in Zurich with Greek and Turkish leaders, as well as representatives of the British government. They came to ratify a previously agreed plan whereby independence would be granted to Cyprus under conditions that would satisfy all sides.

The British were to retain two bases and a numbr of other military sites as part of the agreement. Cyprus would not enter into a political or economic union with Turkey or Greece, nor agree to be partitioned. Political power was to be shared on a proportional basis, although with less than 20% of the total population, the Turkish Cypriots were granted 30% of civil service positions, 33% of seats in the House of Representatives and 40% of positions in the army.

Ominously, Britain, Turkey and Greece were to be named as 'guarantor powers', which gave any of the three nations the right to intervene in the affairs of Cyprus should it be believed that the terms of the independence agreement were being breached in any way.

A frisky film from 1979, *Emmanuelle: Queen of Sados,* possibly inspired by Aphrodite's exploits, was filmed at the Amathus Beach Hotel in Lemesos and at that famous aphrodisiac location, Larnaka airport.

THE REPUBLIC OF CYPRUS

The birth of the new and independent Republic of Cyprus was realised on 16 August 1960. Transition from colony to an independent nation was not without growing pains, and sporadic violence and agitation continued. The unrest culminated when Greek Cypriots proposed amendments threatening power-sharing arrangements, resulting in Turkish Cypriot withdrawal from government. Serious sectarian violence broke out in 1963, further dividing the Greek and Turkish communities. The UN sent a peacekeeping force to the island in 1964 to support British troops manning the so-called 'Green Line' dividing Lefkosia. The Turkish Cypriots retreated to ghettos and enclaves as a means of protecting themselves against Greek harassment and aggression.

The Cold War was at its peak and Cyprus' strategic value as a radar listening post became vitally important to the British and to the militarily stronger Americans. Both nations relied on Cyprus in order to monitor Soviet nuclear-missile testing in central Asia. The British maintained an air-force garrison on the Akrotiri base that included a nuclear arsenal.

Archbishop Makarios III, then president of Cyprus, played an increasingly risky game of political nonalignment while seeking arms and

1191	**1192–1571**
The English conquer Cyprus; Richard the Lionheart weds Princess Berengaria in Lemesos	Lusignans rule and build churches and castles; Venetians help themselves to the island in 1489

support from communist nations such as the Soviet Union and Czechoslovakia. He also covertly supported further calls for enosis with Greece. As the communist party gained support, Turkey and Turkish Cypriots became increasingly uneasy at the thought of a possible communist-dominated government in Cyprus. The Americans and their British allies felt concern at the possibility of another Cuban crisis – this time in the Mediterranean.

The discussions on the possibility of segregating the two communities began to take on a greater tempo. In 1967, a coup in Greece installed a right-wing military junta. Its relations with Cyprus cooled while the US cosied up to the more accommodating colonels in Athens. Because of his many diplomatic manoeuvres with the Soviets, Makarios' Cyprus became a less and less desirable option for both the Greeks and the Americans. In July 1974, a CIA-sponsored and Greek-organised coup took place in Cyprus with the intention of eliminating Makarios and installing a more pro-Western government.

On 15 July, a detachment of the National Guard, led by officers from mainland Greece, launched a coup aimed at assassinating Makarios and establishing enosis. They laid waste to the presidential palace, but Makarios narrowly escaped. A former EOKA member, Nikos Sampson, was proclaimed president of Cyprus. Five days later, Turkish forces landed at present-day Kyrenia (Girne) to overturn Sampson's government. Despite vigorous resistance, the Turks were successful in establishing a bridgehead around Kyrenia and linking it with the Turkish sector of North Nicosia (Lefkoşa).

On 23 July 1974, Greece's junta fell and was replaced by a democratic government under Konstantinos Karamanlis. At the same time, Sampson was replaced in Cyprus by Glafkos Clerides, the president of the House of Representatives. The three guarantor powers, Britain, Greece and Turkey, as required by the treaty, met for discussions in Geneva, but it proved impossible to halt the Turkish advance until 16 August. By that time Turkey controlled the northern 37% of the island. In December, Makarios returned to resume the presidency. Cyprus was divided.

TAKSIM

The 1974 division of Cyprus has continued to this day. While the arrival of the Turkish army was seen as a godsend by harried and harassed Turkish Cypriots, it was viewed as an enormous disaster by the 200,000 Greek Cypriots who then lived in the northern third of Cyprus. Many were caught up in the onslaught and killed; most were evacuated or fled south to what remained of the Republic of Cyprus. Similarly, some 100,000 Turkish Cypriots from the Republic of Cyprus fled, or were forcibly evacuated, to Northern Cyprus.

The economic cost to the island and lack of stability brought about with division, and the number of refugees this caused, was enormous. The now-truncated Greek Republic of Cyprus was deprived of some of its best land, two major towns, its lucrative citrus industry and the bulk of its tourist infrastructure.

While the forced division of Cyprus served certain short-term military and political purposes, and Turkish Cypriots received protection from

The Cyprus Conspiracy by Brendan O'Malley and Ian Craig details the role of the British, the CIA, Makarios and the junta colonels of Greece in the events in Cyprus from the 1950s up to 1974.

Under the Stars is a Cypriot road movie from 2001 about two Greek Cypriots whose lives have been torn apart by the Turkish invasion of the island in 1974.

1571	1878
The Ottoman Empire takes over Cyprus	Britain takes over from Turkey as the island's administrator and annexes Cyprus formally in 1914

RAUF DENKTAŞ: PORTRAIT OF A RENEGADE

Viewed as the bane of Cypriot society by Greeks and saviour of the nation by many Turks, Rauf Denktaş used to, and still does, provoke strong feelings among Cypriots. Before he stepped down as president of the self-proclaimed independent republic in 2005, this one-time lawyer was matched in resilience and political longevity by few neighbouring Middle Eastern political leaders. He used charisma and stubbornness to lead the Turkish Cypriot community from well before the forced division of Cyprus in 1974. Until Mehmet Ali Talat beat him in the 2005 election, he had been leader for 31 years.

Mercurial in character, Denktaş was born near Pafos on the island's southern coast and trained as a barrister in London before commencing his long political career. As leader of the Turkish Communal Chamber from 1960, he was in and out of the spotlight – and trouble – until 1974, when he became leader of the partitioned Turkish Cypriots.

Denktaş was known for his persistence and perceived intransigence in seeking a solution for reuniting Cyprus. He dodged and wove, teased and tested the will of both the Republic of Cyprus' political leadership and that of the intermediary nations or organisations who vainly attempted to broker numerous peace deals.

His drive to seek a mutually acceptable solution to the political impasse was compromised by an obdurate steadfastness and unwillingness to deviate from the long-held party line. At thrice-weekly talks held in the UN buffer zone during the spring and summer of 2002, Denktaş refused to concede any ground from the entrenched position of his party and his Turkish-mainland backers who prefer a bizonal, bicommunal state with a large degree of autonomy and separation between the two communities. These talks sputtered on into 2003 without any progress.

In 2003, lead by motives still questioned by many leaders, particularly in the South, Denktaş made a surprise announcement that he would ease border crossings between the two parts of the island, with immediate effect. This decision, however politically 'suspicious', marked a major point in Cyprus' history; Denktaş' failure to get re-elected two years later indicated the possibility that, despite how entrenched things may sometimes seem in Cyprus, they might still change.

Turkey, the final result was ultimately a Pyrrhic victory for the Turks. Makarios escaped assassination by the coup plotters, the military junta collapsed and the desire for enosis dissipated, as Cyprus became preoccupied with its internal problems.

The declaration of a Turkish Republic of Northern Cyprus (TRNC; KKTC in Turkish) by President Rauf Denktaş in 1983 was recognised by no nation other than Turkey. The Cold War came to an end in 1991, by which time half the population of native Turkish Cypriots had fled the island for the UK, Canada and Australia.

CYPRUS TODAY

The Greek Cypriots quickly regrouped and put their energies into rebuilding their shattered nation. Within a few years the economy was on the mend, and the Republic of Cyprus continues to enjoy international recognition as the sole legitimate representative of Cyprus. The economy is booming: the Cyprus Stock Exchange opened in mid-1999 and initially absorbed vast amounts of private funds. Later, the stock exchange took a nose dive and many Cypriots lost huge amounts of money. Tourism is generally buoyant, though 2002 saw a downward trend sparking some concern in the industry.

1955–1960	1963–1964
EOKA begins guerrilla warfare against the British; Makarios becomes the first president of independent Cyprus	Intercommunal fighting after Makarios' proposals of constitutional changes; Turks retreat into enclaves; UN peacekeeping force arrives

---

A GREEN LIGHT ON THE GREEN LINE: THE FIRST CYPRIOT CROSSINGS

It all happened in a matter of hours. On 23 April 2003, Rauf Denktaş, then leader of the Turkish Cypriots, made the surprise announcement that the Green Line (the boundary separating Greek Cypriot Lefkosia from Turkish Cypriot North Nicosia) would open that day for all Cypriots to cross from 9am to midnight. The Greek Cypriot government, gobsmacked by the news, was silent. No-one knew how the Cypriot people would react and what the consequences of this decision would be. Would there be riots or civil unrest? After all, no-one had crossed the Green Line for 29 years, except for the occasional diplomat or at times of emergency. Many still had friends, relatives and homes they missed on the 'other side'.

Starting with a few eager early-morning visitors, the checkpoints swelled with thousands of people over the coming days. Crossing over to the South, the Turkish Cypriots were enchanted by the comparative wealth of the smart shops and restaurants on Lefkosia's glitzy Leoforos Arhiepiskopou Makariou III (Makarios Ave). Greek Cypriots wandered through the run-down streets of North Nicosia, surprised at the way time had stood still over the last thirty years. Friends and families met, and many tears were shed. Greeks and Turks visited their former homes and were welcomed by the current inhabitants, reportedly inviting them in for coffee and sending them home with presents of citrus fruit and flowers. The two peoples treated each other with studied civility and kindness, and, three years after the checkpoints' opening, no major incidents have been reported.

It is estimated that more than 28,000 people, equivalent to 35% of Cyprus' entire population, crossed in the first two weeks. Allegedly, 25,000 Turkish Cypriots applied for a Cypriot passport in 2003 alone. Many Turkish Cypriots now cross the line every day, on their way to work in the southern part of the island. Serdar Denktaş, the son of Rauf and the man behind the realisation of the border opening, dubbed the events 'a quiet revolution'. Many compared it to the fall of the Berlin Wall in 1989, minus the dramatic knocking down of the buffer zone, an event some eagerly await.

The crossing frenzy subsided slightly in the following years, and the attitude to crossing has normalised. However, many report a sense of disappointment that nothing more has been done off the back of the initial enthusiasm, and that the lack of any real solution simply confirms the island's existing separation and status quo. With the reshuffles in European and world politics over the next ten years, it remains to be seen what the future of Cyprus will be, and whether the dividing line will be truly erased once and for all.

Known by most foreigners simply as 'Northern Cyprus' and by Greeks as the 'Occupied Territories' *(ta katehomena)*, the northern segment of Cyprus as a separate entity defies logic; despite international economic sanctions, it continues to survive and develop, supported largely by its client and sponsor nation, Turkey.

Talks to reunite Cyprus have taken place sporadically since 1974 but little ground has been gained, with both sides presenting an entrenched and uncompromising point of view. The UN has maintained peace along the Green Line since 1964; in 1974, it was called on to patrol and monitor the cease-fire line, now called the Attila Line, the border that runs the entire length of the island.

When Cyprus and Turkey were seeking entry to the EU, the leaders of both the South and the North had thrice-weekly talks during the spring and summer of 2002 aimed at reunification, but talks became bogged down in the fine print. The first real changes in the relations between the

1974	**1983**
Greek military junta organises a coup against Makarios; Turkish army invades/intervenes, taking over the northern third of Cyprus	Turks unilaterally proclaim the Turkish Republic of Northern Cyprus

two communities started in April 2003, after a surprise announcement
by Rauf Denktaş stated a decision to 'amend travel' and allow Cypriots
from both sides to visit the opposing parts of the island, so long as they
returned home by the end of the day. Since then, four checkpoints have
been opened along the border, and visiting time has been extended to
up to three months.

During this period Kofi Annan, the UN secretary-general, tried to broker an agreement that would allow a referendum on reunification, which
was rejected by a vast majority of Greek Cypriots (nearly 76%) and endorsed by more than half of Turkish Cypriots (65%). While Turkey's application for admission to the EU was deferred in January 2003, Cyprus'
application (with or without the North) was approved and the southern
Republic of Cyprus alone became a part of the EU in May 2004.

The following April, the 30-year Turkish Cypriot leader, Rauf Denktaş,
lost the presidential elections to his prime minister Mehmet Ali Talat.
Talat, a more modern leader and head of the centre-left Cumhuriyetçi
Türk Partisi (CTP; Republican Turkish Party), is a supporter of unifica-
tion and was vocal in his support of Kofi Annan's plan.

Cyprus' relationship with Turkey is also looking to improve following the commencement of the formal talks on Turkey's EU admission,
which started in 2005 and are predicted to go on for ten years. Turkey's
controversial EU entry rests on several conditions, one of which is its
eventual recognition of the Republic of Cyprus. It remains to be seen
how the Cyprus problem will be solved after this.

Echoes from the Dead Zone: Across the Cyprus Divide by Yiannis Papadakis is about the author's journey from the Greek to the Turkish side of the border, and the overcoming of prejudices and finding understanding.

2003	2004
Borders open for the first time in 30 years	UN referendum for reunification, rejected by the Greeks, endorsed by the Turks; the Republic of Cyprus joins the EU

The Culture

THE NATIONAL PSYCHE

The Cypriot character has been moulded by the many different nations who have coveted, fought for and possessed the island over the centuries. And it's because of this history that Cypriot identity is as divided as the country itself. Although politics play an important part in every Cypriot's life and the scars of 1974 are still very much alive in the people's minds, a peaceful mentality was evident when borders opened in 2003 and Cypriot Greeks and Turks met each other again for the first time in 30 years. Despite the political and emotional difficulties of the long division, the Cypriot people were kind and civil to each other.

The Cyprus problem (*kypriako* in Greek) is an issue that all Cypriots have grown up with and lived with on either side of the Green Line, and the bitterness that they feel in relation to this subject cannot be overestimated. In that light, and while politics are discussed widely on both sides of the Green Line, the Cyprus problem is a very sensitive issue – particularly for Greek Cypriots – and one that travellers should approach with tact and understanding.

Both Greek and Turkish Cypriots can be quite frank and forthright in discussing the issue, but it's better to let them take the lead rather than initiate a discussion yourself. Considering the internal divisions, it is then surprising to know that Cyprus' inhabitants see themselves as Cypriot first and Greek or Turkish second.

Since 1974, there has been a creeping Turkification of the North. Greek place names have been converted to Turkish so that anyone familiar with the pre-partition names may find it difficult to find their way around the North without a Turkish-language map. Greek road signs and wall signs of any description have completely disappeared and visitors cannot help but feel that they are in a region of Turkey.

Likewise, there has been a near-total Hellenisation of the South. Even the former city names of Nicosia, Limassol and Paphos have been officially changed to their Greek versions, something that may catch out the unaware traveller. Other than in the UN-controlled village of Pyla (p168), where one can see Turkish and Greek Cypriots still living together, there are few signs of the Turkish language or culture anywhere in the South.

While British domination was understandably rejected by Cypriots in the late 1950s, there is still a lingering 'Britishness' about Cyprus in both the North and the South, such as neighbours who'll call each other up on the phone before popping over for a coffee, a custom not usually practised in other Mediterranean countries.

There are a number of second-generation Cypriots who grew up in foreign countries (many of them in the UK) and who are now returning to live on the island. They are generally regarded as semiforeigners by the locals and often find themselves struggling to fit in.

Greek Cypriots are very traditional and protective of their 'national purity' and many *xeni* (foreigners) who have married locals and stayed on the island report a long and difficult 'initiation' into the family and local community. Despite this, Cypriots are a friendly and welcoming people who will show kindness to strangers.

Cypriot men on both sides of the Green Line are the face of machismo: hairy and often moustachioed (especially the older generations), they drive their cars fast, wear their chains gold, comb their hair back, and

The Internet has opened all kinds of possibilities for dialogue, one of them being www.talkcyprus.org/forum, a website for Cypriots to discuss their country's political situation online.

WHAT'S IN A NAME?

The issue of place names is a thorny one in Cyprus, pregnant with political, cultural and linguistic overtones and potential pitfalls. To avoid treading on too many peoples' toes, we have adopted a few ground rules to make navigating this maze a little easier.

In general, we have adopted a bilingual approach to towns and villages that were once bi-communal, and a trilingual approach where some towns had Anglicised versions of their name. In Northern Cyprus (referred to throughout this book as 'the North'), we list major tourist towns by the Anglicised names, followed by their Turkish and Greek names, while villages are listed by their Turkish name followed by the Greek name. This occurs out of a need to assist travellers to navigate Turkish-language destination signs rather than to make a political statement. Without this knowledge, and with Greek-only place names in our guide, navigating Northern Cyprus would be totally unfeasible. Thus Kyrenia is known as Girne in Turkish and Keryneia in Greek, Famagusta as Mağusa in Turkish and Ammohostos in Greek.

In the Republic of Cyprus (referred to throughout this book as 'the South'), we have used the new, approved Hellenised place names for cities and towns. Thus, South Nicosia is known as Lefkosia; Paphos as Pafos and Larnaca as Larnaka. Road signs these days tend to use the new names, though you will occasionally see the old names on older signs.

For the Republic, we list Greek versions of names as well as the Anglicised and Turkish ones, where appropriate. Thus Pafos is known also as Baf in Turkish, Limassol as Lemesos in Greek and Limasol in Turkish. While we acknowledge the Turkish Cypriots' right to call a town or village by a Turkish name, this can lead to problems for a publication such as this guide where many of the former Greek villages of Northern Cyprus are still known internationally by their Greek names and are still shown as such on many maps.

The Turkish Republic of Northern Cyprus has never been recognised by any other authority than itself and Turkey. It is not Lonely Planet's intent to 'recognise' states as such and thus confer implied legality on them, but to describe a given situation as fairly as possible and allow readers to reach their own conclusions. In this book we refer to Northern Cyprus as the territory currently occupied by the Turkish military, and to the Republic of Cyprus as the territory not occupied by the Turkish army.

love to think that women (particularly Western women) adore them. So, if you're a woman travelling alone in Cyprus, keep in mind that you'll get plenty of male attention, and from all generations.

LIFESTYLE

The Cypriot standard of living has rocketed in the last five to ten years, and particularly so in the Republic. Years of tourist interest have resulted in lucrative land sales, development opportunities and a general rise in wealth. Compared to the Cyprus of the 1950s when most people immigrated to the West to try and earn a living, this wealth has given the country a standard of living that matches most European countries, and, frankly, exceeds some too. In fact, Cyprus has the third-highest standard of living in the Mediterranean. Once a country of immigrants, the island has become an attractive destination for many people from the developing world and poorer countries of the EU who move here seeking work. A live-in nanny seems to be the national 'must-have', with an influx of people from Southeast Asia aiming specifically for this calling. Eastern Europeans and Russians are mainly employed as catering staff in tourist destinations. This has meant that seeds of cosmopolitanism have been planted in this formerly homogenous society.

Northern Cyprus, on the other hand, has a much lower standard of living than the Republic, with a GDP roughly one-third of the South. Despite this, the Turkish Cypriot economy grew by 2.6% in 2004, fuelled by the construction and education sectors, along with the increased employment of Turkish Cypriots in the Republic of Cyprus.

Although many mainland Turks come to Northern Cyprus to work, the North is heavily dependent on financial transfers from Ankara – around US$300 million a year. Tourist development has increased since the borders have opened, yet there is a danger that too much growth can ultimately work against the North, as the island overdevelops and loses its individuality.

The Cypriot reputation for hospitality is well known. Although this is waning slightly, you may be still be invited into a stranger's home for coffee, a meal or even to spend the night. In case you are invited by a host who is poor, it is considered offensive to offer money. The most acceptable way of saying thank you is through a gift, perhaps to a child in

---

GETTING HITCHED IN CYPRUS

Maybe it's the dreary weather and the strong likelihood of a rainy wedding day that's behind the Brits' desire to get loved up, pop the question, and tie the knot somewhere in Cyprus. So many of them get married on the island that the American Express Travel Weddings and Honeymoons League 2005 named Cyprus the second most popular place in the world for getting married; the island is ranked sixth for honeymoons. The UK-based First Choice and Thomson travel agencies have also rated it as their top wedding destination.

Some seem to think that the spirit of Aphrodite has a little to do with it. After all, the goddess did emerge from sea foam (think Bo Derek in *10,* minus the braids) and entertained lovers left, right and centre, leaving behind her an amorous scent that has continued to intoxicate paramours ever since. But Cyprus' history as a wedding nest was officially begun by Richard the Lionheart who married his wife Berengaria at Lemesos fortress in the 12th century.

It's no surprise that the Brits love Cyprus so much: the prices are low, the weather is excellent and wedding regulations are easy. If you're thinking of getting hitched in the Republic of Cyprus, here's what you have to do: when you arrive, apply in person to the marriage officer of the relevant region with your passport and birth certificate, and fill in a Notice of Marriage form. Then, make a declaration under oath in front of the marriage officer, stating that you know of no legal impediment to your marriage, supported by documents proving you're not a serial bigamist; if you're divorced or widowed, you need to show the appropriate papers. If you don't have any papers to prove your marital status, the Cypriots are pretty flexible; you just have to sign a legal declaration stating that you are definitely, cross-your-heart-and-hope-to-die, single. The cost of making this application is UK£75.

Once all that is complete, you can get married anytime between 15 days and three months later. Note that if you miss the three-month limit, you'll have to apply all over again. However, if you want to get married quickly, simply pay UK£165 and you can have your big day 48 to 72 hours later.

A number of hotels have built chapels on site to make the procedure as hassle-free as possible, while the reception often takes place in the hotel itself. The superluxurious Anassa Hotel in Polis (see the boxed text Spa Life, p125), where even the Beckhams have holidayed, is a place where you can have a glitz-a-tastic wedding; then there is the Elysium in Pafos, the Columbia Beach Resort in Pissouri, the Palm Beach in Larnaka and the Amathus Beach hotel in Lemesos (p88), all of which are four-star establishments at least. There are numerous online wedding agencies such as the **Wedding Company** (www.the-weddingcompany.com) or **Weddings in Cyprus** (www.wedding.cyprushotels.org.uk) that help organise the whole shebang, from the hors d'oeuvre to the wedding band.

There's only one glitch in this beautiful scene: an apparent shortage of priests. A solitary priest covered the entire area of Agia Napa and Protaras in 2004; despite interventions by the Cyprus Tourism Organisation, the church seems reluctant to part with its pastors.

the family (particularly if you happen to have a Nintendo Playstation III handy). A similar situation arises if you go out for a meal with Cypriots; the bill is not shared as in Western European countries, but paid by the host. But do offer to pay in any case.

The contrast between a Cypriot home in a village and one in an urban area can be astounding. The city dwellers, particularly those in Lefkosia (South Nicosia), put their suits on, get their 'skinny lattes to go' and rush down the street in pursuit of prosperity and career. Youngsters hang out in bars and clubs and covet designer items displayed in tempting shop windows; restaurants, bars and clubs are the modern churches of these trendy, classy urbanites. In the villages, the local *kafeneio* (coffee shop) is packed with men of all generations – from boys, usually serving the customers, to middle-aged men on their way to work, to old men. They all sit in the shade of the vine leaves, and the action centres around pairs playing backgammon. Haloumi (helimi), tomatoes, olives, coffee and ouzo are consumed, and many cigarettes are smoked while dice are thrown and backgammon positions are counted in whispers. Come lunchtime, only the echo of chatter and lingering cigarette smoke remain; the men have stampeded home, where the wife has prepared a nice pot of *fasioli* (beans) and tomatoes.

While you may occasionally see two men holding hands on the Turkish side of the island (and this is normal in many Asian countries), homosexuality is largely frowned upon in the traditional parts of Cyprus. Cities like Lefkosia, Lemesos and Pafos have several gay bars and clubs, and the atmosphere in these places is more relaxed; however, it is never advisable to be too obvious, since macho attitudes are prevalent.

Despite its overt Western outlook, Cyprus is steeped in traditional customs. Name days, weddings and funerals have great significance. Weddings are highly festive occasions, with dancing, feasting and drinking sometimes continuing for days. In Cypriot villages, it is common for the whole village to be invited to the wedding.

A favourite Cypriot pastime is having a *souvla* (barbecue or spit-roast) on the beach. There's a joke that the Cypriot's favourite vehicle (and in fact the best-selling one) is a pick-up truck, because twenty chairs, a table and the entire barbecue set can be stacked on the back of it when the family goes out on the weekend. And indeed, the smoke and the smell of delicious food often tickle one's nostrils on Cypriot beaches.

Cypriots are a little more formal in their interpersonal relations than their mainland brethren. People are commonly addressed with a title, such as Mr (*kyrie* before the person's name in Greek; *bey* after the name in Turkish) or Mrs (*kyria* in Greek; *hanım* in Turkish); the use of first names alone is considered too familiar. Appointments are usually kept to the agreed time, and in small towns it is not unusual for villagers to phone each other before visiting even if they live next door to each other.

You may have come to Cyprus for sun, sand and sea, but if you want to bare all other than on a designated nude beach, remember that Cyprus is a traditional country, so take care not to offend the locals.

'A favourite Cypriot pastime is having a *souvla* (barbecue or spit-roast) on the beach'

POPULATION

Cyprus is primarily made up of Greek and Turkish Cypriots who together constitute a total population of 780,133. The Greeks are descendants of the early settlers who intermingled with the indigenous population around 1100 BC and subsequent settlers who came to Cyprus up to the 16th century AD. The Turkish Cypriots are descendants from Ottoman settlers who first arrived in Cyprus in 1570 following the Ottoman conquest of the island.

Around 18% of the population is Turkish Cypriot; immigrants from mainland Turkey since 1974 are thought to make up to about 50% of that total. A large number of Cypriots left the island as refugees in 1974, but many have since chosen to return home permanently.

Most Cypriots in the Republic of Cyprus speak English and many road signs are in Greek and English. In Northern Cyprus, this is not the case outside the tourist areas and you'll have to brush up on your Turkish. In both areas, the spelling of place and street names varies enormously.

The division of Cyprus in 1974 made the country's population more or less ethnically 'clean': the southern, Greek part of the island is populated by the Greeks, and the northern, Turkish side is mainly Turkish. But things are never that simple. Although Greek Cypriots in particular demonstrate preservationist tendencies when it comes to Greek national purity, Cypriot society is more cosmopolitan than one may think. The wealth acquired through tourist development has moved Cypriot life several steps up, and tourism provides employment for an average of 37,000 people a year, or 13% of the general workforce, many of them immigrants.

There has been a large influx of Russians to the island, particularly in some parts of Lemesos and Pafos. The question, and for some the 'problem', of the Pontian Greeks (ethnic Greeks from Russia who have the right to Cypriot and Greek nationality) has become a sensitive social issue on the island. Complaints of racism and discrimination can be heard from the Pontians, many of whom struggle with unemployment and poverty, while the Cypriots complain of disruptive and socially problematic behaviour from the Pontians.

A dominant socio-political problem in Cyprus is the status and the future of the large minority of mainland Turks, who have gradually settled on the island since 1974.

TURKISH SETTLERS: THE ELEPHANT IN CYPRUS' LIVING ROOM

The easing of border crossings in 2003 brought the Cyprus problem, and its solution, into the international public eye once again. As Greeks and Turks crossed and continue to cross the Green Line, the mainland Turkish settlers (or naturalised Turkish Cypriots, depending on your view) have been left on the fringes of the discussions and hopes for the island's reunification. The *Turkiyeli,* as they are known in Northern Cyprus, have also been physically left out of the recent changes since they are unable to cross over the Green Line, as the Greek Cypriots don't recognise the validity of their documents.

Arriving in gradual waves from mainland Turkey since 1974 as population boosters introduced by Denktaş, the settlers were given Greek Cypriot properties, mainly in rural, deprived areas undesirable to Turkish Cypriots. The number of settlers is one of the most debated and politically manipulated issues in Cyprus – the Greek Cypriots claim there are 119,000 on the island, whereas independent researchers in the North put the figure down to 50,000.

Although many of the settlers married Turkish Cypriots and some have grandchildren on the island, they are largely rejected and looked down upon by Turkish Cypriots, particularly the middle classes; as is often the case with discrimination, the settlers get the blame for increases in crime rates and social problems.

There is hardly any public debate on the issue of the Turkish settlers, and their identity and future represent the elephant in Cyprus' living room. Aside from throwing statistics at each other, governments on both sides of the Green Line have given no indication on how they intend to approach the future and status of these people.

RELIGION

About 78% of Cypriots belong to the Greek Orthodox Church, 18% are Muslims and the remaining 4% are Maronite, Armenian Apostolic and other Christian denominations. These days, the Muslims live mainly in the North and the Greek Orthodox in the South. The Maronites have traditionally been centred on the village of Koruçam (Kormakitis) in the North, and there are small non-Orthodox Christian communities on both sides of the border.

Greek Cypriots are more pious than their Turkish Cypriot compatriots, and church visits are a regular thing; even McDonald's offers special Lent dishes during Easter week. The presence of the Orthodox Church is strong both in politics and ordinary life, and the Orthodox Christians are by and large intolerant towards most non-Christians, particularly Muslims. The Greek year is centred on the festivals of the church calendar. Most Greeks, when they have a problem, will go into a church and light a candle to the saint they feel is most likely to help. Sunday afternoons are popular times for visiting monasteries, and the frescoed Byzantine churches in the Troödos Massif are often packed with elderly weekend pilgrims.

Turkish Cypriots are generally more secular and can often be heard complaining of their Turkish mainland brethren being 'too religious'. They are mostly Sunni Muslims and, while religion plays an important part in Turkish Cypriot culture, the more conservative Islamic culture seen elsewhere in the Middle East and in rural Turkey is not so obvious in Cyprus. Alcohol, for example, is widely available and frequently consumed by Turkish Cypriots and women dress more casually than their Turkish mainland counterparts. A large number of Orthodox churches in the North were destroyed by the Turks and Turkish Cypriots in the wake of the 1974 partition.

WOMEN IN CYPRUS

While traditional ideas about women die hard in Cypriot villages, where women mainly stay at home, cook and look after the house and the family, women in the cities are dressed up to highest fashion standards, frequent the beaches in skimpy bikinis, work, and go out. The pressure to look good and 'look after yourself' (which involves a lot of designer-label wearing) is perhaps as present as the traditional pressure to be able to cook and keep the house clean and tidy.

Sexual liberation and education may have given Cypriot women a certain degree of freedom and independence, but there is still a long way to go when it comes to combating the occupational segregation of the sexes. In 2001, Cyprus came second on a list of the worst places in Europe for women's pay discrimination, after Portugal.

During the same year, women occupied around 10% of positions in the public sector, and there were no female ministers in the Cypriot government. Things are looking up, however, and it was expected that women's participation in all political spheres would count at 30% by the end of 2005.

The traditional ideas of women as 'mother' or 'sex object' are still dominant on both sides of the Green Line. Running a 'cabaret' (brothel) is a lucrative business, and women-trafficking is a serious problem. The feminist movement never really took off in Cyprus, but there is a strong women's movement for peace and reunification of the island, run by women from both sides of the Green Line and fronted by an NGO called **Hands Across the Divide** (www.handsacrossthedivide.org).

As in many Middle Eastern countries, people in Cyprus believe in the 'evil eye'. Avoid praising things too much, as this attracts envy and the 'evil eye'.

An NGO project entitled 'Take Our Daughters to Work' (www.amade -mondiale.org) tackled gender inequality in Cyprus in 2000 and 2003, by taking 500 girls, aged from nine to 15 to work for a day in traditionally male jobs.

ARTS
Literature

Cyprus has produced a sprinkling of literary illuminati, and the literature scene is actively promoted and encouraged by the government of the Republic, with competitions and accompanying awards organised annually. However, little Cypriot literature is available in translation and, where it is available, its circulation is limited and usually restricted to Cyprus. Home-grown talent of the 20th century includes Loukis Akritas (1932–65), who made his mark mainly in Greece as a journalist and writer, and later championed the cause of Cypriot independence through letters, rather than violence. His works include novels, plays, short stories and essays.

Theodosis Pierides (1908–67), who wrote actively from 1928 onwards, is one of Cyprus' national and most respected poets. His *Cypriot Symphony* is considered to be the 'finest most powerful epic written by a Greek poet about Cyprus', according to contemporary and fellow poet Tefkros Anthias (1903–68). Anthias himself was excommunicated by the Orthodox Church and internally exiled by the British administration in 1931 for his poetry collection *The Second Coming*. He was arrested during the liberation struggle of 1955–59 and imprisoned. While in prison he wrote a collection of poems called *The Diary of the CDP*, which was published in 1956.

The North supports a small but healthy literary scene with more than 30 'name' personages. Nese Yasin (1959–) is a writer, journalist and poet, and a founding member of a movement known as the '74 Generation Poetry Movement. This was a postdivision literary wave of writers that sought inspiration from the climate generated after Cyprus was divided. Her poems have been translated and published in magazines, newspapers, anthologies and books in Cyprus, Turkey, Greece, Yugoslavia, Hungary, the Netherlands, Germany and the UK.

Hakki Yucel (1952–) is a poet, literary researcher and eye specialist. His poems and essays have been published in magazines and newspapers in Cyprus, Turkey, the UK and Hungary. He is one of the leading members of the '74 Generation Poetry Movement and has been active in the promotion of Cypriot culture and literature in Turkey.

For a taste of Cypriot folk music, go to www .zypern.com, where you can listen online.

Music

Greek Cypriots have tended to follow the musical preferences of mainland Greece. Conversely, Cyprus has also produced some of its own home-grown musicians who have made successful careers in Greece as well as in their homeland.

The bouzouki, which you will hear all over Cyprus, is a mandolin-like instrument similar to the Turkish *saz* and *baglama*. It's one of the main instruments of *rembetika* music – the Greek equivalent of American blues. The name *rembetika* may come from the Turkish word *rembet*, which means outlaw. Opinions differ as to the origins of *rembetika*, but it is probably a hybrid of several different types of music. One source was the music that emerged in the 1870s in the 'low-life' cafés, called *tekedes* (hashish dens), in urban areas and especially around ports such as Pireus in Greece. Another source was the Arabo-Persian music played in sophisticated Middle Eastern *amanedes* (music cafés) in the 19th century. *Rembetika* was originally popularised in Greece by the refugees from Asia Minor and was subsequently brought to Cyprus.

Today's music scene in Cyprus is a mix of old and new, traditional and modern. Young Greek Cypriots are as happy with *rembetika* or *demotic* (folk) songs as they are with contemporary Greek rock music. One artist to look out for is Pelagia Kyriakou and in particular her contribution to two albums known as *Paralimnitika 1 & 2*, a superb collection of Cypriot *demotic* songs from the beginning of the 19th century, sung in Cypriot dialect. Mihalis Violaris is an exponent of folk and modern songs who was especially popular during the 1970s and '80s. Two songs he made famous (which you'll inevitably hear somewhere in Cyprus) are 'Ta Rialia' (Money) and 'Tyllirkotissa' (Girl from Tylliria), again sung in Cypriot dialect.

Of the more modern singers, Anna Vissi sings contemporary Greek music and has appeared on albums released by top Greek singer Georgos Dalaras, as well as producing her own albums. Alkinoös Ioannides is a young Lefkosian who sings emotional ballads of his own composition that occasionally border on rap and rock, and has released three excellent albums. His first, *O Dromos o Hronos kai o Ponos* (The Road, the Time and the Pain), is worth picking up for an introduction to the music of this talented Cypriot.

Georgos Dalaras, while not a Cypriot, has devoted much time and energy to the Cypriot cause. His album *Es Gin Enalian Kypron* (To Sea-Girt Cyprus) is a poignant tribute to the trials and tribulations of modern-day Cyprus, set to the music of Cypriot composer Mihalis Hristodoulidis. Finally, Cypriot singer and lyricist Evagoras Karageorgis has produced some excellent music. His work is best represented on a fine album that is little known outside Cyprus called *Topi se Hroma Loulaki* (Places Painted in Violet), which is definitely worth seeking out. It's a nostalgic and painful look at the lost villages of Northern Cyprus sung in a mixture of Cypriot dialect and standard Greek accompanied by traditional and contemporary instruments.

In the North, musical trends tend to mirror those of mainland Turkey. However, Greek music is still admired and quietly listened to on radio broadcasts from the South (radio thankfully knows no boundaries), and both cultures share a remarkable overlap in sounds and instrumentation. Among Turkish Cypriot musical personalities, Yıltan Taşçi has made something of a name for himself locally, and helped create and play in such bands as Golgeler, Ozgurler, Kalender5 and Letul. Taşçi's first recording, *Bana Seviyorum De,* came out in March 1995 and contains seven songs that he composed and performed.

Germany-based French horn player Turgay Hilmi is originally from Northern Cyprus but now plies his trade playing classical music with renowned orchestras, such as the Nüremburg Chamber Orchestra, and contemporary material with his brass quintet. He visits Cyprus whenever he can and in 1998 participated in the first performance of the opera *Othello* in Cyprus at the Bellapais Music Festival (p195).

Lovers of jazz will have to keep their ears to the grapevine for possible jazz venues or festivals. The Paradise Jazz Festival near Polis (p136) is held in September, but you will be hard-pressed to find anything similar in the North.

Tim Boatswain's *A Traveller's History of Cyprus* is an excellent source of concise and structured history and a useful read for anyone heading to the island.

Painting & Sculpture

In the Republic of Cyprus, painting enjoys a healthy patronage. One of the more famous exponents of the art neither runs a gallery nor participates in art festivals. He is Father Kallinikos Stavrovounis, the aged priest of Stavrovouni Monastery (p151), situated between the cities of Lefkosia and Lemesos. Father Kallinikos is regarded as the most superb contemporary icon painter of the Orthodox Church. Icons are made to order and the money received is ploughed back into the Orthodox Church for the upkeep of the Stavrovouni and other monasteries.

Athos Agapitos is a contemporary Greek Cypriot painter who was born in Lefkosia in 1957. His art portfolio runs the gamut from realism and naive painting to expressionism in more recent years. His work was exhibited at the Florence Biennale of International Contemporary Art in 1999.

Among the foremost sculptors is Fylaktis Ieridis, whose talent finds its most natural expression in bronze. He has been commissioned to complete several busts and reliefs for monuments to local heroes.

Folk Art

Cyprus has particularly well-developed folk-art traditions, with lace and basketry prominent among items produced. Lefkara lace, from the village of the same name in the southern Troödos foothills (p152), is one of Cyprus' most famous folk-art export commodities. Large, woven bread baskets are on sale all over Cyprus and are characterised by their intricate and multicoloured patterns.

Fashion designer Hussein Chalayan, controversial British artist Tracey Emin, and musicians George Michael (Giorgos Panayiotou) and Cat Stevens (Stephanos Georgiou) all have Cypriot origins.

The Cyprus Handicraft Service (CHS) in the South has been instrumental in promoting and preserving these arts that, without this support, may well have taken the road to oblivion like folk arts in other industrialising nations. The service runs shops in the major towns and sells the wares of the artists that it supports, such as *sendoukia* (ornate bridal chests). The town of Lapta (Lapithos) in the North used to be the island's centre for *sendoukia*-making but the industry has taken a downturn following the events of 1974.

Pottery

Well-made and often highly decorative pottery is produced in Cyprus and is worth seeking out. You can hardly miss the enormous *pitharia* (earthenware storage jars), which are often used as decorative plant pots outside rural houses. Originally used for storing water, oil or wine, they have fallen victim to more convenient methods of storage and packaging. Their sheer size and volume, though, render them all but impossible to take home. The village of Kornos, between Lemesos and Larnaka, is still an active pottery-making community, as is the Pafos region; in Pafos town, you will find shops selling all kinds of multicoloured, functional and decorative pottery pieces.

Cinema

In Cyprus, cinema is a relatively recent phenomenon – hardly surprising given the turbulent and disruptive nature of recent Cypriot history. At the end of the 1940s, the British colonial government started to train Cypriot film makers in the Colonial Film Unit. With the impetus created by the arrival of TV in 1957, the first home-grown cinema productions began. These were mainly documentaries, and the first independent production was entitled *Roots*. The Cyprus Broadcasting Corporation sponsored most productions over the next two decades, with a 1963 production by Ninos Fenwick Mikellidis called *Cyprus, Ordained to Me* winning a prize at the Karlovy Vary Festival in then Czechoslovakia. George Lanitis' film *Communication* won first prize for a short foreign film at the Thessaloniki Festival in 1970.

Further prizes were awarded in 1985 to Cypriot film makers Hristos Siopahas, at the Moscow Film Festival for his film *The Descent of the Nine*, and Andreas Pantazis, at the Thessaloniki Film Festival for his depiction of the Turkish invasion of Cyprus entitled *The Rape of Aphrodite*. The two film makers were honoured 10 years later at the Thessaloniki Film Festival for their works *The Wing of the Fly* (by Siopahas) and *The Slaughter of the Cock* (by Pantazis), both dealing with the invasion of Cyprus.

The upsurge in film production in the South since 1974 is due primarily to newly found support from the state, which is keen to assist young film directors. Since 1983, an enlightenment committee has been particularly active in the area of cinematography with a view to projecting the Cypriot problem to a wider international audience.

The North does not support a domestic film-making scene; its cinematographic culture is supplied entirely from mainland Turkey.

Several films were produced in 2003 and 2004, in the run-up to the UN referendum, dealing with the division of Cyprus. Some of them raised the hackles of the Cypriot governments on both sides of the Green Line, as well as those of the governments on the Greek and Turkish mainlands.

Camur (Mud), in 2003, was hailed as the first 'united Cypriot' film. Directed by Derviş Zaim, a Turkish Cypriot and produced by Panicos Chrysanthou, a Greek Cypriot, this dark comedy takes place near the Green Line, where black mud in a saltwater lake is thought to have unique healing properties. The film deals with four Turkish friends who are coming to terms with their memories of the partition.

The second film Zaim and Chrysanthou made together is *Parallel Trips* (2004), a documentary that explores the legacy of massacres committed by the Greeks and the Turks on both sides of the island.

Elias Demetriou's *Living Together Separately* (2003) is a humorous documentary recording life in Pyla, the small village in the military zone where Turks and Greeks have continued to live together despite the partition.

Which Cyprus? (2004) by Rüstem Batum is a powerful film of stories about people travelling to 'the other side' and presents the views of politicians, peace activists, journalists and clergymen.

Equally popular on both sides of the border, cinemas abound in Cyprus. Movies are usually shown in the original language with subtitles in Greek or Turkish. Tickets cost about 2YTL in the North and CY£3 in the South.

> 'Films dealing with the division of Cyprus raised the hackles of the Cypriot governments on both sides of the Green Line'

Theatre

Theatre in the South is a flourishing industry, with the Theatre Workshop of the University of Cyprus (thepak) very active in the performance of works written by Greeks and Cypriots.

The biannual Kypria Festival hosts performances from a variety of domestic theatre groups. The Cyprus Theatre Organisation performed Aristophanes' *Peace* and the Eleftheria Theatre of Cyprus presented Euripides' *Phoenician Women* at the 2004 Kypria Festival.

Theatre in the North can be said to have started with the arrival of the Ottomans in 1570 and with the importation from the Turkish mainland of the Karagöz puppet shadow theatre. This theatre tradition is shared by the Greeks, who call it Karagiozis. Theatre in the contemporary sense started on the island with British influence after 1878, but only really took off after independence in 1960, when amateur theatre groups were established in most Turkish Cypriot communities.

Independence also saw the flourishing of a new generation of playwrights, such as Hilmi Özen, Üner Ulutug and Ayla Haşmat. In 1964, the Department of Education provided the Atatürk İlkokulu salon for the use of the Turkish Cypriot Theatre, now called the Turkish Cypriot State Theatre, which is still active and successful.

Going to the theatre is certainly popular among Cypriots, however unless you speak Greek or Turkish, the entertainment value is likely to be limited. Check local newspapers or look out for street posters advertising performances that may appeal.

Dance

The origin of Cypriot folk dancing dates back centuries. It may even be said to be related to shamanist ceremonies and early religious and incantational worship. There are references to Cypriot dances in Homer's works, and one of these, the *syrtos*, is depicted on ancient Greek vases. Many Greek folk dances, including the *syrtos*, are performed in a circular formation; in ancient times, dancers formed a circle in order to seal themselves off from evil influences.

Different regional characteristics may be noticed. In the Republic, musical and dance traditions follow those of mainland Greece to some degree. There is of course a wide range of indigenous Cypriot dances that are only seen these days at folk festivals or specially staged dance performances. The most famous of these is the *kartzilamas*, in effect a suite of up to five different dances that usually ends with the more familiar *syrtos* or *zeïmbekikos*. Cypriot dances are commonly 'confronted pair' dances of two couples, or vigorous solo men's dances in which the dancer holds an object such as a sickle, a knife, a sieve or a tumbler. Shows at popular tourist restaurants frequently feature a dance called *datsia* where the dancer balances a stack of glasses full of wine on a sieve. Another is a contrived dance in which diners are invited to try to light the tail – usually a rolled-up newspaper – of the solo male dancer who will attempt to dance and bob his way out of being set alight.

Dances in the North share very similar patterns of development and execution to those in the South, the only real difference being the names. Thus the *kartzilamas* is the North's *karşilama* and the *tsifteteli* is the *ciftetelli*. In addition there is the *testi*, the *kozan*, and the *kaşikli oyunları*, a dance performed with wooden spoons. However, it is unlikely you will come across much Turkish dancing, unless you happen upon sporadic summer folk festivals at either Kyrenia (Girne) or Famagusta (Mağusa), or the harvest festivals that occasionally take place in country towns and villages. Restaurants with floor shows are most likely your best opportunity to sample some of the northern variants of Cypriot dancing.

'In ancient times, dancers formed a circle in order to seal themselves off from evil influences'

Environment

THE LAND

The saucepan shape of Cyprus reflects its geology. In the North, a 100km-long mountain chain, known as the Kyrenia (Girne) Range, runs more or less parallel to the northern coastline. It is the southernmost range of the great Alpine-Himalayan chain in the eastern Mediterranean and is made up of thrust masses of Mesozoic limestone.

South of the Kyrenia Range lies a vast plain known as the Mesaoria (Mesarya in Turkish). It stretches from Morfou (Güzelyurt) in the west to Famagusta (Mağusa) in the east. The divided capital Lefkosia/North Nicosia lies more or less in the middle of the plain. The Mesaoria is the island's principal grain-growing area. Around half of its 188,385 hectares are irrigated; the remainder is given over to dryland farming.

The south of the island is dominated by the Troödos Massif, a vast, bulky mountain range towered over by Mt Olympus (1952m). To the east is a small, lower plateau where most of the South's tourist industry is now based.

The Troödos Massif is made up of igneous rock and was originally formed from molten rock beneath the deep ocean that once separated the continents of Eurasia and Afro-Arabia. Since antiquity the mountain range has been known to be particularly rich in minerals, with abundant resources of copper and asbestos. Other natural resources include chromite, gypsum and iron pyrite. Marble has also been mined here for several thousand years.

For the best choice of rural accommodation in sustainable, traditional houses, visit www.agrotourism.com.cy.

WILDLIFE
Animals

Birds travelling between Africa and Europe use Cyprus as a stepping stone on their migratory path. Bird-watchers have an excellent window onto both more exotic migratory species and local birds such as griffon vultures, falcons and kestrels.

The island's mammals include fruit bats, foxes, hares and hedgehogs. There are a few snake species and, although you are unlikely to cross their paths, it is worth noting that the Montpellier snake and blunt-nosed viper are poisonous and can inflict nasty bites. Lizards are the most obvious of Cyprus' fauna species and they are everywhere. Don't be afraid of the pretty geckos in your hotel room; they come out at night to feed on insects.

A handy field companion is *Butterflies of Cyprus* by John Eddie and Wayne Jarvis. This comprehensive guide is available quite cheaply in paperback.

RESPONSIBLE TRAVEL

Some might argue that hoteliers and tourist operators have not acted responsibly in the race to develop (in the South at least). However, there is no reason for travellers to behave in the same way.

Travelling light, lean and green is the way to go. Water is scarce in this country so use it sparingly, even in a big hotel. Ordinary Cypriots at home may be on water rations if a drought is biting. Take your rubbish with you when you have finished hiking the Troödos Massif or the Akamas and Karpas (Kırpaşa) Peninsulas. Locals take pride in their countryside so follow their example. Don't pick the wildflowers in spring; others may want to enjoy them too. Spread your spending money around, and support small businesses and local artists. Visit village tavernas, not just hotel restaurants. Get to know Cyprus – not just the facilities at your hotel.

ENDANGERED SPECIES

The moufflon is Cyprus' best-known endangered species. Widespread shooting by farmers and hobby hunters over the years has reduced the numbers of this indigenous wild sheep drastically and now they are rarely, if ever, spotted wild in the Pafos Forest. A small herd is kept under protection at the Stavros tis Psokas forest station in the Pafos Forest. It is estimated that from near-extinction in the early part of the 20th century, the current moufflon population is around 10,000 (see p137 for more information).

Green and loggerhead turtles breed and live on the beaches. These endangered animals enjoy some protection in Cyprus; conservation programmes in the North and the South are in place to ensure their continuing survival (see the boxed text, p216).

Another endangered species is the monk seal, which can be spotted off parts of the coast.

> Cypriot hunters love shooting, and attempts by environmentalists to get a restriction on killing migratory birds have all been unsuccessful.

Plants

The diversity of Cyprus' flora is not immediately obvious to first-time visitors. In summer the island is arid, but spring sees an explosion of colour from its endemic flora, particularly its wildflowers. The island is home to some 1800 species and subspecies of plants, of which about 7% are indigenous to Cyprus. Plants can be found in the five major habitats that characterise Cyprus' flora profile: pine forests, *garigue* and maquis (two types of thick scrubby underbrush found in the Mediterranean), rocky areas, coastal areas and wetlands. The main places for endemic or indigenous plant species are the Troödos Massif and its western extension (the Pafos Forest), the Karpas (Kırpaşa) Peninsula and the northern coastal strip, and the southern strip of the Cape Greco Peninsula in the southeast.

About 45 species of orchids are found in Cyprus and one of these, Kotschy's bee orchid, is unique to the island. Cyprus boasts some 130 endemic plants of which 45 are found only on the high slopes of the Troödos Massif. A further 19 endemic species are found only in Northern Cyprus, with Casey's larkspur perhaps the rarest plant on the whole island. For more information see opposite.

The country's flora profile is a result of the catastrophic ice ages when much of the flora of northern and central Europe was covered in ice sheets and glaciers, while the Mediterranean basin escaped unscathed, providing a haven for the further evolution of plant life. As an island, Cyprus became rich in endemic flora and home to a large number of varied species that are typical of the Mediterranean area as a whole.

The best time to see Cyprus' wildflowers is in early spring (February and March) when most of the species enjoy a short period of blossoming and take advantage of the usually moist climate at this time of the year. There is a second period in late autumn (October and November) when flowers can also be enjoyed.

During the arid summer months only a few hardy flowers, found chiefly in the mountain regions, and colourful thistles on the Mesaoria plains provide any relief from what can seem like a botanical desert to the untrained eye.

> For fuller coverage of wildlife, the colourful photo guide *Collins Complete Mediterranean Wildlife* by Paul Sterry probably has the most comprehensive information on the region.

NATIONAL PARKS & RESERVES

The previously neglected topic of the island's national parks is now receiving some serious attention. In the South, the areas under study for inclusion as national parks include the Akamas Peninsula, the Akrotiri

BLUFF YOUR WAY TO FLOWER SPOTTING

In order to get the best out of flower spotting, enthusiasts will need to spend plenty of time trekking and searching carefully, since many species are limited to small geographical areas, sometimes to only a few hundred square metres. So arm yourselves with patience and good eyesight.

Orchids are the most popular wildflowers for enthusiasts. The one endemic orchid, Kotschy's bee orchid, is an exquisite species, looking much like a bee both in its shape and patterning. It is fairly rare yet can be found in a variety of habitats all over the island. The Troödos helleborine, while not endemic, grows mainly on the slopes of Mt Olympus. Other orchid varieties include the slender, pink Troödos Anatolian orchid, the cone-shaped pyramidal orchid, the giant orchid and the colourful woodcock orchid.

The delicate white and yellow Cyprus crocus, from the iris family, is an endangered species protected by law and is generally found at high altitudes in the Troödos Massif. The delicate, dark-red Cyprus tulip is another rare species protected by law and is today restricted to the Akamas Peninsula, the Koruçam (Kormakitis) Peninsula and parts of the Beşparmak (Pentadaktylos) Range. A member of the borage family is the endemic Troödos golden drop, a small, yellow, bell-shaped flower appearing in leafy clusters. This endangered species is confined to the highest peaks of the Troödos Massif.

In the North, the unlikely sounding St Hilarion cabbage is found mainly on rocky outcrops near St Hilarion Castle. This large endemic cabbage flower grows to 1m in height and has spikes of creamy white flowers. Also found near St Hilarion is Casey's larkspur, a late-flowering species that carries a dozen or more deep-violet, long-spurred flowers atop a slender stem. Its habitat is limited to the northern extremity of one small rocky peak 1.5km southwest of St Hilarion.

While it is only possible to scratch the surface here, there are some good publications available for the seriously botanically minded. When looking for wildflowers, travel light and on foot. Only take photos of the flowers you spot; leave the flowers themselves, as their existence may be tenuous at best. Other people will no doubt want to enjoy their beauty as well.

Salt Lake and Fassouri Marsh, and the Platys Valley. Two forest nature reserves have already been established at Tripylos (including Cedar Valley) and at Troödos. There is one marine reserve, the Lara Toxeftra Reserve on the west coast, which was established to protect marine turtles and their nesting beaches. There are also six national forest parks that have been set up in recent years.

In the North, plans are afoot to declare the far eastern section of the Karpas Peninsula as a nature reserve. Marine turtles nest on beaches on the northern and southern sides of the peninsula.

ENVIRONMENTAL ISSUES

Like most modern nations today, Cyprus is feeling the pinch in matters relating to urban encroachment, water and air pollution, erosion and deforestation. Significant urban encroachment took place in the South after 1974, when vast hotel complexes were built in pristine or sparsely populated coastal areas, particularly near Lemesos and Agia Napa. While many would argue that the saturation point has been reached, new hotel complexes are still being built to soak up more of the tourist dollar. These complexes use up considerable amounts of energy and, in particular, water, which is in permanent short supply.

In the North, where authorities have not yet experienced the advantages and disadvantages of mass tourism, there's been the chance to monitor encroachment more carefully. In some large areas, notably the Karpas Peninsula, large-scale development is now banned.

To find out whether the beach outside your hotel is clean and safe, go to www.blueflag.org.

THE ODD CAROB

The carob (*Ceratonia siliqua*) is a leguminous evergreen tree native to the coastal regions of the Mediterranean basin. It grows in abundance in Cyprus and was once one of the island's most valuable crops. Its dark green leaves are quite distinctive and the trees can often be found interspersed with the lighter green olive trees along Cyprus' north coast.

The long beanlike pods are not used directly for human consumption, though you can eat the dark-brown dried pods raw – they taste rather like chocolate. They are instead used to produce seed gums and kibble (fruit pulp without seeds). Many products are also made from kibble for human consumption including sweets, biscuits and drinks. The kernels are made into a carob-bean gum and germ meal. The gum from the seeds is used in the food-processing industries in soups, sauces and a large range of manufactured dairy products.

Carobs are polygamous: they can have either a male flower, a female flower or flowers can be hermaphrodite (both male and female). Stop and examine these odd trees and their curious fruit as you drive around the island. Eat a pod or two if you're bold enough.

Overall, authorities on both sides of the border are now belatedly taking a more cautious approach to conservation issues, and there are small but active conservationist groups making waves in the country. As a visitor, be aware that the tourist presence does have an impact on the country and, wherever possible, make sure that your presence is as unobtrusive as possible (see p43).

Food & Drink

One of the best things about Cyprus is its cuisine. The Cypriots love their food; they enjoy it and take it very seriously. Celebrations are never without an army of little plates crowding the long tables. There are endless meze, fresh fish, flavoursome vegetables and fruit dripping with juice. It would be limiting to say that Cypriot food is a combination of Greek and Turkish cuisine only (although these are big mama and papa). Middle Eastern influences are powerful here, the flavours of Syria and Lebanon hard to miss, and the Armenian community, long-present in Cyprus, has added its own touches. And don't forget the Brits. Although they're not renowned for their indigenous cuisine, the British have influenced many restaurant menus in Cyprus, with an English breakfast snuggling up comfortably next to a Cypriot one.

STAPLES & SPECIALITIES

Cypriots generally eat three meals a day, but dinner time is real food time. Breakfast is a combination of olives, grilled or fresh haloumi (in Greek; helimi in Turkish) cheese, bread and tomatoes, and a coffee of course. It's a wonderful combination to start your day.

Lunch is usually eaten at home, and a Cypriot's larder is filled with pulses and grains, which are often eaten as part of this meal. *Pilaf* (cracked wheat, steamed together with fried onions and chicken stock, and served with plain yoghurt) is common at lunchtime, accompanied by meat and vegetables. For a meat-free lunch, *louvia me lahana* (greens cooked with black-eyed beans and served with olive oil and fresh lemon juice) is fantastic. In spring, when the young vines show their sturdy green leaves, the Cypriots pick them and roll them around meat and rice, and cook them in tomato sauce, or just plain, for a dish called *koupepia*. If you like stuffed vegetables, then you'll be in heaven here, with *yemista* (stuffed courgettes) or dolmades (stuffed vine leaves). Tomatoes, onions, courgettes, peppers, aubergines and marrows: everything is subject to stuffing. *Melintzanes yiahni* is a mouthwatering bake of aubergines, garlic and fresh tomatoes. The famous *spanakopitta* is a combination of spinach, feta cheese and eggs, wrapped or layered in paper-thin filo pastry.

A more complicated but equally scrumptious dish that you might be able to try in a Cypriot home is *tava*, a lamb and beef casserole, cooked with tomatoes, onions, potatoes and cumin, and named after the earthenware pots in which it is cooked. Another highlight is *stifado*, a real treat

For a thorough rundown of Cypriot cuisine go to www.cyprus.com, where you can learn how to make Turkish or Greek coffee, step by step.

THE UBIQUITOUS HALOUMI

A Cypriot house without a round moon of haloumi (in Greek; helimi in Turkish) in its fridge is like a church without a crucifix. Officially recognised by the EU as a traditional Cypriot product, and therefore only made in Cyprus, haloumi will feature in most of your meals as an integral part or as a side dish. It's made from goat's or sheep's milk, or a combination of the two, which has been soaked in brine and mint. It's stored in a straw container and matured until it reaches its rubbery texture and mild flavour. You can eat haloumi raw, with olives and tomatoes, or set its taste off against a slice of cool watermelon in the summer. It's particularly delicious when grilled, with some tomato-soaked bread, or in a hot pitta bread, peeking out from underneath a mountain of salad. The Cypriots use haloumi in soups and pasta dishes, or scrambled with eggs for a big breakfast. So, get your chef's hat on and see what you can do with this wonder-cheese.

for the tastebuds: this rich stew, made with beef or rabbit, is cooked with lots of onions and simmered in vinegar and wine. If you're lucky enough to know Cypriots who have a traditional sealed oven in their garden, you might get to try *ofto kleftiko*. For this dish, the meat, usually lamb, comes out juicy and tender, swimming in its own delicious fat. A more basic version of this is *ofto*, a simple meat and vegetable roast.

> If you've always wanted to make your own haloumi (helimi) cheese, check out the recipes on www.gourmetsleuth .com/recipe_halloumi cheese.

If you get a chance, try homemade soup. *Trahana* is a mixture of cracked wheat and yoghurt, and *avgolemono* is chicken-stock soup, thickened with egg plus a bit of lemon for tanginess.

In the North, you'll most likely eat in a *meyhane* (tavern), the no-frills Turkish eatery. The real Turkish culinary expertise lies in kebabs, most of which are made from lamb, although there are also chicken and fish variations. Kebabs are usually wrapped in a flat bread with salad, and accompanied by a cool *ayran*, a salty refreshing yoghurt drink. There are doner kebabs, ubiquitous in Western kebab shops. *Urfa* kebab comes with lots of onions and black pepper, while *Adana*, one of the most delicious of kebabs is slightly hot, with spicy red

---

TRAVEL YOUR TASTEBUDS: EATING MEZE IN CYPRUS

Prepare yourself for an assault by food: a pleasant assault, an exercise in overeating, a sampling and gorging on around thirty different dishes. The small plates may look unthreatening, but they keep on coming, promising a night of indigestion laced with wonderful memories of the delicious contents of meze.

The word meze is short for *mezedes* or 'little delicacies', and is shared by the Greeks and Turks equally. Meze is almost never served for one: two is the minimum, and three's never a crowd but the beginning of a beautiful feast. Try to dine in a larger group, since sharing meze is as integral to the experience of eating it as the variety of the dishes themselves. All the shoving and pushing, passing this and passing that, shouting across the table for more tahini or bread is a true bonding experience that Cypriots share many nights a week.

Think of eating meze as a boxing match, although not painful at all, but extremely enjoyable. In fact, let's take the boxing analogy in relation to the match's rounds. Because that's how the food arrives.

Round one: the waiter brings shiny olives, a salad and fresh bread, along with tahini, tarama-salata, *talatouri* (tzatziki) and hummus for dipping. Pace yourself, go easy on the bread, suck on an olive or two, and crunch on a salad leaf.

Round two: the vegetables. Some are garnished with lemon, some are raw, a few are pickled, or brought with haloumi (in Greek; helimi in Turkish) cheese. The sausages, and Cyprus' own *lountza* (smoked loin of pork), follow behind. Again, eat the veggies, sample a coin of sausage and a strip of cheese, but remember, a bite of each will suffice because the biggies are still to come.

Round three: roll up your sleeves, the meat is here (this doesn't apply for vegetarians, who may be able to order vegetarian meze). A meat meze is a parade of lamb, chicken, beef, pork, souvlaki (char-grilled lamb), *kleftiko* (oven-baked lamb), and *sheftalia* (a kind of spiced, grilled sausage), meatballs, smoked meat, and so on. If you're having fish meze, then expect everything from sea bass to red mullet, prawns and octopus, and of course, *calamare* (squid).

By round four you should already be near knock-out time, and the waiter approaching with fresh fruit and pastries will positively start looking like an enemy of your gut. Assess the situation carefully, and if possible, try some prickly pears – they are a real delicacy.

Be sure not to have any lunch before you go for a meze dinner. Pace yourself and eat slowly or *siga-siga*, as the Cypriots would say.

Taste the dishes, smell them, feel their texture, for there is a lot of food here and you don't want things to end before they've even started, with a full belly and no space for the mains. As with every good meal, a nice wine is recommended, so choose a good bottle and *kali orexi –* bon appétit!

pepper. There is also *şiş köfte,* which is meat barbecued on a flat skewer, and *Adana köfte.*

The Turks have also perfected the art of *patlıcan* (aubergine) dishes, and, like the Greek Cypriots, they love dolmades. The Turkish variant of dolma is meatless and is stuffed with rice, currants and pine nuts.

Cypriot desserts carry in them the rich flavours of Turkey and the Middle East. *Kandaifi* (in Greek; *kadaif* in Turkish) are strands of sugary pastry wound into a roll. *Mahalepi* (in Greek; *muhallebi* in Turkish) is an aromatic Middle Eastern rice pudding sprinkled with rose-water and pistachios. Then there is *galatopoureko* (a sweet, sticky pastry) and *rizogalo* (a simple rice pudding). Despite these sweet delights, fruit is the most common Cypriot dessert on both parts of the island.

But there's one treat that's reserved for dinner alone: meze (see the boxed text, opposite). This Cypriot speciality is unforgettable, as much for its flavours as for the sheer volume of food that crowds your table. Dishes in the North and the South are very similar, with a few local variants to make things interesting. A Turkish addition to the meze menu is *börek* (pastry parcels; either rolled up like cigarettes and known as *sigara böreği,* or cut into triangles like Indian samosas).

Meze Cooking by Sarah Maxwell, praised by gourmets all over the Mediterranean, contains recipes for more than 100 different meze dishes.

DRINKS
Nonalcoholic Drinks

Greek or Turkish coffee should be 'hot as hell, dark as night, bitter as poison or sweet as love' according to aficionados. When you order your coffee, you will be asked how you like it: *glykos* (in Greek), *çok şekerli* (in Turkish) is with sugar (sweet as love); *metrios* (in Greek), *orta* (in Turkish) is medium-sweet; *sketos* (in Greek), *şekersiz* (in Turkish) is unsweetened (bitter as poison).

The younger generations prefer frappé (iced instant coffee), which is seriously popular and really quite refreshing as a pick-me-up on a hot day.

Alcoholic Drinks

Drinking alcohol in the dedicated pub sense – as in the UK or Australia, for example – is generally unknown in Cyprus. Alcohol is normally taken with food or at least meze. Local beer comes in two brands: Cypriot-made KEO, and Danish-inspired but Cypriot-brewed Carlsberg. Other beers, while available, are normally more expensive. In the North you will commonly find Efes or Gold Fassl beer. While they are nominally Muslims, many Turkish Cypriots either drink alcohol or are quite happy to let others enjoy it freely.

Rakı (Turkish) or *zivania* (Greek) is the local firewater made from distilling the leftovers of the grape crushing. It is strong, so beware. It goes well as an apéritif, with meze or any other food. Wine is popular on both sides of Cyprus.

Commandaria from Kolossi, near Lemesos, is Cyprus' most famous export fortified wine; its popularity dates back to the time of the crusades.

CELEBRATIONS

Religious festivals play an important part in Cypriot life and food is prepared to fit and symbolise various parts of the festivities. For Greek Cypriots, celebrations or large family meals are usually accompanied by a *souvla:* large chunks of lamb, flavoured with fresh herbs, threaded onto a spit and grilled over charcoal. Easter is the most important of Greek

Orthodox festivities, so the days preceding and during Easter are filled with food-related activities. The 40 days of Lent are the best time for eating vegetarian food, and Easter Sunday brings dishes such as cheese pies and salads. But the lamb, after so many meatless days, steals the show. Orthodox followers also fast for 40 days before Christmas; then on Christmas Day they slaughter and roast a piglet.

The Muslims in the Turkish Cypriot North also fast, then eat a lot during their religious festivities. During the month of Ramadan (Ramazan in Turkish), observing Muslims eat nothing and drink nothing from sunrise to sunset, but as soon as the cannon announces the İftar (the breaking of the fast), tons of food are brought to the table, and eating commences and goes on into the night. It's a sociable occasion and mealtimes are shared with friends, family and neighbours.

The last three days of Ramadan are called Bayramı, of which there are two 'types': Şeker Bayramı (Sweets Holiday) and Kurban Bayramı (Sacrifice Holiday). The latter, marking İbrahim's near-sacrifice of his son İsmael, is the charitable holiday, with the head of the household (who can afford to) sacrificing a cow or sheep. The meat is then given to the poor, as well as family and neighbours.

Bayramı is a time for home visits. Plenty of sweets are served, the best and most popular of which is baklava.

Geroskipou village (just east of Pafos) broke the world record for the largest slab of Turkish delight in 2004, beating the Australian 1997 world record of 2.349 tons with a slab weighing in at 2.543 tons.

WHERE TO EAT & DRINK

The taverna is where Cypriots go to eat if they don't eat at home, and there is one in every Cypriot town and village. A taverna can be a no-frills village eatery, or a more upmarket restaurant with a traditional leaning. The *psistaria* specialises in souvlaki (char-grilled lamb), and the *psarotaverna* mainly has fish. The Greek word for restaurant is *estiatorio* although every restaurant in Cyprus has an English 'restaurant' sign on it and a menu in English. *Meyhanes* are Turkish taverns where you can eat meze, meat, fish and anything else, and drink lots of *rakı*. In the North, *lokanta* is an informal restaurant and a *restoran* is a more upmarket version, and again English-language signs are everywhere. *Hazır yemek* ('ready food') restaurants specialise in dishes that have been prepared in advance and kept warm in steam trays; these dishes are best eaten earlier in the day when they're fresh. You'll see signs for *kebapçı* (kebab shops) and *ocakbaşı* (fireside kebab shops) where you can watch your kebab being prepared.

The *kafeneio* is central to any self-respecting Greek Cypriot village's existence. Traditionally, *kafeneia* serve coffee and little snacks of haloumi, tomatoes and olives, and they are only frequented by (older) men.

In the North, *pastanes* (patisseries) sell sugary treats, such as biscuits (*kuru pasta*; dry pastry) and cakes and sweet, sweet baklavas (*yaş pasta*; moist pastry). Beware of the difference between *pasta* (pastry) and *makarna* (noodles).

Quick Eats

Traditional fast food in Cyprus is the kebab, or souvlaki. Meat is barbecued, stuffed into a pitta or rolled in a flat bread and accompanied with a big salad, which is garnished with lemon juice. Also, like in most places in the world, Western fast-food chains are mushrooming on the island.

VEGETARIANS & VEGANS

Food for vegetarians is rarely marketed as such. Even restaurants catering primarily for tourists may not make traditional (vegetarian) dishes.

CYPRUS' TOP FIVE

- Seven St Georges' Tavern, Pafos (p126) – everything you eat and drink in this place is grown, dried or pickled organically by the owner
- Tziellari, Lefkosia (South Nicosia; p70) – an atmospheric spot with traditional dancing, meze and Cypriot brandy
- 127, Lemesos (p88) – visit this place for a salad you won't forget
- Oasis at Ayiflon Restaurant, Dipkarpaz (Rizokarpaso; p218) – follow the world's only advert-by-poetry to the best fish on the Karpas (Kırpaşa) Peninsula
- Idris ustanın yeri, Kyrenia (Girne; p190) – try this workers' eatery for simple and delicious food

---

Instead, you can choose dishes made from vegetables or pulses, which will more often than not appear on restaurant menus anyway. Vegetarian meze is available in some restaurants, and vegetarian moussaka is a popular dish on the menu.

EATING WITH KIDS

Children will have a great time eating in Cyprus, as the majority of establishments, and Cypriots in general, are child-friendly. In fact, most waiters and waitresses will probably run around and entertain your children, and you'll just have to hope that nothing gets broken. Menus are generally the same for adults and children, although some restaurants have a children's menu aimed at tourists, with chips and burgers (and fishfingers) as their options.

For more information on travelling with children, see p224.

HABITS & CUSTOMS

The Cypriots eat their lunch around two or three in the afternoon. Most shops and restaurants close after 2pm, when the proprietors go home and have their lunch and a snooze. Dinner is eaten rather late and over a few hours, and restaurants get pretty full after 9pm or 10pm.

Eating out is very popular in Cyprus, and with all the meze, it's a lot of fun.

EAT YOUR WORDS

Want to know a doner from a kebab, or a souvlaki from a *gyros*? Get behind the cuisine scene, by getting to know the language. For pronunciation details see p247.

If you're a vegetarian and you love Greek cuisine, try out Diane Kochikas' Greek Vegetarian Encyclopaedia for a meatless menu.

Useful Phrases

GREEK

Do you have a menu in English?
Έχετε το μενού στα αγγλικά;   e·he·te to me·nu stang·gli·ka

I'd like ...
Θα ήθελα ...   tha i·the·la ...

Please bring the bill.
Το λογαριασμό, παρακαλώ.   to lo·ghar·ya·zmo, pa·ra·ka·lo

I'm a vegetarian.
Είμαι χορτοφάγος.   i·me khor·to·fa·ghos

I don't eat meat or dairy products.
Δε τρώω κρέας ή γαλακτοκομικά προϊόντα.   dhen tro·o kre·as i gha·la·kto·ko·mi·ka pro·i·on·da

TURKISH

I'd like the menu (in English), please.
(İngilizce) Menüyü istiyorum lütfen.
(een·gee·*leez*·je) me·new·*yew* ees·*tee*·yo·room lewt·fen

The bill, please.
Hesap lütfen.
he·*sap* lewt·fen

Do you have any dishes without meat?
Etsiz yemek yemekleriniz var mı?
et·*seez* ye·mek·le·ree·*neez* var muh

I'm allergic to ...
... alerjim var.
... a·ler·*zheem* var

dairy produce
Süt ürünlerine
sewt ew·rewn·le·ree·*ne*

eggs
Yumurtaya
yoo·moor·ta·*ya*

nuts
Çerezlere
che·rez·le·*re*

seafood
Deniz ürünlerine
de·*neez* ew·rewn·le·ree·*ne*

Food Glossary

GREEK

Staples

αλάτι	a·*la*·ti	salt
αυγά	a·vgha	eggs
βούτυρο	*vu*·ti·ro	butter
γάλα	gha·la	milk
ελαιόλαδο	e·le·*o*·la·dho	olive oil
ελιές	e·lyes	olives
ζάχαρη	*za*·kha·ri	sugar
μέλι	*me*·li	honey
ξύδι	*ksi*·dhi	vinegar
πιπέρι	pi·*pe*·ri	pepper
τυρί	ti·*ri*	cheese
ψωμί	pso·*mi*	bread

Meat, Fish & Seafood

αρνί	ar·*ni*	lamb
αστακός	a·sta·*kos*	lobster
βοδινό	vo·dhi·*no*	beef
γαρίδες	gha·*ri*·dhes	prawns
καλαμάρι	ka·la·*ma*·ri	squid
κατσικάκι	ka·tsi·*ka*·ki	kid (goat)
κέφαλος	*ke*·fa·los	grey mullet
κολιός	ko·li·*os*	mackerel
κοτόπουλο	ko·*to*·pu·lo	chicken
λαγός	la·*ghos*	hare
μαρίδες	ma·*ri*·dhes	whitebait
μοσχάρι	mo·*sha*·ri	veal
μπαρμπούνια	bar·*bu*·nya	red mullet
μύδια	*mi*·di·a	mussels
σαρδέλες	sar·*dhe*·les	sardines
φαγρί/λιθρίνι/ μελανούρι	fa·*ghri*/li·*thri*·ni/ me·la·*nu*·ri	sea bream
χοιρινό	hyi·ri·*no*	pork
χταπόδι	khta·*po*·dhi	octopus

Fruit & Vegetables

καρότο	ka·*ro*·to	carrot
κρεμμύδια	kre·*mi*·dhi·a	onions
λεμόνι	le·*mo*·ni	lemon
μελιτζάνες	me·li·*dza*·nes	aubergine (eggplant)
μήλο	*mi*·lo	apple
ντομάτα	do·*ma*·ta	tomato
πατάτες	pa·*ta*·tes	potatoes
πιπεριές	pi·per·*yez*	peppers
πορτοκάλι	por·to·*ka*·li	orange
ροδάκινο	ro·*dha*·ki·no	peach
σκόρδο	*skor*·dho	garlic
σπανάκι	spa·*na*·ki	spinach
σπαράγγια	spa·*rang*·gi·a	asparagus
σταφύλια	sta·*fi*·li·a	grapes
φράουλα	*fra*·u·la	strawberry

Drinks

καφές	ka·*fes*	coffee
κρασί	kra·*si*	wine
(κόκκινο/άσπρο)	(*ko*·ki·no/*a*·spro)	(red/white)
μπύρα	*bi*·ra	beer
νερό	*ne*·ro	water
τσάι	*tsa*·i	tea

TURKISH
Staples

çorba	chor·*ba*	soup
ekmek	ek·*mek*	bread
pirinç/pilav	pee·*reench*/pee·*lav*	rice
yoğurt	yo·*oort*	yoghurt

Meat, Fish & Seafood

ahtapot	ah·ta·*pot*	octopus
alabalık	a·la·ba·*luhk*	trout
barbunya	bar·*boon*·ya	red mullet
çiğer	jee·*er*	liver
çipura	jee·*poo*·ra	sea bream
hamsi	ham·*see*	anchovy
istakoz	ees·ta·*koz*	lobster
kalkan	kal·*kan*	turbot
karides	ka·ree·*des*	shrimp
levrek	lev·*rek*	sea bass
midye	*meed*·ye	mussels
palamut	pa·la·*moot*	mackerel
piliç/tavuk	pee·*leech*/ta·*vook*	chicken
sardalya	sar·*dal*·ya	sardine
ton baliği	ton ba·luh·*uh*	tuna

Fruit & Vegetables

bamya	bam·*ya*	okra
biber	bee·*ber*	pepper
domates	do·ma·*tes*	tomato
elma	el·*ma*	apple
karpuz	kar·*pooz*	watermelon

kavun	ka·*voon*	cantaloupe melon
kayısı	ka·yuh·*suh*	apricot
kiraz	kee·*raz*	cherry
kuru fasulye	koo·*roo* fa·*sool*·ye	white beans
muz	mooz	banana
patates	pa·ta·*tes*	potato
portakal	por·ta·*kal*	orange
salata	sa·la·*ta*	salad
salatalık	sa·la·ta·*luhk*	cucumber
soğan	so·*an*	onion
taze fasulye	*ta*·ze fa·*sool*·ye	green beans
zeytin	zay·*teen*	olive

Drinks

bira	bee·*ra*	beer
buz	booz	ice
maden suyu	ma·*den* soo·*yoo*	mineral water
meyve suyu	may·*ve* soo·*yoo*	fruit juice
şarap	sha·rap	wine
su	soo	water
süt	sewt	milk

The Republic of Cyprus

CHRISTINA DAMEYER

Lefkosia (South Nicosia)
Λευκωσία Lefkoşa

If you get tired of the coast's lazy, beach-bum lifestyle, and even if you don't, make sure you spend some time in the country's capital, known officially (and to Greek speakers) as Lefkosia. The city been labelled with the beaten cliché of 'the last divided capital', a reality that, although still present, is slowly changing thanks to 24-hour checkpoint crossing into its northern half. Clichés aside, Lefkosia (population 213,500) is an attractive, enticing city and the country's cultural heart; it's ideal for experiencing what modern Cyprus is all about. There are great restaurants here, from dark taverns with dancing families and bouzouki players beside metres of meze, to ultramodern, fashionable joints, where young Cypriots twitch to the sounds of electronic music. The country's best museum is here, with its extensive archaeological collection. The long, glitzy stretch of Leoforos Arhiepiskopou Makariou III (Makarios Ave) is a consumer's heaven, with chain, designer and local shops displaying goods not for the thrifty-hearted. The Old City with its curious shape that's been likened to a snowflake or a hand grenade is a labyrinth of narrow streets, teeming during the day and ghostly at night. It hides churches, mosques and beautiful, often dilapidated colonial houses.

Lefkosia's high summer temperatures are both a curse and a blessing. It can be painful to traipse along melting pavements at high noon, along with mad dogs and Englishmen, but the heat rescues Lefkosia from the hordes of tourists holidaying on the rest of the island.

The city is split almost evenly between the Turkish-occupied North and the Republican South. The modern parts of (Greek) Lefkosia look like the made up, face-lifted sister of the crackly skinned, traditional (Turkish) North Nicosia, whose streets are full of crafts and faces you may think belong to three centuries ago. Lefkosia/North Nicosia as a whole reflects the story of Cyprus: its two people, divided, hoping for a future that may bring a better solution. With crossing to and fro made easier, in Lefkosia things are already looking up. And what better place to start preparing for the future than in the capital?

HIGHLIGHTS

- Explore the fantastically preserved **Venetian walls** (p61) that surround the Old City
- Delve into the country's ancient past at the **Cyprus Museum** (p63)
- Pamper yourself at the luxurious (yet afford-able) **Omeriye Hammam** (p65)
- Check out **Faneromeni Church** (p64) and its peaceful square, which was once the centre of city activity
- Dine on meze at **Tziellari** (p70) and dance to bouzouki music

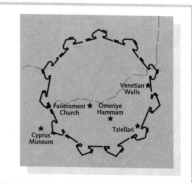

HISTORY

Established in the middle of the wide Mesaoria plain on the Pedieos River for defence purposes, Lefkosia has always been the country's capital. The city was originally known as Ledra, the name kept by one of its major streets, and grew extensively during the Byzantine period. The Venetians, who briefly held Lefkosia from 1489, built the stone defensive walls around the city. But these did little to keep the Ottomans out in 1570. Life in Lefkosia under the Ottomans saw little growth, and only when the British took control in 1878 did the city begin to spread beyond its walls.

Violence inspired by the Ethniki Organosi tou Kypriakou Agona (EOKA; National Organisation for the Cypriot Struggle) against the British in the 1950s and then the Turkish Cypriots in the '60s saw considerable carnage on the streets of Lefkosia. Intercommunal disturbances between Greek and Turkish Cypriots in 1963 brought a de facto partition of the city. The so-called 'Green Line' came into being at this time when the British military defined the Greek and Turkish areas using a green pen on a military map. The name has stuck to this day. The Turkish invasion of 1974 finally divided the city and it has remained so ever since, chaperoned by the watchful but increasingly weary eyes of UN peacekeeping forces. In 2003, crossing the Green Line was made easier, and now numerous Turkish Cypriots from the northern side of the city come to work in the southern side of the capital. Many protests take place in Lefkosia for the abolishment of the Green Line and the buffer zone, but so far to no avail.

ORIENTATION

The most interesting part of the city for visitors is the Old City, inside the 16th-century Venetian walls. Reduced in height and dissected by wide thoroughfares, the walls are hardly visible in places. The town centre is Plateia Eleftherias on the southwestern edge of the walls. Fireworks are held here on New Year's Eve. The UN crossover point (the Ledra Palace Hotel crossing) is at the far west, and Famagusta Gate is near the Caraffa Bastion to the east. At the base of the walls there are car parks and municipal gardens. See p174 for orientation tips on that half of the city.

The New City sprawls outwards south of the Venetian walls, and its main artery is the modern Leoforos Arhiepiskopou Makariou III (Makarios Ave) where dozens of cafés, bars, restaurants and shops attract Lefkosians.

Maps

The Cyprus Tourism Organisation (CTO; p61) has a fairly reasonable map of Lefkosia city centre and, on the reverse side, greater Lefkosia. This is available free from all CTO

LEFKOSIA IN...

Two Days

Start your day walking along the **Venetian walls** (p61), the city's guardians for centuries. Go to **Famagusta Gate** (p62), where concerts and other events are often held. Visit **Faneromeni Church** (p64), and have a fresh juice at the **Double Six Coffee Bar** (p71). Check out the views of the city from the **Ledra Museum-Observatory** (p64) and see the Green Line. Visit the **Cyprus Museum** (p63), where the oldest artefact dates back to 8000 BC. Dine to *rembetika* music at **Tziellari** (p70), and have some drinks at **Hammam** (p72).

On day two, visit the extravagant **House of Hatzigeorgakis Kornesios** (p65) and the **Archbishop's Palace** (p65) fronted by the looming statue of Archbishop Makarios III. In the afternoon, have a luxurious Turkish bath in the **Omeriye Hammam** (p65). Dine at the **Syrian Arab Friendship Club** (p71) and check out the bars on the trendy Leoforos Arhiepiskopou Makariou III (Makarios Ave).

Four Days

Follow the two-day itinerary, then on your third day visit **North Nicosia** (Lefkoşa; p172) for the day. On the fourth day visit the **Lefkosia Arts Centre & Library** (p66) and then relax in the leafy **municipal gardens** (p68). Dine on brilliant pizza at **Da Paolo** (p70) and drink at **Plato's** (p73), a place reminiscent of a Parisian bistro.

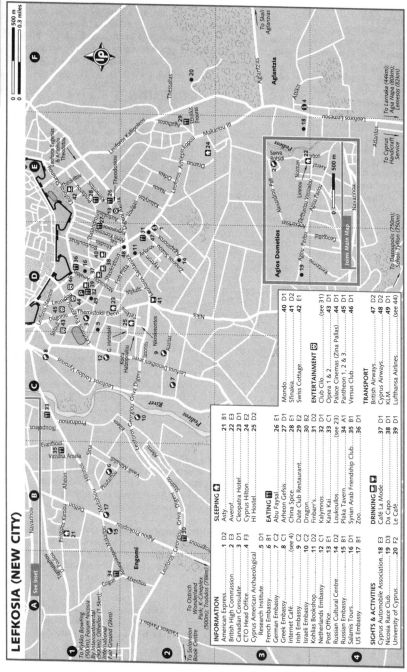

LEFKOSIA (NEW CITY)

INFORMATION
American Express.............................1 D2
British High Commission....................2 E3
Canadian Consulate...........................3 D1
CTO Head Office...............................4 F3
Cyprus American Archaeological
  Research Institute............................5 D1
French Embassy.................................6 B1
German Embassy................................7 C2
Greek Embassy...............................(see 4)
Internet Café.....................................8 C1
Irish Embassy.....................................9 C2
Israeli Embassy................................10 D2
Kohlias Bookshop.............................11 D2
Netherlands Embassy........................12 C1
Post Office..13 E1
Russian Cultural Centre....................14 D2
Russian Embassy..............................15 B1
Salamis Tours...................................16 D1
US Embassy......................................17 B1

SIGHTS & ACTIVITIES
Cyprus Automobile Association......18 D2
Nicosia Race Club.............................19 D3
University of Cyprus.........................20 F2

SLEEPING
Asty...21 B1
Averof...22 E3
Cleopatra Hotel................................23 D1
Cyprus Hilton..................................24 E2
HI Hostel...25 D2

EATING
Abu Faysal......................................26 E1
Arheon Gefsis..................................27 D1
China Spice.....................................28 E1
Date Club Restaurant......................29 E2
Dragon..30 B2
Finbarr's..31 D2
Kalymnos...32 C1
Kana Kai..33 C1
Loukoullos....................................(see 23)
Plaka Tavern...................................34 A1
Syrian Arab Friendship Club............35 B1
Zoo...36 D1

Mondo...40 D1
Sfinakia...41 D2
Swiss Cottage..................................42 E1

ENTERTAINMENT
Club Clio......................................(see 31)
Opera 1 & 2.....................................43 D1
Palace Cinemas (Zina Pallas)............44 D1
Pantheon 1, 2 & 3............................45 D1
Versus Club......................................46 D1

TRANSPORT
British Airways..................................47 D2
Cyprus Airways.................................48 D1
KLM...49 D1
Lufthansa Airlines.........................(see 44)

DRINKING
Café La Mode...................................37 D1
Da Capo...38 D1
Le Café..39 D1

offices. The *Street & Tourist Map of Nicosia* has much better coverage of the outer suburbs and also has a street index. This map is available from most bookshops or stationery shops in Lefkosia.

Some bookshops stock a street directory of sorts, but it is poorly produced and of little practical value. Public street-map displays of the 'You Are Here' kind are found around central Lefkosia.

INFORMATION
Bookshops
There are only a few bookshops in Lefkosia that may be of interest to foreign visitors. Foreign-language newspapers and magazines can be found at either of the Periptero Hellas or Miltis & Evgenis kiosks on the west side of Plateia Eleftherias.

Kohlias Bookshop (Map p58; ☎ 2246 1766; fax 2244 6258; Avlonos 9) Specialises in art books and Cypriot publications.

MAM (Map p60; ☎ 2275 3536; mam@mam.cy.net; Leoforos Konstantinou Paleologou 19) A leading academic bookstore that is worth seeking out.

Moufflon Bookshop (Map p60; ☎ 2266 5155; bookshop@moufflon.com.cy; Sofouli 1) This shop deals primarily in English-language titles (new and secondhand) and stocks a wide range of Lonely Planet guides. It has a good section of books on Cyprus both in English and Greek.

Soloneion Book Centre (☎ 2266 6799; Vyzantiou 24, Strovolos) A little south of the New City, it might also serve your needs.

Cultural Centres
A number of cultural centres offer a wide range of periodicals and books for reference:

British Council (Map p60; ☎ 2266 5152; Leoforos Mouseiou 3)

Cyprus American Archaeological Research Institute (Map p58; ☎ 2267 0832; Andrea Dimitriou 11)

Russian Cultural Centre (Map p58; ☎ 2276 1607; Alasias 16)

Emergency
The general emergency numbers for police and ambulance are ☎ 199 or ☎ 112.

Police station (Map p60; ☎ 2247 7434) Located in the Old City, at the northern end of Ledra, by the barrier.

Internet Access
Internet Café (Map p58; ☎ 2233 9936; Leoforos Lemesou 17a; per hr CY£1; ☺ noon-2am Mon-Fri, 2pm-2am Sat & Sun) In the New City; somewhat inconveniently situated near the CTO.

Nicosia Palace Arcade (Map p60; ☎ 2266 3653; Leoforos Kostaki Pantelidi; per hr CY£1; ☺ 10am-11pm) On the edge of the Old City.

Printways (Map p60; ☎ 2266 1628; Rigenis 63B; per hr CY£1; ☺ 10am-11pm) Close to the Holiday Inn hotel.

Laundry
Express Dry Cleaners (Map p60; Ippokratous 49) In the Old City; will do a service wash for you for about CY£4.

Libraries
At least five public or semipublic libraries in Lefkosia are open for research and reading, although you cannot take books home. The following places are all located on the map of Lefkosia's Old City (p60).

Ahilleios Library (☎ 2276 3033; Leoforos Konstantinou Paleologou 30)

Lefkosia Municipal Arts Centre & Library (☎ 2243 2577; Apostolou Varnava 19)

Makarios Cultural Foundation & Library (☎ 2243 0008; Plateia Arhiepiskopou Kyprianou)

Ministry of Education Library (☎ 2230 3180; Leoforos Konstantinou Paleologou)

Severios Library (☎ 2234 4888; Plateia Arhiepiskopou Kyprianou)

Medical Services
If you need a private doctor or pharmacy, ring ☎ 1432. Visiting hours for doctors are normally from 9am to 1pm and 4pm to 7pm. Local newspapers list pharmacies that are open during the night and on weekends and holidays, as well as the names of doctors who are on call out of normal hours.

Lefkosia General Hospital (Map p60; ☎ 2280 1400; Leoforos Nechrou) West of the Old City.

Money
There are ATMs all over the city that accept most cards. A handy place for cash is the corner of Plateia Eleftherias and Leoforos Konstantinou Paleologou. Banks include the following:

American Express (Map p58; ☎ 2276 5607; Agapinoros 2d; ☺ 8.30am-5pm Mon-Fri, 9am-1.30pm Sat) In the New City.

Hellenic Bank (Map p60; Solonos 1a; ☺ 2.30-6.30pm Mon-Fri Sep-May, 2.30-8pm Mon-Fri Jun-Aug) Near the CTO; provides an afternoon tourist service.

Photography
Andreas Papaeracleous Photostore (Map p60; ☎ 2266 6101; Rigenis 48) In the Old City; this is a well-stocked shop catering to all your photography needs.

LEFKOSIA (SOUTH NICOSIA)

LEFKOSIA (OLD CITY)

300 m
0.2 miles

NORTH NICOSIA (LEFKOŞA)

Post

Post office (Map p60; ☎ 2230 3123; Leoforos Konstantinou Paleologou; ✆ 9am-1pm & 3-6pm Mon, Tue, Thu, Fri, 8.30am-1pm Sat) The central post office is east of Plateia Eleftherias. This is where poste restante mail comes to. There is also a small post office close to the northern end of Ledra near the Green Line lookout, and another branch in the New City.

Telephone

The main telephone centre in Lefkosia is the Cyprus Telecommunications Authority (CYTA; Map p60), which is close to Pafos Gate. It has some phone booths inside and outside the building.

There is no real cause to go there since public phones are found throughout the city, with a large concentration on Plateia Eleftherias.

Toilets

Public toilets are situated near the Venetian walls; the nearest ones to the centre are by Plateia Eleftherias. There are also toilets in Laïki Yitonia, near the CTO office.

Tourist Information

Cyprus Tourism Organisation (CTO; www.visitcyprus .org.cy) head office (Map p58; ☎ 2233 7715; fax 2233 1644; Leoforos Lemesou 19); Old City (Map p60; ☎ 2244 4264; Aristokyprou 11; ✆ 8.30am-4pm Mon-Fri, 8.30am-2pm Sat) The CTO's head office is in the New City, although it is not really geared to handling over-the-counter queries from the public. There's a branch in the touristy, restored area of the Old City.

Travel Agencies

While you'll find a large number of travel agencies throughout Lefkosia, none is likely to offer significant price advantages over the others. One that is helpful:

Salamis Tours (Map p58; ☎ 2276 2323; fax 2275 8337; Arnaldas 7c) In the New City; arranges airline tickets and other travel-related bookings, including cruise tickets for Salamis Lines.

Universities

University of Cyprus (Map p58; ☎ 2289 2000; www .ucy.ac.cy; Kallipoleos 75) The only university in the Republic of Cyprus is on the southeastern side of the New City. It was established in 1989 and admitted its first students in 1992. It currently has around 3000 undergraduate students and 500 postgraduate students.

DANGERS & ANNOYANCES

Lefkosia is a remarkably safe city to walk around. However, the Old City streets, particularly near the Green Line, can appear dingy and threatening at night, and solo women should avoid them. Crossing into the North is allowed only at official checkpoints; you'd be ill-advised to try to cross at any other place. This illegal move would lead to serious trouble.

SIGHTS & ACTIVITIES

The sights in this section are found on the map of the Old City (p60). Allow yourself at least two days to see most of the major sights properly.

Venetian Walls

The Venetian walls are like Lefkosia's logo. They form a border around the Old City that is so unique that when you see it once, on a map or from a high viewpoint, you'll never forget it. And that's partly to do with its odd shape: is it like a snowflake? A star? A hand grenade? Or a horizontally sliced artichoke?

Despite its impressive appearance, this circular defence wall that surrounds both the northern and southern halves of the

---

PREPARING A NEW SQUARE

A massive reconstruction project is about to begin in Lefkosia's Plateia Eleftherias. A sweeping, floor-lit design is intended to paint the capital's main attraction, the Venetian walls, in sharp relief, while remaining in harmony with its ancient surroundings. The architect, Zaha Hadid, is renowned for her socially aware projects. Her impressive CV includes the Strasbourg tram station, a housing project for IBA-Block 2 in Berlin, and the Mind Zone in London's Millennium Dome. Hadid plans to construct a green belt along the moat that surrounds the walls at present, turning the area within into Lefkosia's central park, encircled by a palm-tree-lined pedestrian walkway. She calls the design an 'urban intervention' and hopes that it may become the catalyst for the eventual reunification of the island. A little over-ambitious perhaps, but the designs look promising on paper. Work should start in 2006, so watch this space.

Old City unfortunately failed in the purpose for which it was built. The Venetian rulers erected the walls between 1567 and 1570 with the express aim of keeping the feared Ottoman invaders out of Lefkosia. The appointed engineer Ascanio Savorgnano designed the ramparts and fellow engineer Francesco Barbaro built them to specifications, while adding 11 fortifying bastions spaced equally around the ramparts for added protection. A moat was also dug, although it was apparently never intended to contain water. In July 1570 the Ottomans landed in Larnaka and three months later attacked Lefkosia, storming the fortifications.

The walls have remained in place more or less unchanged ever since. Five of the bastions, **Tripoli**, **D'Avila**, **Constanza**, **Podocataro** and **Caraffa**, are in the southern sector of Lefkosia. The **Flatro** (Sibeli) Bastion on the eastern side of the Old City is occupied by Turkish, Greek Cypriot and UN military forces. The remaining bastions, **Loredano** (Cevizli), **Barbaro** (Musalla), **Quirini** (Cephane), **Mula** (Zahra) and **Roccas** (Kaytazağa), are in North Nicosia.

The city's walls were originally punctured by three gates: the Famagusta Gate (below) in the east, the Pafos Gate (right) in the west, and the Kyrenia (Girne) Gate in the north.

The Venetian walls and moat around Lefkosia are in excellent condition. They are used to provide car-parking space and venues for outdoor concerts, and for strolling and relaxing. In North Nicosia, the walls are in poorer shape and have become overgrown and dilapidated in parts. There are vehicle access points around the walls now, which allow regular traffic access to the Old City.

In the following section, the sights within the walls are organised by interest.

Famagusta Gate

The easternmost **Famagusta Gate** (Pyli Ammohostou; 9am-1pm & 4-7pm Mon-Fri) is the most photographed and best preserved of the three original gates that led into the Old City of Lefkosia. It's in the Caraffa Bastion off Leoforos Athinas. Following more than a century of neglect, the whole structure was renovated in 1981 and now serves as a concert venue and exhibition hall. Its impressive wooden door and sloping façade

open out onto a tunnel that leads through the rampart wall. Outside the tunnel and to the right is a small open-air arena where concerts by visiting artists are held, usually during the summer months. The area surrounding the gate has great trendy eating and drinking places (see p69 and p72).

Bayraktar Mosque & Liberty Monument

West of Famagusta Gate, this prominent mosque, situated on the Constanza Bastion, marks the spot where the Venetian walls were successfully breached by the Ottomans in 1570. The Ottoman *bayraktar* (standard bearer; for whom the mosque is named in Turkish) was immediately cut down by the defending forces, but his body was subsequently recovered and buried on this spot. The small mosque has attracted a lot of unwanted attention. It has been the target for terrorist activity, and in the early 1960s EOKA-inspired attacks damaged the mosque and nearby tomb of the standard bearer. It was eventually repaired and the mosque closed to the general public. In 1999 a plot was uncovered to bomb the mosque.

Close by is the elaborate **Liberty Monument**, on the Podocataro Bastion. It represents Greek Cypriots' liberation from the British Colonial powers, with figures of 14 EOKA fighters being released from prison in 1959, alongside peasants and priests, representing the various strata of Greek Cypriot society. Presiding over it is the Statue of Liberty. The monument, erected in 1973, does not include any figures of Turkish Cypriots, reflecting the divisions between the two communities.

Pafos Gate

This westernmost gate, known by the Venetians as Porta San Domenico, is one of the three traditional entrances to Old Lefkosia. It has been a spot for a kind of flag stand-off since 1963, with the flags of the Republic of Cyprus, Northern Cyprus, Greece and Turkey fluttering defiantly at each other. The gate served as an arsenal warehouse for the Ottomans, and as a police headquarters for the British. The Pafos Gate, left firmly open, guards a narrow pedestrian passage under the wall. The adjoining breach in the wall that allows traffic into the Old City is a much later addition.

Holy Cross Catholic Church

Across the road, east of the Pafos Gate on Pafou, this church is in the uncomfortable position of backing onto the Turkish sector while resting within the UN buffer zone. Despite this, the church still functions as a place of worship on the proviso that the back door leading onto the Turkish-controlled sector remains firmly closed. Mass times are posted inside the front-door vestibule.

Roccas (Kaytazağa) Bastion

The Roccas Bastion was unique throughout Cyprus in that it was the only place where Greek and Turkish Cypriots could eyeball each other at close quarters, before 2003. Now it's hardly an attraction, since it's so easy to actually cross over to the opposite side and eyeball each other face to face. It is interesting, however, as a reminder of the noncontact between the two communities that lasted for around thirty years.

It is situated about 200m south of the Ledra Palace Hotel crossing (below) and is easily identifiable by the no-parking signs along the bastion walls. The UN buffer zone separating the two sides by a normally comfortable margin virtually disappears here for a stretch of about 200m, while the border of Turkish-controlled Northern Cyprus ends at the very edge of this bastion.

If you are in North Nicosia you can easily reach the Turkish-held side of the Roccas Bastion. See the boxed text, p178 for details.

Ledra Palace Hotel Crossing

This is the only spot on the island reserved exclusively for pedestrian and bicycle crossings between the North and the South. Masses of tourists and locals now cross from one side to the other, and many cross in the middle of the night too, after a late night out.

The crossing is partially blocked by a blue-and-white painted wall with graphic posters depicting those missing since the 1974 invasion. There are also posters depicting the murder of three Greek Cypriots by Turkish soldiers near Deryneia in the eastern part of the island at a demonstration in 1996 (see p167). On Sunday mornings Greek Cypriot women gather to remember the 1974 invasion and hand out literature, accompanied by songs of lamentation and protest.

The crossing itself is about 300m long. To the left, as you head north, is the former Ledra Palace Hotel, now renovated and occupied by the UN. The renovation is part of the EU-sponsored 'Nicosia Master Plan' project. Started in 1979, many interesting and valuable buildings in the city have been (and are being) renovated. The project office is just outside the Ledra Palace Hotel, and has displays of all the work completed and planned.

Abandoned shops lie to the right of the hotel. A white iron gate marks the entry to Turkish Cypriot-controlled territory, after which lies the fairly innocuous Turkish Cypriot checkpoint building. A prominent sign welcomes you to the 'Turkish Republic of Northern Cyprus' while another sign reads 'TRNC forever'.

Cyprus Museum

This is the island's most interesting **museum** (☎ 2286 5888; Leoforos Mouseiou 1; admission CY£1.50; ⏰ 9am-5pm Mon-Sat, 10am-1pm Sun) and houses the best collection of archaeological finds in Cyprus. The original building, erected in 1883, is opposite the lovely municipal gardens. It's a 10-minute walk west of Plateia Eleftherias.

Highlights include the remarkable display of **terracotta figures** in room 4, discovered in 1929 at Agia Irini, north of Morfou (Güzelyurt) in the North. The 2000 figures, dating back to the 7th to 6th centuries BC, are displayed as they were found, in a semicircular order. Apart from two female representations, the figures are male and many are warriors. Their war chariots indicate the worship of a warrior god, presumably a centaur or minotaur. There are figures that represent demon-servants of the god; the snake representations symbolise fertility and suggest a deity that was also identified with fertility and the underworld.

Another highlight is the collection of three **limestone lions** and two **sphinxes** found in the Tamassos necropolis south of Lefkosia. The statues, which show a definite Egyptian influence, were only discovered in 1997. They date from the Cypro-Archaic II period (475–400 BC).

Also look out for the famous **Aphrodite of Soli** statue in room 5, widely marketed as the 'goddess of Cyprus' on tourist posters and also depicted on the CY£5 banknote. An enormous bronze statue of **Emperor Septimus Severus**, found at Kythrea (Değirmenlik) in

1928, is the main exhibit in room 6 and can hardly be overlooked.

A couple of lovely mosaics, such as the **mosaic of Leda & the Swan** from Palea Pafos, are displayed in room 7B, alongside various displays of gold.

Faneromeni Church

The centre of the city before Plateia Eleftherias took over in 1974, Plateia Faneromenis is a quiet square, so silent that birdsong can be heard only metres away from the bustle of Ledra street. In the centre is the impressive Faneromeni Church, built in 1872 on the site of an ancient Orthodox nunnery. It is the largest church within the city walls and is a mixture of neoclassical, Byzantine and Latin styles. The **Marble Mausoleum** on the eastern side of the church was built in memory of four clerics executed by the Ottoman governor in 1821, during the newly declared Greek War of Independence.

Arablar Mosque

Alongside Plateia Faneromenis is Plateia Okostïogdois Oktovriou, where this tiny mosque is squirrelled away. A curious building, unfortunately no longer open to the public, it was the church of Stavros tou Misirikou in Lusignan times. Inside, if you manage to find someone to let you in, is a beautiful octagonal dome, on top of impressive colonnaded arches.

Ledra Museum-Observatory

Not really a museum, although it likes to call itself one, **Ledra Museum-Observatory** (☎ 2267 9396; 11th fl, Shakolas Tower, cnr Ledra & Arsinois; admission CY£0.50; ☼ 10am-8pm Mon-Sat, 10am-6pm Sun) is an observatory on top of Ermes (formerly Woolworths) department store (p74). A good vantage point over the city, here you can use telescopes to gaze at the whole of Lefkosia and trace the Green Line. It is also a great place to orient yourself. Explanations of various buildings and neighbourhoods are given in English, French and German.

Leventis Municipal Museum

The small, two-storey **Leventis Municipal Museum** (☎ 2267 3375; Ippokratous 17; admission free; ☼ 10am-4.30pm Tue-Sun) has exhibits dating from before 2000 BC to the present day. Among items on display are household equipment, traditional dress, books and prints. There is also a gift shop.

Laïki Yitonia

Laïki Yitonia, meaning 'popular neighbourhood', was restored after it served for many years as an area for painted ladies and dodgy merchants. This tiny southern part of the Old City is Lefkosia's only tourist area. This means that it's crammed with bad restaurants with tacky water features, where waiters try to lure you in with cheesy greetings, and the food is often overpriced. However, it's

---

WALKING THE GREEN LINE

Despite the fact that crossing into the North is now easy and some of the 'mystery of the other side' has therefore vanished, the Green Line and the spooky buffer zone with its abandoned, crumbling houses still fascinate foreigners. The Green Line is unmissable and it exudes a sense of division. While there's not a lot to see once you are there (save for some creative graffiti work), its mere presence gives Lefkosia its bizarre edge. You'll see the double minarets of the Agia Sofia mosque, North Nicosia's most remarkable landmark, with the Turkish and Turkish Cypriot flags that hang between them like washing. The Green Line embodies the eeriness of the capital's and the country's division, especially when coupled with so many 1974 stories that you hear from every Cypriot.

UN and Greek Cypriot **bunkers** punctuate the line across the city, and you are not supposed to approach them too closely or get your camera out. The CTO-signposted walking tour takes you hard up to the line at the far eastern side of the city close to the military-controlled **Flatro (Sibeli) Bastion**. Take the last turn left off Leoforos Athinas along Agiou Georgiou and look for the little street on the right with Taverna Axiothea (p70). Walk to the end of Axiotheas and squeeze through the gap into the next street, following the walking-tour sign. There is an area of particular desolation and destruction towards the end of **Pendadaktylou** where it meets **Ermou**, the street that originally bisected the Old City more or less equally into two.

It is thought that many of the streets and ruined buildings are booby-trapped with mines.

rather pretty, and a nice place for a short stroll. With so many good restaurants and taverns in the city, try to avoid eating in this area, with the exception of 1900 Paei Kairos (p70).

The CTO has an office here, and you can stock up on most maps and other tourist brochures free of charge.

Cyprus Jewellery Museum
The small **Cyprus Jewellery Museum** (☎ 2266 7278; Praxippou 7-9; admission free; ☯ 10am-4pm Mon-Fri) in Laïki Yitonia presents the history of jewellery from the end of the 19th century to today. The exhibits include ornaments, religious items, silver utensils and old tools.

Cyprus Handicrafts Centre
A government-sponsored foundation aiming to preserve Cypriot handicrafts, **Cyprus Handicrafts Centre** (☎ 2230 5024; Athalassis 186; ☯ 7.30am-2.30pm Mon-Fri, 3-6pm Thu) is well run and nicely presented. Here you can watch pottery, woodwork, embroidery and other crafts being practised and nurtured. Many of the products are on sale for visitors.

Omeriye Mosque
Originally the Augustinian Church of St Mary, the **Omeriye Mosque** (Ömeriye Camii; cnr Tri-koupi & Plateia Tyllirias; ☯ outside prayer times) dates from the 14th century. The church was destroyed by the Ottomans as they entered Lefkosia in 1570. It was subsequently restored as a mosque, based on a belief that this was the spot where the Muslim prophet Omer was buried in the 7th century. Its tall minaret can easily be spotted some distance away; the entrance to the mosque is about halfway along Trikoupi. Today the mosque is used primarily as a place of worship by visiting Muslims from neighbouring Arab countries. Non-Muslims may visit as long they observe the general etiquette required – dress conservatively, leave shoes at the door and avoid official prayer times.

Omeriye Hammam
Switch off your mobile, put your shower cap on, and strip down to your birthday suit for a lovely, relaxing Turkish bath at **Omeriye Hammam** (Ömeriye Hamam; Plateia Tyllirias; admission & Turkish bath CY£10, traditional body peeling CY£6, massage CY£12-25; ☯ 9am-9pm, men only Tue, Thu, Sat, women only Wed, Fri, Sun, tours Mon 11am-5pm). This building

was recently restored and sports a luxurious, stylish design. The domed reception has an enormous chandelier hanging over the circular bar area, while candles, mirrors and a refreshing minty scent accompany the baths themselves. The 16th-century Omeriye Hammam is a safe, popular and relaxing spot, with separate days for men and women, and same-sex masseurs. As you enter, you get a complimentary bottle of water, towels (one large, one small) and a cup of herbal tea to relax with after the bath. Apart from the basic steam bath, you could indulge in body scrub (which comes at an extra cost) or have a Chinese or aromatherapy massage for CY£25 each. If you don't fancy the bath experience, you can take a tour on a Monday.

House of Hatzigeorgakis Kornesios
The well-preserved **House of Hatzigeorgakis Kornesios** (☎ 2230 5316; Patriarchou Grigoriou 20; admission CY£0.75; ☯ 8am-2pm Mon-Fri, 9am-1pm Sat) belonged to Kornesios, the Great Dragoman of Cyprus from 1779 to 1809. A dragoman (tercüman in Turkish) was an interpreter or liaison officer between the Ottoman and Orthodox authorities. Kornesios, originally from Kritou Terra village, accumulated his vast wealth through various estates and tax exemptions, and became the most powerful man in Cyprus at the time. But, as you may guess, his extravagance was his undoing. A peasant revolt in 1804, aimed at the ruling classes in general, forced him out of Cyprus and to Istanbul. Returning from exile five years later, he was accused of treason, his property was confiscated, and he was beheaded. The house itself is more beautiful and interesting than any of the exhibits inside. Only one room is set up as mock living quarters, with plush floor cushions and nargileh (Middle Eastern water pipes) for smoking. The rest of the mansion is given over to displays of antiques and Ottoman memorabilia.

Archbishop's Palace
A mock Venetian building on Plateia Arhiepiskopou Kyprianou, this was the scene of much of the fighting in 1956, as well as during the 1974 military coup and subsequent Turkish invasion of the North. The palace was almost totally destroyed by EOKA-B (the postindependence reincarnation of EOKA,

which mostly fought Turkish Cypriots) while they attempted to kill Archbishop Makarios on 15 July 1974, but it was rebuilt during the 1980s. The building, which is generally closed to the public, is the official residence of the Archbishop of Cyprus. The palace (and everything else in the vicinity) is overshadowed by a hideous black **statue of Archbishop Makarios III**, which looms across the square. See the boxed text, p110, for more about the life of this revered archbishop-president.

Makarios Cultural Foundation

This complex of the **Makarios Cultural Foundation** (☎ 2243 0008; Plateia Arhiepiskopou Kyprianou; admission CY£1; 🕑 9am-4.30pm Mon-Fri, 9am-1pm Sat) consists of three main exhibition areas. The **European Art Gallery** presents 120 oil paintings of various European schools of art from the 16th to the 19th centuries. The themes are mainly religious with works by Van Dyck, Rubens, Tintoretto, Lorraine and Delacroix.

Close by is the **Greek Independence War Gallery**, which contains maps, copper engravings and paintings of people and events from the Greek War of Independence in 1821. The **Byzantine Art Museum** has the island's largest collection of icons related to Cyprus. There are some 220 pieces in the museum, dating from the 5th to the 19th centuries. Among the more interesting items on display are the icons of **Christ & the Virgin Mary** (12th century) from the Church of the Virgin Mary of Arakas at Lagoudera, and the **Resurrection** (13th century) from the Church of St John Lambadistis Monastery at Kalopanayiotis. In addition, there are six examples of the Kanakaria Mosaics, which were stolen from the Panagia Kanakaria (Kanakaria Church) in Northern Cyprus after the 1974 Turkish invasion.

Ethnographic Museum

Close to the Makarios Cultural Foundation, the small **Ethnographic Museum** (☎ 2243 2578; Plateia Arhiepiskopou Kyprianou; admission CY£1; 🕑 9am-5pm Mon-Fri, 10am-1pm Sat) houses the largest collection of folk art and ethnography in the country. The building dates back to the 15th century, although some later additions have been made. Here you will see fine examples of embroidery, lace, costumes, pottery, metalwork, basketry, folk painting, leatherwork and woodcarving.

National Struggle Museum

This display is really for die-hard history buffs. The **National Struggle Museum** (☎ 2230 5878; Kinyras 7; admission CY£0.25; 🕑 8am-2pm Mon-Fri, 3-7pm Thu) exhibits documents, photos and other memorabilia from the often bloody 1955–59 National Liberation Struggle against the British.

Lefkosia Arts Centre & Library

For something a little less cerebral than the museums, duck into the small arcade to the right of the National Struggle Museum and head along Apostolou Varnava for one block to the rather avant-garde **Lefkosia Arts Centre & Library** (☎ 2243 2577; Apostolou Varnava 19; admission free but donations welcome; 🕑 10am-3pm & 5-11pm Tue-Sat, 10am-4pm Sun). Its air-conditioned interior contains an occasionally bizarre but mostly interesting collection of art. The permanent collection includes paintings and sculpture, and other works from the Dimitris Pierides Museum of Contemporary Art in Greece. Exhibitions vary monthly. The centre also has a coffee shop and art library for visitors.

Panagia Chrysaliniotissa

The church of **Panagia Chrysaliniotissa** (Arhiepiskopou Filotheou) is dedicated to the Virgin Mary, and its name means 'Our Lady of the Golden Flax' in Greek. It's considered to be the oldest Byzantine church in Lefkosia and was built in 1450 by Queen Helena Paleologos. It is renowned for its rich collection of old and rare icons.

Chrysaliniotissa Crafts Centre

This small **arts centre** (Dimonaktos 2; 🕑 10am-1pm & 3-6pm Mon-Fri, 10am-1pm Sat) is worth dropping into for its display of Cypriot arts and crafts. Eight workshops and a coffee shop surround a central courtyard in a building designed along the lines of a traditional inn.

WALKING TOUR

This tour goes along the Old City's main streets and past many of its museums.

Starting from Plateia Eleftherias follow Ledra and turn right onto Ippokratous. At No 17 is the **Leventis Municipal Museum** (**1**; p64), which traces the city's development from prehistoric times to the present.

Continue along to the end of Ippokratous, turn left onto Thrakis and take the dogleg onto Trikoupi. Soon you'll see the

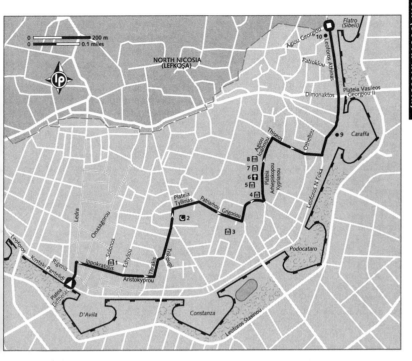

WALK FACTS

Start Plateia Eleftherias
Finish Flatro (Sibeli) Bastion
Distance 2km

Omeriye Mosque (**2**; p65) on your right. Turn right onto Plateia Tyllirias and shortly after you will reach Patriarchou Grigoriou. About 125m along this street on the right is the 18th-century **House of Hatzigeorgakis Kornesios** (**3**; p65), which is now a museum.

The next left leads you to Plateia Arhiepiskopou Kyprianou, dominated by the **Archbishop's Palace** (**4**; p65) and a colossal statue of Makarios III. Here you'll find the **Makarios Cultural Foundation** (**5**; opposite), comprising the European Art Gallery, Greek Independence War Gallery and Byzantine Art Museum. In the grounds of the foundation is **Agios Ioannis Church** (**6**), which was built in 1662 and has wonderful frescoes dating from 1736. Next door is the **Ethnographic Museum** (**7**; opposite), and also nearby is the **National Struggle Museum** (**8**; opposite).

Continue north along Agiou Ioannou and turn right onto Thiseos, which leads onto Leoforos N Foka. Turn left and you'll see the imposing **Famagusta Gate** (**9**; p62), which was once the main entrance to the city. From here it's a 400m walk past Lefkosia's trendy night-time dining area along Leoforos Athinas to where the street abruptly ends at the barbed wire and UN watchtowers of the **Flatro (Sibeli) Bastion** (**10**). The most direct way back to Laïki Yitonia is to take Leoforos N Foka, following the signposts to the CTO. Check out the Venetian walls along the way.

LEFKOSIA FOR CHILDREN

Unlike the seaside towns and resorts, Lefkosia's appeal to children is rather low, although Lefkosians are child-friendly, like most Cypriots. There are no professional baby-sitting services in the city, as so many families seem to have their own, live-in nannies. The CTO has a list of events taking place throughout the year, and will know what's on while you are around. Ask about watching a traditional Cypriot shadow-puppet theatre show.

Ostrich Wonderland Theme Park (☎ 2299 1008/9; Agios Ioannis Maloundas; adult/child CY£1/0.50; ☼ 9am-7pm May-Oct, 9am-5pm Nov-Apr) This theme park might tickle your fancy. It's reputedly the biggest ostrich park (and farm) in Europe and is 25 minutes outside Lefkosia. Your kids can learn everything there is to know about the powerful speedy birds and their eggs too, and use the park's playground; a sightseeing tour is included in the admission price. To get here, follow the Troödos highway, take the Palehori exit and follow the signs to Agios Ioannis Maloundas.

Kykko Bowling (☎ 2235 0085; Archimidous 15-19, Engomi; ☼ 1.30pm-1.30am) This 19-alley bowling centre, sitting behind the Hilton, is a great place to get your kids to wear uncomfortable shoes and share in Homer Simpson's great passion. The café with snacks and drinks will allow them to share his other passion (the fast food one).

Cyprus Classic Motorcycle Museum (Map p60; ☎ 2268 0222; Granikou 44; admission CY£1; ☼ 9am-1pm & 3.30-7pm Mon-Fri, 9am-1pm Sat) Although this place attracts kids of all ages, it's a great stop to make with young ones, obsessed as they probably are with vehicles of all kinds. This is a private museum whose owner is more than happy to chat extensively about his collection. It may just keep the parents happy too.

Municipal Gardens (Map p60; Leoforos Mousieou) This is a lovely spot for a walk and a rest on a hot summer's day, and the playground can be used for some fun on the slide.

TOURS

The **CTO** (Map p60; ☎ 2244 4264; Aristokyprou 11; ☼ 8.30am-4pm Mon-Fri, 8.30am-2pm Sat) runs free guided walks on Monday, Thursday, and Friday, all starting at 10am, from the CTO office in the Old City.

'Chrysaliniotissa & Kaimakli: the Past Restored' is a bus and walking guided tour that runs on Monday; Thursday is a walk through Old Lefkosia; Friday is 'Nicosia – Outside the Walls', a bus and walking guided tour. All walks last two hours and 45 minutes, and have a 30 minute break in the middle.

Alternatively, pick up a CTO walking-tours brochure or follow our walking tour around the Old City (p66).

FESTIVALS & EVENTS

The **Cyprus International Film Festival** (www.ciff2006 .com), first held in March 2006, emphasises

Cyprus' position as a middle-ground between the West and the Middle East. It screens contemporary film and video productions from around the world related to dialogue among civilisations. Events also take place in Larnaka and Lemesos.

The **Cyprus State Fairs Authority** (☎ 2235 2918/2316; www.csfa.org.cy) takes responsibility for three annual fairs and exhibitions. The biggest event is the annual **Cyprus International Fair** that takes place between May and June; the **Motorshow** takes place in the first week of November; **Offitec** is a tech-fest of computers, office machines and telecommunications equipment. All events are held at the International Fair Grounds in the western suburb of Makedonitissa.

SLEEPING
Budget

There is very little budget accommodation left in Lefkosia. Most of what once existed has either closed down or been upgraded to a midrange category.

Tony's Bed & Breakfast (Map p60; ☎ 2266 6752; fax 2266 2225; Solonos 13; s/d CY£18/28; ⊠) This is one of those places that seems to have been forgotten by time and redecoration, although the air-conditioning units would suggest otherwise. The old building, bang in the centre of the Old City, is in a fantastic location. The prices are low, and the beds feel as if they've been there since 1974. Nice little balconies compensate for the dodgy showers. Each room comes with a semicold fridge and a fuzzy-picture TV.

HI Hostel (Map p58; ☎ 9943 8360; Tefkrou 5; dm CY£5) In a quiet part of the New City about six blocks from Plateia Eleftherias. You can have a double or single room here, but you have to book in advance. Follow the signs from Hatzidaki, off Themistokli Dervi. It's basic but quite reasonable for a cheap sleep.

Midrange

Midrange hotels are the most common accommodation in the city. But, as in many other places in Cyprus, hotels at this price range aren't too used to dealing with solo travellers, or those who don't look particularly groomed (or who look a bit scruffy). So don't be surprised if you don't get the 'feel at home' treatment that's advertised.

Classic Hotel (Map p60; ☎ 2266 4006; www.classic .com.cy; Rigenis 94; s/d CY£54/65; ⊠) This three-star hotel, close to Pafos Gate, is a member of the 'Small Luxury Hotels of the World' group, and you can see why. Everything, from the reception to the rooms, is done up in relaxing creamy, wood colours; the design is minimalist; the rooms are smart and comfortable. The 59 Knives restaurant, part of the hotel, specialises in *haute cuisine,* adding its own contribution to the Classic's luxuries.

Castelli Hotel (Map p60; ☎ 2271 2812; hinnicres@ cytanet.com.cy; Ouzounian 38; s/d CY£99/114; ✷ ▣ ▤) Next door to the Holiday Inn, and close to the Classic, this is a hotel aimed at the business lot and therefore slightly aloof towards dishevelled-looking travellers, so don your suit before you ask about vacancies. The rooms are smart and comfortable and have Internet ports. The hotel also has a sauna, particularly handy as a hangover cure after too many cocktails at the Pago Pago Polynesian restaurant-bar downstairs (p71).

Cleopatra Hotel (Map p58; ☎ 2235 6666; cleo hotel@cleopatra.com.cy; Florinis 8; s/d CY£58/75; ✷ ▤) The Egyptian Pharaoh would not have approved of the lack of luxury and rather boring, impersonal rooms in this (again) business-oriented hotel. The pool looks more ravishing than any other feature in the building and on a hot Lefkosia day, could be a life-saver. Travellers with scruffy bags or clothes may be frowned upon or ignored altogether.

Averof (Map p58; ☎ 2277 3447; www.averof.com .cy; Averof 19; s/d CY£26.75/39; ✷) Close to the Old City, near the British High Commission and in a quiet part of Lefkosia, this place prides itself on its rather kitsch rustic décor and 'personal touch'. The mock-traditional rooms are clean and bright.

Asty (Map p58; ☎ 2277 3030; fax 2277 3311; Pringi- pos Karolou 12; s/d CY£38.50/63; ✷) This two-star place promises peace and quiet, plus some comfortable rooms over in Engomi.

Top End

Lefkosia's top-end hotels are all the usual suspects, with luxurious comfort and design, but there is a lamentable lack of imaginative and original establishments in the city.

Cyprus Hilton (Map p58; ☎ 2237 7777; www.hilton .com; Leoforos Arhiepiskopou Makariou III; s/d CY£169/204; ✷ ▤) This premier five-star hotel was apparently the gathering-ground for eastern and western spies during the Cold War, when Cyprus' strategic position was invaluable.

Who knows what political manoeuvring went on in its luxurious rooms, indoor and outdoor pool, tennis and squash courts and in-house restaurants. With a knowing smile, ask about the discounts that apply from 1 July to 31 August, when rooms can go down to as low as CY£95 a night.

Holiday Inn (Map p60; ☎ 2271 2712; hinnicres@ cytanet.com.cy; Rigenis 70; s/d CY£150/188; ✷ ▤) The great location could perhaps justify the extortionate room prices, but a serious lack of imagination makes this hotel sterile and indistinguishable from most top-end chain hotels. Lefkosia's Holiday Inn is most popular for the restaurants that it cradles, such as the Japanese restaurant Bonsai (p71). Guests get to use the indoor pool, gym and sauna.

Forum Nicosia By Intercontinental (☎ 2235 6666; forum@louishotels.com; Leoforos Georgiou Griva Digeni; s/d from CY£65/112; ✷ ▤) Four star; the only one of the bunch that is a little way out of town, in the western suburb of Engomi. It has excellent rooms and facilities, and a 30% discount applies from 1 July to 31 August.

EATING

Lefkosia offers three basic locations for eating: the Old City, the New City, and the burgeoning suburbs to the east or west. While we stick mainly to the Old and New Cities, suburbs such as Engomi to the west or Strovolos to the south have their own culinary enclaves, and a drive to either may turn up some surprising finds.

Dining in Lefkosia can be a real treat. Because the city is not a prime tourist target, it is thankfully bereft of low-quality, high-cost tourist traps that pander to foreign palates. The growing internationalism of Cyprus, coupled with the fact that many Cypriots now hanker after food other than their own, means that there is a wide array of ethnic cuisines available. Chinese and Indian restaurants are among two of the main growth areas.

A word of warning: many restaurants in Lefkosia close down for a couple of weeks in August for the annual holidays. Phone beforehand to be on the safe side.

Old City

Dining in the Old City is centred on two main areas with a sprinkling of low-frills, cheap eateries scattered in between. Laïki Yitonia

---

THE AUTHOR'S CHOICE

Tziellari (☎ 2243 1099; Koraï 24; meze per person CY£10; ☽ dinner) You won't have to look hard to find this place. All you have to do is open your ears as you get to the murky night-time Plateia Achiepiskopou Kyprianou, then follow the sound of the bouzouki down a dark alley and push the heavy doors into Tziellari. There is such a distinct atmosphere in this restaurant that you might feel as if you'd walked onto a film set from the 1930s: dark wooden walls, demure lighting, and often entire families dining and Greek dancing, arms outstretched. The meze is as typical as you get, starring the Cypriot favourites such as olives, grilled haloumi, souvlaki and *seftalia* (grilled Cypriot sausage). There is house wine, *zivania* (local firewater) and Cyprus brandy, all of which will come in handy if you try to master some of that dancing.

---

is mainly popular with the lunchtime crowd of day-trippers, who then normally retreat to the coast, while the Famagusta Gate strip is full of bars and restaurants and attracts evening revellers, most of whom are locals. The eateries in this section are found on the Old City map (p60).

RESTAURANTS
Greek Cypriot Cuisine
Zanettos Taverna (☎ 2276 5501; Trikoupi 65; mains CY£2.50-3) This place has a great reputation in the city, as it is allegedly one of the oldest traditional taverns. The locals flock here in their dozens, and it's definitely worth joining them. A great place for meze, it's hidden away in a slightly shady part of town, where the painted ladies sit in their doorways, waiting for business.

1900 Paei Kairos (☎ 2266 7668; Pasikratous 11-15; meze CY£2.50-4.50; ☽ dinner) The only place in the tourist part worth going to. It's a pretty little Greek-style *mezedopolio* (a small restaurant specialising in *mezedes*). It serves mix-and-match *mezedes* such as *stryftari* (a pie made up of five cheeses), eggplant stuffed with cheese in filo pastry, and eggplant patties. Have a tipple of *tsipouro* (a clear, distilled spirit) or try a selection of the mainly Greek wines on offer.

To Steki tis Loxandras (☎ 2267 5757; Faneromenis 67; meze CY£6.50; ☽ dinner) Live traditional music, good quality Greek-style *mezedes* and lots of people is the standard at Loxandras. Booking is an absolute must for dining on weekends.

Erodos (☎ 2275 2250; Patriarchou Grigoriou 1; mains CY£4-8; ☽ lunch & dinner) This is certainly the loveliest front yard in the Old City, on Plateia Tyllirias, abutting the Omeriye Hammam. The food is reasonable, although by no means exquisite.

Orfeas (☎ 2234 3447; Leoforos Athinas 23; meze CY£7.50, grills CY£4; ☽ dinner) A sprawling taverna with tables in the park, always packed full of Cypriots coming to eat their national favourite: souvlaki. An old solitary mama observes the evening activity from inside, reading a newspaper, unperturbed by her successful business.

Odos Othellou (Othellou 1; meze CY£8; ☽ dinner) This small Greek blue-and-white house is like an apparition on the dimly lit street. The little wooden tables outside are perfect for a quiet dinner or drink (p73), away from traffic and people. Like most traditional outfits, this place serves meze, but the emphasis is on the mainland Greek version, which is all about grilled meat. For CY£12.50, you can eat, have one free drink and listen to bouzouki (inside the restaurant only).

Taverna Axiothea (☎ 2243 0787; Axiotheas 9; mains CY£3-4; ☽ dinner) A little, unassuming joint on the last street before the barricades. It is good for low-priced and tasty *mezedes*.

Egeon (☎ 2243 3297; Ektoros 40; meze CY£7-12; ☽ dinner) The ever-so-discreet yet very popular Egeon draws a faithful following of mainly local devotees. You dine in an atmospheric old house on a rich platter of imaginative *mezedes*. Bookings are essential.

Also worth checking out is **Estiatorio Savvas** (☎ 2276 3444; Solonos 65; mains CY£5; ☽ noon-4.30pm Mon-Sat), unadorned, simple and basic but offering good home-cooked dishes, just like **Agios Georgios Taverna** (☎ 2276 5971; Plateia Paliou Dimarhiou 27; grills CY£2.50-4.50) on the northern side of the market.

International Cuisine
Da Paolo (☎ 2243 8538; Leoforos Konstantinou Paleologou 52; mains CY£5.50; ☽ lunch & dinner) A small Italian place with pizza that smells so divine you will throw caution to the wind and forget all

about your low-carb diet. The interior (only used in winter) is a red-brick room, with high ceilings and tall, wooden-shuttered windows. Everything smells of the herbs and garlic that dangle above the ovens. Waiters risk their lives carrying your food across the street to the summer garden, which sits right on top of the Venetian walls. Wood-fired brick ovens bake your pizza, and the pasta is always *al dente*.

Bonsai (☎ 2271 2712; Rigenis 70; mains CY£5-9; ☺ lunch & dinner) The best Japanese place in town. Sitting deep inside the Holiday Inn (p69), Bonsai serves tasty sushi that goes around the counter, as you sit on high stools and get hypnotised by the moving choice. *Nigiri* sushi (CY£11.60) consisting of raw tuna, hamour, sword fish, omelette, salmon, mackerel, octopus, shrimp, squid and California rolls is a delicacy. An all-you-can eat sushi buffet (CY£12.50) is on offer every Monday and Thursday lunchtime from 12.30pm to 2pm, and Tuesday dinner time from 7.30pm to 11.30pm.

Pago Pago (☎ 2271 2812; Ouzounian 38; mains CY£7.50-10; ☺ lunch & dinner) Put on your grass skirt and grab a pineapple and umbrella-adorned cocktail as you wait for a table. Pago Pago is located in Castelli Hotel (p69). Tahitian duck (CY£10) is recommended, as is lots of dancing to live Cuban music.

CAFÉS
Double Six Coffee Bar (☎ 2266 8998; Faneromenis; snacks CY£1.50-2; juice CY£1.50; ☺ 8.30am-7pm Mon-Sat) A great café decked out in smooth ebony furniture, hauled from Bali by Vassos, the owner. The atmosphere is relaxed, there are cushions to recline on and delicious fresh juices to boost your system. Try sweet Cypriot prickly pear, hydrating watermelon, or delicious kiwi juice. Breakfast on haloumi, tomato and *lountza* (pork-loin sausage) sandwiches, and a delicious cappuccino.

QUICK EATS
Nikos (Rigenis 3A; kebabs CY£3-5; ☺ 11.30am-11pm) A quick, quality kebab for a hungry, wandering traveller.

Pahit Ice (☎ 2267 7141; Ledra 120; ice cream CY£1; ☺ noon-10pm) So many ice-cream flavours, so little time. A local ice-cream maker whose outside tables are always full of kids, families and just about anyone on the hot summer days.

New City
All the eateries in this section are found on the New City map (p58).

RESTAURANTS
Greek Cypriot Cuisine
Zoo (☎ 2275 8262; Leoforos Stasinou 15; mains CY£5-7; ☺ 9pm-1am) Great for romantic dining, the restaurant overlooks the Old City from the 4th floor, and serves a modernist, Mediterranean menu. Laid out in chrome and steel, it has a reputation for being one of Lefkosia's better places to eat. After dinner, for a bit of indigestion, go dancing in the club downstairs (p73).

Date Club Restaurant (☎ 2237 6843; Agathonos 2; mains CY£4-6; ☺ lunch & dinner; ☒) Flashy and a little hard to find, this place is really popular with the well-heeled of Lefkosia, including prime ministers and presidents who come for the casserole lunches. The vanilla-white interior is a little glitzy, so dress up before you come to eat here.

Kalymnos (☎ 2247 2423; Zinas Kanther 11; fish per kg CY£10-18; ☺ lunch & dinner) A fish tavern that also attracts the Cypriot high-flyers, as well as el Presidente; it's a modest little place and the fish is to die for. There's a small bar for a predinner drink.

Loukoullos (☎ 2267 1000; Florinis 8; mains CY£4-6; ☺ lunch & dinner) The management of Cleopatra Hotel may be stuffy, but it doesn't stop its in-house restaurant from being considered one of Lefkosia's better hotel restaurants. In summer, dine on *mezedes* or European cuisine next to the pool.

Plaka Tavern (☎ 2244 6498; Plateia Arhiepiskopou Makariou 8, Engomi; meze CY£7; ☺ dinner Mon-Sat) If you have plenty of time in the city and fancy a change, head west of the centre and dine at this superb little taverna. It's best visited during the summer months when dinner is served on the square. The *mezedes* are best here but be warned: there are many of them and you'll need a big appetite.

International Cuisine
Syrian Arab Friendship Club (SAFC; ☎ 2277 6246; Vasilisa Amalia 17; ☺ 11am-midnight; meze CY£10) Apart from being one of the best places to eat in Lefkosia, this is the ideal place for vegetarians. The meze is massive, so approach it with respect, and if you come for lunch, you won't be eating dinner. The large garden is laden with cooling fans and greenery,

and children are welcome to play. The service here is superfriendly, and the wonderful food is an experience of its own: green beans, chick peas, *tabouleh* (bulgur-wheat and parsley salad) and plenty of meat too. Try the delicious *mahalabia* (a light, rice custard, which is served cold) dessert and, once you're so stuffed you can't move, puff on a nargileh.

Abu Faysal (☎ 2276 0353; Klimentos 31; meze CY£7; ❧ lunch & dinner) Lebanese cuisine is a gourmet's heaven, and if you want to sample or simply indulge in some fantastic Lebanese dishes, this is Lefkosia's best place. Three blocks south of the Constanza Bastion, the restaurant is an old house in a quiet backstreet with a leafy courtyard. The *mezedes* are recommended, as is a bottle of Lebanese Ksara Riesling.

Arheon Gefsis (☎ 2245 2830; Stasandrou 29; mains CY£4-8; ❧ dinner) 'The root of all pleasures is the satisfaction of the stomach' said Epicurus (341–270 BC). The owners of this place have taken this to heart and offer up foods that the ancient Greek philosopher himself may have feasted upon. Dine on dishes featuring figs, nuts, honey, beets, chickpeas and olives.

China Spice (☎ 2287 5875; Pindarou 26; mains CY£7-10; ❧ lunch & dinner) Chinese cuisine like they eat it in the posh parts of Shanghai or Hong Kong perhaps. The décor is minimalist, with black wood, white walls, and beige cushions, and a plant adorns the centre of each table. The delicious, elegantly presented dishes are prepared by nine Chinese chefs.

Finbarr's (☎ 2237 6625; Leoforos Arhiepiskopou Makariou III 52b; mains CY£5-7; ❧ lunch & dinner) This Irish pub (see opposite) is an up-market version of its more 'earthy' clones around the world. The menu is all Irish cuisine: either traditional, or 'fusion', such as beef-and-stout pie, or a jazzed up basil-and-chicken boxty (stuffed potato pancake).

Dragon (☎ 2259 1711; Leoforos Georgiou Griva Digeni; mains CY£6-8; ❧ lunch & dinner) If you fancy a Chinese takeaway, try this place. There is a good range of dishes, all cooked by a Chinese chef.

Kana Kai (☎ 2277 3820; Metohiou Hilonos 25; set menu for 2 CY£8.80-10.80; ❧ lunch & dinner) An intimate place close to the Old City, which does a mean Peking duck. You can order takeaway chicken dishes for around CY£4.

CAFÉS

The following places are open from 9am to 11pm.

Le Café (☎ 2275 5151; Leoforos Arhiepiskopou Makariou III 16; snacks CY£2-3) This is the place to be seen for everyone who's anyone in Lefkosia's fashionable elite. Witness the Prada and Gucci brigade nibble on salads, or businessmen deep in conversation on their mobiles while eating pasta dishes, as you sip your frappé. No alcohol is served.

Swiss Cottage (☎ 2243 3000; Leoforos Stasinou 31; cakes CY£1.50-2) On the corner of Theokritou close to the Old City, this place is great for late-night coffee and cake. The Swiss-trained pastry chef makes some exquisite European-style tarts and flans, but prices tend to be a little steep.

Leoforos Arhiepiskopou Makariou III is packed with cafés and bars, so for a bit of guidance, sample the following:

Da Capo (☎ 2275 7427; Leoforos Arhiepiskopou Makariou III 30B) The mother of all trendy Leoforos Arhiepiskopou Makariou III cafés. This is the place that started the sipping-coffee-outdoors trend. It also has wi-fi Internet points.

Mondo (☎ 2277 8044; Leoforos Arhiepiskopou Makariou III 9A) A spacious café and bar with an upstairs terrace, catering for all types and not only the usual plenty of lip-gloss and blonde-highlights girls, or muscle and designer-wear boys.

Café La Mode (☎ 2251 0788; Leoforos Arhiepiskopou Makariou III 12A) Believe it or not, Marks & Sparks hosts one of the city's most stylish cafés. Alongside delicious coffee, this place also serves rather swish food.

DRINKING

If you're about to hit the streets of Lefkosia for a night out, consider this: to really fit in, you must really dress up. Designer stuff is big here, and Lefkosia is the only place on this small island where there are any so-called 'trendies' to be found. If you're not the dressing-up type or you didn't bring your Prada outfit along, well, you'll survive. But don't say you weren't warned…

From the Famagusta Gate area in the Old City, to bars alongside Leoforos Arhiepiskopou Makariou III, you can have lots of fun exploring the city through an alcoholic blur. Usually, none of the following places show signs of life before 9pm and don't close until around 2am.

Hammam (Map p60; ☎ 2276 6202; Soutsou 9) Right behind Omeriye Hammam, this heavenly old colonial house, with a grand arched door and beautifully tiled floors, is perfect for sitting under the stars and sipping a cocktail beneath the aromatic fig tree. The music is good and the atmosphere relaxed.

Plato's (Map p60; ☎ 2266 6552; Platonas 8) Hidden inside an old house, this place feels like a jazz joint or a bistro that wouldn't be out of place in Montmartre. Beer from all over the world is served, but only to those who are respectably dressed: no shorts or T-shirts allowed (miniskirts are OK, though).

Bastione (Map p60; ☎ 2243 3101; Leoforos Athinas 6) A neat little bar built into the wall next to Famagusta Gate, catering mainly for an older crowd wanting a quiet drink.

Ithiki (Map p60; ☎ 2243 4193; Leoforos N Foka 33) This popular street-bar is on the corner of Leoforos N Fokas and Thiseos, with funk music and keen-to-party Lefkosians.

Odos Othellou (Map p60; Othellou 1) A gorgeous little house, one block west and just away from the main drag, this is a haven for a quiet drink under the stars. It serves great food too (p70).

Erotiko (Map p60; ☎ 2234 8111; Athinas 2-3) Although it's by Famagusta Gate, this place feels and looks like a beach bar. There's loud house music, the garden is surrounded by bamboo fences, and the crowd is young and jolly (although not wearing bikinis).

Sfinakia (Map p58; ☎ 2276 6661; Santaroza 2) In the New City, Sfinakia is a popular, buzzing preclub bar that packs in a crowd of people-watchers and posers.

Finbarr's (Map p58; ☎ 2237 6625; Leoforos Arhiepiskopou Makariou III 52b; pint of Guinness CY£2.70) Posh Lefkosians check each other out, while some expats drink Guinness and Caffrey's and chill with a newspaper or a magazine. There is a 'happy hour' from 4.30pm to 8pm.

Kyklos Café (Map p60; ☎ 2266 9998; 36 Ippocratous; nargileh CY£3.50) A great place for the gap-year crowd and backpackers who want to chat to their mates, smoke lots of nargileh (the really *in* thing to do), and play backgammon 'til late.

ENTERTAINMENT

For listings, particularly for classical-music concerts and the theatre, pick up *Nicosia This Month* and the *Diary of Events* pamphlets, available from the CTO. Note that some events may not be listed in the latter publication as this goes to print several months before the events take place.

Nightclubs

Zoo (Map p58; ☎ 2275 8262; Stasinou 15) Under the Zoo restaurant (p71), Zoo club is the embodiment of style and sophistication on Lefkosia's club scene (although its '70s 'flower power parties' put a bit of a blemish on that image). The music ranges from international to Greek pop.

Red (Map p60; ☎ 2276 7711; Dionysou 15) A live-music venue and nightclub in a former warehouse with a great atmosphere and eclectic music choices, such as R&B, Greek pop, and trance.

Club Cilo (Map p58; ☎ 2276 0061; Leoforos Arhiepiskopou Makariou III 52) Garage on Friday, house on Saturday; great for after some drinks at Finbarr's Irish pub, which is next door.

Live Music

Lefkosia occasionally hosts classical-music concerts; the best way to find out about them is to look in the local press. Other than this, watch for posters or drop by the Lefkosia Municipal Theatre box office (p74), diagonally opposite the Cyprus Museum on Leoforos Mouseiou, or visit Virgin Records (p74).

The best way to get to see and hear some traditional music is to head for any of the restaurants offering live music in Laïki Yitonia. Otherwise keep your eyes peeled for posters over the summer advertising visiting musicians from Greece.

Concerts are commonly held at the **Skali Aglantzias** (www.aglantzia.com) outdoor venue in Aglantzia and the **Scholi Tyflon** (School for the Blind) outdoor theatre near the southern suburb of Dasoupolis.

If you're keen, get in touch with promoters **Papadopoulos & Schinis Productions** (☎ 2537 2855; schinis@cytanet.com.cy) for interesting upcoming events.

Cinemas

K-Cineplex (☎ 2235 5824; www.kcineplex.com; Makedonitissis 8; ☒ 5-10.30pm) The best cinema experience to hit Lefkosia, 2.5km out of the city in Strovolos. Sporting multiple screens, K-Cineplex runs all the latest-release movies and provides movie-goers with ample parking, a cafeteria and hi-tech sight-and-sound systems.

There are a number of other cinemas scattered around Lefkosia that show varying permutations on the latest films and sometimes reruns of English-language movies. Foreign-language films are subtitled in Greek.

Among these cinemas (all on the New City map, p58) are the following:

Opera 1 & 2 (☎ 2266 5305; Hristodoulou Sozou 9)

Palace Cinemas (Zina Pallas; ☎ 2267 4128; Theofanous Theodotou 18)

Pantheon 1, 2 & 3 (☎ 2267 5787; Diagorou 29)

Admission to K-Cineplex is normally around CY£3 per person; other cinemas are slightly cheaper.

Theatre

There is a thriving local theatre scene. However, plays performed in Lefkosia are almost always in Greek.

Theatre Workshop of the University of Cyprus (thepak; Map p60; ☎ 2243 4801) Regularly puts on good shows at its little theatre close to the Green Line northwest of Famagusta Gate.

Theatro Ena (Map p60; ☎ 2234 8203; Leoforos Athinas 4) Also try this theatre in the Old City for any productions that may meet your linguistic needs.

Lefkosia Municipal Theatre (Map p60; ☎ 2246 3028; Leoforos Mouseiou 4) Opposite the Cyprus Museum. At the handy box office you can find flyers for all upcoming events – musical as well as theatrical – and buy your tickets.

Sport

Football (soccer) is the main spectator sport in Lefkosia. The football season is from September to May. Check out **Takis-on-Line** (http://soccer.kypros.org/cyprus_links.htm) for the lowdown on the nation's teams. The 16-times champion, APOEL Nicosia, held the top place for many years. The city is also home to clubs Omonia and Olympiakos.

Nicosia Race Club (Map p58; ☎ 2278 2727; www.nicosiaraceclub.com.cy; Grigoriou Afxentiou 10-12) In the western suburb of Agios Dometios, this club caters for keen horse punters. Meets are normally held on Wednesdays and Sundays in winter and Wednesdays and Saturdays in summer, starting at 4pm.

SHOPPING

With its army of designer babes around, it's no wonder that Lefkosia rules when it comes to clothes shopping. The so-called 'discount stores' offer clothes and shoes at 30% to 80% off their original price, and many a Lefkosian can be found elbowing their way to the best bargain. Join them if you have the time and energy, so that you can return home with a new outfit and boast about your bargain-spotting skills.

Otherwise, there are two main shopping areas. Ledra street in the Old City has lots of old-style shoe and clothes shops, and it's home to the swish Ermes department store. Leoforos Arhiepiskopou Makariou III in the New City is a mecca for chain-stores, which are not always the best value (the prices are not converted into Cyprus pounds in some British chains, so they end up being more expensive). Tourist shops tend to be centred on Laïki Yitonia and generally sell all the same things as any other tourist shops around the island at the same high prices.

Cyprus Handicrafts Centre (☎ 2230 5024; Athalassis 186; ⏱ 7.30am-2.30pm Mon-Fri, 3-6pm Thu) Get your Cypriot lace and embroideries here at decent prices, as well as leather ware, mosaics, ceramics and pottery. Even better, watch these products being made at various workshops.

Ermes (Map p60; ☎ 2244 7801; Shakolas Tower, Ledra) The former Woolworths is a classy department store selling anything from food and cosmetics to clothes and stationery.

Virgin Records (Map p60; ☎ 2276 1190; Arnaldas 8) A place that music-lovers might want to head for, just off Leoforos Stasinou near the D'Avila Bastion. Here you can get all the latest Greek and non-Greek releases as well as buy tickets for the many music acts that come to Lefkosia in the summer.

GETTING THERE & AWAY

Air

Lefkosia's international airport is in the UN buffer zone and is no longer a functioning airport. All air passengers for Lefkosia will arrive at Larnaka airport in the South.

Most airlines that serve the Republic of Cyprus have offices or representatives in Lefkosia:

Alitalia (Map p60; ☎ 2267 4500; www.alitalia.com; Leoforos Evagorou I 54-58)

British Airways (Map p58; ☎ 2276 1166; www.britishairways.com; Leoforos Arhiepiskopou Makariou III 52a)

Cyprus Airways (Map p58; ☎ 2275 1996; www.cyprusairways.com; Leoforos Arhiepiskopou Makariou III 50)

KLM (Map p58; ☎ 2267 1616; www.klm.com; Zinas Kanther 12)

Lufthansa (Map p58; ☎ 2287 3330; www.lufthansa.com; cnr Leoforos Arhiepiskopou Makariou III & Leoforos Evagorou I)

Olympic Airlines (Map p60; ☎ 2267 2101; www.olympic-airways.com; Leoforos Omirou 17)

Bus

There are many private companies oper-ating out of Lefkosia. Most buses depart from one of three areas (Map p60): Plateia Solomou, abutting the Tripoli Bastion; Leo-nidou near the corner of Leoforos Stasinou; and the bus lot next to the Constanza Bas-tion, 700m further east.

Other services have their own departure points.

Agia Napa & Paralimni

Eman Buses (☎ 2372 1321; Constanza Bastion) One bus at 3pm Monday to Friday to Agia Napa (CY£2.50, one hour).

PEAL Bus Co (☎ 2382 1318; Leoforos Stasinou 27) Runs a bus at 1.30pm Monday to Friday to Paralimni and Protaras via Agia Napa (CY£2.50, 1¼ hours).

Larnaka

Intercity Buses Co (☎ 2266 5814; Plateia Solomou) Six buses run Monday to Friday and two on Saturday (CY£1.50, 45 minutes).

Lemesos

Alepa Buses (☎ 9962 5027; Plateia Solomou) There are two buses a day (2.45pm and 3.45pm, one hour) on Monday, Tuesday, Thursday and Friday and one at 12.45pm on Wednesday and Saturday (CY£2, one hour).

Intercity Buses Co (☎ 2266 5814; Plateia Solomou) Seven buses run Monday to Friday and two on Saturday (CY£1.50, one hour).

Pafos

Alepa Buses (☎ 9962 5027; Plateia Solomou) There is a service at 3.45pm on Monday, Tuesday, Thursday and Friday (CY£3, 1¾ hours) and at 12.45pm on Wednesday and Saturday (CY£3, 1¾ hours).

Nea Amoroza (☎ 2693 6822; Plateia Solomou) A bus runs at 6.30am from Monday to Friday via Lemesos and at 7am on Saturday (CY£3, 1¾ hours).

Solis (☎ 2266 6388; Plateia Solomou) A minibus runs at noon Monday to Saturday (CY£5, 1¾ hours).

Troödos

Clarios Bus Co (☎ 2275 3234; Constanza Bastion) Has a bus to Troödos at 11.30am Monday to Friday (CY£1.50, one hour) and up to 12 buses a day in summer to Kakopetria (CY£1.20).

Kambos Buses (Leonidou) Runs a bus to Kykkos Monastery at noon Monday to Saturday (CY£1.90).

Pedoulas–Platres Bus (☎ 9961 8865, 2295 2437; Leonidou 34) Runs a bus at 12.15pm Monday to Saturday to Pedoulas and Platres (CY£2). The Saturday bus doesn't continue to Platres.

Car & Motorcycle

Traffic approaching Lefkosia tends to come from either the Troödos Massif to the west, or Larnaka and Lemesos in the south. The Larnaka–Lemesos motorway ends fairly abruptly on the outskirts of Lefkosia about 6km south of the Old City. By following the extension of the motorway into the city centre, you will eventually reach Leoforos Arhiepiskopou Makariou III, the main thoroughfare in the New City. Traffic from Troödos will enter the city along Leoforos Georgiou Griva Digeni.

Parking is most easily found at the large car parks abutting the city bastions, to the right of Leoforos Arhiepiskopou Makariou III, or to your left if you approach from the Troödos. The most convenient one for new arrivals is the large lot between the D'Avila and Constanza Bastions on Leo-foros Stasinou. Parking costs a minimum of CY£0.30 for two hours. Buy a ticket from the machine and display it on the inside of your windscreen.

Getting out of Lefkosia is made easy by the prominent signs all along Leoforos Stasi-nou. Be wary, however, of the many one-way streets and the numerous on-street parking restrictions. Avoid the peak period of 11am to 1pm on weekdays when traffic can be very slow.

Service Taxi

All service-taxi destinations are handled by **Travel & Express** (Map p60; ☎ 7777 7474; Municipal Parking Place, Leoforos Salaminos) just next to the Podocataro Bastion. Rates are CY£4.50 to Lemesos (1½ hours), CY£3.50 to Larnaka (45 minutes to one hour) and CY£9 to Pafos (2½ hours). Although Travel & Ex-press will pick you up at an appointed time from anywhere in urban Lefkosia, delays of up to 30 minutes are the norm. Be prepared and leave at least an hour extra if you're getting a service taxi to the airport.

Passengers boarding at the Podocataro Bastion will usually spend up to 30 minutes picking up other passengers before actu-ally departing Lefkosia. Service taxis de-liver passengers to both Larnaka and Pafos airports.

Things have changed significantly when it comes to crossing into the North. Cross-ing via the Ledra Palace Hotel, as a pedes-trian, is hassle-free. To take a rented car, or indeed a car of your own, refer to the boxed text The Elusive Insurance, p175. Otherwise, the easiest thing to do, if you have luggage and don't want to walk, is to get a taxi to take you anywhere in the North. Most drivers should be happy to do this, but if one refuses, try another. A journey from Lefkosia to North Nicosia should cost anywhere between CY£10 and CY£15, and a journey from Lefkosia to Kyrenia should be no more than CY£25. Also, most taxi drivers who go to the North regularly will have the visa leaflet that you will need to fill out. For more info, see the boxed text Crossing the Thin Green Line, p235.

GETTING AROUND
To/From the Airport
There is no public or airline transport between Lefkosia and Larnaka or Pafos airports. You can, however, take a service taxi to either airports, but do make sure you leave at least an hour for your journey, as picking up and dropping off the other passengers can take a long time. This applies particularly to those flying from Pafos airport, because passengers travelling from Lefkosia to Pafos with a service taxi have to change in Lemesos, which can sometimes include a wait of around 30 minutes.

A service taxi to Larnaka airport will cost around CY£3.50, and around CY£9 to Pafos airport.

Bus
The urban bus station is at Plateia Solomou. **Lefkosia Buses** (☎ 2266 5814) operates numerous routes to and from the city and suburbs. Because most of the major sites and hotels are within walking distance of each other, urban buses are of limited use.

Car & Motorcycle
At Plateia Solomou is the urban bus station, **A Petsas & Sons** (Map p60; ☎ 2246 2650) where you can hire cars. There are no bicycles for rent in or around the Old City.

Taxi
There is a large taxi stand on Plateia Eleftherias (Map p60). Some local taxi companies:
Apostrati (☎ 2266 3358; Plateia Eleftherias)
Elpis (☎ 2276 4966; Leoforos Arhiepiskopou Makariou III 63c)
Ethniko (☎ 2266 0880; Plateia Solomou)

AROUND LEFKOSIA

The plain of the Mesaoria (which means 'between two mountains') is a sprawling, parched landscape during the summer months, when the land is totally exposed to the relentless sun. But come spring and winter, the Mesaoria, like most of Cyprus, transforms into a green, fertile plain. The two mountain ranges surrounding the plain are the Kyrenia (Girne) Range to the north and the Troödos Massif to the south. For the visitor wanting to explore the Mesaoria, there are a couple of ancient archaeological sites and a sprinkling of churches and monasteries. Note that for some of the churches and monasteries, you need to be in a group to be of any interest to those with the keys to unlock the buildings.

Getting There & Around
A car will be necessary to see some of the sites listed in this section. While public buses (often colourful and old-fashioned) connect most of the Mesaoria villages with Lefkosia, they're basically scheduled to service workers and schoolchildren, and not curious travellers, so will be of limited use. Generally, you'll need your own transport here, but if you have the time and patience you should be able to get around, perhaps fitfully, by hitching. Locals hitch fairly regularly and you might find it an interesting diversion to pick up someone yourself, if you have your own wheels. However, bear in mind the dangers of hitching; see p242 for more.

Cycling in the area is easy because of the mostly gentle gradients, but it is not recommended: the weather gets very hot in summer and the traffic on the main highways to Troödos can be heavy and dangerous.

ANCIENT TAMASSOS
Homer mentioned **Ancient Tamassos** (admission CY£0.75; ☯ 9am-3pm Tue-Fri, 10am-3pm Sat & Sun) in *The Odyssey*, where it is referred to as Temese. The goddess Athena says to Odysseus' son, Telemachus: 'We are bound for the foreign port of Temese with a cargo of gleaming iron, which we intend to trade for copper.' The site of this otherwise obscure and little-known city kingdom is on a small hillside about 17km southwest of Lefkosia next to the village of Politiko. Tamassos' main claim

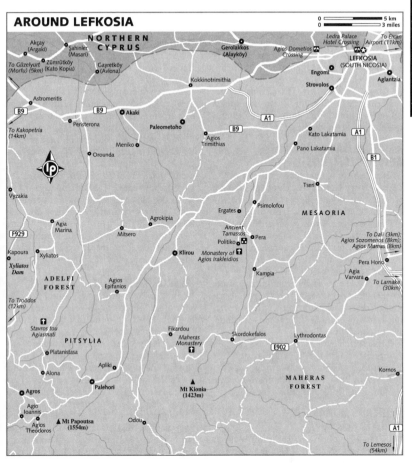

to fame was its seemingly endless supply of copper – the mineral from which the name of Cyprus (Kypros in Greek; Kıbrıs in Turkish) is derived. A copper-producing settlement here dates from at least the 7th century BC, and production of copper ran well into the Hellenistic period. Excavations of the remains of the citadel began in 1889, and two tombs dating back to the 6th century BC were discovered. Today these two tombs constitute the site's major attraction, as the citadel itself is little more than a scattering of nondescript foundations.

The tombs probably contained the remains of the citadel's kings. Looters have long since spirited away the rich burial treasures that may once have been buried here.

A hole in the roof of the larger tomb shows where grave robbers broke in. The walls are unusually carved in such a way as to imitate wood – a feature that some archaeologists have linked to a possible Anatolian influence at the time of the citadel's zenith. Some theorists suggest that Tamassos was even part of the Hittite Empire.

MONASTERY OF AGIOS IRAKLEIDIOS

Easily combined with an excursion to Tamassos is a visit to the nearby **Monastery of Agios Irakleidios** (☉ groups 9am-noon Mon, Tue & Thu). St Irakleidios was born in Tamassos and guided St Paul and St Barnabas around Cyprus. He was later made one of the first bishops in Cyprus by Barnabas. The bishop has been subsequently attributed with performing a number of miracles, including exorcisms.

The original church was built in the 5th century AD, but the current monastic buildings date from the late 18th century. The church today boasts the usual panoply of frescoes and icons. On a table to the eastern side of the church you can spot a reliquary containing one of the bones and the skull of St Irakleidios.

AGIOS MAMAS CHURCH AT AGIOS SOZOMENOS

This is the somewhat forgotten site of the 16th-century Gothic church of **Agios Mamas**, whose arches were never finished in the first place; it's like an exercise in nonstarters. Perhaps that's why the beautiful arches have a sense of nostalgia about them. The church was built in retrograde Lusignan style and, although the site is locked and cannot be entered, the arches, the nave, and two aisles can be easily seen and admired. The isolated ruins are in the deserted mud-village of Agios Sozomenos, an area that has been abandoned since some intercommunal incidents in 1964.

The church and village can be reached from Lefkosia on the A1, taking exit 6 (for Potamia), and going on to a minor, paved road about 2km before Potamia, following a sign for Agios Sozomenos.

MAHERAS MONASTERY
MONH TOY MAXAIPA

It's a fair hike out to the sprawling **Maheras Monastery** (🕑 9am-noon Mon, Tue & Thu), perched in the foothills of the eastern spur of the Troödos Massif and under the all-seeing radar installation on Mt Kionia (1423m) to the southwest. The Maheras Monastery was founded in a similar way to the Kykkos Monastery (p110). In 1148 a hermit named Neophytos found an icon guarded by a sword (*maheras* means knife or sword in Greek) in a cave near the site of the present monastery. The monastery developed around the icon and flourished over time. Nothing remains of the original structures; the current building dates from around 1900.

The monastery is a popular outing for Cypriots who come as much for the cooler climate as for spiritual enlightenment. There is a small cafeteria in the grounds, and pilgrims may stay overnight. One less spiritually

inspired visitor was Grigoris Afxentios during the EOKA uprising of 1955–59. The fearsome EOKA leader hid out in a cave just below the monastery, but was eventually tracked down and killed by British soldiers in 1957. A huge black statue of the hero now looms over a commemorative shrine.

The monastery is open for visits by groups of parishioners only at certain times. Ask locally or perhaps at the CTO in Lefkosia on how you might join one of these groups, which will mostly consist of Cypriot pilgrims. Visits should be conducted with reverence and solemnity. Maheras Monastery is best approached via Klirou and Fikardou, since the alternate route via Pera and the E902, while very pretty, is winding and tortuously slow.

Drivers up this way might look out for the Skordokefalos picnic area east of the Maheras Monastery.

MESAORIA VILLAGES

Renting a car and driving around the Mesaoria is a good way to see the area's villages, but keep in mind that roads tend to fan out haphazardly along roughly defined valleys and ravines, and cross from one valley to another. The journey can therefore be slow as the roads are narrow and winding. So-called 'safari' tours often take travellers to see some of the villages of the Mesaoria as part of a wider tour around Cyprus.

One of the more popular villages is **Pera** (population 1020), a couple of kilometres from Tamassos. While there are no specific sights here, Pera is nonetheless pretty. A stroll through the cobbled backstreets leads photographers to some particularly captivating scenes: old houses covered in bougainvillea, ancient stone jars, pretty doors and cats on walls, the stuff that postcards of rural idyllic scenes are made of. Visitors stop at the *kafeneio* (coffee shop) for refreshments, while the locals and often the village priest sip coffee and engage in gossip in a world where time means little.

The villages of **Orounda** (population 660) and **Peristerona** (population 2100), west of Lefkosia, both have interesting and photogenic churches. The village of **Lythrodontas** (population 2620), 25km south of Lefkosia, is a cool, get-away-from-it-all kind of place.

The postcard-pretty village of **Fikardou** (population 6) is close to the Maheras

Monastery (opposite), and visits to both are easily combined. Fikardou is the 'official' village in a clutch of well-preserved villages in the eastern Troödos Massif. Its Ottoman-period houses with wooden balconies are a visual relief after the cement structures of many modern Troödos mountain villages. That said, there's not a lot to Fikardou and few people live here permanently.

The central strip is no more than a few hundred metres long, and photo opportunities are frustratingly elusive. Most visitors (many on Troödos 'safaris') content themselves with sitting idly at the village's café-cum-restaurant while awaiting the next move. Still, if you are in the region, a visit is recommended since there are few places left in Cyprus that retain at least a tenuous architectural link with the past.

From these villages, roads lead in various ways to the higher reaches of the Troödos, via the Pitsylia region, offering a slow but scenic route into the mountains. This option is particularly useful on weekends when Lefkosians in their hundreds storm the Troödos via the main B9 road (through Astromeritis and Kakopetria) for picnics and a day out in order to escape the city heat.

You will find a tavern or restaurant in most villages and even in out-of-the-way places along the road. Many Lefkosians come to the country to eat on weekends and usually have their favourite haunts. Advertised widely around **Agia Marina** (population 630) is **Katoï** (☎ 2285 2576; Agia Marina Xyliatou; mains CY£5-7), overlooking the village itself. Its lights are visible from afar at night and it commands a great view over the Troödos foothills and the Mesaoria. The restaurant serves solid Cypriot staples and a pretty imaginative selection of *mezedes*.

Around here, you can have some pleasant picnics at picnic grounds, usually situated in cool and leafy spots. Try the **Xyliatos Dam** near the village of the same name, or **Kapoura** on a picturesque back road (F929) linking Vyzakia with the B9, or even high up in the Maheras Forest south of Pera, at **Skordokefalos** along the E902 that leads to the Maheras Monastery. All picnic grounds in this area have barbecue areas, tables, chairs and, most importantly, shade.

Agrotourist lodgings are your best bet for accommodation in the Mesaoria, although there is really only one place that serves the region. Close to the Maheras Forest, **Avli Georgallidi** (☎ 2265 5100; www.yourcyprus.com/agro tourism/lythrodontas.htm; Markou Drakou 3l; tw CY£20, ste for up to 5 people CY£38) is situated in the village of Lythrodontas. It can sleep up to 14 people in self-contained rooms and has a courtyard, phones, central heating and log fires.

Lemesos & the South Coast

The physical heartland of the island, Lemesos and the south coast is one of Cyprus' richest areas for archaeological remains. In this region, there are also a dozen beaches to sprawl your limbs on; you can tap into the city's club scene and spend sleepless nights; or you can tuck into some sophisticated cuisine that just might ruin your beach-body. The Lemesos area shelters the country's second-biggest city and its main port, which also makes Lemesos an economic centre of the Republic of Cyprus. In addition, it holds one of the most important military bases in the whole of the Mediterranean region. The Troödos Massif meets the sea and presents its villages like offerings for tourists to explore. And tourists there are many; so many that sometimes you forget quite where you are. But fear not, there is also tranquillity to be found.

The most impressive and important archaeological site in the area is Ancient Kourion, perched on a bluff overlooking the azure waters of Episkopi Bay, west of Lemesos, which was significant for its role in the spread of Christianity throughout the island. Ancient Amathous, to the east of Lemesos, was one of Cyprus' four original city kingdoms. Richard the Lionheart first set foot in Cyprus in the 12th century – perhaps the island's first British colonist – and liked the country so much he kept it for himself. The English are still here, and occupy the whole of the Akrotiri Peninsula, where housing estates more reminiscent of England's home counties than the eastern Mediterranean are not uncommon.

The area makes a great base for visitors wishing to be in easy reach of all of Cyprus. Take your time to explore its many facets.

HIGHLIGHTS

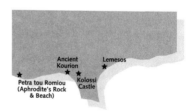

- Stroll around Lemesos' renovated Old City, a much underrated part of town, and visit **Lemesos Medieval Castle & Museum** (p84), the scene of a 12th-century wedding between Richard the Lionheart and Berengaria

- Enjoy an evening concert or play in the amphitheatre at **Ancient Kourion** (p94)

- Discover the roots of Commandaria, a sweet wine first produced by the Knights Hospitaller, at **Kolossi Castle** (p96)

- Swim and picnic at **Petra tou Romiou** (Aphrodite's Rock & Beach; p93), the spot where, apparently, the goddess Aphrodite emerged from the sea

- Eat in one of Lemesos' **Old City restaurants** (p88), and spend an evening at **Notes Studio** (p90) dancing to bouzouki music

LEMESOS & THE SOUTH COAST

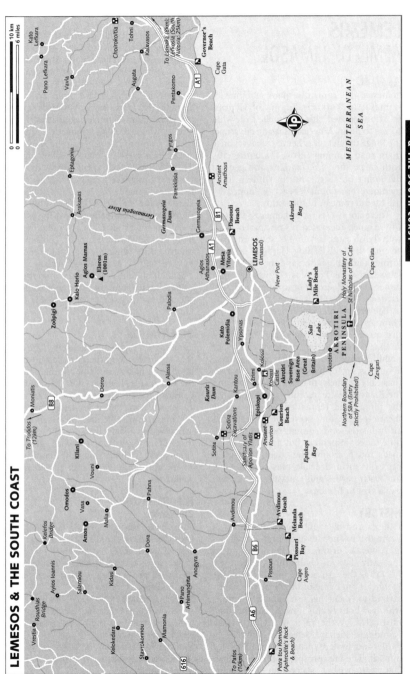

0   10 km
0   6 miles

Kato Lefkara
Pano Lefkara
Vavla
Choirokoitia
Tohni
Kalavasos
Governor's Beach
To Larnaka (8km);
Lefkosia (South;
Nicosia) 25km
Cape Gata

MEDITERRANEAN SEA

Eptagonia
Pentakomo
A1
Pyrgos
Arakapas
Parekklisia
Ancient Amathous
Germasogeia River
Germasogeia Dam
Germasogeia
B1
Dasoudi Beach
Akrotiri Bay
Agios Mamas
Eloros (1001m)
Agios Athanasios
A1
Mesa Yitonia
LEMESOS (Limassol)
New Port
Lady's Mile Beach
Holy Monastery of St Nikolas of the Cats
Cape Gata
Kalo Horio
Zoöpigi
Palodia
Kato Polemidia
Ypsonas
Salt Lake
AKROTIRI PENINSULA
Doros
Alassa
Kourri Dam
Kantou
Kolossi
Erimi
Kolossi Castle
Akrotiri Sovereign Base Area (Great Britain)
Akrotiri
Cape Zevgari
Moniatis
B8
To Troödos (12km)
Sotira
Sotira Excavations
Episkopi
Ancient Kourion
Kourion Beach
Sanctuary of Apollon Ylatis
Northern Boundary of SBA (Entry Strictly Prohibited)
Kilani
Vouni
Patima
Avdimou
Episkopi Bay
Omodos
Vasa
Malia
Dora
Avdimou Beach
Melanda Beach
Kelefos Bridge
Arsos
B6
Pissouri Bay
Agios Ioannis
Salamiou
Kidasi
Anogyra
Pissouri
Cape Aspro
Vretsia
Roudhias Bridge
Kelokedara
Pano Arhimandrita
A6
Mamonia
Stavrokonnou
616
To Pafos (10km)
Petra tou Romiou (Aphrodite's Rock & Beach)

LEMESOS

ΛΕΜΕΣΟΣ LIMASOL

pop 94,600

Lemesos, still known to many as Limassol (Limasol in Turkish), is one of Cyprus' most underrated cities. Modelled on what seems to be an American seaside cityscape, the long stretch that is Lemesos has its busy main road running across the entire city, with cafés, shops, restaurants and general life going on to the north, while a long, mediocre but popular beach is lapped by the Mediterranean to the south.

There are two parts to Lemesos: the Old City, a much-renovated, historic part of town with stylish cafés, restaurants, shops and bars around the Old Fishing Harbour and the former Turkish quarter; and the tourist area (also known as Potamos Germasogeias), a rather abysmal stretch of town around 3km to the east of the Old City.

The second-biggest city in the country, Lemesos has several reputations: 'the city that never sleeps' is one, and the cliché is thanks to the tourist area's exuberant nightlife, rivalled only by that of Agia Napa; another is 'sex town', with the many 'cabarets' (basically brothels) that dot the area around the Rialto Theatre, recently reclaimed from the pimps and rebranded for respectable theatre-goers. Some see Lemesos mainly as an industrial and commercial centre with little to recommend it. But if you like a city that's rough around the edges, with great places to eat and drink, plus several spots for beach parties and fantastic sights, then pay a visit to Lemesos.

HISTORY

Little is known about the early history of Lemesos; its neighbours, first Amathous and later Kourion, stole the limelight in the early days of civilisation in the area. In 1191, the crusader king Richard the Lionheart put Lemesos on the map when he arrived to rescue his sister and his fiancée, who had both been shipwrecked, and then mistreated by the ruler of Cyprus, Isaak Komninos. Richard defeated Komninos in battle and took Cyprus and Lemesos for himself. The city prospered for more than 200 years with a succession of Knights Hospitaller and Templar as its rulers until earthquakes, marauding Genoese (1373) and Saracens (1426) reduced Lemesos' fortunes to virtually zero. The city was still creating a bad impression in the mid-20th century: Lawrence Durrell, writing in 1952 in *Bitter Lemons of Cyprus*, noted upon arrival in Lemesos that '…we berthed towards sunrise in a gloomy and featureless roadstead, before a town whose desolate silhouette suggested that of a tin-mining village in the Andes'.

Lemesos grew up quickly following the Turkish invasion of Cyprus in 1974, as it was required to replace Famagusta (Mağusa) as the nation's main port. It was also obliged to shoulder the mantle of the tourist boom in the Republic. Originally comprising what is today known as the Old City, radiating out from the Old Fishing Harbour, Lemesos has outgrown its original geographic limits to now encompass a sprawling tourist suburb. The tourist centre is a riotous confusion of bars and restaurants, and you could be excused for forgetting that the sea is there at all.

ORIENTATION

Lemesos is a highly walkable city. The road that stretches along the city's length has a good, well-lit walking and cycling path on the beach side. Lemesos' Old City is fairly compact, but the New City now extends for 12km east along the seafront, encompassing the main tourist centre. Buses and taxis arrive within a short distance of each other in the Old City; the New Port, where all ships dock, is about 3km to the southwest. There are handy car parks all along the waterfront.

INFORMATION

Bookshops

Anna's Book Swap (☎ 2559 0093; 28 Oktovriou) A fantastic little bookshop based on the ingenious idea of 'recycling' your books. You buy the first one at full price, and once you've read it and come back to return it, you get 40% towards the price of the second book. It's located by the Ermes Olympia department store.

Kyriakou Bookshop (☎ 2574 7555; Griva Digenis) A good bookshop; the best in town for English language bestsellers (all those beach-reads), with an exhaustive section on Cyprus-related titles.

Marilyn's Book Swap (☎ 9941 6823; Kitiou Kyprianou 51) The sister bookshop to Anna's Book Swap, functioning on the same principle.

Emergency

In case of emergency, call ☎ 199 or ☎ 122.
Police station (cnr Griva Digeni & Omirou) On the Lefkosia road.

Internet Access

CyberNet (Eleftherias 79; per hr CY£2; ⊙ 1-11pm Mon-Fri, 10am-11pm Sat & Sun) A convenient Old City location.

Explorer (Agias Zonis; per hr CY£2; ⊙ 10am-11pm Sat & Sun) Another Old City Internet café.

Laundry

There are at least four laundrettes scattered around Lemesos. Costs range from CY£2 for a DIY service to CY£4 for a service wash done by the laundry staff. The two most central:

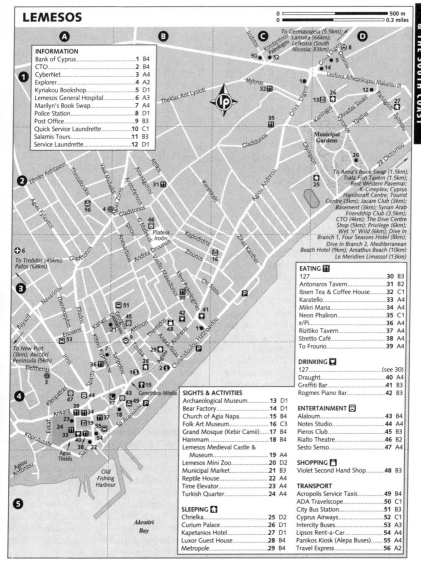

LEMESOS

LEMESOS & THE SOUTH COAST

Quick Service Laundrette (☎ 2558 7056; Griva Digeni 145)

Service Laundrette (Anastasi Sioukri 20) Near the Curium Palace hotel.

Medical Services

Lemesos General Hospital (☎ 2533 0777; Arhie-piskopou Leontiou I) Situated 1km northwest of the Old Fishing Harbour.

Night pharmacy assistance (☎ 1415)

Money

You can change money on arrival at the New Port, but there are plenty of banks around the centre of the Old City and in the tourist centre equipped with ATMs for cash withdrawals.

Bank of Cyprus (cnr Saripolou & Agiou Andrea) Probably the most convenient bank in the Old City.

Post

Post office (Kitiou Kyprianou) The main post office is centrally located in the Old City, a block north of the pedestrian zone. Poste restante mail is also held here.

Tourist Information

Cyprus Tourism Organisation (CTO; ☒ 8.15am-2.30pm & 4-6.15pm Wed, Thu & Sat-Mon Jun-Aug) town centre (☎ 2557 1868; fax 2574 6596; cnr Nikolaidi & Spyrou Araouzou); tourist centre (☎ 2532 3211; fax 2531 3451; Georgiou 1, 22a) Has many branches in Lemesos. Opening hours outside of summer are subject to change.

Travel Agencies

ADA Travelscope (☎ 2534 3111; evie@travelscope.com .cy; Konstantinou Paleologou 25b) Not far from the Archaeo-logical Museum; offers a wide variety of services and can book discounted airline tickets for most destinations.

Salamis Tours (☎ 2535 5555; fax 2536 4410; Salamis House, 28 Oktovriou) Maintains its head office here, close to the CTO, and issues tickets to transport your vehicle to Greece or Israel.

DANGERS & ANNOYANCES

We don't recommend visiting any of the city's 'cabarets', but if you do decide to go, keep in mind the stories of being charged several hundred pounds for a couple of beers at the end of a night. And woe betide those who refuse to pay.

SIGHTS & ACTIVITIES

Lemesos Medieval Castle & Museum

The city's most popular tourist attraction is **Lemesos Medieval Castle** (Irinis; grounds admission free; ☒ 9am-5pm Mon-Sat, 10am-1pm Sun), and its alluring gardens, on the west side of the Old City, are a shady haven in the summer heat. The structure, built in the 14th century over the remains of a Byzantine castle, has been used and plundered by many throughout Cyprus' exciting history. The Venetians vandalised it; the Ottomans gave it a face-lift for military use; and the Brits used it as a prison during their colonial rule. According to history and legend, Richard the Lionheart married Berengaria in the chapel of the original castle in 1191, where he also crowned himself King of Cyprus and his wife Queen of England. The chapel and Byzantine castle have long since gone, and in their place now stands the current structure.

Although the castle doesn't really look like a massively grandiose structure from the outside, it's worth going inside and exploring. The gardens hide an old **olive oil press** that dates from the 7th to 9th centuries. The oil press is based on a simplified version of a Hellenistic and Roman trapetum, a mill that uses only one millstone.

In order to appreciate the castle, don't miss the **Medieval Museum** (☎ 2533 0419; admission CY£1; ☒ 9am-5pm Mon-Sat, 10am-1pm Sun). The museum building is an intriguing collection of vaults and air shafts, and its artefacts, transferred from the original Lefkosia Medieval Museum in 1974, are often fascinating. The museum's interior is divided into a series of rooms and chambers on varying levels. All have thematic displays of Byzantine and medieval objects, including Ottoman pottery, gold religious objects, tombstones, suits of armour and weapons. In the Grand Hall, to the right and on a lower level as you enter, there is a good display of black-and-white photos of Byzantine sites all over Cyprus. Climb up to a rooftop terrace, where you can get good views over the city.

Archaeological Museum

The city's **Archaeological Museum** (☎ 2533 0157; cnr Vyronos & Kaningos; admission CY£0.75; ☒ 9am-5pm Mon-Sat, 10am-1pm Sun) has a largish collection of pottery, and a collection of items dating from Neolithic and Chalcolithic times (primarily of shards and implements for domestic use) through to Mycenaean pottery. A multitude of terracotta figures exhibited are thought to be the remains of votive offerings. There is a display of classical pottery, jewellery and oil lamps, as well as curiously modern-looking glass bottles and vials. Although it pales in comparison to Lefkosia's Cyprus Museum (p63), it's worth a browse; and if you've been doing nothing but sunbathing and clubbing for a week, the museum offers a nice, refreshing change of scene.

Folk Art Museum

Lemesos has a somewhat mediocre **Folk Art Museum** (☎ 2536 2303; Agiou Andreou 253; admission CY£0.50; ☒ 8.30am-1.30pm Mon-Fri, 3-5.30pm Mon-Wed & Fri, 4-6.30pm Mon-Wed & Fri Jun–mid-Sep), which is housed in an old mansion not far from the city centre. It has displays of woodwork, traditional dress, jewellery and household utensils. There is a guidebook for sale at the ticket desk, which is the only thing that explains what you're looking at.

Grand Mosque

Set in the midst of the old Turkish quarter, the **Grand Mosque** (Kebir Camii; Genethliou Mitella) is surrounded by palms almost as tall as its minaret. It is used by the remaining Turkish Cypriot population and Muslims from the Middle East who live in Lemesos. As with any mosque, visitors are requested to dress conservatively, leave shoes by the door and avoid visiting at prayer times. There are no fixed opening hours – if the gate is open, step inside the courtyard and take a look.

Hammam

This tiny **hammam** (☎ 9947 4251; Loutron 3; steam bath & sauna/massage CY£5; ☒ 2-10pm) is located near the mosque. It isn't really a tourist site, and visitors are not encouraged to go in and 'have a look', since many count on privacy when going in for a steam bath. Don't go there expecting any luxury; it's a back-to-basics place where people go to relax. Keep in mind that all sessions are mixed. Also on offer are full-body massages, shiatsu, Swedish massage, Indian head massage, and anti-stress massages for CY£10.

LEMESOS FOR CHILDREN
Time Elevator

You'll see lots of advertisements for the **Time Elevator** (☎ 2576 2828; fax 2576 2829; Vasilissis 1; adult/child CY£7/CY£5; ☒ 10am-8pm) in Lemesos, which is slightly worrying, but also symptomatic of the kind of lightweight approach to the island's history and culture by many a package tourist, at whom this kind of thing is ultimately aimed. But the history of Cyprus, from 8500 BC to AD 1974 compressed into 40 minutes, is great if you're trying to force some history on your kids. You get water, wind and lots of jostling, so much so that it's recommended that pregnant women and sufferers of motion sickness should watch the show from static seats. Shows start on the hour.

Wet 'n' Wild

As Lemesos' reputation as a 'good time gal' has to be maintained to compete with that of its younger sister, Agia Napa, so too Lemesos has to have a crazy water theme park. It actually has three, but **Wet 'n' Wild** (☎ 2531 8000; www.wetnwild.com.cy; 13 yrs & over/2-12 yrs/under 2 yrs CY£12.50/6.25/free; ☒ 10am-6pm Apr-Oct) is particularly special. It's in the middle of the tourist centre, and is set back a few hundred metres from the beachfront. There are raft rides, inner-tube rides, body flumes, speed slides, a 'lazy river', wave pool, activity pool, kiddies' pool and 'wet bubble'. And if that doesn't get your kids to sleep like logs at night, we don't know what will.

If you are coming to Lemesos by car, exit at the Mouttagiaka exit (junction 23) on the A1 motorway. There's no public transport to get here.

Bear Factory

Nothing to do with either the sea or Cyprus, but always guaranteed to make the little ones drool, are teddy bears. And here, at the **Bear Factory** (☎ 2534 1040; Leoforos Arhiepiskopou Makariou III; ☒ 8.30am-1pm & 4-7pm Mon, Tue, Thu, Fri, 8.30am-2pm Wed & Sat May-Sep, 8.30am-5.30pm Mon, Tue, Thu, Fri, 8.30am-2pm Wed & Sat Oct-Apr), children can choose the kind of teddy bear they want. They can choose the 'skin' or the softness of the material, how hard or soft the bear's 'insides' are, and even a 'heart'. Oh, and they can implant sound devices too. Then they get to choose its name, and watch it being sewn up, so they can feel the bear is truly their creation. And they get to take it away in its very own box, with, wait for it, a birth certificate! (Parents note: all major credit cards are accepted, so no wrangling.)

Lemesos Mini Zoo & Reptile House

Also good for kiddies, although slightly small is the **Lemesos Mini Zoo** (Municipal Gardens;

LEMESOS & THE SOUTH COAST

GOING UNDER: THE BEST DIVES IN CYPRUS

What's an islander to do with all that water? Well, dive in it, of course. If you love discovering remains, rocks or shipwrecks at the bottom of the sea, Cyprus is a perfect spot for a varied and interesting choice of dives. Either Larnaka or Lemesos is a good base for diving.

The prime location is the shipwreck of the **Zenobia**, rated as one of the world's top-ten diving wrecks. Situated off the coast of Larnaka, this sunken cargo ship is almost completely the same as it was when it sank in 1980. You have to be a qualified diver to go to the depths of 17m to 43m. The ship is around 200m long and still has its cargo on board. The fish have made the wreck their home, and you'll see beautiful creatures such as giant tuna, barracuda, amberjack and eel swimming in and out of the Zenobia's nooks and crannies.

Another fascinating shipwreck is the site of the **Vera K** in Pafos (10m below sea level), which touched bottom in the 1970s. It has since been used as a military practice target; and its two arches have served as a romantic background for underwater photography.

Officially called the Helicopter Wreck, a British Army Air Corps helicopter wreck is an attraction for divers off the coast of Larnaka. Located 16m below sea level, this place is a magnet for creatures like octopus, jack and groper.

A more recent wreck is **M/Y Diana** in Lemesos, a 50ft Russian yacht, discovered in 1996. It was found sitting upright on the seabed, 21m below sea level. Apart from being used as a training spot for divers for wreck and night dives, the yacht is home to elegant sea creatures like large squid.

The **Pharses II** wreck in Lemesos (21m below sea level) is so busy with marine life that you might witness some sea rage on this cargo ship. The wreck is around 1000 tonne in weight and is intact. It rests on its starboard, and entry is strictly supervised.

But it's not all shipwrecks under the sea. The Cypriot Mediterranean hides some beautiful underwater caves such as the Big Country (23m below sea level), a multilevel cave site near Lemesos, and Akrotiri Fish Reserve (9m below sea level), a dive ideal for the inexperienced but enthusiastic, also near Lemesos. You can hand-feed lovely fish, like groper, eel, sea bass, and sometimes octopus too. But if you love octopus, go to the obviously named Octopus Reef in Larnaka (10m below sea level), where schools of the multilimbed creatures relax in the water.

For serious divers, Mushroom Rocks (50m below sea level) offers a real challenge, as well as large-fish sighting. The name comes from the mushroom-shaped rock, growing from the sea floor near Larnaka. And for those who want to see some underwater ancient history, the **Amphorae Reef** in Pafos (5 to 10m below sea level) is the perfect place. There is an abundance of pottery lying around in the shadow of a massive ship beached on the reef, shed by this and other similar unfortunates.

If you're a qualified diver, you'll know what to do. But if you're in Cyprus on holiday and want to try it out, check out the island's best known diving company **Dive-In** (www.dive-in.com.cy), which has branches in Larnaka, Lemesos and Pafos.

Try-dives (in a pool) usually cost around CY£20 to CY£25. Internationally recognised PADI courses teach you the basics of diving in open water. They last around five days and cost between CY£180 and CY£190.

admission CY£0.50; ⊙ 9am-noon & 3-7pm May-Sep, 9am-6.30pm Oct-Apr), which has not much more than a sweaty giraffe and some cheeky cheetahs.

You may also want to take your kids, if they like blood and gore, to the **Reptile House** (☎ 2537 2779; admission CY£1.50; ⊙ 9am-6pm) situated on the roundabout in the Old Fishing Harbour, where numerous thick-skinned creatures are kept, and squeaking mice are fed to snakes for dinner.

TOURS

To stretch your legs, there are three different types of walk in Lemesos, all organised by the CTO. They're free, but it's wise to book in the high season.

'A Stroll in Neapolis, Nemesos, Limassol', at 10am on Mondays, takes you around Lemesos' historic centre, its monuments, craft shops, markets and traditional shops. As a bonus, local gossip from (some of) the CTO guides is thrown in.

At 10am every second Wednesday from October to April, 'Germasogeia: A Village Blessed by Water' goes to, you guessed it, Germasogeia village, where the water theme is covered by a visit to the village dam. You also get to see the village itself, its architecture and street life.

'Discover the Natural Environment of Germasogeia', at 10am every second Wednesday from October to April, is a walk in the hills (a bit of fitness required), following a nature trail laid out by the Forestry Department.

FESTIVALS & EVENTS

The **Lemesos Wine Festival** is an orgy of (obviously) wine, wine and wine. Held in the Municipal Gardens annually from 30 August to 11 September, it's a chance to sample cheap and also more expensive local wines. As you might predict, the festival is extremely popular with young, fun-seeking tourists, who use the opportunity to get completely sloshed. Nevertheless, the atmosphere in the city is good during the festival: there's Cypriot food, traditional music and dancing, and, did we mention wine?

Lemesos is the only town in Cyprus with a full-blown carnival atmosphere, enjoyed particularly by the little ones. The 11-day **Lemesos Carnival**, held 50 days before Easter, starts with the 'King Carnival' entering town, escorted by a motley parade.

There is a children's carnival parade, and the festivities close with a fancy-dress explosion. Watch out Rio, Lemesos Carnival is on the loose!

SLEEPING

The good news is that there are plenty of hotels in Lemesos. The bad news is that they are all along a 9km tourist strip to the northeast of the Old City, and are often crowded and overpriced. The Old City doesn't feature many high-quality establishments, but hotels in this area are more used to walk-in travellers and are likely to have rooms vacant.

Budget & Midrange

The cheapest hotels are clustered in the Old City, to the east of the castle.

Luxor Guest House (☎ 2536 2265; Agiou Andreou 101; s/d CY£6/12) This place is like a dinosaur surrounded by modern animals, but in a good way. The Luxor is the only truly budget place in the city, and possibly in the country. The rooms are airy and spacious, with painted wood-board ceilings and little balconies. The bathrooms are mostly shared, and there are no cooking facilities apart from a small breakfast kitchen. This dying breed of budget accommodation may soon be altogether extinct, since the owner, who complains of a serious lack of independent travellers, is thinking of converting the place and raising the prices as early as 2006.

Metropole (☎ 2536 2686; Ifigenias 6; s/d CY£17/22) Once a little more budget-oriented, the Metropole became a three-star general after a refurbishment in 2004. It's a comfortable place with a rather classic décor where navy bed quilts match the curtains. The bathrooms are en suite. The hotel's location is supercentral, so it's a pretty good choice if you want to be in the Old City.

Kapetanios Hotel (☎ 2558 6266; kapetdev@spider net.com.cy; Panagioti Symeou 6; unrenovated s/d CY£30/38; renovated s/d CY£34.50/42.50; 🔲 🖳) A three-star hotel in a tall building, this place has cheaper older rooms, which are decent enough, and new, renovated ones, which feel a bit more comfortable. All rooms have phones, minibars, satellite TV and balconies, and there is a small swimming pool downstairs too. The Kapetanios is a little beyond the zoo on the east side of the Old City, but still within reasonable walking distance.

Curium Palace (☎ 2536 3121; www.luxuryhotels oftheworld.co.uk/Europe/Cyprus/hotels/curium-palace .asp; Vyronos 2; s/d CY£48/62; 🔲 🖳) This four-star establishment is a gleaming white marble palace that looks down on a weary traveller and up at a groomed, designer-luggage-laden one. An extremely comfortable, almost luxurious hotel, with a large restaurant terrace, pool and a swish evening bar. Rich Russians seem to like this place, and many package-tourists come here for their bit of lavishness. Opposite the Municipal Gardens.

Best Western Pavemar (☎ 2532 4535; fax 2558 7711; 28 Oktovriou; s/d CY£48/67; 🔲 🖳) On the edge of the tourist centre and handy for checking out both sides of town, the Pavemar is not a stylish or interesting place, and has slightly cheap-looking décor. But there is a pool and a nice roof terrace on the building's top floor, where an evening drink comes with a good view of the sunset.

Chrielka (☎ 2535 8366; www.chrielka.com.cy; Olympion 7; 2-person ste CY£48-65; ⊠ ⓡ) This place is great if you'd like to self-cater and stay in a decent place. The 33 apartments vary in size and level of 'luxury', but all are tastefully decorated, with a balcony, kitchenette and satellite TV. There's a guest pool, and the location is central, with some apartments overlooking the Municipal Gardens.

Top End

Lemesos' plushest hotels are located at the far northeastern end of the tourist centre. Discounts of between 30% and 40% apply at both these hotels out of season.

Amathus Beach Hotel (☎ 2532 1152; www .amathushotel.com; per person s/d CY£119/158) This is a super-duper lavish place, where that 'bit' of extra cash is well worth spending. For a start, why not exchange your restaurant buffet breakfast for a lazy breakfast in bed. Smell the roses on the desk in your room, and head for a spa treatment that you'll probably never want to finish. Have dinner on your balcony, and watch the endless Mediterranean and the stars that'll be looking down at you from above. Sunbathe and swim on the smooth, sandy beach. And if you do all this during low season (swapping the sea-swimming with indoor-pool swimming) and you do it as a couple, you get almost 50% off.

THE AUTHOR'S CHOICE

127 (☎ 2534 3990; Eleni Paleologinas 5; salad/sandwich CY£4.50/2.50) In a country of meze and meat-eaters, 127 is a place with a serious difference. Vintage furniture adorns the three rooms inside, with comfy old sofas and rugged leather armchairs, and bowling pins sit on the 'mantelpiece'. Exposed-brick walls provide the backdrop, and some are painted in mossy greens, raspberry pinks and melon yellows. There is a lovely large garden for lunch or dinner. And the food is all about salads. But don't go expecting a bit of rocket or lettuce and a slice of tomato. The people in this place know how to make a salad (and how to make your mouth water): the seafood salad is swamped with succulent prawns, thin slices of salmon and bits of squid, all drizzled with balsamic vinegar that really brings out the taste.

Le Meridien Limassol (☎ 2586 2000; www.lemeri dien-cyprus.com; s/d CY£168/371.50; ⊠ ⓡ ⓐ) This is another luxury giant, a little more kitsch than the Amathus, and a little more expensive, with grottos and fountains spurting water in the large pools. There's a range of room choices, from standard to 'Jacuzzi cabanas' (where you can sit in your Jacuzzi and watch the world from the window next to you) to presidential suites offering masses of opulence, to two-bedroom Citrus Garden Villas housing up to seven people where extravagance will be coming out of your ears. Le Meridien also has special luxury rooms for disabled travellers.

EATING
Restaurants

As always, meze rules. Eating in Lemesos offers variety and quality with a modern touch, particularly in the Old City. The restored Old Carob Mill next to the fort has several restaurants (as well as housing the Time Elevator, p85) and bars, all of which are top-notch places to eat and are very popular with Lemesians.

Karatello (☎ 2582 0464; Vasilissis 1; specialities CY£2.50-5; ⓨ dinner) The tall ceilings of the old mill and the massive space inside gives Karatello a stylish, modern look that goes with the interesting cuisine. Dishes that stand out in tastiness are rabbit in yoghurt and lemon sauce, seasonal greens baked with feta cheese, and a delicious and neatly served *kleftiko* (oven-baked lamb or goat). The menu has little boxes where you tick off your order and hand it over to your waiter.

Trata Fish Tavern (☎ 2558 6600; Ioanni Tompazi 4; fish meze CY£10; ⓨ dinner) Arguably one of Lemesos' best fish restaurants, Trata is choc-a-bloc every night with people wanting some of those fish meze. The décor is minimal and the place looks like an unassuming family restaurant. Booking is advisable on weekdays and essential on weekends. Close to the Ermes Olympia department store and the Holiday Inn hotel.

Mikri Maria (☎ 2535 7679; Agkuras 3; meze per person CY£7, fresh fish from CY£6; ⓨ dinner) This is the quintessential Cypriot taverna with home cooking and fresh food. The guitars on the walls make it look like an Andalusian tapas place where the flamenco dancers might jump out and do a quick dance as you eat.

Syrian Arab Friendship Club (SAFC; ☎ 2532 8838; Iliados 3; meze CY£8; ☯ lunch & dinner) Sister of the Lefkosia restaurant (p71) and just as good, the SAFC is a delight to all lovers of Arab cuisine that's rich with chick peas, beans, herbs, spices, grilled and marinated meats and sweet desserts. And here the meze will blow your tastebuds. A nargileh (Middle Eastern water pipe) after eating is a superb treat, and, if you're lucky, you may get to have a belly dancer flex her abdominals at you.

To Frourio (☎ 2535 9332; Tsanakali 18; mains CY£3-8; ☯ Mon-Sat) Priding itself on its setting in an 18th-century historically listed building opposite the castle, To Frourio is popular and a little on the touristy side, but decent. There are meat and vegetarian dishes (such as tasty, aubergine-laden vegetarian lasagne), as well as both variations of meze.

Antonaros Tavern (☎ 2537 7808; Attikis 1; meze CY£6-6.50; ☯ evenings Mon-Sat) For a no-frills, genuinely Cypriot, local-style evening meal. Only *mezedes* are served here. Choose from a wide range of dishes such as snails and mussels as well as fish (CY£11 to CY£20 per kilogram). The handwritten notes on the wall are Greek philosophical sayings.

Rizitiko Tavern (☎ 2534 8769; Tzamiou 4-8; mains CY£3.50-5; ☯ dinner) This is an excellent, low-key establishment, tucked away by the mosque, which spills out onto the narrow street at night. The *afelia* (pork cooked in red wine and coriander seeds) and *kleftiko* are homemade quality and worth every cent.

Neon Phaliron (☎ 2536 5768; Gladstonos 135; mains CY£7-9; ☯ 10am-4pm & 6.30pm-midnight, closed Wed & Sun) A high-class gourmet dining option that specialises in Mediterranean-European fare, such as marinated salmon kebabs (CY£6.50) and stuffed mushrooms (CY£4), and an extensive wine cellar for committed oenophiles. Neon Phaliron is popular with Cyprus' posh dinner crowd.

Cafés

The following cafes are open from 10am to 11pm.

Stretto Café (☎ 2582 0465; Vasilissis) Cafés in Lemesos don't come any more fashionable than this. Part of the Old Carob Mill, it has tall ceilings and comfy sofas, beautiful people in real life and on TV. Sounds intimidating? Fear not, the atmosphere is good and relaxed, and its icy frappé on a hot day will make you come back for more.

Ibsen Tea & Coffee House (☎ 2534 0714; Mylonas 6) A café dedicated to the dark Norwegian playwright in the middle of sex-town Lemesos? The name is enough to make you want to try this place out. And lovely things you'll find too, such as Norwegian coffee and waffles.

π/Pi (☎ 2534 1944; Kitiou Kyprianou 27; snacks CY£2-3) A relaxed, jazzy café with a small, cosy garden in the back where you can lounge during the day, or come after dinner for a sharp drink.

DRINKING

Time to test out that 'party town' theory.

Most places in Lemesos are quiet until at least 10pm. We've avoided making specific bar recommendations on the tourist strip, where a conglomeration of pubs with names such as the Blu Bar, Downunder, Leprechaun, West End, Lucky, Full Monty and Woody's makes you feel that you've been there before. And it was bad enough the first time.

These are great bars in the Old City.

Rogmes Piano Bar (☎ 2534 1010; Agiou Andreou 197) A highly praised bouzouki bar. It has a mad, wonderful tempo on weekend nights when the musicians stay and play as loud and as late as the crowd wants it, like in the good old days. Book a table on Saturdays when the locals pour inside for singing and dancing 'til dawn.

Graffiti Bar (Agiou Andreou 238) Silky drops hang over cushioned sofas in a very Middle Eastern style. Nargileh smoke billows over the cocktail-drinking customers, and the garden where all this happens is behind an old mansion that the becomes the bar's location during the winter months.

Draught (☎ 2582 0470; Vasilissis) Yet another listing in the Old Carob Mill complex, this time a bar. The Carob Mill people seem to know what they're doing, don't they? Once ultra-fashionable, Draught is a bit less maniacally sought after now. That means it's a pleasant place to have a drink, while it still has a nice buzz; it gets really busy only on weekends. Massive copper vats line the wall, where the decent in-house ale is brewed.

127 (☎ 2534 3990; Eleni Paleologinas 5) Although many come for the food (opposite), just as many come to lounge on the sofas and drink long cocktails while playing a game of backgammon, or just smooching in the darker areas of the lovely back garden.

ENTERTAINMENT
Nightclubs
Notes Studio (☎ 2534 4344; cnr Irinis & Eleftherias 5; admission CY£15) If you're serious about experiencing Cyprus (or at least the Greek part), then a bouzouki club is a must. And what great fun it is too. Notes Studio specialises in live performances, bringing over Greek performers, who hurl themselves about (and you, if you let them) until dawn. It's your chance to try yourself at *Zorba the Greek* dancing, but beware: strong thighs are necessary. Your first drink is included in the admission price.

Sesto Senso (☎ 2587 9080; Eleftherias 45) The in-est place in town, where the crowd is so beautiful and admiring of itself, it finds it hard to dance. The décor is also beautiful, and the drinks are expensive (which is not so beautiful), but if you want to see who's in and what it's all about, check this place out. If they let you in, that is. Aside from the whole looks thing, the sounds in this place are the best in town if you like good dance music.

Basement (☎ 2587 3380; Potamos Germasogeias) A predominantly young crowd hangs out in this small, busy club, where a be-young-and-beautiful dress code applies.

Privilege (☎ 2563 4040; Loura) Near the five-star St Raphael Resort, at the far eastern end of the tourist centre; an indoor and outdoor club with various bars and dance areas. The music mix is Greek and European chart sounds.

Gay & Lesbian Venues
Alaloum (☎ 2536 9726; Loutron 1) Situated near the hammam in a renovated old mansion, this is the town's oldest and favourite gay club. Gay, lesbian, bi: everyone parties hard and stays up very, very late.

Jacare (☎ 2532 0635; Popiland 67, Georgiou, Potamos Germasogeias) Right in the middle of the tourist area; popular with a relaxed, young gay crowd.

Pieros Club (☎ 9989 5737; Georgiou Gennadiou 10) If you are up for a more mixed crowd, although still predominantly gay, with a good atmosphere, check out this club.

Cinemas
K-Cineplex (☎ 2543 1955; www.kcineplex.com; Ariadnis 8, Mouttagiaka; ☼ 5-10.30pm) As in Lefkosia and Larnaka, the cinema scene in Lemesos is now dominated by the multiscreen K-Cineplex, which features many new-release movies. It's in the middle of the tourist centre and is best reached by taxi. See the website for current showings.

SHOPPING
Most of Lemesos' clothes, shoes and appliance shops are clustered along the pedestrianised street of Agiou Andreou in central Lemesos, but also filter out through most of the backstreets of this area. Some fun places to spend a bit of your holiday dosh:

Cyprus Handicraft Centre (☎ 2530 5118; Themidos 25; ☼ 8.30am-1pm & 4-7pm Mon, Tue, Thu, Fri, 8.30am-2pm Wed & Sat May-Sep, 8.30am-5.30pm Mon, Tue, Thu, Fri, 8.30am-2pm Wed & Sat Oct-Apr) As in other cities across Cyprus, this government-sponsored centre is the best place for getting your traditional handmade stuff. You can be sure you're not being ripped off and that what you buy won't fall apart as soon as you take it home.

Violet Second Hand Shop (☎ 2574 6748; Salaminos 10; ☼ 10am-2pm & 4-7pm Mon-Sat) A great place for clothes and jewellery, with possibilities for finding some interesting Cypriot vintage pieces.

GETTING THERE & AWAY
Air
The office of **Cyprus Airways** (☎ 2537 3787; www.cyprusairways.com; Leoforos Arhiepiskopou Makariou III 203) is a 20-minute walk northeast of the main CTO office. Lemesos is more or less equidistant from Pafos and Larnaka airports. Service or private taxis are the only way to reach either and will charge you CY£5.10.

Boat
CRUISES
Expensive two- and three-day cruises depart from Lemesos all year. They go to Haifa (Israel), Port Said (Egypt), a selection of Greek islands, and sometimes (in summer) to Lebanon. You can book at any travel agency, but you cannot use these cruises to exit Cyprus, unless you decide to jump ship (see p234).

INTERNATIONAL FERRY
In late 2001, international passenger-ferry services from Cyprus to Israel and Greece were suspended indefinitely, which has

made it impossible to enter the Republic of Cyprus by ferry. Travellers bringing in a vehicle to Cyprus must now send their vehicle independently by ship and fly to Cyprus to collect it (see p238).

Bus

Intercity Buses (☎ 2266 5814; cnr Enoseos & Irinis) runs frequent daily services to Lefkosia (CY£1.50, 1 hour) from its bus stop north of the castle.

Intercity Buses also has services to Larnaka (CY£1.70, 45 minutes) from the Old Fishing Harbour or from outside the CTO. Both **Alepa** (☎ 9962 5027) and **Nea Amoroza** (☎ 2693 6822) have daily buses to Pafos (CY£2, 45 minutes). Alepa leaves from the Panikos kiosk on the promenade, while Nea Amoroza leaves from the Old Fishing Harbour.

There is a bus to Platres (CY£2.50, 1 hour) that leaves from the Municipal Market every day at 9.30am.

Service Taxi

Travel & Express (☎ 7777 7474; Thessalonikis 21) has regular service taxis to Lefkosia (CY£4.50, one hour 30 minutes), Larnaka (CY£3.50, one hour) and Pafos (CY£3.50, one hour). Another taxi option is **Acropolis Service Taxis** (☎ 2536 6766; Spyrou Araouzou 65), which departs regularly for the same destinations.

GETTING AROUND

The city bus station is located on Georgiou Gennadiou, close to the municipal market. Bus 1 goes to the port; buses 16 and 17 to Kolossi; and bus 30 runs northeast along the seafront and passes not far from the entrance to Ancient Amathous. The CTO gives out a useful timetable of urban bus routes.

Buses also run at 10am, 11am and 1pm from the castle to Ancient Kourion and its beach, via Episkopi (return CY£1.60, 30 minutes). Return times are 11.50am and 2.50pm. From April to October, there's a daily Governor's Beach bus (return CY£2, 20 minutes) that leaves from the Old Fishing Harbour at 9.50am, making stops at about 23 locations along the seafront, with the last one being at Le Meridien hotel. The bus returns at 4.30pm.

Lipsos Rent-a-Car (☎ 2536 5295; cnr Richard & Berengaria 6), opposite the castle, is the only car-rental place in the Old City. The tourist centre has many other rental agencies.

AROUND LEMESOS

For travellers, there's lots to do and see in the area around Lemesos, such as excellent beaches that beckon tan seekers and ancient ruins galore for lovers of history.

Getting There & Around

You really need to have your own transport to explore this area. Other than Ancient Kourion, Episkopi and Ancient Amathous, which are linked to Lemesos by daily public buses, and Governor's Beach, which is served by a daily private bus, reaching any of the other places described in this section is going to require hired transport or expensive taxis. Cycling in and around Lemesos is fairly easy once you have cleared the confines of the city, where traffic is intense. The terrain is reasonably flat, until you encounter the first slopes of the Troödos Massif.

BEACHES

Lemesos' city beaches are popular enough and decent for a quick swim. But if you'd like to lounge on a nice beach all day, with a little privacy thrown in, you'll have to move out of town where you can stretch out on sand and pebble.

Lady's Mile Beach

This shadeless 7km stretch of hard-packed sand and pebble is the town's closest beach. Named after a horse owned by a former colonial governor who exercised his mare on the beach, it runs south beyond Lemesos' New Port along the eastern side of the British-controlled Akrotiri Peninsula. There is a rather awful power station at its eastern end; the beach (and the view) get better the further south you go. On summer weekends, the citizens of Lemesos flock here in large numbers to relax in the rather shallow waters. A couple of beach taverns serve the crowds and provide some respite from an otherwise barren beachscape. Bring your own shade if you plan to sit on the beach all day. Getting here requires your own transport.

Governor's Beach

Lemesos' tourist appeal starts 30km east of the city, at Governor's Beach. With a private bus serving the area from Lemesos (see left), many decide to spend their day chilling out

LEMESOS
& THE SOUTH COAST

(or, more appropriately, baking) on the several coves of dark sand, contrasted by the white chalk cliffs behind them. There are a couple of restaurants here and at least one place to stay, though the overall ambience is slightly marred by the sight of the large Vasilikos power station looming 3km to the west. Beach techno parties are frequent during the summer here, so keep an eye out for leaflets advertising such events across the island.

Campers can hole up here at **Governor's Beach Camping** (☎ /fax 2563 2878; tent & 1 person CY£2.50). The site is OK, but is more attuned to caravanners than to campers.

Kourion Beach

This is a lovely beach of grey sand and small pebbles, with waves soaking the sand. The area is windy and attracts windsurfers and other wind-dependent sportspeople, as well as the general public, who come here for the stunning lack of visual clutter or buildings. Kourion Beach is around 17km west of Lemesos, within the British Sovereign Base Area (SBA), which is partly responsible for the lack of development in this pocket of the island. The beach can be reached by public transport from Lemesos (p91), although the locals like to drive their cars and 4WDs practically up to the water's edge. There is no shade, apart from the escape offered by several tavernas. The eastern end of the beach (prominently marked) is unsafe for swimming, so head for the western end. This beach is best combined with your trip to Ancient Kourion (p94).

Avdimou Beach

The closest thing to a deserted beach in this part of the island is Avdimou. As you park your car (which is the only means of getting here), a massive sign warns those inclined to nudism that there will be a heavy punishment if they even think of stripping here. As things go, this is a good indication that hardly anyone comes to this place, and that the beach is a peaceful and quiet one. Like most other beaches in Cyprus, it has no shade, and is a combination of small pebbles and sand. The sea is not as choppy as at Kourion Beach and, with a good umbrella, this is the place for super-relaxation.

Kyrenia Beach Restaurant (☎ 2521 1717; mains CY£2.50-3) is the only place to eat on the beach,

with a wooden terrace and friendly service. A refreshing snack of haloumi (helimi), olives, tomatoes and bread is always a treat.

Melanda Beach

This small, narrow sand and pebble beach is close to Avdimou, but accessible only by turning inland and looking for the signposted turn-off. Due to its exposed position, there is often a fair amount of seaweed. There are windsurfers, banana rides and even jet skis here. Like Avdimou Beach, it is favoured by RAF personnel.

Pissouri Bay & Village

As you leave the peaceful and deserted beaches of the Akrotiri Peninsula, you enter the package-tourist area, where the Pissouri Bay resort, 10km west of Avdimou, has jet skis, surfing, banana rides and other entertaining sea activities. At the western end of the bay, you can rest under the shade of olive trees.

If you choose to stay by the sea, **Kotzias Hotel** (☎ 2522 1014; fax 2522 2449; 1-/2-bedroom apt CY£26/32) rents spacious apartments five minutes from the beach.

If you are travelling by car and you fancy staying somewhere with a bit more character, go to Pissouri village and stay at the **Bunch of Grapes Inn** (☎ 2522 1275; Ioannou Erotokritou 9; d CY£27). Formerly run by an English owner who apparently repelled customers with his snootiness, the inn has now been taken over by a friendly Cypriot family. This old mansion, once the home of a wealthy Pissourian, was built around 200 years ago, and was rediscovered and renovated by a Dutch man some thirty years ago. It has served as an inn since. Its nine basic rooms (doubles only; no air-conditioning, fans only) have stained-glass windows, and look out onto the wooden porch. If you don't choose to stay here, then try at least to visit the restaurant, open from noon to 3pm and 5.30pm to 10pm. Under the thick shade of figs, lindens and planes, you can eat things like crispy roast duck in apricot brandy sauce (CY£7.95). Cypriots flock here from all over the island to sample the Bunch of Grapes' menu.

Down by the beach, the best place to eat is **Limanaki** (☎ 2522 1288; 11-12.15am Tue-Sun, 6.30pm-12.15am Mon; mains CY£7-9), which was once a taverna, and before that a carob mill. People from Pafos and Lemesos come here to eat. The restaurant is famous for its homemade curries, and more elaborate Middle Eastern dishes such as lamb cubes cooked in yoghurt sauce and garnished with dry mint and pine nuts, served with basmati rice.

Symposio (☎ 2522 1158; grills CY£4-6) is slap-bang on the beach and is a popular spot with the tourists taking a lunch break from sunbathing. The moussaka (meat or vegetarian) is a favourite.

Petra tou Romiou (Aphrodite's Rock & Beach)

Possibly the most famous and mythical beach in Cyprus, Aphrodite's Beach is most certainly one of the island's most beautiful. Driving along the old B6 road from Lemesos to Pafos (a highly recommended journey), you'll stop in awe as you see the vast indigo expanse of the Mediterranean beneath the intense blue of the cloudless summer sky, the white rock and the beach that curls around it. The view from the road is stunning. The two upright rocks look as if they might just walk out of the water. Mysteriously, swimmers sit on top of them, making the less-acrobatic wonder how they've managed to climb all the way up. The sea here is cool and fresh, and the beach is wonderful for a picnic and a day of semisolitude.

The name of the place in Greek, Petra tou Romiou (Rock of the Greeks), has nothing to do with Aphrodite, but alludes to the Greek folk hero, Digenis Akritas. He apparently used to hurl large rocks, like the ones here, at his enemies. The actual rock that he is supposed to have thrown is the westernmost one and not the others that seem to be somehow split down the middle. All are equally beautiful.

The reason the spot is called the 'Rock of Aphrodite' in English is because legend has it that Aphrodite, ancient patron goddess of Cyprus, emerged from the sea at this point in a surge of sea foam before, no doubt, going off to entertain some lovers. The same thing is claimed by the residents of the island of Kythira in Greece. But who's to say she didn't do it in two places? She was a goddess, after all.

Most visitors either stop when they are driving and have a swim, or come for the spectacular **sunset**, best seen from either the **tourist pavilion**, or from a roadside car park

about 1.5km further east. Skip any kind of eating at the tourist pavilion cafeteria, where you will be charged extortionate amounts for awful snacks. Bring your own food and have a picnic instead. An underground tunnel leads from the cafeteria and car park to the beach on the other side of the road.

ANCIENT AMATHOUS

This archaeological site, about 11km east of Lemesos, belies its original importance. **Ancient Amathous** (admission CY£0.75; ☒ 9am-7.30pm Jul-Aug, 9am-5pm Sep-Jun) was one of Cyprus' original four kingdoms (the others were Salamis, Pafos and Soloi). Legend has it that the city was founded by Kinyras, the son of Pafos. It is also said that Kinyras introduced the cult of Aphrodite to Cyprus (see the boxed text, p132). Founded about 1000 BC, the city had an unbroken history of settlement until about the 14th century AD, despite depredation at the hands of Corsairs during the 7th and 8th centuries. In 1191, when Richard the Lionheart appeared on the scene, the city was already on the decline. Since its harbour was silted up, King Richard was obliged to disembark on the beach to claim the once proud and wealthy city. He promptly applied the royal *coup de grâce* by destroying it, and Amathous was no more.

It is rather difficult to understand the site without visual guidance, since much of the stone and marble has long been looted and carted away for other building projects. Most of Amathous' best treasures were removed by the infamous American consul of Larnaka, Luigi Palma de Cesnola (see also p145). As you enter the site, there is an explanatory pedestal with a schematic map of the area. This will help you to understand how the city was originally laid out. Excavations only started in earnest in 1980. To date, the two main visible features are an **early Christian basilica** in the so-called lower city, and the remains of a sanctuary to Aphrodite on the **acropolis** immediately behind the lower city.

The full extent of the ancient city has yet to be discovered. Excavations are made difficult by the considerable growth of tourist hotels on both sides of the site. The remains of the **ancient harbour** have been found offshore. Occasional free summer concerts are held within the grounds of Amathous. Look for posters at the site or check with the CTO in Lemesos.

If you're travelling by public transport, local buses 6 and 30 from Lemesos will drop you off around 800m from the entrance.

EPISKOPI

pop 3110

One of the main reasons for visiting the village of Episkopi, 14km west of Lemesos, is the **Kourion Museum** (☎ 2593 2453; admission CY£0.75; ☻ 9am-2.30pm Mon-Fri, 3-5pm Thu Sep-Jun). The collection mainly comprises terracotta objects from Ancient Kourion and the Sanctuary of Apollon Ylatis, and is housed in what used to be the private residence of archaeologist George McFadden. The museum is signposted off the Lemesos–Kourion road, as well as in Episkopi itself.

If you decide to stay in Episkopi, **Antony's Garden House** (☎ 2593 2502; www.agrotourism.com .cy/DestinationMgr/Property_Card.aspx?HotelID=15; r per person CY£15-25; 🏊) is a wonderful little agro-tourism hotel built around a cool, leafy garden. There are beautiful double rooms and a self-contained studio. It is relatively easy to find, as it's well signposted from the Lemesos side of Episkopi.

The owner of Antony's Garden House (and he should know) recommends the **Old Stables** (☎ 2593 5568; kleftiko CY£4.50; ☻ evenings Mon-Sat). The *kleftiko* is tender and juicy, and the *mezedes* are good. Takeaway is also available. It's out on the Lemesos–Pafos road opposite the Mobil petrol station.

Episkopi is served by bus from Lemesos (see p91).

ANCIENT KOURION

Defiantly perched on the hillside overlooking the sea, **Ancient Kourion** (☎ 2599 5048; admission CY£1; ☻ 8am-7.30pm Jul & Aug, 7.30am-5pm Sep-Jun) is a spectacular site whether you're an archaeology lover or not. It attracts lots of visitors every day, so if you want to view it with a modicum of peace and quiet, come early in the morning or late in the afternoon, although buses with groups often arrive in the afternoons, when the really hot part of the day is done. If you want to take photographs, mornings and afternoons are better anyway. Ancient Kourion is close to two other attractions in the immediate vicinity, the Sanctuary of Apollon Ylatis (p96) and Kolossi Castle (p96). All three can be visited in the same day; as a cooling break, incorporate a swim at Kourion

Beach (p92), spread out temptingly below the ancient site of Kourion itself.

Ancient Kourion was most likely founded in Neolithic times, probably because of its strategic position high on a bluff overlooking the sea. It became a permanent settlement in about the 13th century BC, when Mycenaean colonisers established themselves here.

The settlement also prospered under the Ptolemies and Romans. A pre-Christian cult of Apollo was active among the inhabitants of Kourion in Roman times, as documented by the nearby Sanctuary of Apollon Ylatis. Christianity eventually supplanted Apollo and, despite the disastrous earthquakes in the region, an **early Christian basilica** was built in the 5th century AD, testifying to the ongoing influence of Christianity on Kourion by this time. Pirate raids 200 years later severely compromised the viability of the now-Christian bishopric; the Bishop of Kourion was obliged to move his base to a new settlement at nearby Episkopi (meaning 'bishopric' in Greek). Kourion declined as a settlement from that point on and was not rediscovered until tentative excavations at the site began in 1876.

The early Christian basilica displays all the hallmarks of an early church, with foundations clearly showing the existence of a narthex, diakonikon (a storage area for agricultural products used by priests and monks), various rooms, baptistery and atrium. Some floor mosaics are also visible among the remains.

The site is dominated by its magnificent **amphitheatre**. This is a reconstruction of a smaller theatre that existed on the same site, high on the hill overlooking the sea, which was destroyed by earthquakes during the 3rd century AD. Nevertheless, it gives a good idea of how it would have been at its peak. Today it's used for cultural events such as plays and music concerts by Cypriot and visiting Greek singers and bands.

Nearby is the **Annexe of Eustolios**, probably a private residence dating from the 5th century. Its colourful, Christian-influenced mosaic floors are well preserved, and make a mention of the builder Eustolios and the decidedly non-Christian patron Apollo. Look for the Christian motifs of cross-shaped ornaments and fish.

Northwest is the **House of the Gladiators**, so called because of two fairly well-preserved

ANCIENT KOURION

0 ⟝━━━━━━━━━ 50 m

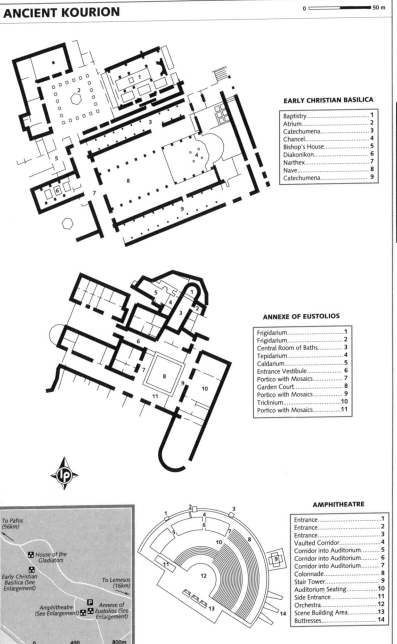

EARLY CHRISTIAN BASILICA

Baptistry	1
Atrium	2
Catechumena	3
Chancel	4
Bishop's House	5
Diakonikon	6
Narthex	7
Nave	8
Catechumena	9

ANNEXE OF EUSTOLIOS

Frigidarium	1
Frigidarium	2
Central Room of Baths	3
Tepidarium	4
Caldarium	5
Entrance Vestibule	6
Portico with Mosaics	7
Garden Court	8
Portico with Mosaics	9
Triclinium	10
Portico with Mosaics	11

AMPHITHEATRE

Entrance	1
Entrance	2
Entrance	3
Vaulted Corridor	4
Corridor into Auditorium	5
Corridor into Auditorium	6
Corridor into Auditorium	7
Colonnade	8
Stair Tower	9
Auditorium Seating	10
Side Entrance	11
Orchestra	12
Scene Building Area	13
Buttresses	14

To Pafos (56km)

House of the Gladiators

Early Christian Basilica (See Enlargement)

To Lemesos (16km)

Amphitheatre (See Enlargement)

Annexe of Eustolios (See Enlargement)

0   400   800m

floor mosaics depicting gladiators in combat dress. Two of these gladiators, Hellenikos and Margaritis, are depicted practising with weapons.

SANCTUARY OF APOLLON YLATIS

About 2km west of Kourion's main entrance and prominently signposted off the highway is the **Sanctuary of Apollon Ylatis** (☎ 2599 5049; admission CY£0.75; ✆ 9am-7.30pm May-Sep, 9am-5.30pm Oct-Apr), which is part of the larger site of Kourion. The precinct was established in the 8th century BC in honour of Apollo, who was considered god of the woods (*ylatis* means 'of the woods' in Greek). The once woody site now has far less vegetation, but retains a good scattering of remains that give a reasonable idea of the layout of the original sanctuary. The remnants that you see are Roman structures that were levelled by a large earthquake in AD 365.

Kourion's **main sanctuary** has been partly restored; the beautiful, imposing standing columns mark the extent of the restoration. Also discernible are the **priests' quarters**, a **palaestra** (sports arena) and **baths** for the athletes, and a rather depleted **stadium** 500m to the east, which once seated up to 6000 spectators.

KOLOSSI CASTLE

Less of a castle and more a fortified tower house, **Kolossi Castle** (☎ 2593 4907; admission CY£0.75; ✆ 9am-7.30pm Jul-Aug, 9am-5pm Sep-Jun) perches incongruously between the vineyards and houses of the village of the same name. It is an interesting reminder of the rule of the Knights of St John in the 13th century, who started producing wine and processing sugar cane at a commandery that stood on this land. The famous Cypriot wine, Commandaria, took its name from here. However, the Mameluke raids of 1425–26 compromised the knights' prosperity and no doubt damaged the infrastructure. The current structure dates from 1454 and was probably built over the older fortified building.

Kolossi Castle is accessible by a short drawbridge that was originally defended by a machicolation (a parapet for protecting the castle) high above, through which defenders would pour molten lead or boiling oil on the heads of unwanted visitors. Upon entering, you come across two large chambers, one with an unusually large fireplace and a spiral

staircase that leads to another two chambers on the second level. The chambers are empty, so it is hard to imagine what they would have been like in their heyday. The only tangible remains of occupation is a mural of the crucifixion in the first-level main chamber. The spiral staircase leads to the roof, where the battlements, restored in 1933, lend a final touch.

To the east of the castle is an outbuilding, now called the **sugar factory**, where cane was processed into sugar.

AKROTIRI PENINSULA
Akrotiri Sovereign Base Area

Cyprus' past is full of stories of colonisers, raiders and armies generally coveting the small island's strategic position. So when Cyprus finally and belatedly received its independence from colonial administration in 1960, Britain negotiated terms that saw the newly formed Republic of Cyprus ceding 158 sq km (99 sq miles) of its territory to its former colonial master. This territory, now known as the Sovereign Base Areas (SBAs), is used for military purposes by the British, who have a couple of well-established and solidly entrenched garrisons on the two SBAs in Cyprus. A large chunk of these areas occupies the Akrotiri Peninsula, immediately southwest of Lemesos, while the border of the Akrotiri SBA territory runs as far west as Avdimou Beach (p92).

The only indication that you are on 'foreign soil' is the odd sight of British SBA police, who patrol the territory in special police vehicles. So, if you are booked for any traffic infringement while driving in the area, you'll be booked by British military police. To the immediate west of the peninsula, along the old Lemesos–Pafos road, you will come across green playing fields, cricket pitches and housing estates more reminiscent of Leicester than Lemesos.

The lower half of the peninsula is out of bounds since it is a closed **military base**, complete with its own large airfield. The village of **Akrotiri** itself is the only true settlement within the SBA (borders were set in order to exclude most settlements); its only substantial claim to fame is that its inhabitants are accorded the privilege of dual citizenship. British military personnel often eat here at the several tavernas; they may be seen on their days off riding flashy mountain bikes and tackling the dirt tracks surrounding the large salt lake in the middle of the peninsula.

The area's only real sights are the **Fassouri plantations**, a large swath of citrus groves across the north of the peninsula, interwoven with long, straight stretches of road overhung by tall cypress trees. They create wonderfully cool and refreshing corridors after the aridity of the southern peninsula.

Holy Monastery of St Nicholas of the Cats

A wonderful and bizarre story lies behind the name of this place. The monastery and its original little church were founded in AD 327 by the first Byzantine governor of Cyprus, Kalokeros, and patronised by St Helena, mother of Constantine the Great. At the time, the Akrotiri Peninsula and indeed the whole of Cyprus was in the grip of a severe drought and was overrun with poisonous snakes, so building a monastery was fraught with practical difficulties. A large shipment

of cats was therefore brought in from Egypt and Palestine to combat the reptilian threat. A bell would call the cats to meals, and the furry warriors would then be dispatched to fight the snakes. A Venetian monk visiting the monastery described them all as maimed, one missing a nose, another an ear, and some were completely blind as a result of their selfless battles.

The peninsula was in fact known for a time as 'Cat Peninsula' before reverting to plain 'Peninsula'. There is a little renovated church that dates from the 13th century and a sprawling monastery building that received a much-needed refurbishment in 1983. The many cats that you'll find snoozing in the shade of the monastery colonnades far outnumber the four solitary sisters who now look after the monastery.

Positioned on the edge of the salt lake with its back to the SBA fence, it can be reached by a good dirt road from Akrotiri or via a not-so-obvious route west from Lady's Mile Beach.

Troödos Massif

For a small country, the variety of landscape in Cyprus is sometimes quite astounding. And the Troödos Massif, holding up the country's highest peak, Mt Olympus, like a proud beacon, offers the perfect antidote to the hot, lazy life of the beach. When temperatures in the high thirties blister the backs of the tourists and parch the island's soil, the atmosphere in the Troödos relieves and refreshes even the most heat-muddled mind. Cool shade and the smell of the tall pines beckon many Cypriots, who spend their summer holidays in the lap of the mountain. And, come winter, they take up their skis and submit themselves to gravity and snow (sometimes with entertaining effects).

But it hasn't always been an area for frolicking in the shade or snow. Over the years, the mountains have provided refuge to religious communities and various underground fighters on the run, as well as the wealthy of the Levant and the colonial civil servants who also tried to get away from the heat. And in their wake, they left magnificent frescoed village churches, unexpected mansions and some quite bizarre museums. But what has also remained, thanks to Troödos' mountain remoteness, is the essence of Cypriot life, most often undisturbed (or, at least, not as disturbed) by the rampaging tourist industry.

Visiting the Troödos during the summer is great for hiking and cycling, simple relaxing, and visiting the frescoed churches and monasteries that date from at least the 15th century. The churches' magnificent frescoes are unique in Cyprus.

Driving is a good way to see all of the little villages, and the roads, although windy, are good. Apart from services to and from the villages of Kakopetria, Troödos, Platres and Pedoulas, public transport to the Troödos is sketchy at best and cannot be relied upon for properly exploring the area.

HIGHLIGHTS

- Get divine inspiration at the Unesco World Heritage–listed **Byzantine churches** (p100)
- Breathe fresh air while **hiking** (p101) and **cycling** (p102) the green spaces in the shadow of Mt Olympus and explore the region's natural beauty
- Stay in some of the island's most authentic accommodation and get a taste of Cyprus' rural life in villages like **Treis Elies** (p106), **Kakopetria** (p111) and **Pedoulas** (p108)
- Sample away at the **krasohoria** (p107), the wine-producing villages on the southern Troödos slopes

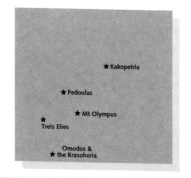

CENTRAL TROÖDOS
ΚΕΝΤΡΙΚΟ ΤΡΟΟΔΟΣ

Mt Olympus sits at the top of the central Troödos region, watching over settlements, ski runs, hiking trails and picnic grounds. The peak itself is inaccessible, but you can admire the gigantic golf ball balanced on top, which might look like a loving tribute to the great golfing nations but is in fact a military radar installation.

From January to the beginning of March you can usually ski on the slopes of 1952m-high Mt Olympus, known in Greek as Hionistra.

Troödos village itself is a bit of a non-entity, but it's the centre for all skiing and hiking activities. Although it is cooler up on the Troödos than on the plains, hiking is probably best undertaken in spring or autumn, when there is no summer heat haze and the superb views can be better appreciated.

This area consists primarily of two settlements: Troödos village, just below the summit of Olympus; and the larger village of Platres (sometimes Pano Platres on maps), 10km further down the southern slope. Central Troödos can be reached by way of a reasonably fast road from Lemesos (the B8) or by the B9 up the mountain's northern flanks from Lefkosia.

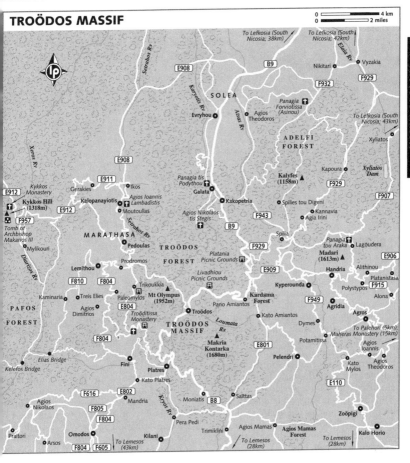

TROÖDOS MASSIF

THE FRESCOED BYZANTINE CHURCHES OF CYPRUS

For many people, the main reason for visiting the Troödos region is a series of remarkable small churches that were built and decorated with vivid frescoes between the 11th and 15th centuries. These are the frescoed churches of Cyprus and 10 of them have been designated by Unesco as World Heritage sites. The churches covered in this chapter are Arhangelos Mihail (p108), Agios Ionnis Lambadistis Monastery (p109), Agios Nikolaos tis Stegis (p112), Panagia tis Podythou (p113), Panagia Forviotissa (Asinou; p113), Stavros tou Agiasmati (p115) and Panagia tou Araka (p115).

By the time the French Catholic Lusignan dynasty took control of Cyprus in 1197, work on a series of small churches in the mountains had already begun. But it was the repression and discrimination exercised by the Lusignans against the Orthodox Greek Cypriots that prompted the Orthodox clergy, along with artisans and builders, to retreat to the northern slopes of the Troödos Massif. Here they built and embellished private ecclesiastical retreats where Orthodoxy flourished undisturbed for some 300 years.

What came out of this activity were many churches built in a similar fashion. Most were little bigger than small barns; some had domes, some did not. Because of the harsh winter weather, large, steeply inclined, overhanging roofs were added to protect the churches from accumulated snow. Inside, skilled fresco painters went to work producing a series of vivid images.

Not all churches were lavishly painted, but the Unesco-designated churches described in this chapter represent the finest examples. The frescoes are remarkable for their clarity of detail and the preservation of their colour. The later didactic-style frescoes are unusual in that they are painted almost like a cartoon strip, ostensibly to teach the illiterate peasants of the time the rudiments of the gospels.

You would need at least two days to visit all the churches, bearing in mind that a lot of time will be spent in tracking down caretakers, as a number of churches are kept locked. Donations of CY£0.50 to CY£1 are appreciated and generally expected. You'll need a car to visit most of the churches, as public transport in the area is scarce.

Central Troödos can also be accessed from the east (Pitsylia) and from the west (Pafos and the Pafos hinterland) by good but often winding and slow roads. At peak times, such as Sunday evenings, traffic can be very heavy on the roads to the coast or Lefkosia.

TROÖDOS ΤΡΟΟΔΟΣ
pop 15

With its souvenir shops, restaurants and scattered public buildings, Troödos may look like an improvised main street. Yet it draws multitudes of activity-seeking tourists, who flock to this central mountain town for the hiking trails, and for skiing in the winter months, when Troödos becomes the Cypriot centre of all snow-related activity. There are also enough forest roads and trails to keep even the most fanatic mountain biker happy for a week.

But don't expect any wild nights in Troödos (apart from being chased by a wild boar perhaps). Everyone is so tired after the day's activities that, come midnight, they are snuggled up in bed.

Orientation

From Troödos, one road leads north towards Lefkosia, while another heads west to Prodromos and further afield. The third approach road, to Lemesos and Platres, goes south. There are plenty of road signs, some of them totally confusing. Troödos itself centres around the little main square with its restaurants and souvenir shops, and the visitor centre, which sits to the south of the square. The Jubilee Hotel and HI Hostel are to the north, as are the skiing facilities.

Information

The town has a small store with a post office agency, and there are several prominent old UK-style phone boxes.

It's really worth visiting the **Troödos Visitor Centre** (☎ 2542 0144; admission CY£0.50; ◷ 10am-4pm), just down from the Troödos main street. Although the display of stuffed animals is a little eerie, the graphic outline of the region is rather informative and there is good information on the fauna and flora of the Troödos National Forest Park. There is also a minitheatre where a 10-minute video is shown to visitors. Do go on the 300m botanical and geological trail that runs around the centre. It displays examples of all the plants that grow in the region, although in high summer most of them are either dead or simply twigs.

You can pick up information on the Troödos hiking trails here too.

Activities

HIKING

The following four trails give you a good overall picture of the Troödos. Many of the trees and plants you pass are marked with their Latin and Greek names, and there are frequent wooden benches conveniently positioned beneath shady trees to allow you to catch your breath or simply to admire the views.

A useful booklet published by the Cyprus Tourism Organisation (CTO), *Nature Trails of the Troödos,* outlines all the trails and gives a description of the flora and natural features to be found along the way. Detailed, though not professional, maps of the trails accompany the text.

Artemis Trail

Of the four trails, this is the one that you should perhaps tackle first. It is the newest of the trails and takes you around the summit of Mt Olympus in a more or less circular loop.

The trail begins and ends at a little car park off the Mt Olympus summit road; it's

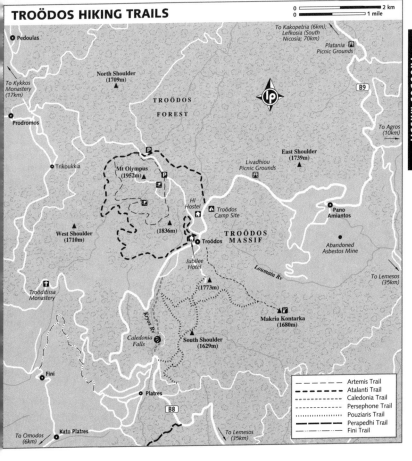

TROÖDOS HIKING TRAILS

TROÖDOS MASSIF

Legend:
- – – – – – Artemis Trail
- – – – – – Atalanti Trail
- – · – · – · – Caledonia Trail
- – – – – – Persephone Trail
- · · · · · · · · Pouziaris Trail
- ▬▬▬ Perapedhi Trail
- – — – — Fini Trail

better to get there by car to avoid the 1.5km walk along the often busy highway. A sign directs you to walk clockwise, though there is no reason why you should not tackle it anticlockwise. The end of the trail is unmarked and on the opposite side of the Mt Olympus summit road.

The complete walk should take 2½ to 3½ hours, allowing for stops along the way. It is 7km long with very little climbing. The track runs alternately through partly shaded and open areas, and the views on the south side of the mountain, over the foothills, are spectacular indeed. Look out for signs to the **giant pine trees**. Take care not to lose the trail around the ski runs on the south and north sides. There is no water along the route so take your own supplies.

Atalanti Trail

This trail is for people who like walking. Starting at the square in Troödos, it involves a fair hike along the main Prodromos–Troödos road to get back to the village. The Atalanti Trail, named in honour of the ancient forest nymph, runs at a lower altitude than the Artemis Trail but follows roughly the same route. It is relatively easy going and is well marked. There is a spring with drinking water some 3km from the trail's beginning.

The views are not as spectacular as those from the Artemis Trail higher up but it is a most enjoyable walk. Allow five hours for this 12km walk.

Caledonia Trail

The 3km Caledonia Trail is perhaps the most enjoyable of the four Troödos trails. It begins about 1km or so down the hill from Troödos and conveniently ends up near the Psilo Dendro Restaurant (p105), just outside Platres. The trail follows the course of the **Kryos** river – in reality a gurgling stream – as it winds its way down a thickly wooded, shady valley to Platres. There are many stream crossings via stepping stones and makeshift log bridges, and the trail is steep in parts. It's best tackled from north to south (Troödos to Platres) as it drops some 450m throughout its course. About 1km from the trail's southern end are the **Caledonia Falls**, a 35m drop of cascading water. The trail is shaded for the most part (great for those really scorching

days) and is well marked. You can return the way you came or arrange to be picked up in Platres. If you have a car, leave it at the Platres end and hitch a lift up the hill to the starting point. You can also try using the local bus service (make a booking), although times may be inconvenient. Allow 1½ to two hours for a comfortable hike.

Persephone Trail

This is probably the easiest trail to undertake if you are based in Troödos without transport. Known in Greek as the **Makria Kontarka Trail** (named after the mountain it ascends), it is a simple out-and-back hike through attractive pine forest and some open areas. The trail is 3km long and it should take you about 45 minutes to reach the **lookout** at the top of Makria Kontarka, the end point of the walk. From here you can gaze out over the southern foothills or, if you look to your left, you will see the enormous scar caused by the now closed asbestos mine at Pano Amiantos. The marked trail begins opposite the Troödos police station. From the main street, walk south along the narrow road heading upward to the left and you will quickly find the trail after about 200m.

CYCLING

Mountain bikers have a choice of forest tracks to ride along. A *Cycling Routes* booklet, with detailed information on bike tracks in Troödos and around the island, is available at the visitor centre and any CTO office. Bicycles can be rented at the **Jubilee Hotel** (☎ 2542 0107), 350m from the village along the Prodromos road, for CY£10 a day and CY£5 a half-day. There is nowhere for repairs and spare parts, so have a basic repair kit with you.

HORSE RIDING

The small horse-riding outfit next to the public toilets on the south side of the village is best if you want to give your kids a little introduction to riding, or if you don't expect any galloping chases. Choose between a 10-minute escorted ride around Troödos for CY£3, or go wild and have yourself a 20- to 25-minute ride for CY£5.

PICNICKING

Having a picnic is a wonderful way of spending the day here. You can set up almost anywhere, but bear in mind that lighting open fires is not allowed, so a picnic ground is the best solution if you wish to join Cypriots in grilling chops or spit-roasting some *konto-souvli* (large chunks of lamb).

Fortunately, there are plenty of well-organised picnic grounds on the approach roads to the Troödos summit. A particularly good picnic ground is the **Livadi tou Pasha**, 3km down the Troödos–Lefkosia road (B9) on the left, thankfully before you reach the ghastly sight of the former Pano Amiantos asbestos mine. There is a barbecue area, and fixed benches and tables are scattered among the pine trees.

Further along the Lefkosia road, about 8km from Troödos, is the very popular **Platania** (Plane Trees) picnic ground. This place gets inundated with weekend revellers, but is well organised and has plenty of shaded facilities, including a children's adventure park. Get there early if you want a good position.

Sleeping & Eating

Jubilee Hotel (☎ 2542 0107; jubilee@cytanet.com.cy; s/d CY£30.50/53, 6-12 yrs/under 6 yrs half-price/free) A surprisingly stylish and elegant hotel, 350m from the village along the Prodromos road. Outside the hotel there are deck chairs for reclining and enjoying the fresh air. Inside is a soothing lounge in dark wood, decorated with shadow puppets and furnished with inviting armchairs. The rooms are comfortable and cosy, and there is central heating in the winter. A family-friendly place, this is probably not suitable for those looking for peace and quiet during the holiday season.

Camp site (☎ 2242 1624; tent sites CY£2; ☾ May-Oct) A kilometre or so north of Troödos along the Lefkosia road and in a pine forest, this good camp site is a really popular spot with many Cypriots, who come here to relax and escape the beach crowds. There is an on-site restaurant and a minimarket.

HI Hostel (☎ 2542 0200; dm 1st/subsequent nights CY£5/4; ☾ usually May-Oct) If you'd like a cheap indoor place to sleep, the Troödos hostel, with its 10 bunk beds, is your best bet. It's airy and clean and there's a big common area with a kitchen. Ignore the conflicting signposting in Troödos village; the hostel is set back 200m on the left as you head down the Lefkosia road.

Your eating choices are, frankly, abysmal. But if you're desperate perhaps try a kebab at

Fereos Restaurant (☎ 2542 0114; full kebab CY£5) or a below-average meal at the **Dolphin Restaurant** (☎ 2542 0215; mains CY£4-6), near the visitor centre. A wide range of mediocre Cypriot and international dishes is served, with large buffets on weekends and public holidays.

Getting There & Away

There is a **Clarios Bus Co** (☎ 2275 3234) service that leaves the Constanza Bastion in Lefkosia at 11.30am (Monday to Friday) for Troödos (CY£1.50) via Kakopetria. It departs from Troödos for Lefkosia at about 6.30am, but only if reservations have been made in advance. Service taxis do not operate out of Troödos.

PLATRES ΠΛΑΤΡΕΣ
pop 280

«Τ' αηδόνια δε σ' αφήνουνε να κοιμηθείς
στις Πλάτρες.» ('The nightingales won't
let you sleep in Platres.')
Georgos Seferis, 'Eleni', 1953

Platres has its roots in British colonial times, when it was the most chic mountain vacation resort for the well heeled and well connected of the era. This included such 'celebrities' as the Nobel Prize–winning Greek poet Georgos Seferis, who wrote poems about the place, and King Farouk of Egypt. But beach holidays suddenly started to look more attractive to many and Platres became a little forgotten. Modelled on the colonial hill stations of India, it has all the trappings of a cool mountain retreat: forest walks, gurgling streams, relief from the searing heat of the plains, and gin and tonics that are drunk on the balconies of old-world hotels catering to their guests' every wish.

Today, it's a little less elegant, and hikers, retirees, and travellers who still prefer the hills to the beaches make up the numbers. It's a nice enough place to base yourself for a couple of days, staying in one of the few very good hotels.

Orientation

At first sight, Platres is confusingly strung out around a series of snaking roads, just off the main Lemesos–Troödos highway. Platres basically consists of an upper road, which is home to a number of hotels, and a lower road, which is the town's main street and home to its restaurants, shops and bars.

TROÖDOS MASSIF

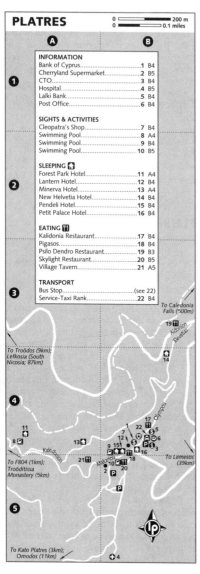

PLATRES

0 _____ 200 m
0 _____ 0.1 miles

INFORMATION
Bank of Cyprus...............................1 B4
Cherryland Supermarket.................2 B5
CTO...3 B4
Hospital..4 B5
Laïki Bank.......................................5 B4
Post Office.......................................6 B4

SIGHTS & ACTIVITIES
Cleopatra's Shop.............................7 B4
Swimming Pool...............................8 A4
Swimming Pool...............................9 B4
Swimming Pool.............................10 B5

SLEEPING
Forest Park Hotel...........................11 A4
Lantern Hotel.................................12 B4
Minerva Hotel................................13 A4
New Helvetia Hotel.......................14 B4
Pendeli Hotel.................................15 B4
Petit Palace Hotel.........................16 B4

EATING
Kalidonia Restaurant.....................17 B4
Pigasos...18 B4
Psilo Dendro Restaurant...............19 B3
Skylight Restaurant......................20 B5
Village Tavern...............................21 A5

TRANSPORT
Bus Stop...................................(see 22)
Service-Taxi Rank.........................22 B4

To Caledonia Falls (500m)

To Troödos (9km);
Lefkosia (South
Nicosia; 87km);

To F804 (1km);
Troöditissa
Monastery (5km)

To Kato Platres (3km);
Omodos (11km)

To Lemesos (39km)

TROÖDOS MASSIF

Information
There are ATMs at the Bank of Cyprus and
the Laïki Bank, close to each other on Platres' main street.

The **Cyprus Tourism Organisation** (CTO; ☎ 2542
1316; platresinfo@cto.org.cy; ◷ 9am-3.30pm Mon-Fri,
9am-2.30pm Sat, closes 30min earlier Jul & Aug) is well
stocked with brochures both on the Troödos

hiking trails and the rest of Cyprus, and the
staff are very willing to help with queries.

The police station and post office are
near the CTO office. The hospital is about
600m south of the village centre, just off
the main road to Kato Platres and Omodos.
Call ☎ 1407 to report a forest fire.

Some English-language newspapers may
be purchased at the little shop opposite the
Bank of Cyprus or at the **Cherryland Supermarket** (Makariou).

Sights & Activities
Offering the temptation of drinking brandy
sours in the company of a good novel around
one of the three outdoor **swimming pools**, Platres is ideal for a relaxing break away from
the torrid heat of summer. In winter you
can go **skiing** or simply relax around a roar-
ing log fire.

Visitors can undertake the four **hikes**
(p101) around Troödos village. Other options include hikes from Platres to Fini (a
longish 9km downhill route to the west perhaps requiring a taxi or lift back), Platres
to Perapedhi (slightly shorter at 7km) or
Platres to Pouziaris (shorter at only 3km,
but uphill). These hikes and others are described in greater detail in the CTO brochure *Platres*, which also contains a map
of the village.

Make sure you pop into the fabulously
strange **Cleopatra's Shop** (Makariou; ◷ 9am-6pm
summer, closed Feb & Mar), in the village centre
opposite the Petit Palais Hotel. Located in
a gorgeous, envy-provoking mansion, this
shop is run by two charming ageing sisters
who are happy to pass on little details about
the history of Platres. The mansion is a sight
in itself, and you may find an unusual souvenir among the many knick-knacks.

Sleeping
Reminders of colonial Britain still linger,
particularly in the hotels, where the history is sometimes more appealing than the
rooms. Discounts apply to all these hotels
out of high season.

Minerva Hotel (☎ 2542 1731; minerva@globalsoft
mail.com; Kaledonion 6; s CY£20, d Sep-Jun/Aug CY£28/38,
Ⓟ) This is the loveliest hotel in Platres. The
reception feels like a shrine to wildflowers,
with pictures covering every inch of the walls.
The rooms and the minisuites are great:
many have antique wrought-iron four-poster

BRANDY SOUR & THE ROYAL CONNECTION

Touted as Cyprus' national cocktail, a brandy sour goes down perfectly after a hard day on the beach or hiking through the forests. Like so many alcoholic concoctions, it has a story behind its origins.

One of the regular visitors to Cyprus in the 1930s was the young King Farouk of Egypt. He liked to stay at the then new and fashionable Forest Park Hotel in Platres. Following a state visit to the UK, he stopped off in Platres, where he was due to meet a delegation of Cypriot VIPs and foreign dignitaries. A Western-educated and rather worldly royal, Farouk was not averse to the odd tipple or two. Not wishing to cause a scene by appearing to drink alcohol in public (as he was Muslim), he had his aide instruct the head barman at the Forest Park, a chap by the name of Stelios, to whip up a cocktail that looked like iced tea.

Without shifting his shaker an inch out of sync, Stelios proceeded to mix two parts of the best Cypriot brandy with one part of fine lemon squash. He then added two drops of Angostura bitters and poured it all over ice cubes, topping up the mixture with soda water. A slice of lemon completed the illusion. King Farouk got his tipple, the dignitaries were none the wiser and the Cypriot brandy sour was born. Cheers!

---

beds, towering antique wardrobes, TVs and telephones. Two-bedroom family houses can be rented for CY£14 per person.

Pendeli Hotel (☎ 2542 1736; pendeli@cylink.com.cy; Makariou; s/d CY£40/55; ☒) A decent three-star hotel with neat, luminous rooms that have lovely views of the forest and valley from the balconies. Each room has a fan and TV.

New Helvetia Hotel (☎ 2542 1348; helvetia@ spidernet.com.cy; Elvetias 6; d CY£50) This isolated, quiet three-star place is at the northeastern end of the village near the main highway. All rooms are double and have TVs, phones and small balconies. Perhaps the best thing about the New Helvetia is the bar, which is dark and broody, with a wonderful terrace, surrounded by pines.

Forest Park Hotel (☎ 2542 1751; www.forestpark hotel.com.cy; s/d CY£49/78; ☒) A place with more history than charm, but with a great setting. This place has hosted Greek, Egyptian and British royalty, the former Indian prime minister Indira Ghandi, the former West German chancellor Willy Brandt, and the East German leader Erich Honnecker. But its appeal has since diminished and its character paled. It does have two pools, a gym, a massage parlour and a sauna, and the rooms are reasonable. The hotel is popular with prosperous Cypriots.

Petit Palais Hotel (☎ 2542 1723; petitpalais@spider net.com.cy; r per person CY£18) A palace it may have been once, but it has now lost some of its grandeur. The rooms are slightly dingy, but they do have two balconies each, TVs and odd-looking space-age telephones.

Lantern Hotel (☎ 9945 2307; Makariou 6; r per person with/without Jacuzzi & TV CY£19/15) This is the cheapest of Platres' hotels. The rooms are quite basic, although the Lantern also offers 'luxury' rooms with Jacuzzis and satellite TVs.

Eating

Fish and creatures from the woods find their way onto many restaurants' plates.

Psilo Dendro Restaurant (☎ 2542 1350; Aïdonion 13; trout CY£5.75; ☽ 11am-5pm) This is the best place to eat in Platres, and the most difficult to find. Behind a bend in the road above Platres, it's hidden behind an inconspicuous house. This restaurant is also a trout farm, so the fish is fresh and tasty.

Village Tavern (☎ 2542 2777; Makariou; mains CY£5; ☽ lunch & dinner) Get your whiskers into a juicy *stifado* (beef and onion stew) or feast on some *kleftiko* (oven-baked lamb) here after a hard day's hiking. Try the house red wine.

Kalidonia Restaurant (☎ 2542 1404; Olympou 41; mains CY£4.50-7; ☽ lunch & dinner) The usual meze and souvlaki draw the Cypriots here, which is always a sign that an establishment knows what it's doing.

Pigasos (☎ 2542 1744; Faneromenis 1; sandwich CY£2; ☽ breakfast & lunch) Pigasos is really only good for a quick snack and a cold beer, and it's located right in the centre. You can breakfast on haloumi (helimi) and *lountza* (smoked loin of pork) sandwiches, or *lahmajoun* (pitta bread stuffed with spicy mince).

TROÖDOS MASSIF

TROÖDOS MASSIF

Getting There & Away

The Lemesos–Platres bus (CY£2.50) leaves from Lemesos at 9.30am and arrives in Platres an hour later, Monday to Friday. It returns to Lemesos at 3.15pm. There is also a very early morning bus between Platres and Lefkosia (CY£2.50), via Pedoulas and Troödos, Monday to Friday. You'll need to make a reservation. For more information, phone the **bus service** (☎ 2357 0592). There are no buses on weekends and public holidays. All public transport arrives at and departs from the area adjoining the CTO office.

Service taxis (☎ 2542 1346) regularly run between Platres and Lemesos for CY£2.50 per person. The service-taxi rank is next to the CTO office.

AROUND PLATRES

Platres is an ideal base for day trips to the surrounding mountain slopes or to the sunny villages of southern Troödos, known locally as the *krasohoria* (wine villages). Exposed to the southerly sun, vines grow here in abundance and many vineyards have taken the opportunity to produce some of Cyprus' best wines, including the famous rich, red dessert wine Commandaria. You can visit a number of these wineries and sample their produce.

You will need your own transport to explore this area, so go easy on the wine.

Mountain Village Driving Tour

The F804 road creates an elongated circle on the west side of Mt Olympus, taking in some of the lovely villages that dot the western flanks of the mountain.

Travelling anticlockwise, the first point of interest along this route is the 13th-century **Troöditissa Monastery** (☉ 6am–noon & 2-8pm), gorgeously located amid thick pines at the top of a steep gorge. Founded after the discovery of a miraculous icon of the Virgin, the monastery's buildings date from the 18th century. The silver icon was discovered in a nearby cave, which had been guarded by two hermits until their death in the 13th century. The icon is said to be helpful to those wishing for children. It's quite difficult to go inside the monastery, as it is a working religious establishment, not too inclined to receive curious onlookers.

Continue along the very pretty mountain road, passing a couple of idyllic, shaded **picnic** areas in cool pine forests, until you reach the village of **Prodromos** (population 150). This small village to the west of Troödos used to have a sizable hill-station clientele, but has not weathered the changes as well as Troödos and Platres. The main claim to fame of this quiet little backwater is that, at 1400m, it is officially Cyprus' highest village.

Loop back and down at this point, following signs to **Paleomylos** (population 30) and **Agios Dimitrios** (population 55), a pair of timeless villages barely touched by tourism and almost buried beneath the greenery of fruit trees and grapevines.

A little further on, **Fini** (population 445) is a great place for tasting some *loukoumades* (Turkish or 'Cyprus' fritters with honey), said to be the best in the country. This village is quite popular with visitors, particularly for its handmade **pottery** and **pithoy** (large clay olive oil storage jars). If you choose to have some lunch here, eat at **Neraida** (☎ 2542 1680; meze CY£10; ☉ lunch Thu-Tue, dinner Fri & Sat), which has some fantastic meze and trout. It's on the western side of the village.

Treis Elies

Southwest of Prodromos, on the F810, is Treis Elies, a small hamlet with a wonderful place to stay. If getting away from the crowds and tourists is what you want, this village is ideal. It is unscathed by people, and its calm atmosphere is perfect for relaxation. There are hiking trails around the village and a small river. It is also close to the wonderful **Venetian bridges**, which are ideal for hikes.

Once upon a time, when the Venetians ruled Cyprus, a Venetian camel-caravan route passed near to Treis Elias village, leaving in its wake three impressive Venetian bridges: **Kelefos**, **Elias** and **Roudhias**. The hunch-backed beasts (the camels, not the Venetians or the bridges) transported copper from the Troödos down to Polis and Pafos, and the path they walked has been all but lost.

All three bridges are connected by a nature trail marked E4. There is also a sealed road between them, if you choose to drive. Closest to Treis Elias village is Elias bridge, after the village of Kaminaria. Elias bridge is the smallest of the three and was the easterly link of the caravan route. It's set in dense forest, with a fresh stream flowing underneath. Kelefos bridge is the loveliest of the three, with a strong, single pointed arch. This is a great picnic spot. To reach Kelefos bridge by car from Treis Elias, follow the signs for Agios Nikolaos. The trek from Elias to Kelefos should not take you more than two hours. It is possible to reach Roudhias bridge from Kelefos via a trail going past the Pera Vassa forestry station, but trekking this distance will take a good few hours.

To Spitiko tou Arhonta (☎ 9952 7117, 2546 2120; www.responsibletravel.com/Accommodation/Accommodation100227.htm; 1-/2-bedroom apt from CY£35/57) is a traditional house converted for ecotourism. Cypriots who want to revisit their roots flock up here during the summer and at Christmas. Perched almost on top of the village, with a shady front yard, the house has two one-bedroom apartments and one two-bedroom apartment, all self-catering and decorated like a bucolic paradise. The friendly owner Androulla may even give you a lesson in *kleftiko* cooking if you've developed a taste for Cypriot cuisine.

Omodos & the Krasohoria
Ομοδος και τα Κρασοχώρια

The shimmering, brilliant vineyards lie spread out across the land around the village of **Omodos** (population 310), situated on the southwest flank of the Troödos Massif. Coming from Lemesos, the landscape on the drive to the village is mesmerising. The village itself, which has a central area paved with cobbled stones and accessible to pedestrians only, is slightly too geared towards the tourist, and souvenir stalls and shops dot the streets.

Omodos is built around a monastery – it's very unusual in the Greek world that a monastery is at the centre of a settlement. The Byzantine **Moni Timiou Stavrou** (Monastery of the Holy Cross), was built around 1150 and was extended and extensively remodelled in the 19th century.

One good shop for souvenirs is **Socrates Traditional House** (admission free; 9.30am-7pm), signposted prominently in and around the back streets of Omodos. You can taste and buy bottles of the homemade Commandaria wine here, and you can also take a look at the ornaments, photos, wedding attire, wine and *zivania* (Cypriot firewater) presses, loom, corn mill and other items of rural life.

And what would be the point of visiting a wine region if you didn't sample any wine?

Pitsylia Winery (☎ 2537 2928; tsiakkas@swaypage .com), located between the villages of Platres and Pelendri, on the southeastern side of the Troödos, is particularly welcoming to visitors. The local grapes Mavro Ambelissimo, Xynisteri, Ofthalmo and Pambatzies make pretty palatable reds, whites and rosés. Visiting times are fairly loose, so it's a good idea to ring beforehand. You'll probably be expected to buy a bottle.

To reach the Pitsylia Winery from Platres, turn left onto the E806 before you get to Trimiklini. The winery is just before Pelendri village.

To Katoï (☎ 2542 1230; Omodos; 2-4 person apt CY£15-20 per person) has spacious apartments with shady front yards and conveniences like TVs and washing machines. Its pleasant little stone-and-wood taverna is good at making hearty village sausages and garlic mushrooms; snacks are CY£1.20 to CY£3.50. It's open from 11am to 4pm and 7.30pm to midnight.

Giannis Agathokleous (☎ 2542 1376; Omodos; apt CY£30) is just next door, with an eight-person apartment for rent year-round.

MARATHASA VALLEY
ΚΟΙΛΑΔΑ ΜΑΡΑΘΑΣΑΣ

The beautiful Marathasa Valley cradles some of Troödos' most important and impressive sights: the giant Orthodox Kykkos Monastery, the wonderful frescoed church of Arhangelos Mihail in the amphitheatrical village of Pedoulas (the valley's tourist centre), and the impressive Agios Ioannis Lambastidis monastery in Kalopanayiotis. From Pedoulas, at the valley's southern end, the plains open out onto Northern Cyprus. The Setrahos river flows through the valley and empties into Morfou Bay in the North.

There is some good accommodation to be found in agrotourism-restored traditional houses, and spring and autumn, when wildflowers display their colours like fireworks, are particularly romantic times for visiting.

While not physically within the confines of the Marathasa Valley – it is actually out on the edge of the Tyllirian wilderness – the Kykkos Monastery is accessible from Kalopanayiotis. Although the monastery was once reached by pilgrims through this valley, most visitors now head up the newly improved side road via Gerakies.

PEDOULAS ΠΕΔΟΥΛΑΣ
pop 190

Pedoulas, at the southern end of the valley before the rise over the Troödos ridge, is a good base in the Troödos Massif, with a good choice of eating and sleeping options. It is the main settlement and tourist centre in the Marathasa Valley, and has banks and a post office. Wonderful cool air and a bracing climate make it an attractive place to sleep on summer nights. It is also famous for its spring water, which can be found on sale all over Cyprus.

Sights

Most people to Pedoulas for the gable-roofed church of **Arhangelos Mihail**, one of ten Unesco-listed churches in Cyprus. It sits in the lower part of the village, and dates from 1474. The **frescoes**, restored in 1980, show a move towards the naturalism of the post-Byzantine revival, and are credited to an artist known only as Adam. Depicted are, of course, the Archangel Michael, who looms above the faithful, the sacrifice of Abraham, the Virgin and Christ, and a beautiful baptism scene where a naked Christ is coming out of River Jordan, fish swimming at his feet. There are also paintings of Pontius Pilate and the denial of Christ.

The key to the church is with the (very) old lady about 10m up the road, who walks painfully down to unlock the door.

Sleeping & Eating

The sleeping options here are decent, although none are outstanding in décor or comfort.

Capuralli Hotel (r per person CY£12) This is the cheapest place in the village, and has the best views of the valley. The corridor and little lounge leading into the rooms look like a typical Cypriot village living room, with white tiles and lace tablecloths, and a TV in the centre. The rooms have a slightly retro feel, but are clean and basic. The food in this place is all homemade and traditional, great for sampling local specialties like preserved sweet aubergines.

Mountain Rose (☎ 2295 2727; fax 2295 3295; r per person incl half-board/full board CY£15/25) A hunters'

lodge kind of place, with a stuffed eagle pointing its claws at you as you enter the reception area, which is cluttered with soft toys, bizarre murals and hanging baskets. The rooms are a bit stuffy, and the ones not front-facing are rather dark. All have fridges and TVs. The hotel is full board in August, and half-board during the rest of the year.

Central (☎ 2295 2457; fax 2295 3324; d CY£35) This place feels a lot like a hostel, but without the hostel prices. Nature posters adorn the slightly run-down halls, rooms have sliding doors, and families are crammed together on wobbly beds. The large terrace is comfortable and populated by a collection of senior citizens who listen to bouzouki full blast, the sound interfered with only by the noise of backgammon dice scrambling against the wooden board.

Rooms to Rent (☎ 2295 2321, 9955 9098; r per person CY£10) Many rooms sleep three or four in this small, basic place. It's on the south side of the village, and is run by the people from the Platanos restaurant.

The eating choices are rather limited.

Platanos (☎ 2295 2518; mains CY£2-4) Where would a Cypriot village be without a restaurant called Platanos (plane tree)? And under a plane tree it certainly is. It offers nice kebabs, and the old chef makes the coffee on the hot ashes on the terrace, the traditional way.

Mountain Rose (☎ 2295 2727; mains CY£3-4) Part of the hotel, and really rather touristy and of dubious quality, it serves things like *pastitsio* (an oven-cooked dish of minced meat and vegetables), *sheftalia* (pork sausages), and *koupepia* (stuffed vine leaves). It also sells cheap wine – CY£5 for a bottle of red.

Getting There & Away

There is a daily bus from Lefkosia to Pedoulas (CY£2) via Kalopanayiotis at 12.15pm Monday to Saturday, which continues on to Platres (except Saturday) via Troödos village. The bus returns to Lefkosia from Pedoulas the following morning at 6am. For information ring ☎ 2295 2437 or ☎ 9961 8865.

KALOPANAYIOTIS ΚΑΛΟΠΑΝΑΓΙΩΤΗΣ
pop 290

The village of Kalopanayiotis, although not as generous in its number of accommodation options, nevertheless has at least one good-quality agrotourism place to stay, and dinner can be had in Pedoulas' Platanos tavern. It's a quiet, genuine place to stay for a few nights, as no day-trip buses arrive here to vomit out the crowds. Kalopanayiotis is home to one of Cyprus' most remarkable monasteries and a fabulous museum, which has the most enthusiastic guide you will ever meet.

Sights
Unesco-listed **Agios Ionnis Lambadistis Monastery** (donation encouraged; ☺ 8am-noon & 1.30-6pm May-Sep) is signposted from the long main street of Kalopanayiotis and is reached by following a road downwards and then upwards again at the opposite side of the valley. Built in the traditional Troödos style with a large barnlike roof, it is actually three churches in one, built side-on to one another over 400 years from the 11th century. The original **Orthodox church** has a double nave, to which has been added a narthex and a Latin chapel.

This composite church is one of the better preserved of the Troödos churches and has the most intricate and colourful **frescoes**. The best are the 13th-century works in the main domed Orthodox church, especially those dedicated to Agios Irakleidios. The charming fresco of the entry into Jerusalem features children in black gloves climbing up date trees to get a better look at the donkey-riding Jesus. Other frescoes include the **Raising of Lazarus** and the **Crucifixion**, and the **Ascension**. The wonderful, vivid colour scheme suggests that the artists hailed from Constantinople.

More frescoes can be viewed in the narthex and **Latin chapel** and date from the 15th and 16th centuries. The frescoes in the Latin chapel are said to be the most developed Italo-Byzantine frescoes in Cyprus, meaning that the artist had spent some time in Italy. The scenes represent the **Akathistos** hymn, which praises the Virgin Mary in 24 verses; there are, in turn, 24 pictures, each beginning with a letter of the Greek alphabet. The **Arrival of the Magi** depicts the Magi on horseback, wearing crusader armour. They flaunt red crescents, which are said to have been a Roman symbol before being taken on by the Byzantines and, later, the Turks.

The monastery keys are with the village priest, who can be found in the local *kafeneio* (coffee shop) during the spring and summer months. From October to April you will have to seek him out in his village house. Photographs are not allowed.

As part of the monastery, there is also an **icon museum** (admission CY£0.50; ☺ 9.30am-5pm Mar-May, 9.30am-7pm Jul-Sep, 10am-3.30pm Oct-Feb). Its main display is the collection of 15 icons, discovered in 1998, that date from the 16th century. As the informative and enthusiastic guide will tell you, the icons stood underground for many years, buried when the Orthodox priests ran from the invading Ottomans. Some of these icons went on tour in London in 2001.

The iconostasis (the screen holding the icons) has its top covered in carvings of the ferns that grow in abundance by the river in Kalopanayiotis, showing its local origins.

Sleeping
Olga's Katoï (☎ 2295 2432; fax 2235 1305; d CY£35) A wonderful agrotourism traditional house, this place has 10 spacious double rooms and balconies overlooking the valley and the monastery. Breakfast is served on the terrace, and there is an overpriced dinner, not quite worth the money.

Polyxeni's House (☎ 2249 7509; fax 2235 4030; 4-person house CY£40) This two-bedroom house, also part of the agrotourism scheme, is on the Lefkosia side of the village. The house is decorated with traditional furniture, and large wooden doors open onto a peaceful, sunny courtyard. There is also a kitchenette and a large bathroom.

Kastalia (☎ 2295 2455; fax 2235 1288; s/d CY£15/30) An elegantly decorated old house with oval portrait paintings and quaint chaise longue–style seating in the living-room area. The rooms are small but clean and neat, and there is a fresh and airy conservatory hallway, full of plants, and a nice shared balcony. Most rooms are doubles and families are welcome.

Getting There & Away
There is a daily bus (12.15pm, Monday to Saturday) from Lefkosia to Kalopanayiotis, which continues on to Pedoulas and, Monday to Friday, Platres and Troödos. For information ring ☎ 2295 2437 or ☎ 9961 8865.

Visitors to Kykkos can save some time by taking the newly upgraded road from Kalopanayiotis to Kykkos, via Gerakies. There's no public transport to the monastery.

TROÖDOS MASSIF

AROUND KALOPANAYIOTIS
Panagia of Kykkos Monastery
Μονή Παναγίας Κύκκου

The richest and most famous of Cyprus' religious institutions had humble, if rather odd, beginnings. The founder of the **monastery** (admission free; ☉ dawn-dusk) was a hermit called Isaiah, who lived in a cave near the current site in the 11th century. One day, while out hunting, the Byzantine administrator of Cyprus, Manouil Voutomytis, crossed paths with Isaiah. Because of his ascetic vows, Isaiah refused to talk to the self-important Voutomytis, who promptly beat up the hermit.

Later, while suffering an incurable illness in Lefkosia, Voutomytis remembered how he had mistreated Isaiah and sent for him in order to ask for forgiveness, on the off chance that his act of charitable penance might also restore his failing health.

In the meantime, God had already appeared to Isaiah and asked him to request Voutomytis to bring the icon of the Virgin Mary to Cyprus from Constantinople. This icon had been painted by St Luke.

After much delay and soul-searching by Voutomytis, the icon was finially brought to Cyprus with the blessing of the Byzantine emperor, Alexios I Komninos. The emperor's daughter developed the same illness that had afflicted Voutomytis and was cured after Isaiah's timely and, by extension, divine intervention. The icon now constitutes the *raison d'être* for Kykkos Monastery, which has guarded it, sealed in a silver-encased box, for more than four centuries.

However, history is one thing. At present, this imposing, modern-looking monastery structure dating from around 1831 is swarming with tourists eager to go inside.

ARCHBISHOP MAKARIOS – PRIEST & POLITICIAN

Archbishop Makarios III, ethnarch and religious leader of Cyprus for its brief period of independence as a united island, was born Michael Hristodoulou Mouskos on 13 August 1913 in Pano Panagia, a small village in the western foothills of the Troödos Massif. He studied in Cyprus and at Athens University, and graduated from the School of Theology at Boston University. In 1946 he was ordained the Bishop of Kition, and in 1950 he became archbishop.

It may seem strange that a religious leader could also be the political leader of a nation, but Makarios was only carrying on a tradition that had begun long ago during Cyprus' domination by foreign powers. In those dark times, Greek Orthodox Cypriots looked to their clergy for leadership and guidance. Makarios represented the culmination of the people's aspirations for independence and identity.

Makarios was initially associated with the movement for enosis (union with Greece). He was opposed to the idea of independence, or Commonwealth status for Cyprus, as well as *taksim* (the Turkish demand for separation). During the three-year uprising of the 1950s, the British suspected him of collaboration with the terrorist pro-enosis movement Ethniki Organosi tou Kypriakou Agonia (EOKA; the National Organisation for the Cypriot Struggle), and he was exiled in the Seychelles. However, Makarios was a politician, not a terrorist, and was brought back to Cyprus in 1959. He negotiated an independence agreement with the British and was elected president of the newly independent state of Cyprus on 13 December 1959.

Distancing himself from the extremes of the enosis movement, Makarios tried to appease the Turkish Cypriot minority in Cyprus and forge a foreign policy of nonalignment. However, he was seen by the Turkish Cypriots as being anti-Turkish, and serious sectarian violence broke out in 1963, leading to the ultimate division of Cyprus 11 years later.

The Americans and the West saw him as being too accommodating to Communism and feared another Cuba crisis, this time in the Mediterranean. The Greek junta, abetted by the CIA and pro-enosis EOKA-B (the postindependence version of EOKA) activists in Cyprus, launched a coup in 1974 with a view to assassinating him and installing a new government. The coup backfired; Makarios escaped, the Turks invaded the north of Cyprus, the junta fell and Makarios returned to preside over a now-truncated state.

He died on 3 August 1977 and is buried in a site of his own choosing on a hill top close to the Kykkos Monastery. He is still remembered fondly as Cyprus' greatest leader and statesman.

They are often turned away by bored guards for wearing short sleeves and above-the-knee shorts (men and women). The visitors then go to the stalls outside where clever entrepreneurs hire (yes, hire) long trousers and shawls.

This is an unattractive place, especially compared with the exquisite architecture and peace of the small churches and monasteries in the surrounding villages. But the importance of Kykkos in the island's Orthodox hierarchy cannot be underestimated.

The fabulous wealth of the monastery is displayed in the **Byzantine Museum** (☎ 2294 2736; admission CY£1.50; ☉ 10am-6pm Jun-Sep, 10am-4pm Nov-May), along with an extensive collection of Byzantine and ecclesiastical artefacts. There is a small antiquities display, on the left after you enter; a large ecclesiastical gallery with early-Christian, Byzantine and post-Byzantine church vestments, vessels and jewels; a small circular room with manuscripts, documents and books; and a rich display of icons, wall paintings and carvings in a larger circular chamber.

A comprehensive visitors guide in English and other languages is available from the ticket office for CY£3.

Tomb of Archbishop Makarios III

If you have made the trip out to Kykkos and have a little extra time on your hands, visit the tomb of Archbishop Makarios III (see the boxed text, opposite) on Throni Hill, 2km beyond the monastery.

Follow the road past the main entrance of the monastery until it bends right and heads upwards. There is a little parking area at the top with a mobile cafeteria. Take the road to the right to reach the tomb by a shortcut.

The tomb, which is rather unimpressive and was apparently prepared in haste due to Makarios' sudden death, is a stone sepulchre overlaid with a black-marble slab and covered by a round stone-inlaid dome.

Further up the hill is the **Throni Shrine** to the Virgin Mary, which in itself is not particularly attractive. However, it has some great, endless views, and you can clearly see the long serpentine road leading to Kykkos from the east snaking over the ridge tops. A touching detail is the wish tree, where the pious have tied little bits of tissue, paper and cloth to mark their wishes to the Virgin.

SOLEA VALLEY
ΚΟΙΛΑΔΑ ΣΟΛΕΑΣ

This sunnily named valley has a revolutionary past: it served as the prime hideout area for EOKA insurgents during the anti-British campaign of the 1950s, mainly because of its proximity to Lefkosia. Now it's packed with less dangerous visitors – weekend tourists from the capital, and foreign visitors looking for a bit of rural character.

The Solea Valley, bisected by the Karyiotis river, has some lovely frescoed churches, having been an important stronghold of the late-Byzantines. The main village here is Kakopetria, which has the best hotel in the Troödos Massif and good tourist facilities. It's possible to exit the valley via picturesque mountain roads to both the east and west.

KAKOPETRIA ΚΑΚΟΠΕΤΡΙΑ
pop 1200

Kakopetria, or *kaki petra* (meaning wicked stone), gets its name, according to legend, from a line of stones along the ridge above the village, which brought good luck to newlyweds. Then, one day, perhaps during an earthquake, some of the stones fell onto a hapless couple and killed them, and the village's name was born. A bizarre and morbid story.

But nowadays life is safe for newlyweds in this village, which sits on two banks of the Karyiotis river. There is a constant flow of visitors here, especially during the summer. The main village of the Solea Valley, Kakopetria has two wonderful hotels and a couple of good restaurants, banks (with ATMs), petrol stations, and a small old quarter, which retains its charm despite the tourists. It is a good place from which to explore the area and see the Byzantine churches.

Sunday picnickers often stop here for a coffee and a stroll on their way between the Troödos and Lefkosia.

Sleeping

Kakopetria is the only place in the mountains with two excellent hotels right opposite each other.

THE AUTHOR'S CHOICE

Linos Inn (☎ 2292 3161; www.linos-inn.com
.cy; Palea Kakopetria 34; per person d/studio/ste
CY£22/27/32, villa per day CY£160-260; 🖭 🖭)
Stay here, if you possibly can, just to experience the wonderful combination of a
rustic room laden with antique furniture,
four-poster beds covered in woven white
linen, fireplaces, old wooden radios and
heavy black telephones that remind you of
those in films about the Gestapo. In suites
and studios, you get plasma-screen TVs and
Jacuzzis; the villas have swimming pools.
This is the most tasteful and most comfortable place of its kind in the country, and
you will have to book in advance if you are
visiting on a weekend. The original architecture has been retained wherever possible.
The restaurant serves quality Cypriot food
(see below).

Mill Hotel (☎ 2292 2536; www.cymillhotel.com;
Mylou 8; per person r/junior ste/ste from CY£23/29/39.50;
🕑 closed 20 Nov-20 Dec) Perched high up on the
hillside overlooking the village, opposite
the Linos Inn, this stylish hotel is situated in
a tall wooden building where a lift will take
you to the reception from the leafy ground
floor. The hotel is decorated in plush, neo-
colonial style, with plenty of wood everywhere. The large rooms are exceptionally
comfortable, and have views across the valley. The restaurant is good.

Ekali (☎ 2292 2501; www.ekali-hotel.com; Grigoriou
Digeni 22; s/d CY£29/47) A renovated three-star
place that has decent rooms decorated in
dark-red hues, and laminated-wood flooring. The rooms also have baby-monitoring
facilities. Out of high season (July and August) the prices go down considerably.

Eating

As with sleeping, the eating choices are good,
but almost limited to the two main hotels.

Linos Inn Taverna (☎ 2292 3161; www.linos-inn
.com.cy; Palea Kakopetria 34; 🕑 lunch & dinner) The
most atmospheric, best-quality place to eat
in the village, so book your table in advance.
Cypriot food is good here, and the Cyprus
plate (CY£2.75), consisting of taramasalata
(dip made of fish roe), cured ham, haloumi,
smoked pork slices, *koupepia*, cucumber, tomatoes and olives, is a good starter. The os-

trich stir-fry is a speciality (CY£8.50) and the
mixed grill has a good reputation (CY£7.50).
The wine list here has one of Cyprus' best
reds, Ktima Malia (CY£12), a rich, red Caber-
net from the Lefkada grape, and a choice of
Italian, Argentine, Chilean and Greek wines.
There is also a café and bar, where nargileh
(Middle Eastern water pipes) are smoked.

Mill Restaurant (☎ 2292 2536; www.cymillhotel
.com; Mylou 8; mains CY£3.50-7.50; 🕑 lunch & dinner,
closed 20 Nov-20 Dec) The large terrace is shady
and cool, and the little river trickles past,
barely turning the once-functioning mill
wheel below. In the winter, you eat by the
fireplace, which is just as good. Trout is a
big thing here, and it comes in two forms:
grilled and 'special'. The chefs won't reveal
the secret of the 'special' but its tastiness
speaks for itself. As with the Linos Inn, it's
good to reserve a table on weekends.

Village Pub (mains CY£4-6) When all you want
is a simple summer meal, this is a great place
for a plate of white beans or some lentils. The
trout is recommended.

Getting There & Away

The valley is served by **Clarios Bus Co** (☎ 2245
3234) buses, which run up to nine times daily
between Lefkosia and Kakopetria (CY£1.10)
in summer, the first bus leaving Lefkosia
at 6.10am and the last one at 7pm. There
are two buses on Sunday (CY£1.90) in July
and August, leaving at 8am and 6pm. Seven
buses leave Kakopetria for Lefkosia between
4.30am and 8am on weekdays, with two
later services at 1.30pm and 2.30pm. In July
and August there are departures on Sunday at 6am and 4.30pm only. The 11.30am
service from Lefkosia continues to Troödos
village except on weekends. It returns from
Troödos at 6.30pm.

There's no public transport to the lovely
Unesco-listed churches in the valley.

AROUND KAKOPETRIA
Agios Nikolaos tis Stegis
Άγιος Νικόλαος της Στέγης
This **church** (donations welcome; 🕑 9am-4pm Tue-Sat,
11am-4pm Sun) is the more easily accessible (with
road signs) and interesting of the two Unesco-
listed churches close to Kakopetria. Known as
St Nicholas of the Roof in English, this tall,
barnlike church, founded in the 11th century,
was named for its large, heavy roof. The dome
and narthex came later, and the characteristic

Troödos pitched roof was added in the 15th century as protection against the heavy snows that sometimes fall in the area.

As in other Troödos churches, the art of icon and fresco painting flourished here in the Middle Ages, when Orthodoxy sought refuge from Cyprus' then-dominant Latin church administration. The **frescoes** at Agios Nikolaos are the usual convolution of images and styles, but among those worth seeking is a depiction of the **Virgin Mary breastfeeding Jesus**. Look out also for images of the **Crucifixion**, the **Nativity** and the **Myrrh Carriers**, which shows an angel on top of Christ's empty tomb. Photos (without flash) may be allowed, but the fussy caretaker may subtly suggest you make a donation to the collection box.

The church is prominently signposted from Kakopetria and lies about 3km southwest of the village on the Pedoulas mountain road.

Panagia tis Podythou
Παναγία της Ποδύθου
One less commonly visited Unesco-listed church (or rather duo of churches) is this rather charming pair, made up of **Panagia tis Podythou** (☎ 2292 2393; upon request) and **Panagia Theotokou (Arhangelou)**, a few kilometres north of Kakopetria (the signpost is easy to miss). The main church was established in 1502 by Dimitrios de Coron, a Greek military officer in the service of James II, the king of Cyprus at the time. Up to the 1950s, the building was occupied by monks. The church itself is rectangular, with a semi-circular apse at the eastern end. A portico, built at a later date, surrounds the church on three sides. Again, you'll see the characteristic pitched roof with flat tiles, and the floor inside is covered with baked terracotta tiles. The church's interior was never completed, yet **frescoes** cover the pediments of both the east and west wall. Two 17th-century frescoes on the north and south wall depicting the **Apostles Peter & Paul** were never completed. The fresco style is of a Renaissance-influenced Italo-Byzantine painter, who used vivid colours and a three-dimensional treatment of the subject matter.

The smaller and often overlooked Panagia Theotokou nearby is in fact more impressive, with vivid didactic-style panels, quite striking in their freshness even today.

Dating from around 1514, the interior frescoes depict a rather fascinating panoply of images from the **life of Christ**.

Seek out the caretaker of both churches at the *kafeneio* next to the Lambrou supermarket in Kakopetria. Bring a torch as neither of the churches has electric lighting.

Panagia Forviotissa (Asinou)
Παναγια Φορβιωτισσα (Ασινου)
This beautiful Unesco-listed **church** (☎ 9983 0329; donations welcome; 9.30am-12.30pm & 2-4pm Mon-Sat, 10am-1pm & 2-4pm Sun) on the perimeter of the Adelfi Forest, 10km northeast as the crow flies from Kakopetria, is easily accessible from Kakopetria or Lefkosia. It has arguably the finest set of Byzantine **frescoes** in the Troödos and, if you feel that you have overdosed elsewhere, its calm rural setting makes for a delightful day out. A visit to the church could also be combined with a picnic in the adjoining forest.

The styles and motifs of the frescoed interior cross several artistic generations and are quite arresting. Most of the interior images date from the 14th and 15th centuries, and portray themes found elsewhere in the Troödos Byzantine churches. However, it's the sheer vibrancy of the colours that make the Asinou frescoes so appealing.

Father Kyriakos of nearby village of **Nikitari** (population 430) is the priest and caretaker of the church and, if he is not already tending to groups of Cypriot pilgrims at the church, he can be found in the village itself; ask at the *kafeneio*.

The Panagia Forviotissa is reached by a circuitous route over the mountain ridge east of Kakopetria, or by a well-signposted fast route off the B9 from Lefkosia, via Vyzakia. If you would prefer to walk here, there is a pleasant forest hike from the village of Agios Theodoros to the west, off the B9. There's no public transport.

PITSYLIA ΠΙΤΣΥΛΙΑ

The wide-reaching region of Pitsylia is the least visited and most remote part of the Troödos Massif. It stretches from the start of the E909, north of Troödos village, to the Maheras Monastery in the east. The northern slopes of Pitsylia are covered in tall, aromatic pines to the north, and vines grow here too.

TROÖDOS MASSIF

A number of frescoed Byzantine churches are dotted around the region, and there are challenging walks for longer-distance hikers.

Pitsylia's de facto centre is the sprawling, amphitheatrical village of **Agros**. Other villages are **Kyperounda** (population 1500), **Platanistasa** (population 170), **Alona** (population 130) and **Palehori** (population 410).

Hiking

The CTO has created marked hiking trails in the Pitsylia region. Except for two short circular trails, they generally require an out-and-back approach, unless you're prepared to keep hiking to the next village or transport link. Most are about 6km or less, so require a few hours trekking to complete. Trails take hikers through forests, orchards, villages and mountain peaks, and offer some of the best recreational hiking in Cyprus.

A short description of the trails in the region follows:

Trail 1: Doxasi o Theos to Madari Fire Station (3.75km, two hours) A panoramic ridge-top hike with excellent views. It begins about 2km from Kyperounda.

Trail 2: Teisia tis Madaris (3km, 1½ hours) A continuation of the above trail, it involves a circular cliff-top hike around Mt Madari (Adelfi; 1613m) with excellent views.

Trail 3: Lagoudera to Agros (6km, 2½ hours) A longish hike through vineyards and orchards, with spectacular views from the Madari–Papoutsas ridge.

Trail 4: Panagia tou Araka (Lagoudera) to Stavros tou Agiasmati (7km, three hours) The longest hike, it links two of the most important Troödos Byzantine churches via a forest, vineyards and stone terraces.

Trail 5: Agros to Kato Mylos (5km, two hours, circular) An easy hike through cherry and pear orchards, vineyards and rose gardens.

Trail 6: Petros Vanezis to Alona (1.5km, 30 minutes, circular) Involves a short hike around the village of Alona, passing through hazelnut plantations.

Trail 7: Agia Irini to Spilies tou Digeni (3.2km, 1½ hours) An easy out-and-back hike to the secret caves of Digenis, where EOKA resistance fighters hid during the insurgency of 1955–59.

The CTO pamphlet *Cyprus: Nature Trails* describes these hikes in some detail and provides basic maps, but hikers would be advised to take along a more detailed map of the region.

Getting There & Away

Public transport into and out of the region is strictly functional, designed to get people to and from Lefkosia for work or business. There is a Monday to Saturday bus from Agros to Lefkosia (CY£1), via Lagoudera, at 7am, which returns from Lefkosia at midday. Other colourful, old-fashioned local buses link most major Pitsylia villages with Lefkosia, but usually leave early in the morning and return to the villages in the early afternoon. Seats need to be booked, and visitors should not rely on these services for planned day trips to the region.

This is an area where you need time and energy; hiking from one village to another or perhaps hitching to a better-served transport artery are probably your best bets. For more information on hitching in Cyprus, see p242.

AGROS ΑΓΡΟΣ
pop 840

Poised high on the mountains (1000m), Agros is a breezy, largish village, convenient for hiking or driving forays into the surrounding hills. While not a particularly beautiful place to spend your holidays, it is an alternative to the better-known village of Platres to the west. The less-frequented surrounding villages and Byzantine churches make it a good base for discovering the island away from the rest of the mountain visitors.

Sights

Agros is known across the island for its cottage industries that make rose products, bottled fruit, and sausages. Local entrepreneur Chris Tsolakis runs an unusual yet thriving industry in the village: **CNT** (☎ 2552 1893; www.rose-tsolakis.com; Anapafseos 12; ☒ 8am-7pm) is a rose-product and pottery business. Visit the workshop and learn what can be made out of roses: rose- and flower-water, rose brandy, skin cleansers, candles, rose liqueur and even a rose-infused Cabernet Sauvignon wine. Decorative ceramic bottles and other pottery items are also made in the workshop.

A wonderful Mediterranean way to put some sweetness into your life is preserving fruit, so that in winter when, for example, figs are but a distant dream, you can dip into a jar of fig preserve and beat the winter blues. **Niki's Sweet Factory** (☎ 2552 1400; prices CY£0.70-3) dedicates its entire business to this tasty therapy, and sells products like orange marmalade, fig preserve and diabetic walnut sweets. Ask about the healing properties of some of the preserves. Niki sells her products all over Cyprus and even exports as far as Australia.

Less glamorous perhaps but no less tasty are the products made by the **Kafkalia Sausage Factory** (☎ 2552 1426; prices according to weight CY£4.50-11). All products, including *lountza*, *hiromeri* (traditional smoked ham), *loukanika* (village sausages), *pastourmas* (spicy smoked beef) and bacon, are made on the premises. Ask to see the dark and hot smoke room next to the busy little shop.

Sleeping & Eating

Rodon (☎ 2552 1201; fax 2552 1235; www.swaypage .com/rodon; Agros; s/d CY£32/50; 🏊) This is a gigantic three-star hotel, communally owned and run. Its unconventional manager, Lefkos Christodoulou, is a keen advocate of green tourism and has worked hard to promote Agros as an alternative tourist destination. The Rodon's rooms have seen a little wear and tear, thanks to catering to large groups of package tourists, but guest facilities include a good restaurant, a bar, two pools and tennis courts. Mr Christodoulou has revived many of the area's walking paths, and he has maps detailing walks around Agros, which he happily hands out to interested guests.

Two places at the northeastern end of the long, snaking main village drag vie for lunchtime and evening customers. The **Agros Village Restaurant & Pub** (☎ 2552 1558; mains CY£3-4; 🕒 Mon-Sat) is probably marginally better than the nearby **Kilada Restaurant** (☎ 2552 1303; grills CY£3.50- 4.50).

STAVROS TOU AGIASMATI
ΣΤΑΥΡΟΣ ΤΟΥ ΑΓΙΑΣΜΑΤΗ

This Unesco-listed Byzantine **church** (admission free but donations welcome) is famous for the **frescoes**, painted by Filippos Goul in 1494, that decorate its gable roof. Access to the church requires some forethought; you must obtain the key from the priest at Platanistasa village 5km away and, of course, return it. The church is somewhat remote, hidden along a sealed side road off the Orounda–Platanistasa (E906) route, though it can also be approached by a signposted but unsealed road from the next valley to the west through which the Polystypos–Xyliatos (E907) road runs.

PANAGIA TOU ARAKA
ΠΑΝΑΓΙΑ ΤΟΥ ΑΡΑΚΑ

This more accessible and more frequently visited Unesco-listed **church** (donations welcome; 🕒 9am-6pm) looks, from the outside, more like a Swiss cattle stable than a place of worship. Its enormous all-encompassing snowproof roof and surrounding wooden trellis all but conceal the church within. The paintings inside are a wide selection of neoclassical works by artists from Constantinople.

The vivid images on display run the usual thematic range, with the impressive Pantokrator in the domed tholos taking pride of place. Look out also for the **Annunciation**, the **Four Evangelists**, the **Archangel Michael** and the **Panagia Arakiotissa**, the patron of the church.

The unusual name of the church (*arakiotissa* means 'of the wild pea') owes its origin to the vegetable that grows in profusion in the district. If things are quiet here, it might be possible to take nonflash photos, but only if the watchful caretaker approves.

TROÖDOS MASSIF

Pafos & the West

For centuries, this attractive part of the Republic of Cyprus was considered to be the island's Wild West thanks to its physical and cultural isolation from the heartland of the country. The region gained a reputation as backward and introspective, particularly as the Greek and Turkish dialects of the west were among the most difficult for an outsider to understand (the Greeks had even retained parts of Homeric vocabulary). Its people were considered canny yet uneducated, and they became the butt of the island's jokes. They were not bothered by this at all, and in fact considered themselves a notch above the rest of the island in intelligence.

The west's large Turkish population reluctantly moved to the North in 1974, leaving the area solely populated by Greeks. The 1983 construction of Pafos International Airport, a small hutlike structure, means that the region is no longer considered a backwater, and it now attracts an increasing share of the tourist influx, as demonstrated by the rows of resort hotels that stretch north and south from Pafos, the region's capital.

Despite the aesthetic assault that you might experience upon visiting Kato Pafos (Lower Pafos) and the tourist resorts in the area, the wilderness of the western region, particularly the Akamas Peninsula, is beautiful and romantic. It is in fact the most remarkable part of the Republic of Cyprus, with fantastic, remote beaches, villages full of character(s), and long, charming walks. To the east, the vast Pafos Forest melts almost imperceptibly into the sombre tracts of the Tyllirian wilderness. Pafos itself has some great sights, such as the extensive Pafos mosaics and mysterious Tombs of the Kings. Ktima, the old part of Pafos, less crushed by the tourist building boom, breathes a bit of history. The small, pretty town of Polis, recently deserted by package tourists, is a perfect base for the independent traveller.

HIGHLIGHTS

- Explore Pafos' ancient past by visiting the Roman **Pafos mosaics** (p121) and the **Tombs of the Kings** (p120) necropolis

- Wander the wild and rugged **Akamas Peninsula** (p131)

- Relax in lovely **Akamas Heights** (p129), spending time in its beautiful old villages and swimming on **Lara Beach** (p131)

- Catch a glimpse of an endangered **moufflon** (p137) in Pafos Forest

- Hear some jazz in September at **Paradise Jazz Festival** (p136) in Pomos

- Eat the best meze on the island at Pafos' **Seven St Georges' Tavern** (p126)

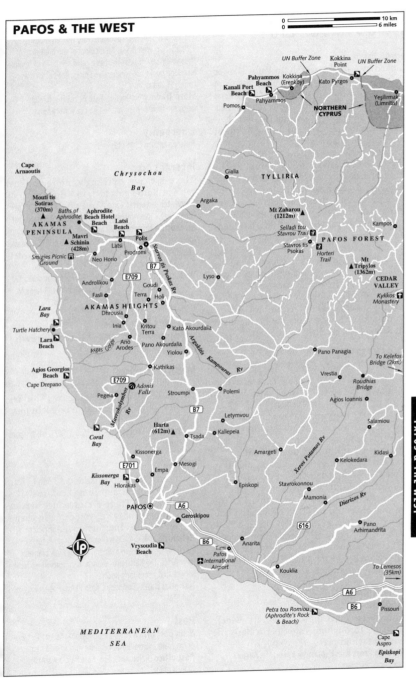

PAFOS & THE WEST

PAFOS ΠΑΦΟΣ BAF

pop 40,000

Linked by a road artery, Kato Pafos (Lower Pafos) and Ktima (Upper Pafos) form an interesting whole. Kato Pafos, the tourist centre, has endless neon lights, bad music, and bars and clubs promising to cover their customers in suds; yet it has the South's most fascinating archaeological sites. When you're standing (relatively) alone in the midst of the Pafos Archaeological Site, surrounded by acres of history, a vast blue sky and the wild fennel and caper plants that grow on the Mediterranean's edges, you feel thousands of years away from the tourist paraphernalia.

Ktima, the real centre of Pafos, has managed to escape the tourist building boom; it's a calmer place where 'real Pafiots' go about their daily business. It has lovely colonial buildings housing government institutions and many of the town's museums. Its old Turkish quarter, Mouttalos, is run-down and slightly deserted, but gives an idea of how things looked 30 years ago. But the highlight of Ktima is its excellent restaurants.

ORIENTATION

Pafos' two distinct sections are 3km apart. Intercity buses and service taxis arrive at Ktima; to get to Kato Pafos, catch bus 11, walk or take a taxi. Leoforos Apostolou Pavlou links the two parts of Pafos, and Leoforos Georgiou Griva Digeni leads east from Ktima towards Lemesos. Leoforos Evagora Pallikaridi heads north from Ktima to Polis.

Kato Pafos centres on Posidonos, and many hotels, bars and restaurants are dotted on this long street. Ktima's main shopping street is Leoforos Arhiepiskopou Makariou III. The two other central streets in Ktima are Gladstonos and Nikodimou Mylona, and both run off Makariou III. Tafon Ton Vasileon, otherwise known as Tombs of the Kings Rd, runs from Kato Pafos towards Coral Bay and has many restaurants and bars.

INFORMATION
Bookshops

Foreign-language newspapers are widely available throughout Pafos, particularly the British tabloid press.

Foreign Press Kiosk (Main Sq, Ktima) Has foreign-language newspapers.

Moufflon Bookshop (☎ 2693 4850; Kinyras 30, Ktima; ◷ 8.30am-1pm & 4-7pm Mon, Tue, Thu, Fri & Sun, 8.30am-2pm Wed & Sat) An offshoot of the bookshop of the same name in Lefkosia; has a good selection of foreign-language books, newspapers and magazines as well as Lonely Planet titles.

Stazo Trading (Posidonos, Kato Pafos) Has foreign-language newspapers; located on the waterfront.

Emergency
Police station (☎ 112; Main Sq, Ktima)

Internet Access

There are, unsurprisingly, more Internet cafés in Kato Pafos than in Ktima.

Baywatch Internet Cafe (Konstantias 1, Kato Pafos; per hr CY£2; ◷ 10am-midnight) With the tacky Baywatch bar.

Maroushia Internet (per hr CY£3; ◷ 10am-11pm Mon-Sat, 3-10pm Sun) Kato Pafos (☎ 2691 0657; Poisidonos, Kato Pafos); Ktima (☎ 2694 7240; Plateia Kennedy 6, Ktima) Has branches in both Kato Pafos and Ktima.

Webstation C@fe (☎ 2695 2220; Agiou Antoniou 12, Kato Pafos; per hr CY£2; ◷ 10am-midnight) A large place on the main tourist strip.

Internet Resources
www.paphosfinder.com Lists a lot of useful services for visitors to the city.

Medical Services

Information about private doctors on call can be obtained by ringing ☎ 1426. You can also obtain information on night pharmacies on ☎ 1406.

Pafos General Hospital (☎ 2680 3100/3264; Ahepans, Anavargo)

Money

There are plenty of banks and ATMs in Kato Pafos and Ktima, and along Leoforos Apostolou Pavlou. There are exchange services in both parts of town; you can also change money at Pafos International Airport.

Hellenic Bank Kato Pafos (Posidonos, Kato Pafos); Ktima (Leoforos Georgiou Griva Digeni, Ktima) Both branches have ATMs. The Kato Pafos branch has a foreign-exchange service that keeps long hours.

National Bank (Posidonos, Kato Pafos) Has an easy-to-find ATM.

Post

Main post office (Nikodimou Mylona, Ktima) Just west of the main square. Poste restante mail is held here.

Post office (Agiou Antoniou, Kato Pafos) A smaller branch office.

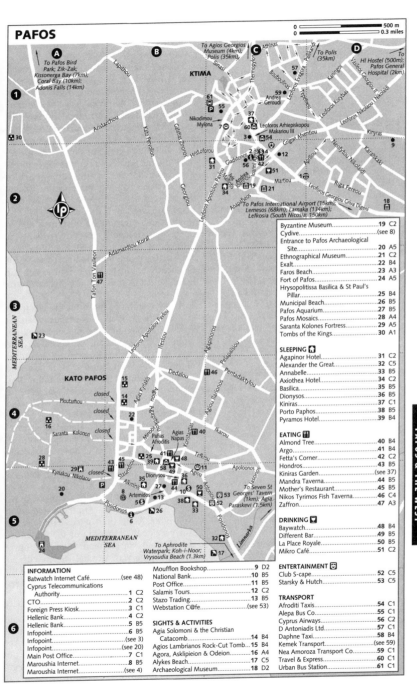

PAFOS

Telephone

Public phones are everywhere; the most convenient phones are on the waterfront in Kato Pafos, close to the harbour.

Cyprus Telecommunications Authority (CYTA; Leoforos Georgiou Griva Digeni, Ktima) You can make phone calls here.

Tourist Information

There are three Infopoint touch-screen electronic information booths in town. One is on the main square in Ktima and the other two are on Posidonos in Kato Pafos: one at the entrance to the Pafos Archaeological Site and the other on the main promenade. The information is in English, Greek and German.

Cyprus Tourism Organisation (CTO; www.visitcyprus .org.cy) airport (☎ 2642 3161; Pafos International Airport; ◷ 9.30am-11pm); Kato Pafos (☎ 2693 0521; Posidonos, Kato Pafos; ◷ 8.15am-2.30pm & 3-6.30pm Mon-Sat, closed Wed & Sat afternoons); Ktima (☎ 2693 2841; Gladstonos, Ktima; ◷ 8.15am-2.30pm & 3-6.30pm Mon-Sat, closed Wed & Sat afternoons) The CTO has decent maps, useful brochures and booklets on hiking, biking and agrotourism, a hotel guide, transport information and tons of other useful information about Cyprus.

Travel Agencies

Salamis Tours (☎ 2693 5504; fax 2693 5505; Leoforos Georgiou Griva Digeni 44, Ktima) A branch of the Lefkosia agency. It can issue cruise tickets for Greece and Egypt as well as air tickets to most destinations outside Cyprus.

SIGHTS
Tombs of the Kings

Imagine yourself surrounded by ancient tombs in a desertlike landscape, with waves crashing on rocks the only sound. If you're here in the summer, the sun will beat hard on you, making you seek shade down in the cool tombs. This is a fascinating and mysterious place.

The **Tombs of the Kings** (☎ 2694 0295; admission CY£0.75; ◷ 8.30am-7.30pm May-Sep, 8.30am-5pm Oct-Apr), a Unesco World Heritage site, is Pafos' main attraction. Two kilometres north of Kato Pafos, the site contains a set of well-preserved underground tombs and chambers used by residents of Nea Pafos from the 3rd century BC to the 3rd century AD, during the Hellenistic and Roman periods. Despite the name, the tombs were not actually used by royalty; they earned the title 'Tombs of the Kings' for their grand appear-

ance and the Doric pillars that help support the structures. Members of the higher social classes were buried here.

The seven excavated tombs are scattered over a wide area and all are accessible to the public. The most impressive is No 3, recently restored, which has an open atrium below ground level, surrounded by impressive Doric columns. A wooden staircase has been added for easier entrance. Other tombs, accessible by stone stairways, have niches built into the walls where bodies were stored. Most of the tombs' treasures have long since been spirited away by grave robbers – notably the late-19th-century American consul of Larnaka, Luigi Palma de Cesnola.

The tombs are unique in Cyprus due to their peristyle court structure, which was influenced by Egyptian architecture. The ancient Egyptians believed that tombs for the dead should resemble houses for the living, and this tradition is reflected in the Pafos tombs.

Allow at least two hours for the site; try to visit during the early morning as it can get very hot walking around the sprawling necropolis. Bring a hat and bottled water, and be very careful when descending into some of the tombs, as the stone steps are large and uncomfortable. To get here from Kato Pafos, jump on bus 15, heading for Coral Bay.

Pafos Archaeological Site

Nea Pafos (New Pafos) is the name given to the sprawling **Pafos Archaeological Site** (☎ 2694 0217; admission CY£1.50; ◷ 8am-7.30pm), which occupies the western segment of Kato Pafos. Nea Pafos is the ancient city of Pafos, founded in the late 4th century BC. Palea Pafos (Old Pafos) was in fact Kouklia, southeast of today's Pafos, and the site of the Sanctuary of Aphrodite. At the time of Nea Pafos, Cyprus was part of the kingdom of the Ptolemies, the Graeco-Macedonian rulers of Egypt whose capital was Alexandria. The city became an important strategic outpost for the Ptolemies, and the settlement grew considerably over the next seven centuries.

The city was originally encircled by massive walls and occupied an area of about 950,000 sq metres, reaching several hundred metres east of today's Leoforos Apostolou Pavlou. The streets were laid out in a rectangular grid pattern, and archaeological excavations have shown evidence of commercial and cultural activity over the life of the city. Nea Pafos was ceded to the Romans in 58 BC but remained the centre of all political and administrative life in Cyprus, reaching its zenith during the 2nd or 3rd century AD. It was during this time that the city's most opulent public buildings were constructed, including those that house the famous Pafos mosaics (below).

Nea Pafos went into decline following an earthquake in the 4th century that badly damaged the city, as well as many other cities on the island. Subsequently, Salamis in the east became the new capital of Cyprus, and Nea Pafos was relegated to the status of a mere bishopric. It was at this time that the fine Hrysopolitissa Basilica (p123) was built. Arab raids in the 7th century set the seal on the city's demise and neither Lusignan settlement (1192–1489) nor Venetian and Ottoman colonisation revived Nea Pafos' fortunes.

The archaeological site is being excavated slowly since it is widely believed that there are many treasures still to be discovered. Visitors can spend a busy half-day exploring the digs. Access to the Pafos Archaeological Site is via the entrance at the western end of the large harbour car park.

The following sections detail the major sights in the Pafos Archaeological Site.

PAFOS MOSAICS

This mesmerising collection of intricate and colourful mosaics in the southern sector of the archaeological site, immediately to the south of the Agora, is a pleasure to discover. Found by accident during levelling operations in 1962, these exquisite mosaics decorated the extensive floor area of a large, wealthy residence from the Roman period. Subsequently named the **House of Dionysus** (because of the large number of mosaics featuring Dionysus, the god of wine), this complex is the largest and best known of the mosaic houses.

The most wonderful thing about the mosaics is that, apart from their artistic and aesthetic merits, each tells a story. In particular, many are based on Greek myths.

The first thing you'll see upon entering is not a Roman mosaic at all, but a Hellenistic monochrome pebble mosaic, showing the monster **Scylla**. Mentioned by Homer, among others, this creature was once a young girl who was the object of Glaucus' affections, but she did not care to return his love. Distraught by her rejection, he went to seek help from the witch Circe who, as fate would have it, was herself in love with Glaucus. Jealousy and black magic being a bad combination in the hands of a witch, Circe poured a dodgy potion into a bay that Scylla frequented for bathing. When Scylla dipped into the sea, her lower body was transformed into that of a long-tailed beast. Scylla, a miserable monster forever on, vented her anger at her fate by sinking passing ships. This mosaic was discovered in 1977, 1m underground in the southwestern corner of the atrium.

The famous tale of **Narcissus** is depicted in a mosaic in room 2. This beautiful, vain man was so attractive that he loved no-one. Instead, he fell in love with himself and spent his entire life gazing at his image in a puddle, pining away with desire. The gods took pity on him, turning him into a yellow flower that only grows near water so he could look at his reflection.

The wonderful **Four Seasons mosaic** (room 3) depicts Summer holding a sickle and wearing ears of corn, Spring crowned with flowers and holding a shepherd's stick, Autumn crowned with leaves and wheat, and Winter as a bearded grey-haired man.

Phaedra & Hippolytos (room 6) is one of the most important mosaics in the house. The mosaic depicts the tragic tale of a stepmother's bizarre love for her stepson. Theseus married Phaedra after abandoning his first wife, the Amazon Antiope, the mother of Hippolytos. Phaedra, tormented by her love, wrote a letter to Hippolytos declaring her affections.

The mosaic depicts the moment when the panicked Hippolytos reads the letter, and Phaedra, waiting to hear his reaction, is burned by Eros' torch of love. The spurned Phaedra told her husband the story, only switching facts and telling him that his son had in fact declared his love to her. Outraged and hurt, Theseus prayed to his father, the sea god Poseidon, for punishment, and Hippolytos was killed by a wild bull that attacked him one night. But, after his death, the truth was revealed, and Phaedra, wracked with guilt, ended her own life.

One of the best mosaics in the house is the **Rape of Ganymede** (room 8). Ganymede, a beautiful young shepherd, was so desirable that not even Zeus could resist him. Zeus turned himself into an eagle and lifted Ganymede to Olympus, where the boy became the cupbearer of the gods. The mosaicist had apparently miscalculated the space allowed to him, which is why the eagle's wings are cropped.

In the Western Portico (room 16) is a mosaic based on a tale familiar to any lover of Shakespeare: the story of **Pyramus & Thisbe**. Told by Ovid in his *Metamorphosis*, it was adapted in *Romeo and Juliet* and was performed by the 'mechanicals' in *A Midsummer Night's Dream*. The story tells of two lovers from hostile families who could not make their love public, but who arrange to meet at dawn. Thisbe, having arrived first and wearing a veil across her face, encounters a bloody lioness wanting to drink at a stream. Afraid of the beast, Thisbe runs into a nearby cave, leaving her veil behind. The lioness, doing what lionesses do, rips the veil to shreds. You can guess the rest; Pyramus arrives at this moment and sees the lioness with Thisbe's bloody veil, and thinks she has been devoured by the animal. Unable to imagine life without Thisbe, he draws his sword and kills himself. Thisbe then comes out of the cave and, upon finding Pyramus dead, kills herself with his sword.

For details on other mosaics, buy the excellent official *Guide to the Pafos Mosaics*, on sale for CY£3 at the ticket kiosk.

A short walk away are the smaller **Villa of Theseus** and the **House of Aion**. The latter, a purpose-built structure made from stones found on the site, houses a 4th-century mosaic display made up of five separate panels. The house was named after the pagan god Aion, who is depicted in the mosaics. Although the image has been damaged somewhat, the name Aion and the face of the god can be clearly seen.

The Villa of Theseus is most likely a 2nd-century private residence and is named after a mosaic representation of the hero Theseus fighting the Minotaur. The building occupies an area of 9600 sq metres, and so far 1400 sq metres of mosaics have been uncovered. The round mosaic of Theseus and the Minotaur is remarkably well preserved and can be seen in room 36. Other mosaics to look out for are those of Poseidon in room 76 and Achilles in rooms 39 and 40.

Allow at least two hours to see the three houses properly.

AGORA, ASKLIPIEION & ODEION

The Agora (or forum) and Asklipieion date back to the 2nd century AD and constitute the heart of the original Nea Pafos complex. Today, the Agora consists mainly of the Odeion, a semicircular theatre that was restored in 1970 but does not look particularly ancient. The rest of the Agora is discernible by the remains of marble columns that form a rectangle in the largely empty open space. What is left of the Asklipieion, the healing centre and altar of Asklepios, god of medicine, runs east to west on the southern side of the Odeion.

SARANTA KOLONES FORTRESS

Not far from the mosaics are the remains of the medieval Saranta Kolones Fortress, named for the 'forty columns' that were once a feature of the now almost levelled structure. Little is known about the precise nature or history of the original fortress, other than it was built by the Lusignans in the 12th century and was subsequently destroyed by an earthquake in 1222. The structure had four huge corner towers and another four intermediary towers along the joining walls. A few desultory arches are the only visual evidence of its original grandeur.

Fort of Pafos

This small and empty **fort** (admission CY£0.75; ⌚ 9am-6pm May-Sep, 9am-5pm Oct-Apr) guards the harbour entrance and is entered by a little stone bridge over a moat. Most visitors climb the fort for the good views of the harbour from its roof. The fort also serves as an event venue during the Pafos Aphrodite Festival (p124).

The fort is in fact all that remains of an earlier Lusignan fort built in 1391; the rest of it was destroyed by the Venetians less than a hundred years later. The Ottomans fixed only the roof, on which they built eight cannon slots aiming in all directions.

Agia Solomoni & the Christian Catacomb

This fairly nondescript **tomb complex** (admission free) just off Leoforos Apostolou Pavlou is the burial site of the Seven Machabee Brothers, who were martyred around 174 BC, during the time of Antiochus IV Epiphanes. Their mother was Agia Solomoni, a Jewish woman who became a saint after the death of her seven sons. It is thought that the space was a synagogue in Roman times. The entrance to the catacomb is marked by a collection of votive rags tied to a large tree outside the tomb. This ostensibly pagan practice is still carried out by Christian visitors today. The tomb was used as a church in the 12th century, as shown by the still-visible frescoes.

Agios Lambrianos Rock-Cut Tomb
A little further north, on the side of Fabrica Hill, are a couple of enormous **underground caverns** (admission free) most likely dating from the early Hellenistic period. These are also burial chambers associated with the saints Lambrianos and Misitikos. The interiors of the tombs bear frescoes that indicate they were used as a Christian place of worship.

Hrysopolitissa Basilica & St Paul's Pillar
This fairly extensive **site** (admission free), which is still being excavated, was home to one of Pafos' largest religious structures. What's left are the foundations of a **Christian basilica** (built in the 4th century), which aptly demonstrate the size and magnificence of the original church; it was ultimately destroyed during Arab raids in 653. Green-marble columns from this church lie scattered around the site and **mosaics** from the church floor are still visible. Further incarnations of the basilica were built over the years, leading to the present small **Agia Kyriaki** church. The overall area is loosely roped off, so you can't get a total picture of the remains.

What is visible on the western side of the basilica is the so-called **St Paul's Pillar**, where St Paul was allegedly tied and scourged 39 times before he finally converted his tormentor, the Roman governor Sergius Paulus, to Christianity.

On the northwest side of the site is a tiny **early-Christian basilica**, the entrance to which has been almost completely taken over by the gnarled root of a nearby tree.

Agia Paraskevi
One of the loveliest churches in the Pafos area is the six-domed Byzantine church of **Agia Paraskevi** (admission free; 🕑 8am-1pm & 2-5pm),

in Geroskipou, east of Pafos. Most of the surviving frescoes date back to the 15th century, but many, restored in the 1970s, are covered at present and cannot be seen. The first frescoes visible when entering are the **Last Supper**, the **Washing of Feet** and the **Betrayal**. A primitive but interesting depiction of the **Virgin Orans** (the Virgin Mary with her arms raised) can be seen in the central cupola.

Archaeological Museum
This small **museum** (☎ 2694 0215; Leoforos Georgiou Griva Digeni, Ktima; admission CY£0.75; 🕑 9am-5pm Mon-Fri, 10am-1pm Sat & Sun) houses a varied and extensive collection of artefacts from eras ranging from the Neolithic period to the 18th century. Displayed in four rooms, the collection includes jars, pottery and glassware, tools, coins and coin moulds. Hellenistic and Roman artefacts include a limestone grave stele, marble statuettes, votive objects, pottery from the House of Dionysus (p121) and terracotta figures of dogs and stags. All in all, it's a collection for admirers of archaeological minutiae, although it lacks any outstanding items. It is worthy of a browse before visiting Ktima's other two museums.

The Archaeological Museum is located about 1km from the centre of Ktima.

Byzantine Museum
This noteworthy **museum** (☎ 2693 1393; Andrea Ioannou 5, Ktima; admission CY£1; 🕑 9am-4pm Mon-Fri, 9am-1pm Sat) is south of the main square in Ktima. It is worth visiting for its collection of icons from the 13th and 14th centuries, ecclesiastical vestments, vessels, documents and copies of scriptures. The collection contains a 9th-century icon of Agia Marina, thought to be the oldest icon on the island, and an unusual double-sided icon from Filousa dating from the 13th century.

Ethnographical Museum
Also in Ktima is the privately owned and maintained **Ethnographical Museum** (☎ 2693 2010; Exo Vrysis 1, Ktima; admission CY£1; 🕑 9am-6pm Mon-Sat, 9am-1pm Sun), which houses a varied collection of coins, traditional costumes, kitchen utensils, Chalcolithic axe heads, amphorae and other assorted items. There's more of the same in the garden, including a Hellenistic rock-cut tomb. The CY£3 guidebook available at the entrance helps you sort out the seemingly jumbled collection.

PAFOS & THE WEST

Agios Georgios Museum

Of possible interest to buffs of recent Cypriot history is this rather bizarre and national-istic **museum** (Hlorakas; admission free; 9am-6pm) located on the spot where the caïque *Agios Georgios* (now the museum's prime exhibit), captained by EOKA rebel Georgos Grivas, landed in November 1954 with a large supply of arms and munitions to start the uprising against British colonial rule. Grivas and his band of rebels were finally arrested while at-tempting another landing two months later. The museum walls document the rebels' capture and subsequent trial, and make for some fascinating reading.

The site, known as 'Grivas Landing', is 4km north of Kato Pafos and is easily iden-tified by the large Agios Georgios church, built to commemorate the event. Take Coral Bay bus 10 or 15 to get there. The museum is on the coastal road going northwest, past the village of Lemba, near St George Hotel.

ACTIVITIES
Beaches

The blue waters around Pafos are clean and alluring, and all the beaches listed below have earned EU Blue Flags for cleanliness, so you can swim freely. Keep in mind, how-ever, that the open sea often develops a swell, making swimming a bit of a hit-and-miss affair unless you like choppy seas.

The most popular town beach is the **mu-nicipal beach**. Although it is next to Posido-nos in central Kato Pafos, tourists love it and the swimming is good. You will need a scooter or a car to get to **Faros Beach**, north of the archaeological site. It's an exposed, sandy beach with some sandstone rocks, and a couple of on-site snack bars.

Even further out, around 8km north of Kato Pafos, is the long, sandy undeveloped beach of **Kissonerga Bay**, where you can find banana plantations and solitude. There are almost no facilities, so bring a book, food and water, and relax.

Southeast from Kato Pafos is the handy **Alykes Beach** – this place is nothing special, but it's good if you want to have a swim away from the municipal beach. Further along is **Vrysoudia Beach**; like Alykes, it's not particularly attractive, but the water is clean and fine for swimming when there is no surf. There's a range of facilities, from um-brellas for hire to restaurants and toilets.

Diving

The waters off Pafos are ideal for diving, and with around 30 sites to explore, some with evocative names such as 'Bubbles', the 'Wreck of the Achilleas', 'Stan's Dilemma' or the 'Valley of Caves', there are enough dives to fill a month or more. **Cydive** (2693 4271; www .cydive.com; Posidonos, Kato Pafos) can help you take full advantage of the opportunity. Single dives, including all equipment, cost CY£22 while a package of 10 dives costs CY£200.

For more on the best dives in Cyprus, see the boxed text, p86.

PAFOS FOR CHILDREN

Children won't be bored in Pafos. Like the rest of Cyprus, the town is child-friendly, and there are a few places for them to use up all that energy and be entertained at the same time.

Pafos Bird Park (2681 3852; www.pafosbirdpark .com; Agios Georgiou; adult/child CY£9/£5; 9am-8pm Apr-Sep, 9am-5pm Oct-Mar) may be Cyprus' best zoo and best children's attraction rolled into one. Apart from birds, there are giraffes, antelopes, deer, gazelles, moufflon, reptiles, giant tortoises, emus, ostriches, small goats and so on. There's also a restaurant and snack bar, and a kiddies' playground. It's located on the road to Coral Bay.

Aphrodite Waterpark (2691 3638; Poseidonos; www.aphroditewaterpark.com; 10.30am-5.30pm May & Jun, 10am-6pm Jul & Aug, 10am-5pm Sep & Oct; admis-sion adult/child/under 3 yrs CY£15/8/free) is all-day-entertainment material, where the adults can have a massage while the kids battle the mini volcano. A wristband can keep track of all your daily expenses, which you then pay at the end of the day.

Pafos Aquarium (2695 3920; Artemidos 1, Kato Pafos; adult/child/family CY£3.75/2/10; 10am-9pm) has 72 tanks of all things with a fish face and, scarily, some crocodiles. It's situated very close to the harbour.

TOURS

Exalt (2694 3803; www.cyprus-adventure.com; Agias Kyriakis 24, Kato Pafos) is a Pafos-based outfit that runs hiking and 4WD-based expeditions to the Akamas Peninsula, the Avgas Gorge and the Troödos Massif.

FESTIVALS & EVENTS

In early September, the **Pafos Aphrodite Festival** (www.pafc.com.cy) has opera under the stars. The

festival specialises in classic opera performances, such as Puccini's *Tosca* (2003), and
Verdi's *Rigoletto* (2004) and *La Traviata*
(2005).

Every year, one opera is chosen and performed alfresco in Pafos Castle to enrap-
tured audiences.

SLEEPING

Accommodation in Pafos is designed for
package-tour groups; there are hardly any
places that might be used to independent
travellers. However, hotels will accommodate you if there is space.

The only worthwhile camping ground
nearby is at Coral Bay (p129), 11km north
of Pafos.

Ktima

Kiniras (☎ 2694 1604; www.kiniras.cy.net; Arhiepiskopou Makariou III 91; per person Oct-May/Jun, Jul & Sep/Aug
CY£15/20/25) Bang in the centre of Ktima, Kiniras is passionately run by its house-proud
owner, who painted the Cyprus-themed
pictures on the walls of the bedrooms. The
rooms are decorated in dark-red wood, and
have telephone, radio, TV, fridge and safe
box. The hotel's downstairs restaurant, Kiniras Garden, is a good place to eat (p127).

Agapinor Hotel (☎ 2693 3926; www.agapinorhotel
.com.cy; Nikodimou Mylona 24-25; s/d CY£32/46; P �)
This is a three-star hotel with a large pool
(which is very welcome in inland Ktima),
airy rooms, an evening restaurant, a coffee
shop and guest parking.

Axiothea Hotel (☎ 2693 2866; fax 2694 5790; Ivis
Mallioti 2; s/d CY£23/31.50) This hotel, on the high
ground to the south of the CTO, has a glass-
fronted bar and reception with wonderful
views of the sea – perfect for watching sunset. It's a two-star place that is a reasonable
budget option.

HI Hostel (☎ 2693 2588; Eleftheriou Venizelou
37; dm CY£4.50) Although cheap, this rather
run-down hostel, northeast of Ktima, is a
bit out of the way for the beaches. To get
to the hostel, walk up Leoforos Evagora
Pallikaridi and turn right onto Leoforos
Eleftheriou Venizelou; the hostel is 750m
along on the left.

SPA LIFE

A wonderful new branch of tourism seems to be taking hold in Cyprus, where spa-lovers are
being pampered to death in the island's top hotels. This luxury is best taken advantage of in the
mild winter days, when the stifling heat doesn't undo the effect of all that relaxing.

You can take sanctuary in the **Anassa Hotel** (☎ 2693 8333; www.thanoshotels.com/ans/ansfrm.html;
d from CY£105; ☒), near Polis. Its rooms, overlooking the sea, are endlessly comfortable, and the
spa is built under the hotel chapel. There are large indoor and outdoor pools, steam room, sauna
and Jacuzzi, and a candle-lit room for yoga and meditation classes (Hatha and Kundalini yoga are
practised here). Aromatherapy massage, hand and foot treatments, Indian head massage, reiki,
detox wraps and salt scrubs are all offered, to soothe the body and mind.

Le Meridien Limassol (☎ 2586 2000; www.lemeridien-cyprus.com; d from CY£165) is Cyprus' oldest and
most famous spa. It has 32 treatment rooms, with treatments ranging from the curious-sounding
Hawaiian Wave Four Hand massage (where your hands are covered with frangipani oil and then
rubbed) and Fennel Cleansing Cellulite and Colon Therapy to good old Thai massage.

A haven for those who want to be waited on hand and foot, **Thalassa Hotel in Pafos** (☎ 2662
3222; www.thalassa.com.cy; d from CY£365) provides a private 24-hour butler, reachable by mobile
phone, with your room. The therapies on offer here are innovative: the Trhana Body Ritual has
yoghurt and herbs rubbed over your skin (sounds a little like you're going to get roasted!), and
Kofo Therapia Me Keri uses the old technique of drawing wax out of your ears with a thin candle.
A highlight of this place is that you don't have to be confined to the therapy rooms – you can
have your massages and treatments on the beach.

Columbia Beach Resort (☎ 2583 3000; www.columbia-hotels.com; d from CY£195) in Pissouri has
been praised highly by spa-lovers. It's built in a remote area and has been designed to look like
a traditional village without ending up as a hideous travesty. It is comparatively more affordable
than the other spa hotels. There are around 25 treatments, many of which seem to be named
after abstract ideas and philosophies. The highlights include Chinese Taoist body massage, Metamorphosis massage and Ayurvedic massage.

Kato Pafos

This part of town is a sea of characterless hotels and apartments, and prices generally don't match what's on offer. The following choices are hotels that are used to walk-ins.

Dionysos (☎ 2693 3414; fax 2693 3908; Dionysou 1; s/d CY£56/82; ✷ ✷) Off the main Posidonos avenue, this is the best small hotel in Kato Pafos. The rooms are in white-painted wood, with navy, marine details, and are neat and comfortable. There is a pool and a Jacuzzi in a cool garden, with an open-air dining area and a bar.

Alexander the Great (☎ 2696 5000; www.kanika hotels.com/article.php?id=31; Posidonos; r per person from CY£44.50; ✷ ✷) A stylish four-star place where a dishevelled traveller is not a welcome sight. The rooms are plush, with large silky-quilted beds. It has everything you need if you don't want to leave the hotel: tennis, gymnasium, children's area, restaurant and bar, and it's right on the beach. Discounts of 40% apply out of season.

Annabelle (☎ 2693 8333; www.thanoshotels.com/anna/annafrm.html; Posidonos; r CY£131-174; ✷ ✷) A five-star hotel with wonderfully luxurious rooms, some with private pools. The large hotel pool snakes through the site and the deck chairs that sit on the pool's edge are shaded by tall trees. Discounts of 30% apply out of season.

Basilica (☎ 2693 3500; fax 2693 3110; Alkminis 3; studios & apt from CY£45) This is an apartment complex with a good choice of studios and one- and two-bedroom apartments. All are fully equipped and neat, and allow for self-catering. The location is very central.

Porto Paphos (☎ 2694 2333; porto@spidernet.com.cy; Posidonos; s/d CY£43/62; ✷) Right on the main tourist beat, sandwiched between Pizza Hut and a large hotel, Porto Paphos is a cement-block building, ugly from the outside, a bit better from the inside. The terrace has nice sea views, but as you watch the sun sinking into the sea, you can also gaze at Pizza Hut diners sinking their teeth into their dinner. The hotel has its own pool and the rooms all have balconies. There is also a gym, children's area and restaurant.

Pyramos Hotel (☎ 2693 5161; pyramos@cytanet.com.cy; Agias Anastasias 4; s/d CY£22/28) Having got an extra star after its renovation in 2004, this place has spacious, run-down rooms. The service is friendly and it's right in the centre of Kato Pafos. TV is available on request.

EATING

Pafos' food scene is as random as its sleeping one. The restaurants, particularly in Kato Pafos, are predominantly used to diners seeking low-quality food; we advise you to check a place out before you eat there. Tafon Ton Vasileon (Tombs of the Kings Rd) and the harbour have some good restaurants, but the restaurants in Ktima are the ones you should really go for.

Ktima

Zaffron (☎ 2693 3026; Tafon Ton Vasileon 110; mains CY£7-10; ✷ lunch & dinner Tue-Sun, dinner only Mon) Zaffron has caused a stir among Cypriot gastronomes, and the place is always full of people who want to be spotted in this most fash-

---

THE AUTHOR'S CHOICE

Seven St Georges' Tavern (☎ 2696 3175; Geroskipou village; www.7stgeorgestavern.com; meze CY£10) If only everyone was as loving and meticulous about food production and preparation as George, the tavern's owner. Everything you eat and drink in this place is grown, dried or pickled organically by the owner. He has a herb garden at the back, and a meat-smoking cabin from where drool-provoking smells tickle the nostrils. Even the wine is produced here, from organic home-grown grapes. Your meze, the house speciality, comes in the usual trickle of olives and capers, beetroot and carrot salads, cold meats, casseroles and smoked ham. Everything is season-dependent so you might get hand-picked wild asparagus, herbed wild mushrooms, aubergines in tomato, or fantastically tender *kleftiko* (oven-baked lamb). In terms of food, this is the closest thing to a self-sufficient heaven. The restaurant is in an old house, with a vine-and-palm-leaf-covered terrace. A good, traditional host, George walks around and chats to his guests. His 'food philosophy' is proudly displayed on the website and he's happy to tell you about it himself. And as you'll see once you've eaten here, you'll come out feeling the harmony between your stomach and your soul.

ionable of restaurants. But being seen is not what it's all about: the food is truly delicious. The menu is Mediterranean, so try the rack of lamb with pesto or the homemade pâtés, and end your meal with a chocolate dessert you will remember for months. There is also a good cocktail lounge bar. Basically, in Pafos, this is where it's at.

Fetta's Corner (☎ 2693 7822; Ioanni Agroti 33; mains CY£3-5; ✍ evenings) A little old lady cooks and dishes things out through a low window on the side of the house; the grill's smoke is so thick it makes you think she might come running out with her apron on fire. Through the clouds of smoke, efficient waiters dodge the cars, crossing the little street between the lady's window and the tables sprawled on the pavement and in the little park. The food is simple, meze and grills, but it's cheap and tasty, and the service is great.

Kiniras Garden (☎ 2694 1604; Arhiepiskopou Makariou III 91; mains CY£7.50-12.50; ✍ dinner) This little oasislike restaurant is in the leafy and shaded garden of the Kiniras hotel (p125). The owner demands booking in advance, as he gets his ingredients fresh according to the number of diners booked, a very good sign. The appetisers are named after villages in the North, where the owner was born. *Kleftiko* (oven-baked lamb) is a house specialty and worth coming for – once you eat a good *kleftiko*, you'll become fussy indeed. There are homemade desserts, and the digestive drink is on the house. The wine list has good wines from the Pafos area (CY£7 to CY£15).

Kato Pafos

Hondros (☎ 2693 4256; Leoforos Apostolou Pavlou 96; mains CY£3.50-7.50; ✍ lunch & dinner) A fat Cypriot bloke in an undershirt gives you 'come hither' glances from the big board above Hondros. Below is a lovely terrace shaded by vines. Tables are covered in simple pink checked cloths, the service is good and the food traditional and delicious. The menu offers all the usual Cypriot dishes, with meaty *stifado* (rabbit or beef stew) for CY£6.50 and *kleftiko* for CY£7.50, and a variation on the tasty Turkish dish *Imam Bayildi*, here known as *Imam* (aubergines and courgettes in a tomato and garlic sauce), for CY£4.95. The children's menu ('Kids corner') looks as if it was lifted out of a McDonald's, with

a choice of chicken nuggets, fishfingers and hamburgers, all for CY£3.50.

Koh-i-Noor (☎ 2696 5544; Cleous 7; mains CY£6.50; ✍ dinner) From the dozens of Indian restaurants in Pafos, this is the one that everyone recommends. The North Indian cuisine has aromatic tandoori dishes, and the lamb korma is great. There is also a good wine list, so you could be here for hours.

Mother's Restaurant (☎ 2696 3474; Leoforos Apostolou Pavlou; veg dishes CY£3.90-10.50; ✍ dinner) A good place for a bit of fish, which explains all the cats lounging in the courtyard. The fresh seafood platter is a good starter for two people. It also serves 'vetererian' dishes. It's across the road from Hondros, in the Basilica Centre.

Argo (☎ 2693 3327; Pafias Afroditis 21; 3-course set dinner CY£6; ✍ dinner) Decent *kleftiko* is made freshly and twice a week (Tuesday and Saturday), when it's advisable to book. The moussaka is recommended. The restaurant has a small terrace and is in the (relatively) quiet part of tourist-tastic Kato Pafos.

Almond Tree (☎ 2693 5529; Konstantias 5; mains CY£5-10; ✍ dinner) One of Pafos' better-kept culinary secrets, featuring Cypriot 'fusion' cuisine. Thai-Cypriot tastes titillate the palate along with a smattering of stock Cypriot and international dishes.

Mandra Taverna (☎ 2693 4129; Dionysou 4; mains CY£5.25-9; ✍ dinner) This place sells itself as the 'genuine article' among the vast number of cheap, bad eateries and restaurants by virtue of having been there since 1979 and its name having originated from the word for barn. But it really does look like yet another mass-tourism place. The dozens of tables and chairs scream quantity over quality, but many guests swear by the fish meze.

Nikos Tyrimos Fish Taverna (☎ 2694 2846; Agapinoros 71; fish meze CY£8; ✍ lunch & dinner) You can smell the fresh fish as soon as you walk into this busy place. This is the place in Pafos to come for the creatures of the sea, caught daily from the owner's own boats. Choose from the ones on display (CY£3.75 to CY£8) or settle for an enormous helping of fish meze, consisting of 22 different dishes.

DRINKING

There is not a nontouristy, nontheme, nonspecial-offer, non-blasting-music bar in sight, so don't come here if you're looking for class, fashion or understatement. Places like Woody'z bar or Tropical Nights adorn the once-quiet streets of Kato Pafos, and Bubbles stays true to its name by shooting bubble guns outside to lure customers. Clubs are always promoted by women in bikinis (actual or pictured) and suds and foam parties are a tourist's delight. English pubs are just like back 'ome, but with the added treat of Robbie Williams impersonators (and such like) entertaining the sunburnt crowds. Most bars and pubs are clustered along Agiou Antoniou, known locally as Bar Street.

Mikro Café (☎ 2691 1567; Municipal Gardens, Ktima) A great place for coffee or booze, with wooden chairs and tables under the pine trees, and fabulous pastrami and smoked-cheese walnut-bread sandwiches. There is a children's playground close by, so it's an ideal spot if you have kids.

La Place Royale (☎ 2693 3995; Posidonos, Kato Pafos) This is one of the classiest café-cum-bars, right on the people-watching strip at the eastern end of Posidonos. This little oasis of glass, cane and wrought iron in a shaded paved patio is perfect for a prepub or preclub cocktail.

Different Bar (☎ 2693 4668; Agias Napas, Kato Pafos) 'Different' is different in that it is a gay bar and is not as tacky as all the bars and eateries surrounding it. The front terrace has simple square tables and stools, and a big steel sign.

Baywatch (cnr Konstantias & Agias Napas, Kato Pafos) If bright-green cushioned chairs, pool playing, and large-breasted waitresses are your thing, then this is the place for you. All the tables are facing the street for yet more visual stimulation, and the cocktails just keep on coming.

ENTERTAINMENT
As with the bars in Pafos, clubs are two a penny and mostly all the same. Disco, '70s funk, '80s pop, house, trance, garage and R&B are the usual choices of music. Don't confuse ordinary clubs with 'cabarets', which are basically brothels.

Starsky & Hutch (☎ 9983 8054; Agiou Antoniou, Kato Pafos) It's all about the TV series here, with glitzy décor, sequins and zebra stripes. Diana Ross, ABBA and other '70s biggies dominate the playlist – before you come here, make sure you remember the moves to 'YMCA'.

Zik-Zak (☎ 2694 7127; Tafon Ton Vasileon) This is where the Cypriots live it up at night, particularly the older generations, who do the dances from their youth.

Club S-cape (Agiou Antoniou, Kato Pafos) Two enormous bars (less queuing) and a seated chill-out area mean that once you're danced out, there's plenty of space to rest. Be present for the weekly carwash disco parties (prepare to be sudsed and rinsed!) and enjoy classic tracks from the '70s and '80s, and house music and R&B on the new sound system.

GETTING THERE & AWAY
Air
Pafos International Airport is 8km southeast of the town. Many charter planes and some scheduled planes fly here. There are two offices for **Cyprus Airways** (airport ☎ 2642 2641; Pafos International Airport; Ktima ☎ 2693 3556; Gladstonos 37-39, Ktima) in Pafos.

Bus
Nea Amoroza Transport Co (☎ 2693 6822; Leoforos Evagora Pallikaridi 79) and **Kemek Transport** (☎ 2693 6822; Leoforos Evagora Pallikaridi 79) operate buses to Polis, Lemesos and Lefkosia. The companies' shared office is northeast of Ktima's main square, and buses leave from the urban bus station. There are two services per day to Lemesos (CY£2) and Lefkosia (CY£3), and around 10 buses a day to Polis (CY£1). There are also three buses daily (except Sunday) to Pomos village (CY£1.10), northeast of Polis.

Alepa Bus Co (☎ 2693 1755; Nikodimou Mylona 17) also has daily buses at either 7.30am or 8am to Lefkosia and Lemesos. If you book in advance you can be collected from your hotel; otherwise, buses leave from the urban bus station near Karavella Parking.

Service Taxi
Service taxis are operated by **Travel & Express** (☎ 0777 7474; Leoforos Evagora Pallikaridi 9) in Ktima. Sample rates are CY£3.50 to Lemesos, CY£8 to Larnaka (change at Lemesos) and CY£9 to Lefkosia (change at Lemesos).

GETTING AROUND
There are no buses to the airport. A regular taxi to the airport from Pafos will cost between CY£5 and CY£7 or you can get a service taxi.

The urban bus station in Ktima is near Karavella Parking, behind the Alepa Bus Co office. From here, buses leave for various local destinations. Bus 10 runs every 20 minutes for Coral Bay and its beach (CY£0.50, 25 minutes). Bus 11 leaves every 10 to 15 minutes for Kato Pafos (CY£0.50, 15 minutes).

Bus 15 runs between Geroskipou Beach, 3km to the southeast of Kato Pafos, and Coral Bay, via Kato Pafos. This service is every 15 to 20 minutes and travels along the coastal route, past the major hotel strip. The cost is CY£0.50.

Afroditi Taxis (Georgiou Griva Digeni) is handy for a quick lift if you are up in Ktima, while **Daphne Taxi** (☎ 2624 4013; cnr Pafias Afroditis & Agias Napas) is easy to spot in Kato Pafos.

D Antoniades Ltd (☎ 2693 3301; Leoforos Evagora Pallikaridi 111-113), in Ktima, rents mountain bikes, motorcycles and mopeds.

AROUND PAFOS

The area around Pafos is superb for exploration, beaches and walks. To visit, however, you'll generally need to take a tour or organise your own transport. While a scooter is great for pottering around beach resorts, you won't be able to tour the region on one. A car is best if you want to cover any distance, especially if you want to go around the western Troödos foothills and villages, the wild and desolate Akamas Peninsula or the seldom-visited and sparsely populated Tyllirian wilderness of northwest Cyprus. A small 4WD is ideal for reaching some of the more isolated places, although the roads are generally pretty good. Many private tour companies run 4WD 'safaris' out of Pafos and Polis, should you prefer to let others do all the hard work.

CORAL BAY

Locals talk about how there used to be coral on this beach, now a well-developed and busy stretch. But although rows of umbrellas and crowds of bathers are no longer conducive to finding coral on this lovely beach, the atmosphere is lively and it is good for families. Coral Bay is located 12km west of Pafos, and there are several different stretches of the beach, all accessible from different parts of the approach road. The

cafeterias are indifferent and serve mainly hamburgers and chips or varieties thereof.

Camping Feggari (☎ 2662 1534; tent & 1 person CY£2.50) is about the only worthwhile camping ground in the Pafos region. There are 47 sites and a snack bar.

ADONIS FALLS

This is a tourist trap if there ever was one, although it's a pretty place. This 10m-high waterfall splashes into the so-called Baths of Adonis, a small swimming hole just upstream from the Mavrokolymbos reservoir. Bought by a local entrepreneur who charges CY£4 to go in and have a look or swim, the reservoir is reached by a windy dirt track, for which a 4WD is a must. The journey could last up to 30 minutes, so think carefully before you decide to go. The reservoir is signposted inland off the main Pafos–Coral Bay road, about 1km before Coral Bay.

AKAMAS HEIGHTS

If you're spending any time in the Pafos area, make sure you dedicate your most active and attentive hours to the Akamas Heights area. Most of the villages have great agrotourism-restored traditional houses for rent (check www.agrotourism.com.cy); the food in the taverns, cooked for the locals, is drop-dead delicious; the atmosphere is peaceful; and the hiking possibilities are fantastic. And did we mention the beaches? This area has some of the best beaches in the South. So what are you waiting for?

Villages

The villages of Akamas Heights can be visited en route to Polis, on the picturesque western road (E701/709). There's no public transport to get to these villages, the beaches or Avgas Gorge.

PEGEIA ΠΕΓΕΙΑ
pop 2360

The climb to the heights starts at Pegeia, the largish escarpment settlement populated mainly by wealthier Brits. The main reason to visit Pegeia is the **St George's Fish Tavern** (Agios Georgios; ☎ 2662 1888; fish around CY£10), a basic village tavern that looks like any bog-standard Cypriot eatery. But the fish here is the best in the region – and you know it's good when its just grilled, with nothing but a bit of olive oil and lemon. The squid and octopus are simple and divine. Weekends get busy and you may have to queue for a table, but you can enjoy the sea views while you wait.

From Pegeia you can head northwest towards the southern approach to the Akamas Peninsula.

DHROUSIA, KRITOU TERRA & AROUND
ΔΡΟΥΣΙΑ, ΚΡΙΤΟΥ ΤΕΡΑ
pop 390 & 90

Once you are up on the heights, you will come across a series of villages that enjoy a cool climate, grow fine wine grapes and are prettier than most Cypriot villages. They also make a useful alternative base for travellers wishing to avoid the busy beach scene of the coast further south.

Particularly beautiful are the villages of Dhrousia and Kritou Terra. Few tourists spend their time here, but each village has a lovely place to stay and is a great base for a relaxing holiday.

Dhrousia is a village of winding streets, moustached men sitting outside the *kafeneio* (coffee shop), large fig trees offering their fruit to passers-by, and an occasional donkey standing by the road. To complete the rural idyll, **Sapho Manor House** (☎ 2633 2650; studio CY£33), an old mansion restored in 2002, is the perfect place to stay. It has five studios, all decorated in the traditional style, with doors and windows made out of Cypriot pine. There is a communal garden and a swimming pool, plus a laundry room (CY£3). The *kafeneio* is right opposite, as is the village supermarket.

A little-known local quirk is Dhrousia's 'Magic Road' phenomenon, which occurs at the bottom of the windy road to Polis, by a kiosk called, ehm, Phenomenon. Around 20m after you turn onto the Polis road, switch off your engine, and the car will go by itself to the top of the hill. There have been numerous scientific investigations into this bizarre occurrence, which was discovered by a Dhrousia villager in the '90s. Despite many arguing it is due to magic, it has been attributed to underground water magnetism. And you thought life in Dhrousia was boring?

Kritou Terra, a little east from Dhrousia, is one of the prettiest villages in the region, with some splendid traditional houses tastefully renovated by their inhabitants. **Makrinari**

(☎ 2693 2931) is an agrotourism house where you can spend a relaxing few days. It has lush gardens overlooking a green gorge. The late-Byzantine church of Agia Ekaterini, at the southern end of the village, is a pretty sight.

Two other villages, not far from Dhrousia and Kritou Terra, are **Inia** (population 350) and **Goudi** (population 160), both of which are lovely. **Kostaris** (☎ 2962 6672; www.agrino.org/eleonora; Goudi; 2-person house CY£50; 🖳), located in Goudi, has three beautiful wood-and-stone houses.

KATHIKAS ΚΑΘΙΚΑΣ
pop 330

This is the most easily accessible village from Pafos, famous for its vineyards and wine, and home to a couple of good restaurants.

Loxandra Inn (☎ 9960 8333; www.gmbds.com/lox.htm; 2-person apt CY£18-27) consists of two one-bedroom apartments and a studio built around a large open courtyard. All rooms have a kitchen and fridge, a fireplace, central heating and a TV.

Two good restaurants here attract people from both Pafos and Polis. **Araouzos Taverna** (☎ 2663 2076; mains CY£4-7; 🕑 lunch & dinner, closed Sun evening) has no menu as such, but serves dishes like oven-roasted chicken and stuffed vegetables, and the meze is great value at CY£6 per person. It's in an old stone house, decorated in a rustic style with a massive plough hanging on a wall and local ceramics scattered around the dining room.

Imogen's Inn (☎ 2663 3269; meze CY£7) resembles a French bistro, with the sounds of jazz and blues twinkling into the garden that sprawls out under a large fig tree. There are the usual meze here, but there is also a vegetarian meze option, which includes the Turkish dish *turlu turlu* (baked and spiced aubergines, courgettes, carrots and chickpeas), falafel and *fasioli* (beans) alongside the standard haloumi (helimi) and olives.

PANO AKOURDALIA & KATO AKOURDALIA
ΠΑΝΩ ΑΚΟΥΡΔΑΛΙΑ & ΚΑΤΩ ΑΚΟΥΡΔΑΛΙΑ
pop 25 & 30

From Kathikas you can detour onto the B7 (the direct road between Pafos and Polis) via these two picturesque villages, where you have the option of staying overnight or taking a relaxing lunch.

Amarakos Inn (☎ 2663 3117; www.amarakos.com; Kato Akourdalia; s/d CY£35/55; ⊠ ⊠) has spacious air-con apartments in a wood-and-stone complex of buildings. There is a pool, children's facilities and an in-house restaurant, Vasilikos Drys (Royal Oak). This cosy old house-cum-restaurant, open for lunch and dinner, serves up palate-pleasing fare such as village sausages, and grilled mushrooms and *afelia* (pork cooked in red wine). Mains cost around CY£4 to CY£6.

Olga's Cottages (☎ 2276 1438; lakes@spidernet.com cy; Kato Akourdalia; 2–3-person apt CY£60) is a lovely 200-year-old stone residence that offers relaxed self-contained accommodation.

Beaches

There is a real treat on the southwestern side of the Akamas Peninsula. The long grin that is **Lara Beach**, cupped by lime rocks in a bay, is the most spectacular beach in the South. There is no development on it, the water is clean and calm, and the beach is laid out in small pebbles and sand. The beach also serves as a **turtle hatchery**, so tread carefully at egg-laying times. The path towards the beach is a dirt track, but can be driven on by 'normal' (non-4WD) cars, although you should take care when parking not to get stuck in the sand. A word of warning: try to leave as soon as the sun sets, as colonies of mosquitoes come out to play.

Agios Georgios Beach can be reached by conventional vehicle from Polis (via Pegeia) or Pafos (via Coral Bay). It is a 100m stretch of shadeless sand and rock with a little harbour, but beach umbrellas and loungers are for hire. There is a small beach cantina and a couple of restaurants up on the bluff overlooking the beach to feed hungry bathers. It's not flashy, but it's quiet and clean and some people prefer it that way.

Avgas Gorge

Also known as the Avakas Gorge, this narrow split in the Akamas Heights escarpment is a popular hiking excursion. The gorge is reached by vehicle from its western end via Agios Georgios Beach. You can drive or ride more or less up to the gorge entrance, though low-slung conventional vehicles will have to take care. The hike up the gorge, which becomes a defile with cliffs towering overhead, is easy and enjoyable. There is usually water in the gorge until

at least June. The walk will take no longer than 30 to 40 minutes one way, although some groups do press on upwards – with some difficulty – emerging on the escarpment ridge and then finding their way to the village of Ano Arodes (not much use if your vehicle is at the gorge entrance).

If you have not taken a picnic with you, excellent food is available close to the entrance of Avgas Gorge at **Viklari** (☎ 2699 6088; mains CY£4-5.50) – a great little eating oasis. It provides lunch (only) for hungry hikers. For CY£4 you get a delicious *kleftiko* barbecue and can relax at heavy stone tables while enjoying great views. Look for signs to the 'Last Castle' from the coastal road and seek out jovial owner Savvas Symeou.

AKAMAS PENINSULA

This anvil-shaped chunk of western Cyprus, jutting almost defiantly out into the Mediterranean, is one of the island's last remaining wildernesses. There's at least one reason why the Akamas has remained relatively untouched: the British army has used the interior of the peninsula as a firing range for a long time and has never been too happy about travellers spoiling their games. While not strictly part of the Sovereign Base Area agreements of 1960, the Cypriot government has tacitly allowed the Akamas to be used for this purpose. This hasn't sat well with conservationists, whose outspokenness and lobbying have brought the controversial status of the Akamas into the public consciousness. It could be argued that by isolating the peninsula for such dubious purposes, the wilderness is being preserved. However, the spent (and perhaps even unspent) ordinance littering the land doesn't look too environmentally or politically sound.

Despite this, visitors can still traverse the Akamas as long as they are prepared to walk, ride a trail, bike or bump along in a sturdy 4WD. Visitors with less stamina can take tour boats that sail the Akamas coastline from Latsi, west of Polis. The peninsula can be approached from two sides: from the east via Polis, or from the south via the little village of Agios Georgios. Tracks linking the two entry points are very rough, perhaps deliberately so to discourage traffic. Care should be taken if riding or driving, although this is as much to avoid live firing ranges as it is to avoid becoming stuck in a big rut.

The peninsula's big attraction is its abundant flora and fauna, resulting from Akamas' position as the easternmost point of the three major plant-life zones of Europe. There are around 600 plant species here, and 35 of them are endemic to Cyprus. There are also 68 bird species, 12 types of mammals, 20 species of reptiles and many butterflies, including the native *Glaucopsyche pafos*, the symbol of the region.

The only public transport to the area is the bus from Polis to the Baths of Aphrodite; see p136 for details.

Baths of Aphrodite

The myth surrounding the cool cave that is Baths of Aphrodite (Loutra tis Afroditis) is great advertising. Aphrodite, goddess of love and patron of Cyprus, came to the island in a shower of foam and nakedness, launching a cult that has remained to this day. Legend has it that she came to this secluded spot to bathe after entertaining her lovers.

The baths attract a fantastic number of people, but it is easy to wonder if the visitors expect more than they find. Surrounded by fig trees and filled with the relaxing sound of running water, the grotto is a nice spot away from the heat, but it's far from the luxurious setting that may be associated with a goddess of such amorous prowess.

The baths are 11km west of Polis, along a sealed road. From the baths' car park, follow the well-marked paved trail from the car park for 200m. You are not allowed to swim in the baths.

If you're suitably inspired, you can continue up the path to start the Aphrodite Trail (below), which conveniently starts and ends here.

Hiking

Easily the most popular way to get a taste of the Akamas is to spend a few hours hiking one of the following trails, which run through the northeastern sector of the peninsula. All can start and end at one of two points: the Baths of Aphrodite or the **Smigies** picnic ground, reached via an unsealed road 2.5km east of Neo Horio.

The most popular two trails are those that start and end at the Baths of Aphrodite. They are both longer than the Smigies trails and offer better views. The first is the **Aphrodite Trail**. This is a three-hour circular loop, 7.5km in length. It heads inland and upwards to begin with; as this can be tiring on a hot day, make an early start if you can. Halfway along the trail you can see the ruins of a Byzantine monastery, the so-called **Castle of Rigena**, before you head up to the summit of **Mouti tis Sotiras** (370m). At this point you head eastwards and down towards the

THE CULT OF APHRODITE

Cyprus is indelibly linked to the ancient worship of the goddess Aphrodite (known as Venus in Roman mythology). She is known primarily as the Greek goddess of sexual love and beauty, although she was also worshipped as a goddess of war – particularly in Sparta and Thebes. While prostitutes often considered her their patron, her public cult was usually solemn and even austere.

The name is thought to derive from the Greek word *afros*, meaning 'foam'. Cypriot legend has it that Aphrodite arose from the sea off the south coast of Cyprus. She was born out of the white foam produced by the severed genitals of Ouranos (Heaven), after they were thrown into the sea by his son Chronos (the father of Zeus, king of the Greek gods). The people of Kythira in Greece hold a similar view, and an enormous rock off the south coast port of Kapsali is believed by Kytherians to be the place where Aphrodite really emerged.

Despite being a goddess, Aphrodite was disposed to taking on a few mortal lovers. The most famous of them were Anchises (by whom Aphrodite became mother to Aeneas) and Adonis (who was killed by a boar, and whose death was lamented by women at the festival of Adonia).

The main centres of worship on Cyprus for the cult of Aphrodite were at Pafos and Amathous. Her symbols included the dove, the swan, pomegranates and myrtle.

Greek art represented her as an Oriental nude-goddess type. Ancient Greek sculptor Praxiteles carved a famous statue of Aphrodite, which later became the model for the Hellenistic statue known as *Venus de Milo*.

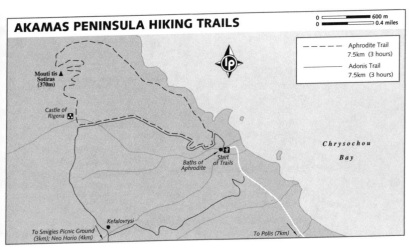

coastal track, which will eventually lead you back to the car park.

The second hike, the **Adonis Trail**, shares the same path as the Aphrodite as far as the Castle of Rigena, but then turns left and southwards before looping back to the car park. Allow at least three hours for this trail, which is also about 7.5km in length. Alternatively, you can turn right (south) just after the village of **Kefalovrysi** and continue on to the Smigies picnic ground if you have arranged a pick-up beforehand.

Water is usually available at the Castle of Rigena and, on the Adonis Trail, at Kefalovrysi. However, don't count on it in high summer. In any case, these trails are best attempted in spring or autumn or, if you must do it in Cyprus' extremely hot summer, just on sunrise.

The CTO produces a step-by-step, plant-by-plant description of these two trails in a booklet entitled *Nature Trails of the Akamas,* available from the main CTO offices. There's no similar brochure for the two trails that commence from the Smigies picnic ground: the circular 5km, two-hour **Smigies Trail** and the circular 3km, 1½-hour **Pissouromouttis Trail**, both of which afford splendid views of Chrysochou Bay and Latsi, and Lara Bay to the west.

POLIS ΠΟΛΙΣ
pop 1890

Polis is an ideal base for hiking or mountain biking in the Akamas, swimming at nearby beaches, touring the wine-making villages of the Akamas Heights or exploring the often wild and rarely visited northwest of Cyprus.

The village also has the island's loveliest camp site, as well as some decent, affordable restaurants.

The sand-and-sea package-tour agencies have turned away from Polis in recent years, and thankfully this little town has managed to evade the overdevelopment and decay of quality that comes from mass tourism. With a small town centre and all the necessary amenities, and situated close to the sea and nature, this is the perfect base in the west.

Polis lies on wide Chrysohou Bay, which runs along the northwest sweep of Cyprus from Cape Arnaoutis at the tip of the Akamas Peninsula to Pomos Point at the start of the Tyllirian wilderness.

Orientation

The town is set back about 2km from the sea on a gradual rise and is fairly compact. Its centre is a pedestrianised zone from which the main streets radiate. Buses from Pafos arrive at the Nea Amoroza bus station on Kyproleontos on the south side of town – one of the two approach roads from Pafos.

Restaurants and accommodation are all within easy walking distance, though the camp ground is a fairly lengthy trek out towards the beach area.

PAFOS & THE WEST

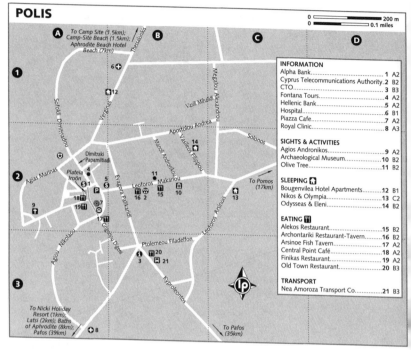

POLIS

0 —————— 200 m
0 —————— 0.1 miles

INFORMATION
Alpha Bank.......................................1 A2
Cyprus Telecommunications Authority.2 B2
CTO..3 B3
Fontana Tours...................................4 A2
Hellenic Bank...................................5 A2
Hospital..6 B1
Piazza Cafe......................................7 A2
Royal Clinic......................................8 A3

SIGHTS & ACTIVITIES
Agios Andronikos...............................9 A2
Archaeological Museum......................10 B2
Olive Tree.......................................11 B2

SLEEPING
Bougenvilea Hotel Apartments............12 B1
Nikos & Olympia...............................13 C2
Odysseas & Eleni..............................14 B2

EATING
Alekos Restaurant.............................15 B2
Archontariki Restaurant-Tavern...........16 B2
Arsinoe Fish Tavern...........................17 A2
Central Point Café.............................18 A2
Finikas Restaurant............................19 A2
Old Town Restaurant.........................20 B3

TRANSPORT
Nea Amoroza Transport Co................21 B3

Information

There are several ATMs scattered around town, as well as banks that exchange travellers cheques. There's a clutch of phones on Leoforos Makariou, with more phones on the road to the camp ground.

Alpha Bank (Plateia Iroón) On the main square; has an ATM.

Cyprus Telecommunications Authority (CYTA; Leoforos Makariou) You can make phone calls from here.

Cyprus Tourism Organisation (CTO; www.visitcyprus .org.cy; ☎ 2632 2468; Vasileos Stasioikou 2; ☑ 9am-1pm & 2.30-5.30pm Sun-Tue, Thu & Fri, 9am-1pm Sat) Very central.

Fontana Tours (☎ 2632 1555; Apostolou Pavlou 147) Books flights and other transport, and organises 'safari' tours and boat trips to the Akamas Peninsula. You can also hire cars here for between CY£14 and CY£46 per day, and rent accommodation ranging in price from CY£17 for a basic room to CY£45 for an apartment for two to three people.

Hellenic Bank (Leoforos Makariou) Centrally located; has an ATM.

Hospital (☎ 2632 1431; Verginas) A small hospital, located between the camp ground and the town centre.

Piazza Cafe (per hr CY£3; ☑ 10am-10pm) Prominently signposted off the pedestrian street, Piazza offers email access.

Royal Clinic (☎ 9962 2331; Efessou 13) Dr Dimitris Polydorou is on call most hours to assist travellers in need of medical assistance.

Sights & Activities

Polis' main attractions are its relaxed atmosphere and its proximity to the Akamas Peninsula and the region's lovely beaches, which are among the most attractive on the island. But if you're dying for some history, visit the **Archaeological Museum** (☎ 2632 2955; Leoforos Makariou; admission CY£0.75; ☑ 8am-2pm Mon-Wed & Fri, 8am-6pm Thu, 9am-5pm Sat), which offers you finds from the nearby graves at Marion and Arsinoe.

The church of **Agios Andronikos**, previously a mosque and the centre of local Turkish Cypriot religious life, has in recent times had some of its Byzantine frescoes revealed. Sitting on the western side of town, by the car park, the 16th-century church can only be visited in groups of ten or more. The key is held at the Archaeological Museum.

The nearest stretch of sand is the **campsite beach** – a good beach and convenient if you don't want to move far from Polis or are camping there. It's sandy and has natural shade, and the scent of the eucalyptus trees that shade the ground is wonderful. There's a beach restaurant and lifeguards. It's a good place to make a day of it with your own picnic.

The best beaches easily accessible from Polis are those on the eastern side of **Latsi**, a small fishing village 2km to the west of Polis. These beaches tend to be mixed sand and pebble, and are somewhat exposed to the vagaries of the weather, but they are popular enough and well serviced with restaurants. You can reach Latsi by bus (see p136).

A lovely, calm beach is the **Afrodite Beach Hotel beach**, on the way to the Baths of Aphrodite. It's good for children, with its clear, swimmable waters and comfortably small pebbles.

There is an extremely old **olive tree** close to the museum, for those interested in such floral phenomena. The trunk of the tree is almost split in two but it is still producing olives after 600 years.

Festivals & Events

In summer, various free concerts take place in the Plateia Iroön (Town Hall Sq) under the banner of **Summer Evenings in Polis**. These range from traditional dancing, music and folkloric events to classical music and jazz concerts.

Sleeping

Bougenvilea Hotel Apartments (☎ 2632 2201; fax 2632 2203; Verginas 13; 2-4 person apt CY£36; 🅿 🖭) Positively the best place to stay in Polis. A flowery path runs alongside the apartments, which have one bedroom, a living room, and a balcony with views of peaceful olive groves. There is a swimming pool, which can get crowded, but the camp-site beach is very close. The price drops by up to 50% out of season. Breakfast is CY£2.

Nikos & Olympia (☎ 2632 1274; nolympia@cytanet.com.cy; Arsinois 1; 2-person apt CY£25; 🅿 🖭) This is another small apartment complex. The studios and one-bedroom apartments here are lovely, with wood-panelled ceilings and balconies.

Odysseas & Eleni (☎ 2632 1172; fax 2632 2279; Vasileos Filippou 8; 2-person apt CY£25-30; 🖭) Bright, airy apartments with everything you need, and friendly service to go with it.

Nicki Holiday Resort (☎ 2632 2226; www.nickiresort.com; apt from CY£25; 🅿 🖭) A large hotel a little out of town on the way to Latsi, with comfortable rooms decorated with clay sunshines and wrought-iron beds. The rooms also have phones and TVs with local and satellite channels. The hotel is used to walk-ins and boasts a restaurant, snack bar and large pool. The service is friendly and the place is open year-round.

Camp site (☎ 2632 1526; sites per tent/person CY£1.50/1) Enshrined by fragrant eucalyptus trees that offer good, thick shade, this lovely camp site has its own quality beach. There is plenty of space, with good facilities. Located about 2km north of Polis, it's signposted from the town centre.

Eating

You'll find that good, affordable restaurants are Polis' trademark.

Archontariki Restaurant-Tavern (☎ 2632 1328; Leoforos Makariou 14; mains CY£4-9; 🕑 dinner) This is a classy and atmospheric tavern where the service is attentive and the food top class. Dine in an old renovated stone house and try chicken stuffed with haloumi and mushrooms, or *kathisto* (octopus cooked in wine and oregano).

Arsinoe Fish Tavern (☎ 2632 1590; Grigoriou Digeni; fish meals CY£4-6; 🕑 dinner) An atmospheric place on the south side of the pedestrian zone, housed in an old stone building. Dining is alfresco, and fish is the speciality. Try the succulent octopus.

Finikas Restaurant (☎ 2632 3403; mains CY£5.60-8.50; 🕑 dinner) This large, airy terrace is a wonderful setting for a dinner of pork marsala or the vegetarian house special. The chef recommends the 'Finikas chicken'. It's located in the pedestrian zone.

Old Town Restaurant (☎ 2632 2758; Kyproleontos 9; mains CY£7-10; 🕑 dinner) A discreet and relaxing place south of Arsinoe, with a leafy, secluded garden. Its specialities include wood-grilled chicken, chicken in a spicy yoghurt sauce and duck breast in black-cherry sauce. There is also a children's menu.

Alekos Restaurant (☎ 2632 3381; Leoforos Makariou 20; mains CY£3-4; 🕑 dinner) Tucked away where almost no-one notices, this budget-minded local eatery serves filling dishes such as black-eyed beans, or garden beans with tomatoes and meat. There's a complimentary litre of house wine for each pair of diners.

PAFOS & THE WEST

Central Point Café (☎ 2681 5032; snacks CY£1-2.40; ☺ breakfast, lunch & dinner) For a quick snack, a beer or two and a spot of people-watching, this café probably has the edge over the other pedestrian-zone eateries in the main square. Sandwiches and pizzas are on offer at reasonable prices.

Entertainment
Call the CTO office for details of events. Ticketed concerts, often given by top-name artists from Greece, take place in the Evkalyptionas (Eucalyptus Grove) at the Polis camp site. These outdoor events can be magical on a hot summer night. Tickets cost between CY£7 and CY£10.

Getting There & Around
Two minibus companies go to Lefkosia (CY£5) via Lemesos (CY£3.50): **Lysos Minibus** (☎ 9941 4777) leaves at 5.30am Monday to Saturday (except Wednesday), and **Solis Minibus** (☎ 2635 2332, 9943 1363) leaves at 5am Monday to Friday (except Tuesday). You can buy tickets on the bus.

Nea Amoroza Transport Co (☎ 2632 1114; Kyproleontos) runs buses more or less hourly to Pafos (CY£1, 40 minutes), and in summer it also has services to Latsi (CY£0.50) and the Baths of Aphrodite (CY£0.50) at 10am, noon and 3pm. Buses return 30 minutes later.

There are plenty of companies that rent cars, motorcycles and mountain bikes. Fontana Tours (p134) rents cars.

TYLLIRIA ΤΥΛΛΙΡΙΑ

If you love untouched, tranquil nature, Tylliria is your heaven. It's a sparsely populated, forested territory with a few desultory beach resorts nestling between Chrysohou and Morfou Bays. Enjoying its wilderness for a few days is highly recommended.

The only public transport in this area is the bus connecting Pomos with Polis and Pafos.

POMOS & PAHYAMMOS
ΠΟΜΟΣ & ΠΑΧΥΑΜΜΟΣ
pop 570 & 100
The trip up the coastal road from Polis towards Tylliria is stunning. The first village on this road is the small village of Pomos. This is an agricultural area, and Pomos is close to the border with the North.

There is a rather good place to swim at **Kanali Port Beach**, a smallish, sheltered pebbly beach just beyond the little Pomos harbour, where you can rent umbrellas. The snorkelling in the rocky sheltered bays here is good. The handmade sign at the beach entrance reads 'Relax to be happy'. Say no more.

Five hundred metres from Kanali Port Beach is **Gabriel Beach Villas** (☎ 2696 2485; www .cyprus4villas.co.uk/Gabriel_Villas_PP.htm; 4-person villa CY£110), a good place for a group of friends wanting some space to themselves. The four villas are fully equipped and there is a pool.

Pomos village has three tavernas but the best one is at Kanali fishing port, where you can enjoy the catch of the day at **Kanali Fish Restaurant** (meze & fish CY£8.50). It specialises in fresh fish, namely sea bass, bream, red snapper and red mullet. The views of the harbour are dreamy at sunset.

Pomos, small though it may be, creates musical waves every year with the **Paradise Jazz Festival** (www.paradise-jazz.com), which takes place in September at **Paradise Place** (☎ 2624 2537; mains CY£3-4.50; ☺ 11am-late Apr-Dec). The rest of the year, this is an outdoor bar-restaurant with a positively loungy, decadent feel – but in a good way. A hammock here, wooden chairs there, local photographers' exhibitions, fantastic music, zucchini-and-cheese fritters and sunsets to die for. No wonder they called it Paradise.

Pahyammos is next up, 5km further eastwards. Pahyammos means 'broad sand', and beach is indeed broad and sweeps around a large bay up to the UN watchtowers that mark the beginning of Kokkina, a Turkish Cypriot enclave.

The beach is made up of darkish sand and there is no natural shade, but the swimming is reasonable. There are no facilities whatsoever on the beach, but there are one or two places to eat in the settlement of Pahyammos, which is strung out along on the main through-road.

KOKKINA (ERENKÖY)
Tylliria really felt the pinch when it was effectively isolated from the rest of Cyprus following the Turkish invasion in 1974. Since that time, this small Turkish enclave, known in Greek as Kokkina and in Turkish as Erenköy, has been surrounded by Greek Cypriot territory.

KATO PYRGOS ΚΑΤΩ ΠΥΡΓΟΣ

pop 1120

This remote beach resort is as far out of the way as you can get in the Republic, yet it attracts a regular summer clientele of Cypriots who come for its isolation, cheap accommodation and food, and laid-back ambience. Kato Pyrgos is like Cyprus used to be, and many Cypriots come here just to get away from the rampant commercialism that they recognise has overwhelmed the more popular coastal resorts of their island.

The breezy village is strung out along a wide bay running from Kokkina Point to where the Attila Line meets the sea. The border's proximity is emphasised by the frequent chatter of UN helicopters that fly in and out of the nearby base. You can bathe at a number of locations along the bay, though the most popular spot seems to be the far eastern end, close to the Attila Line.

Tylos Beach Hotel (☎ 2652 2348; www.tyloshotel .com.cy; Nikolaou Papageorgiou 40; s/d incl breakfast CY£20/40; 🔀) is a very basic, clean place with no décor to speak of, but with wonderful views of the harbour. The rooms all have TV and balcony.

Not too far away from Tylos Beach Hotel, on the main road of Kato Pyrgos, **Ifigeneia Hotel** (☎ 2652 2218; s/d CY£17/34; 🔀) has decent rooms and an in-house restaurant.

Quite near the Ifigeneia and also on the main Kato Pyrgos road, the rooms at **Pyrgiana Beach** (☎ 2652 2322; fax 2652 2306; s/d CY£15/30; 🔀) have harbour views and TV. There's also a restaurant specialising in fresh fish (meals CY£4 to CY£6) – the owner goes fishing daily on his own little boat.

Kato Pyrgos has a fair sprinkling of restaurants and tavernas. **Klimataria** (meals CY£5), at the far eastern end, right on the beach, has the cosiest feel and the food is pretty reasonable.

STAVROS TIS PSOKAS ΣΤΑΥΡΟΣ ΤΗΣ ΨΟΚΑΣ

From Kato Pyrgos or Pahyammos you can strike out southwards into the Tylliria hinterland. Make sure you detour slightly to the lovely forest reserve of **Stavros tis Psokas**, also accessible from Pafos (51km) via a picturesque road that is unsealed for a considerable distance. This vast picnic site is a forest station responsible for fire control in the Pafos Forest. Nature-loving Cypriots come here to walk and enjoy the peace, and they like it so much that there is quite a little crowd in the summer. In a small enclosure, signposted from the main parking area, you can get a glimpse of the rare and endangered native Cypriot **moufflon** (see the boxed text, below). Move quietly and slowly if you want to see them as they get rather skittish at the approach of humans.

You can do some hiking from the Stavros tis Psokas forest station. The **Horteri Trail**, a 5km, two-hour circular hike, loops around the eastern flank of the Stavros Valley. The

PAFOS & THE WEST

THE MUCH-MALIGNED CYPRIOT MOUFFLON

Featured as a stylised graphic on the tail fin of Cyprus Airways' planes, the Cypriot moufflon (*Ovis orientalis ophion*), known as *agrino* in Greek, is Cyprus' de facto national symbol. The moufflon is similar to a wild sheep and is native to the island of Cyprus. It has close cousins on the islands of Sardinia and Sicily, and in Iran. Today, Cyprus' moufflon population is limited to the dense vegetation of the Pafos Forest Reserve on the west side of the Troödos Massif.

The moufflon was once treated as vermin and was fair game for trigger-happy hunters, and by the 1930s there were only 15 alive in Cyprus. Since then an enlightened preservation programme has seen numbers rise to around 10,000. The moufflon is a shy, retiring animal and is rarely seen in the wild as it will disappear into the forest long before your arrival. The male moufflon sports enormous curved horns and, while not aggressive to humans, uses its horns in mating battles with other males.

While numbers have reached stable levels, the moufflon is still considered an endangered species. The main danger nowadays comes from forest fires and poachers. In Sardinia, an Italian biogenetics team in 2001 successfully cloned a Sardinian moufflon, thus setting a precedent for the preservation of other endangered species.

Moufflons can be seen at the Stavros tis Psokas Forest Reserve where they are kept safe from depredation in a secure enclosure.

trail starts at the Platanoudkia Fountain, about halfway along the forest station's approach road, which begins on the main through-road at Selladi tou Stavrou (Stavros Saddle). The hike involves a fair bit of upward climbing and can get tiring in the heat of summer, so tackle the walk early in the day if you can.

The second trail is the **Selladi tou Stavrou**, a 2.6km circular loop of the northern flank of the Stavros Valley. The start is prominently marked from Stavros Saddle (at the junction of the forest station approach road and the main through-road). A longer option (7km, 2½ hours) is to tackle the trail anticlockwise and then branch south (right) to the heliport. From there you can walk along a forest road to the forest station proper.

The CTO brochure *Cyprus: Nature Trails* describes these trails in more detail.

The Stavros tis Psokas forest station has a **hostel** (☎ 2633 2144; r per person around CY£12) with cool rooms that should be booked for the June–September period. You will need your own car to get here.

KAMPOS ΚΑΜΠΟΣ
pop 430

A truly untouristy village, Kampos is the only significant place of habitation in Tylliria. The scenery is beautiful and the locals will be curious to meet you since they don't get to see that many foreigners in these parts. There is a local guest house should you decide to stay put for the night.

Although technically part of the Kykkos Monastery sector of the Troödos, Kampos is stuck out on the southern edge of the Tyllirian wilderness with – these days – only one road out. The road that leads north from the village now comes to an ignominious end after 12km, at the Attila Line.

However, this part of Tylliria is now less isolated than it was, thanks to the completion of the good sealed road that leads across the Tyllirian hinterland and northern extent of the vast Pafos Forest, linking the Kykkos Monastery with Kato Pyrgos and Pahyammos. Take it slow though; the road, while good, is very winding and tiring to drive. Most maps still show it as unsealed. It is a much shorter, if more challenging, route into the Tyllirian wilderness than the traditional road from the southeast via Polis.

WESTERN TROÖDOS

The sparsely populated area flanking the western foothills of the Troödos Massif is home to few attractions other than slow-moving villages, where traditions hold fast and the local Cypriot dialect is just that bit more impenetrable. If you are looking for a route to central Troödos from the west coast you can now easily follow a mixture of good sealed and unsealed roads into the mountains. The best route takes you to the Kykkos Monastery via the village of Pano Panagia.

Pano Panagia Πάνω Παναγιά
pop 560

If you love Archbishop Makarios and Cypriot history makes your heart go 'boom boom' then the village of Pano Pangia will make you a very happy person. This is the **birthplace of Makarios III**, the island's famous archbishop-president (see the boxed text, p110, for more about his life). There is also the **Makarios Cultural Centre** (admission free; ☽ 9am-1pm & 2-5pm), a place for hard-core fans, containing memorabilia from Makarios' life as a politician and priest, including plenty of photos.

Among the odder exhibits are his priestly vestments, overcoat, dressing gown, shoes and slippers. (If only they tried to sell those on eBay!)

Carrying on in the same vein, the **childhood house of Makarios** (admission free; ☽ 10am-1pm & 2-6pm) is quite a large house, containing more photos and memorabilia from the life of the younger Makarios. If the house is locked, obtain the key from the nearby cultural centre.

If you decide to spend the night close to the memory of Makarios, **Arhondiko tou Meletiou** (☎ 2693 5011; fax 2694 7395; 2–3-person apt CY£20) is right next to the house of Archbishop Makarios. The folksy **Stelios House** (☎ 2672 2343; fax 2672 2971; 2-person apt CY£24) is also lovely, as are the spacious apartments of **Palati tou Xylari** (☎ 9961 4673; palati@cytanet .com.cy; 2-person apt CY£25) and the twin apartments of **Liakoto** (☎ 2623 5597; fax 2624 2025; 2-person apt CY£20). All four places are part of the CTO-sponsored agrotourism scheme and represent good value, high-quality accommodation.

A few simple tavernas on the main street provide adequate food.

Cedar Valley

This is the highlight of the western Troö-dos hinterland. This cool valley is home to a large number of the unusual indigenous Cypriot cedars (*Cedrus brevifolia*), a close cousin of the better-known Lebanese cedar. The valley is approached via a winding, un-sealed forest road from Pano Panagia on the Pafos side of the Troödos Massif, or along a signposted unsealed road from the Kyk-kos side of the Troödos. There is a picnic ground here and the opportunity to hike 2.5km to the summit of **Mt Tripylos**.

You'll need a vehicle to see these places, as public transport is patchy or nonexistent. Alternatively you could join a tour from either Polis or Pafos (see p124). Ask at the CTO office for details.

Larnaka & the East

The Larnaka area is often embedded in the tourist's memory as a blurry landscape seen from the inside of a bus. And perhaps this is why, largely ignored by the package-tourist industry, Larnaka town has preserved a quiet yet scruffy charm and some lovely old crafts. Lazarus, who according to the Bible was raised from the dead by Jesus, came to live in Larnaka and brought Christianity to Cyprus. Prophet Mohammed's aunt fell off her mule here and broke her neck; an important Islamic shrine in her honour was built beside a frosty-looking salt lake close to Larnaka airport. For timeless celebrity value, you have to admit that this is pretty good going.

Many architects could learn about unusual buildings from the round stone houses in the Neolithic settlement of Choirokoitia where Cyprus's earliest inhabitants lived. And perhaps the tourists at Agia Napa could have taught the ancient Romans how to party harder than anyone else, if that were chronologically possible. Outside the perennial party-town, the gorgeous sandy coves of Cape Greco are a peaceful space where it's only you and the sea.

Go inland to the Lefkara villages, north of Choirokoitia, and you'll be swarmed by old ladies selling Cyprus' best-marketed craft, lace, worked and perfected by the village's female (sometimes arthritic) hands. Small, timeless villages in the Kokkinohoria area in the east of the region resemble the Australian outback rather than the eastern Mediterranean.

And, thanks to now-relaxed border policies, crossing to the North in this area is as easy as it gets. But the so-called 'ghost town' of Varosia (Maraş), abandoned by the fleeing Greek Cypriots in 1974 and never resettled, is a reminder of the island's physical division. In contrast is Pyla, a village in the east where Greek and Turkish Cypriots still live together in harmony – a reminder of how things used to be.

HIGHLIGHTS

- Enjoy the relaxed lifestyle of **Larnaka** (p142) and walk around its picturesque streets
- Visit Deryneia and get a glimpse of the ghost town of **Varosia** (Maraş; p167), abandoned since 1974
- Swim at some wonderful beaches around Agia Napa, like **Nissi Beach** (p163), **Konnos Beach** (p170) and the beaches of **Cape Greco** (p166)
- Bargain hard for a piece of handmade **Lefkara lace** (p152)
- Party nonstop at **Agia Napa** (p161), the Mediterranean's second-most popular spot for nightlife after Ibiza, then get sporty on the water at **Protaras & Pernera** (p169)

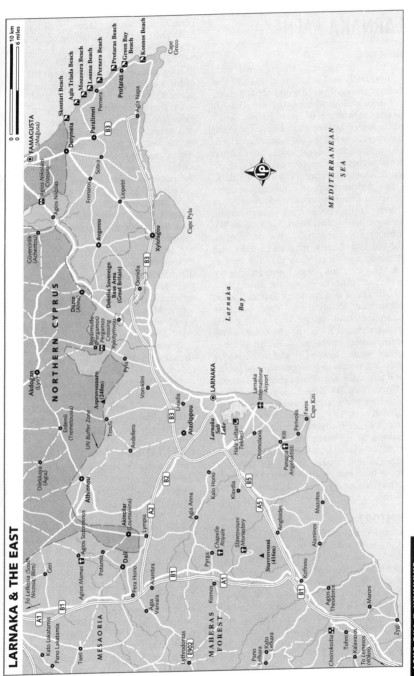

LARNAKA & THE EAST

LARNAKA ΛΑΡΝΑΚΑ

pop 46,700

Larnaka is a rugged, charming town, with a melancholy and seductive character. The main promenade, lined with tall palm trees, is full of cafés and bars; the old Turkish quarter is a maze of quiet streets, small whitewashed houses and ceramics studios; the streets around the old market area have shops with the oldest crafts in Cyprus. Small niches hide ancient men making gigantic church candles. Peep into the dark, shady antique shops, see the ironmongers and pitta-bread makers at work. Nearby, on the city centre's main street, young Larnaka girls get their outfits from chain stores like Zara or Top Shop. So, as the cliché goes, the old and the new meet in Larnaka. But it might be fairer to say that the new is trickling into this sleepy town, and for the most part, it fits in around the old.

Larnaka is also home to Cyprus' largest community of foreigners. Many Lebanese Christians took refuge here during that country's troubles in the 1980s and never went home. In the past, foreign governments tended to use Larnaka as a base for their consulates in preference to the inland and less easily accessible capital of Lefkosia (North Nicosia). Before 1974, the city was also home to a large Turkish Cypriot population that, following the division of the island by their mainland compatriots, was obliged to flee to the North.

Many visitors to this sunny island fly straight to Larnaka. This is the case now more than ever, with visitors to the North preferring to fly here and cross into the North by taxi.

HISTORY

Larnaka was established as a Middle Bronze Age colony sometime between the 14th and the 11th centuries BC. Then known as Kition, the settlement prospered as a port, thanks to the export of copper and other metals mined in the Troödos Massif and Tamassos to the west. The city flourished well into Hellenistic times despite taking the Persian side in the Greek-Persian wars. Kimon of Athens arrived in 450 BC to subdue Kition, but died prematurely outside the city walls. His statue now graces the

Larnaka promenade. Zenon of Kition, the Stoic philosopher and darling of the Athens intelligentsia, was born in Larnaka in 335 BC. His radical philosophies seem not to have pleased Zenon himself at the end of his life; he died by his own hand at the age of 98.

Lazarus brought Christianity to Larnaka and became one of the first bishops of Cyprus. When he died, he was buried in the vault of the church that now carries his name. Little more is known about Kition until the 14th century, when it took the name of Salina because of the nearby salt lake. Larnaka in Greek means 'funerary chest'; it's likely that the city received this name as a result of ancient tombs discovered during its development in the 16th century.

Under the Ottomans' rule, the city was an important port and home to a number of dignitaries. Many of them were emissaries from foreign countries, and a disquieting number were engaged in amateur archaeology. Much of Larnaka's archaeological wealth was secretly sequestered and spirited away during this time.

During the 88 years of British rule, Larnaka gradually fell behind Famagusta (Mağusa) and Lemesos in importance. It only really received a demographic jolt following the influx of refugees from the North in 1974 and the development of its hitherto backwater airfield as the country's prime international airport.

ORIENTATION

Larnaka is a reasonably compact city, and most major sites and facilities are within walking distance of transport terminals and central hotels.

The city centre is encircled by Leoforos Grigoriou Afxentiou to the north, Leoforos Artemidos to the west, Leoforos Faneromenis to the south and Leoforos Athinon to the east. Leoforos Athinon is a landscaped, paved street lined with palm trees, and is usually called the Finikoudes (Palm Trees) Promenade. Within the rectangle formed by these major avenues is the main business and central tourist district. Immediately south of this area and adjoining the seafront is the former Turkish district, the beginning of which is marked by the Grand Mosque and Larnaka Fort.

LARNAKA

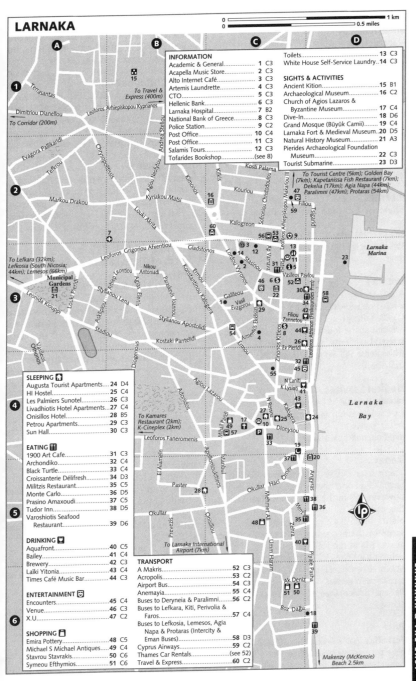

INFORMATION
Bookshops
Academic & General (☎ /fax 2462 8401; Ermou 41) The best place to go for English-language books, stationery and maps.
Tofarides Bookshop (☎ 2465 4912; Zinonos Kitieos 45-47) Located in the city centre, this is another excellent choice with a wide selection of English-language publications.

Emergency
Police station (☎ 2480 4040; cnr Leoforos Grigoriou Afxentiou & Leoforos Arhiepiskopou Makariou III) Easy to find near the yacht marina.

Internet Access
There are a fair number of Internet cafés in town. Try the following:
Alto Internet Café (☎ 2465 9625; Leoforos Grigoriou Afxentiou; per hr CY£4; ☒ 10am-2am) Close to the centre.

Laundry
A full-service wash costs about CY£4, while a self-service wash and dry will cost around CY£2. You can get your clothes washed and pressed at the following:
Artemis Laundrette (Armenikis Ekklisias 12)
White House Self-Service Laundry (Shop 5, Helen Ct, Stasinou)

Medical Services
Larnaka Hospital (☎ 2463 0322; Leoforos Grigoriou Afxentiou) Larnaka's main public hospital is northwest of the city centre.
Night pharmacy assistance (☎ 1414)

Money
There is an ATM and exchange facility at Larnaka airport that is open for all flights; however, it's in the departures area. Within the precinct of the city centre, there are plenty of banks for changing money, and some of them are open afternoons. There are ATMs at the following:
Hellenic Bank (☎ 2450 3000; Zinonos Kitieos) Situated 200m north of the National Bank of Greece, on the opposite side of the road.
National Bank of Greece (☎ 2465 4743; Zinonos Kitieos)

Post
Post office (Plateia Vasileos Pavlou) Close to the CTO office; poste restante mail is held here. There is also a smaller branch close to the church of Agios Lazaros.

Toilets
You'll find signposted public toilets 100m east of the CTO office at the northern end of the city centre.

Tourist Information
Cyprus Tourism Organisation (CTO) airport (☎ 2464 3576; ☒ 8.15am-11pm); Larnaka (☎ 2465 4322; Plateia Vasileos Pavlou; ☒ 8.15am-2.30pm & 3-6.15pm Mon, Tue, Thu & Fri, 8.15am-1.30pm Sat) The city-centre office is two short blocks west of the Sun Hall hotel.

Travel Agencies
Salamis Tours (☎ 2465 6464; fax 2465 0698; Leoforos Grigoriou Afxentiou 7) The Larnaka branch of this travel agency is in central Larnaka. As well as buying cruise tickets to Israel or Egypt, you can take advantage of a wide range of other travel-related services.

SIGHTS & ACTIVITIES
Church of Agios Lazaros & Byzantine Museum
This wonderful **church** (☎ 2465 2498; Agiou Lazarou; admission free; ☒ 8am-12.30pm & 3.30-6.30pm Apr-Aug, 8am-12.30pm & 2.30-5.30pm Sep-Mar), at the southern end of Larnaka, owes its existence to a rather interesting story. Tradition has it that Jesus raised Lazarus from the dead. Immediately after this, Lazarus was expelled from Jerusalem by the Jews and came to Larnaka, where he was ordained as a bishop by St Barnabas. He reportedly remained a bishop for 30 years. After he died (for the second time) he was buried where the current church stands. His relics did not stay entombed for very long after their discovery in 890, as they were transported to Constantinople and subsequently removed to Marseille in 1204.

The church structure itself is a mix of Latinate and Orthodox influences, the most obvious example being the prominent bell tower that is visible from some distance. The church, ransomed from the Ottomans in 1589, was used by Catholic and Orthodox worshippers for some 200 years. This is affirmed by inscriptions in Latin, French and Greek that can be seen in the portico.

The **Tomb of Lazarus**, without Lazarus in it, is under the altar, accessible by stairs to the right. In fact, it comprises just one of several sarcophagi in the catacomb, suggesting that the area was used as a general burial place.

The **Byzantine Museum** (☎ 2465 2498; admission CY£0.50; ☒ 8.30am-1pm & 3-5.30pm Mon, Tue, Thu, Fri & Sun, 8.30am-1pm Wed & Sat) is in the church's courtyard. From 1964 to '74, the museum's original ecclesiastical collection, containing priceless relics and artefacts, was moved and stored in Larnaka Fort, which had come under Turkish administration following the insurgences of the early '60s. In 1974 the administration of the fort reverted once more to the Greeks, but the priceless treasures had apparently disappeared. All that is left of the original collection is in catalogue, and the missing items are still being sought. The present collection was assembled in their place, and it's still a fairly extensive and impressive display of Byzantine ecclesiastical artefacts, icons and church utensils. Many exhibits have been donated by Russian clerics.

Pierides Archaeological Foundation Museum

Dimitris Pierides started his conservation efforts in 1839, as an attempt to salvage artefacts from notorious tomb raiders. Most famous among them was Luigi Palma di Cesnola, Larnaka's first US consul, who spirited away a large number of artefacts, which are now in New York's Metropolitan Museum. The collection was then expanded by Pierides' descendants, resulting in this well-coordinated, bright **museum** (☎ 2465 2495; Zinonos Kitieos 4; admission CY£1; ⏱ 9am-1pm Mon-Sat, 11am-1pm Sun), which is housed in Pierides' old residence, an elegant mansion.

The Pierides Archaeological Foundation Museum, which competes vigorously with the state-operated Archaeological Museum (right) and features artefacts and finds from all over Cyprus, which have detailed explanations in English. There are six rooms in the museum, each arranged chronologically, and the exhibition includes a comprehensive history of Cyprus. The first room, on your left as you enter the building, houses exhibits from the Neolithic period. Here you'll find the famous figure of the **howling man** sitting on a stool, dating back to 5500–5000 BC. The purpose of this statue, found in Souskiou in western Cyprus, is rather ambiguous, although it is evident that water could be poured into his head, which would then come out of his schlong. There is no evidence to suggest whether it was used for religious or secular function.

Room 4 is devoted to a fascinating collection of **Roman glassware**; room 5 is given over to a display of **Cypriot folk art**, with weaving and embroidery, woodcarvings and traditional costumes. The Mycenaean and Achaean periods, the Iron Age, the Roman occupation, through to the later Byzantine, Crusader, Lusignan, Venetian and Ottoman periods are also very well documented.

Archaeological Museum

Larnaka's second significant **museum** (☎ 2463 0169; Kalogreon; admission CY£0.75; ⏱ 9am-2.30pm Mon-Fri, 3-5pm Thu Sep-Jun), this purpose-built place has thorough explanations of the items on display. There is a wide collection of pottery from Ancient Kition and a reconstructed **Neolithic tomb** from Choirokoitia, as well terracotta votive figures, Roman glassware and even folk art. Spread out over five rooms, the collection is worth a browse, although not so much if you have already visited the Cyprus Museum (p63) in Lefkosia.

Larnaka Fort & Medieval Museum

The prominent **fort** (☎ 2463 0576; Leoforos Athinon; admission CY£0.75; ⏱ fort & museum 9am-7pm Mon-Fri) stands at the water's edge separating Finikoudes, Larnaka's promenade, and the old Turkish quarter. Originally a Lusignan-era castle, the present structure is a result of remodelling by the Ottomans from around 1605. It has nice views of the coastal part of town. There is little to see in the castle itself, but the upper floor contains a small Medieval Museum with various displays from Hala Sultan Tekkesi (p150) and Ancient Kition. The open area inside the fort is occasionally used for concerts and other cultural events.

Ancient Kition

Much of present-day Larnaka is built over the original site of **Ancient Kition** (admission CY£0.75; ⏱ 9am-2.30pm Mon-Fri), so no further digging can be done without damaging the city (some work was done by Swedish excavators in the 1920s when the new city didn't extend as far as it does now). It is reported that the British carted off the 'rubble' from the site to fill malarial marshes, and thus regressed this already rather sparse site. What is left of the ancient city is a small site known as **Area II**, a rather nondescript and essentially uninteresting place about 1km northwest of the centre of Larnaka. A raised walkway takes you over what is left of the remains of Ancient Kition, where excavations sporadically continue. Labels or explanations are sparse, so unless you are an archaeologist, the layout may not mean much to you.

Ancient Kition is around 1km northwest of the Archaeological Museum.

Natural History Museum

A small but interesting **collection of exhibits** (☎ 2465 2569; Leoforos Grigoriou Afxentiou; admission CY£0.20; ☺ 10am-1pm & 4-6pm Tue-Sun Jun-Sep, 10am-1pm & 3-5pm Tue-Sun Oct-May) is dedicated primarily to the fauna, flora, geology, insect and marine life of Cyprus. Displayed in a series of eight rooms, the museum is very popular with school groups and is an excellent introduction to the natural history of the island.

This is a wonderful place for children, as there is a little playground, and caged pelicans, flamingos, peacocks and macaws outside the museum, surrounded by a lush garden (part of the Municipal Gardens).

The museum is a little out of the way, off Leoforos Grigoriou Afxentiou at the western edge of town.

Grand Mosque

Standing alone on the periphery of both the former Greek and Turkish quarters of Larnaka is the **Grand Mosque** (Büyük Camii; Agias Faneromenis). Somewhat underused since 1974, the mosque is nonetheless the spiritual home to Larnaka's Muslim community. Built in the 16th century and once called the Latin Holy Cross Church, the current building is the result of 19th-century restoration. The mosque reluctantly accepts visitors, though not during prayer times, and you may also be able to climb the **minaret** for a small fee. The views are quite impressive.

LARNAKA FOR CHILDREN

A little bit overpriced, the **Tourist Submarine** (☎ 2462 2138; www.sadkosub.com; Larnaka Marina; adult/child CY£35/25; ☺ Tue, Thu, Sat May-Jun, plus Wed & Fri Aug) is great fun nevertheless. You and your kids go to the bottom of the Mediterranean to see the shipwreck of the Zenobia – one of the world's top-ten wreck dives. The trips are around one hour long, and start at 9am on the hour every hour, until 12.30pm; the last trip starts at 1.30pm.

TOURS

The **CTO** (☎ 2465 4322; Plateia Vasileos Pavlou; ☺ 8.15am-2.30pm & 3-6.15pm Mon, Tue, Thu & Fri, 8.15am-1.30pm Sat) runs a couple of free, chaperoned walks from its office. This is a painless way to get an introduction to the layout and attractions of Larnaka. 'Larnaka – Its Past & Present' starts at 10am every Wednesday from the CTO; call the CTO office for more information. 'Skala – Its Craftsmen' leaves at 10am every Friday from **Larnaka Fort** (☎ 2463 0576; Leoforos Athinon); call the fort for further information.

FESTIVALS & EVENTS

Most major coastal towns hold an annual **Kataklysmos Festival** in June each year, usually about 50 days after Orthodox Easter, but the festival holds special significance for Larnaka. Kataklysmos means 'deluge' in Greek, and is ostensibly a feast to celebrate the salvation of Noah from the Flood, but is often an excuse for people to throw water at one another and generally have fun. In Larnaka, Finikoudes is given over to a nightly bazaar of stall holders selling snacks and trinkets, interspersed with various concerts. During the day there are water-based activities such as windsurfing and kayak races, as well as swimming competitions.

SLEEPING

Larnaka offers a reasonable range of accommodation, spread out quite evenly across its downtown area, as well as in the hotel stretch northeast of the town centre. A popular sleeping option is a self-contained apartment, which is excellent value if there are at least two of you.

Budget & Midrange

There is only one budget option in Larnaka, as the accommodation scene is pitched firmly at the midrange (family) apartment group and the top-end resort-hotel scene. The best midrange options are self-contained hotel apartments where you can cook for yourself, but usually a minimum stay of two days is required. Advance bookings are always a good idea.

Petrou Apartments (☎ 2465 0600; www.petrou .com.cy; Armenikis Ekklisias 1; 2-person apt CY£30; P ☒) A bright and modern building in the centre, close to the beach and with handy car parking at the rear. The apartments are simple and pleasantly furnished, with phones and TVs; the bathrooms are squeaky clean; and the kitchens have two hotplates for cooking, plus lots of pots and pans. A vending machine by the lift spouts chocolate bars for late-night sugar-fixes.

Les Palmiers Sunotel (☎ 2462 7200; fax 2462 7204; Leoforos Athinon 12; s/d CY£21.50/38) The small, shabby reception is like the rooms, decorated in browns and creams, and the price is a little over-ambitious. A blinding neon light buzzes above your head in the bathroom and the paint on the ceiling hangs in strips. The lamps are bare bulbs, but there is a safe, TV and phone. A good option if nothing else is available. Discounts of 20% may be available in the low season.

Onisillos Hotel (☎ 2465 1100; www.onisillos.com.cy; Onisillou 17; s/d CY£25/34; 🖵) A retro palace, with fake-leather sofas and old Pac-Man game tables, about 500m west of the fort in a very quiet part of town. The rooms are clean and neat, but equally old-fashioned. There is a roof terrace, gym and games room. The rooms come with bathroom, air-con and phone.

HI Hostel (☎ 2462 1188; Nikolaou Rossou 27; dm/family r CY£3/5) The only budget place in Larnaka is hidden in an old hammam – a beautiful building, if a little decrepit. The mixed or single-sex dorms are luminous and pleasant, and there is a little shared kitchen, plus communal showers and toilets. HI cards are not required and there is no discount for holders. East of Agios Lazaros church.

Two other apartment complexes worth checking out are the following:

Augusta Tourist Apartments (☎ 2465 1802; Leoforos Athinon 102; 2-person apt CY£22) Homy apartments here have two balconies with sea views, double bedrooms and neat, small kitchens. Air-con is an extra CY£2.50. It's located right on Leoforos Athinon (Finikoudes).

Livadhiotis Hotel Apartments (☎ 2462 6222; livadhiotishotapts@cytanet.com.cy; Nikolaou Rossou 50; 2-person studio CY£22) Similar to the Augusta but operating more like a hotel, this place has self-contained studios with kitchenette, phone and TV.

Top End

Golden Bay (☎ 2464 5444; www.lordos.com.cy/the goldenbay; d CY£140; 🖳) Larnaka's only five-star giant, on the long and hotel-laden road to Dekelia. The Golden Bay has all the amazing things you would expect from a top-end establishment: loungy halls, elegant corridors,

spacious, bright and comfortable rooms. There's a large pool, a gym, a beauty salon and a stylish restaurant.

Sun Hall (☎ 2465 3341; fax 2465 2717; Leoforos Athinon 6; r CY£62.50-82) A less flashy place, in central Larnaka, which has good rooms with balconies that look over the main promenade. It has earned some high praise from travellers. This four-star hotel offers a 25% off-season discount.

EATING

Larnaka has a diverse and interesting food scene, starting from basic kebab houses to plush fish restaurants. Most places recommended here are in the city itself, with one or two exceptions. They usually open in the evenings only (after 7pm), unless indicated otherwise.

Varoshiotis Seafood Restaurant (☎ 2465 5865; Piyale Pasha 7; fish dishes CY£7-10; 🕙 noon-midnight) Presentation and taste go hand in hand at this chic place on the city's waterfront. Prince's prawns are laid out like orange slices on a bed of wild and white rice, a swirl of soy sauce surrounds a radish and, with a glass of chilled white wine, your palate is headed for a great night out. And that's just the starter.

1900 Art Cafe (☎ 2462 3730; Stasinou 6; mains CY£4; 🕙 9am-2pm & 6pm-midnight Wed-Mon) A Montmartre restaurant-café in the middle of Larnaka: strange but true. A wonderfully atmospheric place on two floors, with art-exhibition posters and paintings covering the walls. If you like reading on the toilet, this place is definitely for you, as there are books on all sorts of subjects. The Art Café opens for breakfast, morning coffee and early lunch, and the doors of the old house are opened again for dinner, when vegetarian and meat dishes are served.

Militzis Restaurant (☎ 2465 5867; Piyale Pasha 42; mains CY£4-6; 🕙 lunch & dinner) This place is really popular with both tourists and locals for Cypriot food. Traditional oven-cooked dishes are good here, such as the delicious *kleftiko* (oven-baked lamb) and *tava* (lamb and beef casserole).

Black Turtle (☎ 2465 0661; Mehmet Ali 11; meze CY£6.50-8; 🕙 dinner) A great quirky little meze taverna featuring live music on Wednesdays, Fridays and Saturdays, when only *mezedes* are served and guests go wild and dance a lot. Don't be put off by the turtle shells on the wall; the owner is really a turtle-lover.

LARNAKA &

Kamares Restaurant (☎ 2436 4400; Hrysoupoleos 24a; mains CY£5-6; ☽ dinner) Few tourists come this far out of town but it's worth the effort, as the quality of the food is excellent. The restaurant faces the impressive Kamares aqueduct, which is romantically floodlit at night. Try *karaolia* (land snails) or *kouloumbra* (kohlrabi cabbage) for a taste of something special. There is live music on Friday and Saturday. Take a cab to get there, and direct your driver towards the nearby K-Cineplex cinema complex (opposite).

Kapetanissa Fish Restaurant (☎ 2464 4254; mains CY£3-6; ☽ dinner) Great, simple food, freshly cooked. This modest place, famous for its tasty fish and unique one-person fish meze, is on the Dekelia road, close to the Palm Beach Hotel.

Tudor Inn (☎ 2462 5608; Lala Mustapha Pasha 28a; steaks CY£11; ☽ lunch & dinner) Missing England? An English country pub, with climbing ivy and all. A Guinness sign beckons knowingly. You can get a steak here for a mighty CY£11, or a vegetarian plate for CY£5.50. The only drawback is that it's closed during August.

Prasino Amaxoudi (☎ 2462 2939; Agias Faneromenis; mains CY£2-3; ☽ noon-10pm) If you like a no-frills good kebab, this is the top place in Larnaka. It looks like kiosk, with a bottle of lemon juice on a plastic tablecloth, and a fridge with drinks where you help yourself. The supertasty grilled haloumi (helimi) in hot pitta has salad erupting from the middle. The tender chicken kebabs are equally scrumptious. It's just by the Grand Mosque in the old Turkish quarter.

Monte Carlo (☎ 2465 3815; Piyale Pasha 28; meat/fish mezedes CY£6.50-8; ☽ lunch & dinner) Situated right on the water's edge, Monte Carlo is a great place to dine in peace and watch the sea. Set menus are a good choice at CY£5.80.

Croissanterie Délifresh (Leoforos Athinon; breakfast from CY£1.70; ☽ 9am-11pm) Although most places along the promenade are very similar (and easily confused), this place is good for the choice of sandwiches and cakes on offer.

DRINKING

Larnaka's drinking scene is plentiful. Finikoudes is lined with bars and cafés from top to bottom. The streets surrounding it hide another few cafés, *kafeneia* (coffee shops) and bars; most are open all day until late.

Times Café Music Bar (☎ 2462 5966; Leoforos Athinon 73) A relaxed, stylish bar with sofas, great for lounging about on a hot summer's night. It's next to Encounters nightclub, with live jazz on Sundays and rock on Wednesdays.

Bailey (☎ 2462 1000; Leoforos Athinon 36) An Irish pub seems inevitable nowadays, wherever you go. And the Bailey's inevitability is increased by its size and popularity. It's decorated so well (or so Irish) that you may forget what country you're in after a few bevvies. There's plenty to wet your whiskers: draught beer, ale, Guinness, booze and more booze.

Aquafront (☎ 2462 5904; Piyale Pasha 54; ☽ 6pm-late) A large veranda with iron chairs and velvety sofas, surrounded by flowers. It's a quieter drinking spot for cocktails than those on the promenade, and it serves food too. The sea is right in front of you, and things don't get much better than a nice drink in the evening breeze. Cocktails are around CY£3, and there's a barbecue night every Wednesday (during the summer, that is).

Brewery (☎ 7777 2444; Leoforos Athinon 77) Not another Irish pub, don't worry. This place is like a temple to beer, with specialist samples, and beer pumps brought to your table so you can pull your own pint. Everybody loves it.

ENTERTAINMENT

If you want all-night decadence, get out of Larnaka. More specifically, go to Agia Napa (p165). Here, it's still all-night, but they go easy on the decadence. Tourists make their own fun in the long strip 8km northeast of the city, while locals and city-oriented travellers hang out along the promenade and the little streets inland from the sea.

Nightclubs

There are several good clubs in the city and, of course, regular beach parties are held at various points along the long Larnaka Bay during summer. Watch out for leaflets advertising when and where.

Encounters (☎ 9963 8986; Leoforos Athinon 76) This is the best place in town for a dance-till-you-drop night out. Once known as Memphis, Encounters has now multiplied and is two places in one: Topaz, on the 1st floor with banging progressive house; and Club Deep, on the second floor, with mainstream, chart, R & B, hip-hop, you name it. The dance floor is on fire when guest DJs from Cyprus and abroad are in town.

X.U. (☎ 9943 7222; Filiou Tsigaridi 2-4) What does X.U. stand for? No idea, but a bit of mystery is always a good thing. Not that this place needs it; it's hip and popular enough as it is. A massive aquarium has techno-loving fish blowing bubbles over the central bar, surrounded by sofas and gentle lighting. DJs from London come and let their tunes loose on a house, hip-hop and R & B dancing crowd.

Corridor (☎ 9967 6134; Karaoli & Dimitriou 8) This spot is pitched at a local Greek clientele, with Greek pop music and dancers, plus some UK dance tunes thrown in for good measure. It's usually closed in high summer.

Venue (☎ 9961 7262; Thermopylon 8) Usually caters for special events or parties, and features house, Greek and Euro pop with an overlay of UK dance.

Cinemas

The smaller cinemas have mostly been overshadowed by the cine-giant, K-Cineplex, which is so packed with activities that you may never return home. All foreign-language films are subtitled into Greek. Admission normally costs around CY£3 to CY£4 per person.

K-Cineplex (☎ box office 2481 9022, cinema 2436 2167; www.kcineplex.com; Peloponisou 1; ☉ box office 8.30am-5.30pm Mon-Fri) Featuring six screens, stereo surround sound, supercomfortable reclining seats and Hollywood blockbusters. There's a bowling alley, Irish pub and a restaurant within the complex. It's a five- to 10- minute taxi ride to the west of the city centre near the Kamares aqueduct.

SHOPPING

Michael S Michael Antiques (☎ 2465 2358; Mihail Paridi 14) This place is a real treat. It's like delving into the town's history through the dusty antiques, old glassware, jewellery and ornaments. The cool, cavernous shop is owned and run by Michalis (Mr Michael), who will give you the lowdown on each item's past. Check out the charming glass paintings by a local artist, which include portraits and depict the circle of life, and lost love. A hurricane lamp (CY£3 to CY£4) makes an excellent souvenir.

Larnaka is good for one thing in particular: pottery. Good quality ceramics are produced in small workshops, most of which are based around Ak Deniz in the old Turkish quarter. Take your time and explore the various styles and prices before you choose. The potters will always give a small gift when you

buy a few things. Check out **Stavrou Stavrakis** (☎ 2462 4491; Ak Deniz 8) with ancient motifs on plates and pots, as well as **Symeou Efthymios** (☎ 2465 0338; Ak Deniz 18) with similar crafts, but with the potter's own touch. **Emira Pottery** (☎ 2462 3952; Mehmet Ali 13) is popular and well signposted, but has less of a workshop and more of a shop feel.

GETTING THERE & AWAY
Air

Larnaka international airport is 7km from the city centre. Most flights to Cyprus arrive and depart from here. There are a couple of offices for **Cyprus Airways** (www.cyprusairways.com; airport ☎ 2464 3313; city centre ☎ 2462 6666; Leoforos Arhiepiskopou Makariou III 21; flight information ☎ 2464 3000).

Boat

Larnaka has an excellent private **marina** (☎ 2465 3110; larnaka.marina@cytanet.com.cy) offering a wide range of berthing facilities for up to 450 yachts. These include telephone, fax and telex services, repair facilities, laundry, showers, lockers, post boxes and a mini-market and provisions store. The marina is an official port of entry into Cyprus.

Bus

Buses to and from Deryneia and Paralimni arrive at and depart from the bus stop opposite the police station.

The stop for **Inter City** (☎ 2464 3492; www.intercitybuses.com) buses to Lefkosia (CY£2.50, one hour, six buses daily, four on Saturday, none on Sunday), Lemesos (CY£1.70, one hour, four buses daily, three on Saturday, none on Sunday), Agia Napa and Protaras (CY£2, five buses daily, none on Sunday), and **Eman Buses** (☎ 2372 1321) to Agia Napa (CY£2.50, 45 minutes, nine buses Monday to Saturday, four buses on Sunday) is almost opposite Croissanterie Délifresh on Finikoudes.

Buses for Lefkara (CY£0.95, one bus daily Monday to Saturday), Kiti (CY£0.50, 12 buses Monday to Saturday), Perivolia and Faros (CY£0.50, three to six buses daily Monday to Saturday) all leave from Plateia Agiou Lazarou, near Agios Lazaros church.

Taxis & Service Taxis

Travel & Express (☎ 2466 1010; cnr Papakyriakou & Marsellou) runs service taxis to major destinations. A trip to Lemesos will cost you CY£4 (one hour), to Lefkosia CY£3.50 (one hour) and to Agia Napa CY£3.50 (45 minutes). There's a second office at Kimonos 2.

A couple of smaller outfits still operate. **Acropolis** (☎ 2465 5555; Leoforos Arhiepiskopou Makariou III) is located opposite the police station, and **A Makris** (☎ 2465 2929) is on the north side of the Sun Hall hotel. Rates are CY£2.60 to Lefkosia and CY£3.10 to Lemesos.

Regular taxis will take you wherever you want. It will cost around CY£5 to get to the airport, CY£12 to Lefkosia, CY£16 to Lemesos and CY£30 to Troödos.

GETTING AROUND
To/From the Airport
Buses 22 and 24 from Ermou and Plateia Palion Finikoundon go to the airport (CY£0.50, 30 minutes). The first bus is at 6.20am and the last one is at 7pm in summer (5.30pm in winter). A private taxi costs around CY£5.

Bicycle
Bicycles can be hired at **Anemayia** (☎ 2465 8333, 2464 5619, 9962 4726; per day CY£4-6), which has its office on the Larnaka–Dekelia road. Call for free delivery, which is promised within 10 minutes.

Bus
Inter City buses run every 30 minutes from the north side of the Sun Hall hotel to the tourist-hotel area on the road to Agia Napa (CY£2 one way, CY£3.50 return).

Car & Motorcycle
Thames Car Rentals (☎ 2465 6333) is next door to A Makris. There are also several car-rental booths at the airport. You can hire motorcycles or mopeds from **Anemayia** (☎ 2465 8333, 2464 5619, 9962 4726; 3hr hire CY£5) on the Larnaka–Dekelia road; ring for free delivery.

AROUND LARNAKA

The sights in the west of the Larnaka region can also easily be visited as day trips from Lemesos or even Lefkosia. Limited public transport does not make it easy to get around, so once again you'll have to rely on your own wheels or inventiveness.

Getting Around
Other than buses 6 and 7, which take you from Larnaka to both the Hala Sultan Tekkesi

and Kiti, transport options for the other sights are thin on the ground. Taking a bus to Lefkara requires an overnight stay there. Your own transport is really your only choice. Even hitching (always a touch-and-go option) is tricky; much of the travelling involves getting on and off at different motorway exits. See p242 for details.

BEACHES
Larnaka's beaches are generally unattractive, especially when compared to those towards Agia Napa and the east. The sand is grey and often hard-packed, but this doesn't stop hundreds of people lounging on deck chairs and swimming in the (shallow) waters. The best beach is **Makenzy (McKenzie) Beach**, 2.5km south of Larnaka. The beach and water along the Finikoudes promenade is quite clean, and the water is shallow and falls away gently, making it ideal for children. There is also the CTO municipal beach on the Dekelia road, favoured by the locals, and backed by dozens of taverns and restaurants.

To the southwest, the minor resorts of **Cape Kiti** and **Perivolia** offer pebbly, narrow and exposed beaches. **Zygi**, a village further west from Cape Kiti, has some of the area's best fish taverns. One particularly yummy option is **Santa Elena** (☎ 2433 2203; fish meze CY£10), on a cobbled street next to the village church. The fish meze is six different types of fresh fish and a big salad; the desserts are all homemade. Sometimes, the ladies may get a bouquet from the owner's rose farm.

HALA SULTAN TEKKESI
Possibly one of the first things you will see on your way from the airport, this most important of Islamic pilgrimage sites in Cyprus looks like an oasis next to the snowy mirage of the adjacent dry salt like. Surrounded by date palms, cypress and olive trees, this **mosque** (admission free, donation expected; ☾ 9am-7.30pm May-Sep, 9am-5pm Oct-Apr) was founded in 674 when Umm Haram, the reputed aunt of Prophet Mohammed, fell from a mule, broke her neck and died. She was buried on the site of the current *tekke* (Muslim shrine), and her tomb and subsequent mosque have become important places of worship for Muslims Hala Sultan means 'Great Mother' in Turkish and refers to Umm Haram.

A rather bored-looking curator gives visitors a quick tour and historical spiel, and takes them over to the tomb and sarcophagus of Hala Sultan herself. The interior is maintained as a working mosque with a layer of prayer mats covering the floor, so remove your shoes before entering.

Local bus 6 drops you off at the approach road to the site; from there it's a 1km walk. Catch the bus from the bus stop on Plateia Agiou Lazarou, near Agios Lazaros church.

LARNAKA SALT LAKE

Shimmering like an ice-skating rink in the height of the summer heat, and housing flamingos and migratory birds in autumn, is Larnaka's salt lake. The lake fills with winter rains and slowly dries up as summer approaches, leaving a thin film of salt. There was salt mining here in the Middle Ages, but pollution from aircraft exhaust in modern times has rendered the salt commercially useless. Signs warn would-be adventure-drivers in 4WDs to keep off, and walkers are not encouraged as the sticky salt-encrusted mud can easily ensnare vehicles and walkers. The lake is right next to Hala Sultan Tekkesi; take the same bus 6 to get here.

KITI ΚΟΙΤΗ
pop 3140

In Kiti village, 7km southwest of Larnaka, you will find the domed, cruciform 11th-century church of **Panagia Angeloktisti** (admission free, donations welcome; ☾ 9.30am-noon & 2-4pm Mon-Sat summer). Literally meaning 'built by angels', the church's highlight is the wonderful 6th-century **mosaic of the Virgin Mary**, standing on a jewelled pedestal with a doll-like baby Jesus in her arms, surrounded by the archangels Gabriel and Michael. This church is a reincarnation of an earlier structure from the 5th century (of which only the apse remains), now incorporated into the current building. The mosaics, which have survived from the original apse, were only discovered in 1952.

The church is a place of worship, so time your visit to avoid a service (unless you choose to participate, which you're free to do). On Sunday, it's open for regular services. Buses 6 and 7 from Larnaka run hourly to and from Kiti.

CHAPELLE ROYALE

This unassuming little church is just off the Lefkosia–Lemesos motorway (A1), close to the village of Pyrga. **Chapelle Royale** (Royal Chapel; admission CY£0.75; ☾ dawn-dusk) is a small Lusignan shrine dedicated to Agia Ekaterini (St Catherine). Established by the Latin king Janus in 1421 (the last of Cyprus' crusader kings), it has interesting French-influenced **wall frescoes**, not all of which are in good condition. There's a funny, rather incomprehensible guide, who points out the paintings of The Last Supper, The Raising of Lazarus, The Washing of Christ's Feet and The Ascension. Note that the inscriptions are in French, not Greek, as this was the official language of Lusignan Cyprus.

The church is best combined with a visit to Stavrovouni Monastery (below) and Lefkara (p152).

Closer to Larnaka, on the Larnaka–Pyrga road, is the pretty village of **Agia Anna**, worth visiting for its pure charm. It has a village tavern and some beautiful stone houses.

STAVROVOUNI MONASTERY
ΜΟΝΗ ΣΤΑΥΡΟΒΟΥΝΙΟΥ

Impressive **Stavrovouni Monastery** (☾ 8am-noon & 3-6pm Apr-Aug, 8am-noon & 2-5pm Sep-Mar), high up in the hills (668m), is the oldest monastery in Cyprus. Legend tells that in AD 327 St Helena, mother of Emperor Constantine the Great, brought a fragment of the Holy Cross here on her way back from Jerusalem. She then erected the cross and founded the monastery (the name means 'cross mountain'). A small piece of St Helena's cross is now preserved in a silver one inside the church.

It's ironic that, since the monastery was founded by a woman, women are not allowed inside. If you're female, save yourself the effort, unless you go for the superb views over the Mesaoria and the Troödos Massif (worth the windy trip uphill).

Colin Thubron documented his stay in the monastery during his trek around Cyprus in 1972 in Journey into Cyprus; he described it as a 'lodestar for pilgrims in the wake of the Crusades'. Stavrovouni is a working religious community consisting of a few young monks who live to follow their ascetic principles. If you visit (and are male), arrive during visiting hours only. Leave your camera behind as photos are not allowed. If you are a genuine or professed pilgrim you may even be invited to stay.

The monastery is located above the Lefkosia–Lemesos motorway (A1), around 11km from Larnaka.

LARNAKA & THE EAST

CHOIROKOITIA

Archaeology buffs and early-history lovers should visit the fascinating Neolithic site of **Choirokoitia** (☎ 2432 2710; admission CY£0.75; ☺ 9am-7.30pm Mon-Fri, 9am-5pm Sat & Sun May-Sep, 9am-5pm daily Oct-Apr), 32km southwest of Larnaka. It's best combined with a day trip to either Lemesos (p82) or Lefkara (below). Dating from around 6800 BC, this Unesco World Heritage site is one of the earliest permanent human settlements in Cyprus. The Choirokoitians lived in round stone huts and practised a relatively sophisticated lifestyle for the time. It's thought they came from Anatolia or the coast of present-day Lebanon. The original settlement was built on an easily defensible hillside, with a large perimeter wall. Inside the wall, around 60 houses have been found, identified by the remains of their circular walls. Reconstructions of the houses have been built at the foot of the hill; they look a bit out of place, but it's worth seeing them as it's difficult to imagine the buildings from their scant remains.

Visitors view the various sections of the site via steps and a series of walkways that overlook the key points of the settlement. Signs give a clear description of the main features of each area, and the walkway finishes at the top of the hill, where the best remains are to be found.

There is ample parking and a snack bar with refreshments. The site is just off the main Larnaka–Lemesos highway.

LEFKARA ΛΕΥΚΑΡΑ

pop 1040

The island's best-known export (except for haloumi cheese, of course) is exquisite lace, which mostly comes from the pretty mountain villages of **Pano Lefkara** and **Kato Lefkara**. The story goes that the women of medieval Lefkara took up lace-making to boost family incomes while the men were away working at sea or on the plains. Enterprising stay-at-home husbands made silverware. Leonardo da Vinci is said to have taken some lace back to Italy; travellers and lace-lovers the world over have being doing the same ever since.

However, this lovely village has capitalised on its lacy fame in a major way, becoming a tourist trap with a vengeance. As you enter on foot, 'STOP AND WATCH' signs blare at you from all corners, as do the lace-makers, busily producing a hand-made original as they try to ply you with one from their shop. The exquisite lace is of high quality, but expensive, so bargain hard if you want a particular piece, or try the nearby villages. Bear in mind that the lace displayed outside the shops is not the good, handmade stuff. You'll only find this inside the shop, away from the sun and dust. A hotelier from Lefkara told us of a shop owner outside the village who encourages people into his shop by telling them that the village has 'closed' or 'moved' or that there is no other shop in Lefkara. So, be warned (and ignore him).

Despite all this, Lefkara is beautiful. Its windy streets are full of character and smell of summer flowers. There are two decent places to stay and eat, and interesting sights. There's a Hellenic Bank ATM in the village.

The wonderful Lefkara **Museum of Traditional Embroidery & Silver-Smithing** (☎ 2434 2326; admission CY£0.75; ☺ 9.30am-4pm Mon-Thu, 10am-4pm Fri & Sat) is in the former house of one of Lefkara's richest families. Set out on two floors, it displays a typical village living room (on the ground floor), with cooking utensils, a workshop and a dining area, and in the corner of the room is what can only be interpreted as a 'poor man's stereo': a bird cage, where a canary once sang. The 1st floor is a grandiose hall and living space, which must be closer to how the original house was furnished. Note the old family photos framed in silk lace.

The village's second museum is the very strange **Fatsa Wax Museum** (☎ 2462 1048; Georgiou Papandreou; admission adult/under 12 CY£5/2.50; ☺ 9am-5pm Nov-Apr, 9am-7pm May-Oct). This extortionately priced museum is hilariously touted as 'Cyprus' answer to Madame Tussauds' (which is how the admission price is justified). Amusing wax figures illustrate a Greek Cypriot propagandist's view of the island's history, with bad sound effects and all.

The best place to stay is the newly reopened **Lefkarama Village Hotel** (☎ 2434 2154; www.lefkarama.com; r CY£25). It was traditionally used as an inn, which is evident from its structure: a courtyard in the centre, where a weary traveller can rest and eat; and the rooms above, on the 1st floor. The rooms, decorated in cooling blues, have wrought-iron beds and good new bathrooms. The downstairs restaurant has traditional and international food.

(Continued on page 161)

PAUL DAVID HELLANDER

Cobbled street, Pera (p78), near Lefkosia (South Nicosia)

PAUL DAVID HELLANDER

Statue of Archbishop Makarios III
(p66), Lefkosia (South Nicosia)

Painted gourd souvenirs, Kakopetria (p111), Troödos Massif

STELLA HELLANDER

Buffavento Castle (p196), near Kyrenia

Traditional gravestone,
Kolossi Castle (p96)

Streetlife, Lemesos (p82)

Facing page: Petra tou Romiou
(Aphrodite's Rock & Beach; p93), near Lemesos

Saranta Kolones Fortress (p122), Pafos

Sanctuary of Apollon Ylatis (p96), near Lemesos

Kykkos Monastery (p110), Troödos Massif

Pedoulas (p108), Troödos Massif

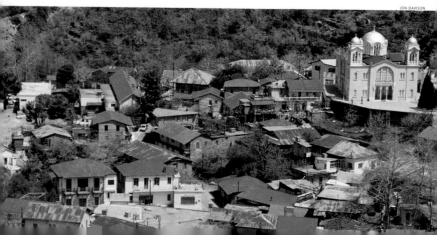

PAUL DAVID HELLANDER

Artemis Trail (p101), Troödos Massif

CHRIS CHRISTO

Fishing boat, Agios Georgios
Beach (p131), near Pafos

Hala Sultan Tekkesi (p150), near Larnaka

PAUL DAVID HELLANDER

Sign at the home of Lawrence Durrell (p194),
Bellapais (Beylerbeyi), near Kyrenia (Girne)

PAUL DAVID HELLANDER

CHRISTINA DAMEYER

Local sweets (p47)

Woman making lace, Lefkara (p152), near Larnaka

ADINA TOVY AMSEL

159

Fountain in the courtyard of the Monastery of Agia Napa (p163), near Larnaka

Mosaic, Basilica of Agia Triada (p217), Karpas (Kırpaşa) Peninsula

Old Harbour, Kyrenia (Girne; p185)

Necropolis of Salamis (Royal Tombs; p213),
near Famagusta (Mağusa)

PAUL DAVID HELLANDER

PAUL DAVID HELLANDER

Interior arcade, Bedesten (p176),
North Nicosia (Lefkoşa)

Kantara Castle (p216), Karpas (Kırpaşa) Peninsula

PAUL DAVID

(Continued from page 152)

But if you really want to eat well, and assuming you've arrived by car, go to **Platanos** (☎ 2434 2160; Kato Drys; mains CY£3-5) in the village of Kato Drys, about 10 minutes' drive from Lefkara. Excellent food is served in a sprawling, cool garden, shaded by a plane tree. Ravish a starter of new potatoes and capers, or dip into tahini and tzatziki. Sample the meatballs with herbs and spices as a main, or an aubergine and courgette bake. For dessert, try the traditional preserved apple and watermelon, with a turbo-strong Cypriot coffee.

Get to Lefkara by a fast road from the Lefkosia–Lemesos motorway (A1), or by a winding and picturesque road from Choirokoitia via Vavla. There's only one daily bus (CY£0.95, Monday to Saturday) between Lefkara and Larnaka. It leaves Lefkara at 7am and returns from Larnaka at 1pm.

AGIA NAPA ΑΓΙΑ ΝΑΠΑ

pop 2680

Ask Cypriots about Agia Napa and they'll all tell you the same thing: 'Before 1974, this was a tiny fishing village, with two houses, a monastery and some fishermen. Look at it now!' Look at it now, indeed. The village started its new life as a tourist resort after the 1974 division, when Famagusta's Varosia (Maraş) beach strip and resort were locked behind barbed wire and oil barrels. Now infamous as the debauched tourist's heaven, Agia Napa shoulders the mantle of Cyprus' top sun-and-fun tourist resort. An entire little town has been made for (package) tourists, and a lot of it is, frankly, horrific. There are bars that look like dodgy sandcastles, and the Flintstones' cave bar that greets you with (if you cringe easily, look away now) a 'Yabba Napa Doo!'. There are pubs with names like the, ahem, 'Organ Grinder'. Tourists wander about in bikinis, sleep their hangovers off on the beach, and go at it again at night. But such is life in Agia Napa, and there are plenty who love it and large it.

If you arrive in high season (mid-July to mid-August), it will be hard to find accommodation. While hoteliers are more used to package-tour visitors, most places will cater for individuals if a room is available.

ORIENTATION

Like washing hung out to dry, Agia Napa is strung out from east to west along the shoreline. Leoforos Nisiou is the main east–west street; arrivals from Larnaka often enter along here. Running north–south at the eastern end of Nisiou is the other main artery, Leoforos Arhiepiskopou Makariou III. Heading east is Leoforos Kryou Nerou. Agia Napa's main focus is Plateia Seferi, known universally as 'the Square'. Several of the streets leading off the Square are pedestrianised. Buses arrive at the southern end of Leoforos Arhiepiskopou Makariou III, near the harbour. Long-distance service taxis arrive and depart near the Square.

INFORMATION

Agia Napa is exceptionally well equipped with banks, ATMs and exchange offices that are open at all hours of the day. ATMs are provided by the **Hellenic Bank** (Leoforos Arhiepiskopou Makariou III) with another branch just south of the Square. There is also a Bank of Cyprus ATM near the harbour.

The police station is north of the Square at the junction of the Larnaka–Protaras ring road and Dimokratias. There are a few laundries fairly close to the town centre.

After-hours pharmacy information (☎ 192)

Agia Napa Clinic (☎ 2372 3222) Also known as the Olympic Napa. Another option for medical care.

Blue Line Laundry (Yuri Gagarin; ☿ 8am-7pm Mon-Sat) Located 600m southwest of the Square. This is a service laundry where you drop your gear off and pick it up 24 hours later.

CTO (☎ 2372 1796; Leoforos Kryou Nerou 12; ☿ 8.15am-2.30pm & 3-6.30pm Mon, Tue, Thu & Fri, 8.15am-2.30pm Wed & Sat) About 200m southeast of the Square.

Elias Travel (☎ 2372 5070; eliastravel@cytanet.com.cy; Eleftherias) A reputable travel agency next to the Square.

IntenCity (☎ 2372 2233; www.intencity.net; Dionysiou Solomou; per hr CY£2.20; ☿ 10am-2am) The easiest Internet café to find; a large, modern, air-conditioned place with 26 terminals.

Paralimni Hospital (☎ 2382 1211; Paralimni) The nearest hospital is about a 15-minute taxi ride away, in Paralimni.

Post office (D Liperti) About 100m east of the Square.

Public telephones (Leoforos Arhiepiskopou Makariou III) Conveniently positioned next to the long-distance service-taxi stand 100m south of the Square.

Wash & Dry Laundrette (Odyssea Elyti 23; wash & dry CY£1; ☿ 8am-7pm Mon-Sat) Located 500m west of the Square, this is a do-it-yourself place.

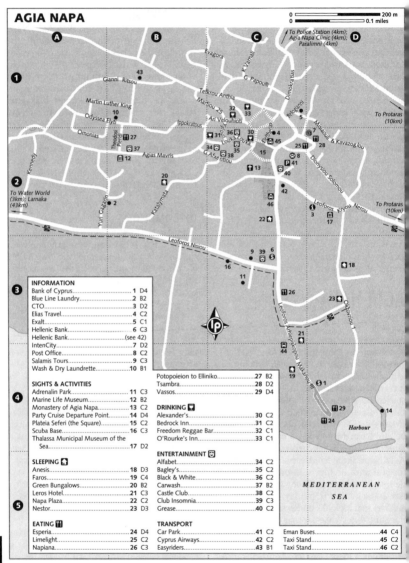

AGIA NAPA

SIGHTS & ACTIVITIES

Thalassa Municipal Museum of the Sea

This very swanky new **museum** (☎ 2381 6366; Leoforos Kryou Nerou 14; admission CY£1.50; ⊙ 9am-1pm & 6-10pm Wed-Sun, 6-10pm Tue, closed Mon May-Oct, 9am-5pm Wed-Sun, 1-5pm Tue, closed Mon Nov-Apr) is dedicated to all things to do with the sea (*thalassa* means 'sea' in Greek). The museum's centre-piece is the amazing reconstruction of a boat that was shipwrecked off the coast of Kyrenia in the 3rd century BC; its original skeleton is displayed in Kyrenia Castle (p187).

The ship was reconstructed using traditional materials and methods. Behind it there is a large video projection of divers supposedly discovering the wreck in 1967.

The museum also has a stylish café, where you can have a quiet coffee, food or drink.

Napa Bungee

What Agia Napa lacks in culture it certainly makes up for in sheer exhilarating, gut-wrenching thrills and spills. For those with faux-suicidal tendencies, head to **Napa Bungee** (☎ 9960 5248; Neofitou Poullou; CY£40-45 for jumping, photo & DVD, plus free drink; ⊗ 10am-6pm May-Sep), where you can hurl yourself from 200ft, alone or in tandem, above the deep blue sea. The staff here are friendly and promise not to push if you get cold feet.

Fast Boat Safari

The high-speed, ex–Formula 3 offshore power boat of **Fast Boast Safari** (☎ 9977 6633; Leoforos Arhiepiskopou Makariou III 39; adult/child 1hr CY£14/£7, 2hr CY£16/£9; ⊗ noon & 3.30pm) takes you around the fascinating sea caves and the harbour. You do get to see the sights, but the speedy boat, which can travel at over 60mph, is the real adventure.

Marine Life Museum

This small private **museum** (☎ 2372 1179; Agias Mavris 25; adult/over 6 yrs/under 6 yrs CY£1/0.50/free; ⊗ 9am-2pm Mon, Tue, Thu & Sat & 3-6pm Mon & Thu), hidden away in the lower ground floor of the modern Agia Napa town hall, is a lot less flashy than the Thalassa museum. If you are into marine biology, fossilised shells, stuffed fish, sharks, turtles and sea birds, then drop in for a quick visit. The display is fairly limited, but well laid out and documented.

Monastery of Agia Napa

Μονή Αγιασ Ναπασ

The beautifully cloistered **Monastery of Agia Napa** (Plateia Seferi; admission free; ⊗ 9am-6pm) is incongruously sited next to the pub-and-club centre of the adjoining Square. Best visited in the early morning, after the revellers have gone to bed, the monastery is an oasis of calm amid the crass commercialism of Agia Napa's entertainment scene.

Built in around 1570 by the Venetians, the monastery is named after the 'holy handkerchief' that was used by St Veronica to wipe the face of Jesus as he carried his cross to Calvary. It is a remarkably well-preserved monastery, and was indeed used as such up until 1790. Visitors enter from either the north or south

side. Outside the south gate is a prominently labelled enormous sycamore tree, which is said to be more 600 years old. A cool, marble fountain is the centrepiece of the courtyard and dates from 1530. It is covered by a large dome, mounted on four pillars.

The church itself, on the west side of the courtyard, is sunken somewhat lower than the courtyard level and is rather dark and gloomy inside.

The monastery is ringed by a stout, protective wall, designed initially to keep marauding pirates at bay, but now ostensibly serving a better purpose in keeping inebriated foreign visitors at a respectable distance from its hallowed ground.

Water World

If you want water but not sand, head 3km west of Agia Napa to **Water World** (☎ 2372 4444; www.waterworldwaterpark.com; Agias Theklis 18; adult/child CY£12.90/6.50; ⊗ 10am-6pm Apr-Oct), supposedly Cyprus' best water theme park. Here you can tube, splash and slide to your heart's content. Expect long queues in peak season.

Beaches

The main beach is usually very crowded and strewn from end to end with umbrellas and beach loungers, but everyone seems to be able to find a spot for themselves somewhere.

Nissi Beach is the most popular of Agia Napa's beaches. It's long, beautiful and sandy, but incredibly crowded. The sea is shallow and calm, and there is a small island about 75m away. Nissi is around 2km from Agia Napa's centre, so a scooter or a bicycle is a great way to get here, or simply grab a taxi.

If you're looking for a bit of solitude, hire a scooter and move on to Cape Greco (p166), or Konnos and Green Bay Beaches (p170) south of Protaras.

Boat Cruises

A large number of boat cruises operate out of Agia Napa's crowded little harbour. Most head out for trips around Cape Greco to the beaches of Protaras and Pernera, advertising their destination as 'Famagusta'. All must turn back before reaching Famagusta of course, since this city is under the control of the Turkish military.

'Party' cruises typically cost CY£4 per adult (CY£2 per child). They include music and drinks (an extra cost) and stops for

LARNAKA & THE EAST

swimming. One outfit that operates these kinds of events is **Party Cruise** (☎ 9963 7233) on the harbour; ask for Nikos. Cruises depart at 11.30am and return at 4pm daily. An evening cruise, dubbed the 'sex cruise', runs every Tuesday, Wednesday and Sunday, departing at 10.30pm and returning at 1.30am. Men pay CY£5; women go for free.

Diving
The waters around Agia Napa and Cape Greco up to Famagusta are perfect for diving. The sea is calm, warm and clear, and a few operators are set up to cater for divers. The **Scuba Base** (☎ 2372 2441; www.thescubabase .com; Leoforos Nisiou 17a) is a reputable local company that organises programmes ranging from an introduction to snorkelling to advanced open-water courses. For information on Cyprus' dive spots, see p86.

TOURS
The Agia Napa branch of Pafos-based **Exalt** (☎ 2372 4390; www.cyprus-adventure.com; Belogianni 10) runs a challenging 12-hour sea and land excursion around Agia Napa.

SLEEPING
At least 90% of visitors come to Agia Napa with booked accommodation. If you turn up between mid-July and mid-August without a booking, you may have trouble finding a bed.

Accommodation ranges from unlicensed rooms (normally a rarity in Cyprus) to five-star hotels. Most hotels will welcome independent travellers if there is space. Prices are cheaper in the off-season, but many hotels only operate from March to October.

Napa Plaza (☎ 2372 1540; blueseasonshotels@cyta net.com.cy; Leoforos Arhiepiskopou Makariou III 12; r per person CY£30; 🔊 🔊) The former Napia Star has changed hands, names and appearances, with the hotel's reception a virginal white with cool marble floors. The pool is busy, and the restaurant has a popular bar that's open most hours. The rooms are in creamy colours and you get slippers and a cosy bathrobe when you arrive.

Faros (☎ 2372 3838; faroshot@spidernet.com.cy; Leoforos Arhiepiskopou Makariou III; s/d CY£43/62; 🔊) A rather swanky place very close to the harbour, with sleek, bright rooms and a great pool surrounded by bungalows.

Green Bungalows (☎ 2372 1511; anastassiadesa@ cytanet.com.cy; Katalymata 19; 2-person apt CY£31; ☼ Apr-Oct) A superior B-class apartment hotel. This place offers cosy apartments and breakfast from CY£2.

Anesis (☎ 2372 1104; fax 2372 2204; 1 Oktovriou 7; s/d CY£29/40; 🔊 🖥) Anesis has plans for renovations in 2006, adding satellite TV channels, a sauna, gym and Jacuzzi separate from the swimming pool. The rooms are decent, and will also be renovated. Prices are supposed to stay as they were at the time of research.

Nestor (☎ 2372 2880; nestor@logos.net.cy; 1 Oktovriou 8; s/d CY£29.50/42; 🔊) This place has large rooms with balconies that overlook the pool, diagonally opposite the Anesis. There are games rooms downstairs.

Leros Hotel (☎ 2372 1126; Leoforos Arhiepiskopou Makariou III 41; s/d CY£17/30; 🔊 🔊) At the bottom of the scale in price and appearance, with a budget look but not a budget price (although it is the cheapest in town). The rooms are a little run-down, but bearable if there is nothing else. There is a small pool and bar.

EATING
Eating in Agia Napa is generally not very good, and is inevitably aimed at the tourist, although you'll never go hungry. The big fast-food chains are all close to each other and there is a place to eat almost every 50m or so. Prices are somewhat higher than elsewhere in Cyprus, but not outrageously so. The following are better than most:

Vassos (☎ 2372 1884; Leoforos Arhiepiskopou Makariou III 51; fish meze CY£8; ☼ lunch & dinner) This place has been around since 1962, so it has a well-tried and successful formula: fresh fish and good service. It looks a rather large, impersonal place during the day, but it's right on the harbour and makes for romantic evening dining.

Esperia (☎ 2372 1635; Leoforos Arhiepiskopou Makariou III 49; fish meze CY£8.75; ☼ lunch & dinner) Closer to the water than Vassos, and boasting slightly more upmarket décor and a marginally better location. Enormous fish and meat dishes sell for similar prices.

Potopoieion to Elliniko (☎ 2372 2760; Theodos Pieridi 2; minimum charge CY£7.50; ☼ dinner) A small evenings-only Greek-style *mezedopolio* (a small restaurant specialising in *mezedes*, with grilled-meat meze, and *zivania* (local firewater), ouzo or wine as accompaniment. There's usually some live music too.

Tsambra (☎ 2372 2513; Dionysiou Solomou 9; pork dishes CY£6-7; ☼ lunch & dinner) For a change in style, try the shaded courtyard of this Lebanese-Cypriot restaurant. Good shish kebabs, barbecued lamb, *tabouleh* (bulgur-wheat and parsley salad), and for dessert, *mahalabia* (a light, rice custard, served cold).

Limelight (☎ 2372 1650; Dionysiou Solomou 10; fish platter CY£12.95; ☼ lunch & dinner) This is an old favourite in town, with charcoal-grilled dishes such as steak, lobster, fish and chicken, as well as succulent suckling lamb and pig. Not a good place for vegetarians.

Napiana (☎ 2372 2891; Leoforos Arhiepiskopou Makariou III 29; ☼ lunch & dinner) A busy establishment with exceptionally attentive service, close to central Agia Napa. Steaks are the big seller here, with the rich Chateaubriand for two at CY£8.50 per person.

DRINKING

For people-watching, choose the balconies of the pubs on the Square.

Freedom Reggae Bar (☎ 2372 2801; Ari Velouhioti; ☼ 9am-2am) A bar with a difference in that it opens for breakfast, when clubbed out punters head here for the exceptionally chilled-out atmosphere. Freedom even serves an early Sunday roast.

Bedrock Inn (☎ 2372 2951; Agias Mavris) This grotesque Fred Flintstone and Barney Rubble–style karaoke palace is extremely popular with the tourists.

Alexander's (☎ 2372 1898; Georgiou Seferi 17) If you don't want to get too involved, but want to see it all, this place has an all-encompassing view of the action. It's a definite voyeur's favourite, located at the top of the Square.

O'Rourke's Inn (☎ 2372 3357; Tefkrou Anthia 13) Serves top Gaelic ales, offers live music and organises beach parties.

ENTERTAINMENT

If you've come to Agia Napa, you're probably here to drink and dance and generally be up all night. The town's bars and music venues are full until around 2am, then it's time to hit the clubs. The central area within 200m of the Square is a riotous confusion of noise, karaoke, disco beats and clinking glasses. There are almost 20 bars and 15 clubs to choose from, and the nightlife never stops.

Nightclubs come and go each year, but the following manage to stick around. Most of these clubs open after 1am; you'll pay between CY£5 and CY£10 for admission.

Alfabet (☎ 2372 5066; Grigoriou Afxentiou 17) Previously the Abyss club, Alfabet has the admiring crowd screaming when Robbie Williams and Tina Turner impersonators burst onto the stage at 3am along with fire-eaters and other circus performances. There's a large dance floor and an outdoor chill-out zone. This is one of the biggest clubs in town and has a mix of house, R&B, old school and garage. Look out for foam parties.

Carwash (☎ 2372 1388; Agias Mavris 24) Two London DJs take the party-goers through a mix of hits from the '70s and '80s from their VW Beetle deck room. Massive queues outside confirm the words of the management that Carwash 'is more like a party than a club'.

Bagley's (☎ 2372 3400; Louka Louka) The old Inferno Club, Bagley's still sports a four-way sound system and DJ Richie P from Shagwells in London. Richie plays the best of the '70s to '90s music. Dress up for the Austin Powers theme night.

Black & White (☎ 2372 3565; Louka Louka 6) The longest-standing venue in town and, according to some hard-core clubbers, the best. It has an eclectic mix of music nights, attracting just about anybody.

Castle Club (☎ 9962 3126; Grigoriou Afxentiou) Housed in a hideous mock castle, this place takes up to 2000 people. And there are still queues outside in summer. It has three separate areas (two dance and one chill-out space); the music is the ever-popular formula of house, R&B, old school and garage.

Club Insomnia (☎ 2372 5554; Leoforos Nisiou 4; ☼ 4am-7am) 'I can't get no sleep' reads the sign outside, like the Faithless hit. This is the place where nightaholics can always seek predawn solace and more drinks. Advertising 'quality chill-out time' and 'happy sunshine music', Club Insomnia is for serious all-nighters.

Grease (☎ 2372 4240; www.3ds.com.cy/grease; Leoforos Arhiepiskopou Makariou III) This place features classic tunes from the '70s to the '90s, plus the soundtrack hits from the movie. Relive teenage bliss and dress up like Sandy and Danny. Rydell High is not out yet.

GETTING THERE & AWAY

Service taxi is the best way to get to Agia Napa from Larnaka, for CY£3.50 (45 minutes); try Travel & Express (p149), which will pick you up and drop you off at the central taxi stand on the Square in Agia Napa. The bus is also good and regular. There are nine direct buses to and from Larnaka (CY£2.50, one hour) in summer, and one daily bus to Lefkosia (CY£2, 1½ hours) at 8am (returning at 3pm). There are more or less hourly (on the hour) buses to Paralimni and Protaras (CY£0.50, 30 minutes). All buses leave from the bus stop between the Square and the harbour.

Private taxis (from the taxi stand close to the Square) vary, with rates from CY£13 to the airport, CY£19 to Lefkosia, and CY£40 to Troödos.

Cyprus Airways (☎ 2372 1265; www.cyprusairways .com; Leoforos Arhiepiskopou Makariou III 17) has an office here.

GETTING AROUND

There's no public transport in Agia Napa, so other than catching a taxi, hiring a scooter or a motorbike is your best option. **Easyriders** (☎ 2372 2438; easyriders@easyriders.com .cy; Gianni Ritsou 1) rents wheels from 50cc scooters (CY£10 per day) to Kawasaki or Suzuki 800cc heavies (CY£25 per day). There is a second outlet at Dimokratias 17.

AROUND AGIA NAPA

Even if you decide to avoid Agia Napa completely, there are some beaches around the place that are worth checking out, and the area near Cape Greco is wonderful. You can also peer over the border into the ghost town of Varosia from vantage points on the Attila Line.

Getting Around

No public transport other than the Protaras–Paralimni–Larnaka bus is going to help you much here. The cheapest option is to hire a scooter in either Protaras or Agia Napa. Rates vary, but are usually very reasonable. Make sure you choose a scooter with some power in its engine: it is a fair haul across the Paralimni region. A scooter is the most suitable option for beach-hopping along the Pernera–Protaras coastal strip.

A car is the best way to see the region in comfort. Rates from smaller companies in Protaras or Agia Napa are usually better than those offered by big-name hire-car companies. A group of four should be able to hire a small open-top 4WD fairly cheaply.

As the whole area is reasonably flat, cycling is an ideal way of getting around the Kokkinohoria. There is a cycle path between Agia Napa and Cape Greco.

CAPE GRECO

The **sea caves**, just a little before the actual land's end that is Cape Greco, are a wonderful sight. If you get to know someone with a boat, make sure you approach the caves by the sea and take a closer look. A constant breeze makes the platform above the caves a perfect place to have a fresh lemonade from the one little lemonade van and enjoy the view. There's no shade here, so bring a hat.

You can't get to the end of the Cape itself, which is a pity. As on Mt Olympus in the Troödos Massif, the Brits have requisitioned the last piece of land to install a radar station that is firmly fenced off from the public.

However, some of the best swimming can be had here if the weather is not too windy. From the shabby car park, walk north towards the little bay and clamber down onto the rocks. A few rock platforms support swimmers who really don't want to be part of the Protaras beach scene. The water is absolutely idyllic here.

A coastal walking and cycling track will take you to the cape from Agia Napa in about 3½ hours, or from Konnos Beach in about one hour. Bicycles should have solid tyres as the track is stony in parts.

Cape Greco is 7km from Agia Napa or 4km from Protaras. A good road, narrow in parts, leads in and out of the area, past a rubbish dump in an ill-chosen location.

PARALIMNI ΠΑΡΑΛΙΜΝΗ
pop 11,100 (including Protaras & Pernera)

Paralimni has reluctantly taken over from Famagusta as the capital of eastern Cyprus. There is nothing in the town itself to have a look at, although you may have to pass through it on your way further east if you are touring the area by scooter.

There is a paved central square with two versions of the church of Agios Georgios (new and old) and a sprinkling of restaurants and shops.

DERYNEIA ΔΕΡΥΝΕΙΑ

pop 1850

People usually come to Deryneia to peer into no-man's-land and stare at the firmly closed 'border' that separates Northern Cyprus from the Republic of Cyprus. During the Turks' second invasion of the North in August 1974, the Turkish army encircled and occupied the deserted holiday resort centre of Varosia. Troops moved towards Deryneia and halted abruptly just below the rise on which the town is located, which now gives it its unparalleled but politically charged view into Northern Cyprus.

There are at least two viewing platforms for looking into the North. **Annita's** (☎ 2382 3003; admission CY£0.50), the top platform, is the better of the two, and is essentially a private apartment block that had the luck or the misfortune not to be occupied by the Turks. From the top-floor platform, you can see the Greek Cypriot barracks, the blue-and-white UN building and, further still, the cream-coloured Turkish Cypriot post with Turkish and Turkish Cypriot flags flying defiantly. Both flags are now safely protected by barbed wire after two violent and fatal incidents in 1996 (see the boxed text, below).

Graphic videos and wall posters in the little viewing platform cafeteria describe events that shocked and still linger in the collective memory of Greek Cypriots. Binoculars are handed out to visitors as part of the entrance ticket. The stark cityscape to the right and north of Deryneia is **Varosia**; it is, to all intents and purposes, dead and abandoned, and has been left the way it was when occupied in 1974. Only rats and a few Turkish military details now inhabit its overgrown streets. The town is important to the Greeks living in this area, and most will be keen to show you the place themselves.

THE DERYNEIA MARTYRS

On 11 August 1996, a Berlin-to-Cyprus peace ride by motorcyclists from around Europe ended at the Greek Cypriot village of Deryneia, which adjoins the Attila Line dividing Northern Cyprus from the Republic of Cyprus. Among the riders that day was a young Greek Cypriot from Protaras by the name of Tasos Isaak. Newly married, his young wife was pregnant with their first child.

At the protest marking the end of the ride, and in memory of the continuing occupation of the North by Turkish forces, a melee developed, with clashes between Greek Cypriots and Turkish Cypriots in the UN buffer zone that separated the two communities. During the running clashes with Turks from the North – many of whom, it is widely believed, belonged to the paramilitary organisation the Grey Wolves from the Turkish mainland – Tasos Isaak was inexplicably cut off from his fellow demonstrators. He was set upon by thugs carrying wooden clubs and iron bars.

Before the astonished eyes of demonstrators and at least one photographer, Isaak was beaten deliberately and viciously to death.

He was unarmed and dressed only in jeans and a shirt. Turkish police stood by and watched. Isaak's lifeless body was later recovered by UN personnel.

Three days later, after Isaak's funeral, a crowd once more gathered at the Deryneia checkpoint to protest against this unprovoked and unwarranted death. Among the protesters this time was Solomos Solomou, a 26-year-old friend of Isaak, who was enraged at the death of his friend. Despite repeated attempts to hold him back, Solomos eluded the UN peacekeepers and slipped across the no-man's-land to one of the flagpoles carrying the Turkish Cypriot flag. Cigarette in mouth, he managed to climb halfway up the flagpole before being struck by five bullets that came from the Turkish Cypriot checkpoint building, and possibly from bushes sheltering armed soldiers. Solomos' bloody slide to death down the flagpole was captured dramatically on video, and is replayed endlessly at viewing points that today overlook the tragic site of the Deryneia murders.

The memories live on vividly in the minds of Greek Cypriots. The graphic photos of Isaak and Solomos, as well as that of an old man caught picking mushrooms in the buffer zone and subsequently shot, are displayed on the Greek side of the Ledra Palace Hotel crossing in Lefkosia. Security is tight at Deryneia now, but tensions run ever high. Life and death here can be as fragile as a Damoclean thread.

DEKELIA SOVEREIGN BASE AREA

Orders for 'Fish and chips!' and 'A cup of tea, please!' can be heard above the rustle of the *Times, Daily Mail, Telegraph* and *Guardian*, as Brits take their lunch break from the beach in the small canteen at Dekelia. The only way to describe this place is 'Britain in Cyprus', and it's almost a sight in itself, in terms of a cultural oddity on the island.

As part of the hard-won deal between the nascent Republic of Cyprus and the UK in 1960, the British were granted rights to two major Sovereign Base Areas (SBAs), and access to retained sites scattered around the country where satellite ground stations and radio listening stations were located.

The Dekelia SBA is the second of the two major base areas taken over 'in perpetuity' by the canny Brits. (See p96 for details about Akrotiri.)

The area comprises a sizable chunk of eastern Cyprus, running from Larnaka Bay to the current Attila Line border with the North. In reality, the Dekelia SBA cuts off the Paralimni district from the rest of the Republic of Cyprus, since the SBAs are deemed to be foreign territory. In practice, there are no 'border' controls, but formidable grey iron gates on the road at the SBA entrances prove that British territorial integrity could be invoked at any time should circumstances require. The British government has stated that it is prepared to cede back a large chunk of this SBA if Cyprus becomes reunified.

You're not supposed to 'tour' the SBA, and taking photographs is a no-no. You can't actually enter the base installations themselves without passes and permits, but you can freely drive around the territory itself. Although the British military play it very low-key and rarely make themselves visible to casual travellers, the installations at Dekelia are still crucial for intelligence-gathering. They continue to play a role in monitoring radio traffic in the Middle East, and keeping a watch on regional military activity with sophisticated over-the-horizon (OTH-B) radar units.

The Attila Line is less rigorously monitored here since there is no closed UN buffer zone. The border-crossing points at Pergamos (Beyarmudu) and Agios Nikolaos are open to casual visitors, but mainly to those in vehicles. See p233 for information about visas.

THE KOKKINOHORIA ΤΑ ΚΟΚΚΙΝΟΧΩΡΙΑ

The Kokkinohoria villages are to Cyprus what Idaho is to the USA – they both produce famous potatoes. Kokkinohoria means 'red villages'; they are so called not because of their political allegiances, but for the colour of the rich earth over which these once backwater but now prospering villages are built. The red soil of the Agia Napa hinterland is striking and appears almost suddenly, soon after the village of Ormidia in the Dekelia SBA. Coupled with a rash of wind-powered water pumps that litter the rolling landscape, this part of Cyprus is in many ways geographically akin to the outback of Australia.

Potatoes and *kolokasi* (a root vegetable similar to the Pacific Islands' taro) grow profusely in the mineral-rich soil. Up to three crops of potatoes are cultivated annually here, no doubt contributing significantly to Cypriots' predilection for chips with everything. The main villages are **Xylofagou**, **Avgorou**, **Frenaros**, **Liopetri** and **Sotira**. While they offer little for tourists per se, other than a glimpse of rural Cyprus or the occasional excellent country taverna, they're great to get around on a scooter, and are in total contrast to the coastal resorts to the east and south. Signposting in the Kokkinohoria is pretty poor at times, so ensure you have a decent map to avoid going around in circles.

PYLA ΠΥΛΑ PILE

pop 1370

The rather unlikely village of Pyla is the only place in Cyprus where Greek and Turkish Cypriots still live together in harmony. Admittedly, that harmony is enforced by the presence of a UN peace-keeping contingent and a watchful Turkish military lookout post on the ridge high above the village, but it works. Pyla is in the UN buffer zone but, unlike elsewhere in Cyprus, this area is open to all and sundry. That means Cypriots from both the North and the South.

The main feature of the village, illustrating the continuing peaceful coexistence of Turk and Greek, is the village square, where a red-and-white Turkish Cypriot coffee shop eyes up a blue-and-white Greek Cypriot *kafeneio* on the other side. Overlooking the middle of the square is the 'referee's' chair, positioned prominently outside the UN watchtower and occasionally occupied by an Irish or Argentinean soldier in a blue beret.

Greeks and Turks live in mixed neighbour-hoods, and by all accounts mind their own business and get on with their lives. Cross-cultural mixing is low-key and not obvious to casual observers. The Greeks are somewhat peeved that they carry the burden of local taxes and utility costs, while the Turks pay nothing and can access both the North and the South. Photography is not allowed.

If you don't want to backtrack to the Larnaka motorway, take the winding road out of Pyla signposted to Pergamos, enter-ing the SBA about 1km outside the village. From here, you can cut across the SBA to the B3 motorway for Agia Napa.

PROTARAS & PERNERA
ΠΡΩΤΑΡΑΣ & ΠΕΡΝΕΡΑ

pop 11,100 (including Paralimni)

Protaras and Pernera are two separate but ever-closer communities; they're geared al-most exclusively to the expat and resort crowd, with sprawling hotels, lawns and swimming pools, and not much to see or do.

The area is a slightly watered-down ver-sion of Agia Napa, and more geared to fam-ilies and couples, with beach resorts that tend to give visitors more breathing space. There seem to be enough restaurants and bars to compensate, though finding one that is be-yond simply adequate can take some doing, as most offer unimaginative meals served by uninspired, non-Cypriot waiting staff.

Orientation & Information
The Protaras–Pernera community hinges upon the main street running through the centre of Protaras. Here is the greatest con-centration of shops, restaurants, bars and hotels. As this is primarily a tourist and not a residential area, little happens here outside of the tourist season. It is approxi-mately 4km from the northern end of Per-nera to the southern end of Protaras.

Sights & Activities
There are some top-class beaches along this strip, if you could only see them for the crowds.

SKOUTARI BEACH
This is an isolated cove surrounded by a cliff. The beach is 50m of hard-packed sand and scruffy rocks, with a sheltered bay, good snorkelling, and a few restaurants nearby.

AGIA TRIADA BEACH
Second along, and used mainly as a boat-launching area, this diminutive beach has shallow water, the sand is a little coarse, and cars tend to be parked along its 200m curv-ing length. Ice-cream sellers are the only source of nourishment.

MOUZOURA BEACH
Blink and you'll miss this next beach. It's small and popular with Cypriot sunbathers, sporting a good but narrow sand strip and some shade under the trees at the southern end. The sand drops away quickly, so it's not suitable for nonswimmers or young chil-dren. There are parking facilities, at least one good restaurant and a large hotel for people who choose to base themselves here.

LOUMA BEACH
Further south is the busy beach zone and the northern extension of Protaras, called Pernera. The 400m curving strand of Louma Beach is protected by an artificial bay. The sand is fine, the water is clean and the beach drops away gently, and there is shade under the trees at the northern end.

Water sports are catered for by Baywa-ter Water Sports, which offers banana-tube rides (CY£3), paragliding (CY£14 a flight), water-skiing lessons (CY£15) or 15 minutes on a jet ski (CY£15). Hire sun-loungers and umbrellas for CY£1.25 each.

PERNERA BEACH
Skipping a fairly lengthy section of coast with few swimming options, the next busy beach is this one, which is a smaller version of Louma Beach. It is a curvy 200m long strip of good, soft sand and shallow water, but with little shade. Five restaurants sur-rounding the beach compete for trade.

The **TABA Diving centre** (☎ 2483 2680) offers single dives for CY£18 or double dives for CY£30.

PROTARAS BEACH
Bypassing a series of open, rocky coves, backed by the lawns of large resort hotels, you arrive at the most popular and frequented of all the beaches on this strip. Protaras Beach is long and sandy, studded with umbrellas and served by a multitude of water sports. The beach is approached by access roads from the main Protaras street inland.

LARNAKA &

THE AUTHOR'S CHOICE

Sirena Bay Hotel (☎ 2382 3502; r CY£35) Get away from the crowds and follow the mermaids. From the main Protaras–Paralimni road, follow the sign for Sirena Bay and then follow the mermaid sculptures, crafted by the owner Irini's Hemingway-esque father. Run by a family of artists, this place is all peace and relaxation. The living room area is jam-packed with the family's art work, woodcarvings and paintings. The rooms are basic, without air-conditioning, but with fans and mosquito nets on the doors. If you don't fancy staying, then this is a good place to just have a drink or some food in the lovely, flowery garden bar and restaurant. People from all over the area come here to relax and eat. There is a little sandy beach, and a couple of stone-surrounded 'pools' in the sea, for children to swim in. The sea is good, although the sand becomes strangely muddy and sticky around 10m into the water.

The most popular part is **Fig Tree Bay** at the southern end, so-named for the single fig tree that used to stand guard at the back of the beach. Unfortunately, the beach is now so swamped with hotels and restaurants, it's anyone's guess where the original fig tree actually is.

GREEN BAY BEACH

'Come and discover a secret beach' reads the road sign. Having invited so many strangers, the beach is no longer a secret, if it ever was. Although less busy than the surrounding beaches, it's laden with umbrellas and sunloungers, and is hardly a haven of peace. If you get in early, you can claim a pleasant spot. Not so prominently signposted, Green Bay is the first obvious beach you will come to if approaching Protaras from Agia Napa.

KONNOS BEACH

This is the best beach in the area, with a Caribbean-like sea, white sandy beach and fantastic swimming. You'll find it about 2km south of Green Bay, signposted 1km off the main road to Cape Greco. The beach is home to **Mike's Water Sports** (☎ 9960 5833). Take a parachute ride (CY£15), a ski tow (CY£15) or a beginner's ski lesson (CY£15), or hire a jet ski (CY£1 per minute).

Sleeping

With one exception, all hotel options are clustered along the Protaras–Pernera strip. Most are resolutely geared to package-tour visitors, and the choice is enormous, with over 90 places on offer. These range from two- to five-star hotels and A- and B-class hotel apartments. Budget accommodation is thin on the ground, with virtually no backpacker scene to speak of. Bookings are recommended in high season, and would-be travellers are advised to get hold of the free CTO *Guide to Hotels and Other Tourist Establishments* that gives a full listing.

Cavo Maris (☎ 2383 2043; cavo@cytanet.com.cy; s/d from CY£46/74; 🏊) A behemoth; good for families who like raucous holidays with lots of activities. It has a couple of pools, a beach, restaurants, bars and night-time activities. It is at the southern end of Protaras, near Green Bay Beach. A 30% discount often applies, even in the high season.

Eating

Eating options are as plentiful as the accommodation possibilities. While hotels all tend to be of uniform quality, some restaurants can be downright bad, so choose prudently. Although by no means fantastic, try these options.

Mouzoura Beach Restaurant (☎ 2382 3333; Vryssoudion 79; fish meze CY£10; 🕑 lunch & dinner) This place tries the 'we are locals, therefore we know what's good' approach, displaying traditional woven tablecloths and waiters with Greek-flag T-shirts. There are nice views of the sea and swaying palms. The fish meze is a speciality.

Olympus (☎ 2383 2262; mains CY£4.90-10; 🕑 lunch & dinner) This is another Greek-style taverna with charcoal-cooked meats and dolmades (stuffed vine leaves). It's located at the southern end of Protaras' main street.

Anemos (☎ 2383 1488; Fig Tree Bay, Protaras; mains CY£4-6; 🕑 lunch & dinner) A large Cypriot family-style restaurant with a wide selection of meat and vegetarian options. For CY£4.75, vegetarians can feast on fried vegetables, haloumi cheese, mushrooms and rice. Amemos has a good range of Hrysorogiatissa wines for around CY£6.

Northern Cyprus

PAUL DAVID HELLANDER

North Nicosia (Lefkoşa)
Lefkosia Λευκωσία

The northern half of Cyprus' capital, known as North Nicosia (Lefkoşa), is a dizzying laby-rinth of narrow, old streets, punctuated by wonderful architecture. The Old City pulses with shoppers in the covered Belediye Pazarı market, and the Büyük Han (Great Inn), recently restored, is a busy centre for tourists and locals alike. The streets of the newly renovated Arabahmet neighbourhood abound with unkempt, screaming children, who want your at-tention and greetings; people sit outside their houses watching the city go by in the heat of midsummer; and women walk past, balancing a load on their heads.

Just as you might have decided, after a walk around the Old City, that here is an old-fashioned place steeped in quaint traditions, you discover a whole part of town that is heaving with shiny, dressed-up youths brandishing mobiles and listening to loud, pump-ing music. And when the call to prayer, blasting from the loudspeakers of the city's many minarets, makes you think that religion is a big thing here, the luring neon winking from the mushrooming casinos offers a different story, with Greek and Turkish men losing big money side by side. Traditional eateries release the aroma of grilled kebabs, and modern restaurants serve top-quality international dishes.

North Nicosia (with a population of around 39,000) has had a much-needed boost in terms of architectural renovation and infrastructure. Brussels is pouring money into the city: along with the already renovated parts of town, the current work on the city's Turkish baths, the legendary Kumarcılar Han, and the beautiful old Bedesten, promises an exciting future for North Nicosia.

HIGHLIGHTS

- Visit the amazing **Büyük Han** (Great Inn; p176), a grand Ottoman structure, full of wonderful craft shops

- Take some time to stroll through the narrow streets of the **Old City** (p178): visit the reno-vated Arabahmet neighbourhood and look for the striking Ottoman and Lusignan buildings on a walking tour

- See the gorgeous Gothic arches of the once church, now mosque, **Selimiye Mosque** (p176)

- Go inside the **Belediye Pazarı** (Municipal Market; p176) and walk between watermelon mountains

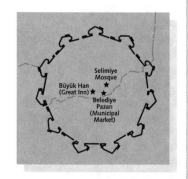

NORTH NICOSIA (LEFKOŞA)

0   200 m
0   0.1 miles

INFORMATION
Australian Embassy......................1 A4
Birinci Turizm...............................2 B5
British High Commission............3 A5
Deep Net City.............................4 B5
Kıbrıs Vakıflar Bankası..................5 B6
Kyrenia (Girne) Gate.................(see 8)
Ledra Palace Hotel Crossing.........6 A5
London Dry Cleaners...................7 C4
NCTO...8 B5
NCTO......................................(see 6)
Parcel Post Office.........................9 C4
Police Station.............................10 B5
Poliklinik...................................11 C4
Post Office.................................12 B5
Rüstem Kitabevi.........................13 B6
TC Ziraat Bankası.......................14 B5
Telecommunications Office........15 C4
US Embassy.............................(see 1)
Virus Net Internet Café..............16 A4

SIGHTS & ACTIVITIES
Bedesten...................................17 C6
Belediye Pazarı (Municipal Market)..18 C6
Büyük Hammam (Great Baths)........19 C6
Büyük Han (Great Inn)................20 C6
Cyprus Turkish Shadow Theatre......(see 20)
Dervish Pasha Museum...............21 B6
Haydarpasha Mosque.................22 B6
Kumarcılar Han (Gambler's Inn)....23 C6
Lapidary Museum......................24 C6
Library of Sultan Mahmut II.........25 C6
Roccas (Kaytazağa) Bastion.........26 A6
Sarayönü Mosque......................27 B6
Selimiye Mosque........................28 C6
Turkish Museum.........................29 B5

SLEEPING
Royal Hotel...............................30 C3
Saray..31 B6

EATING
Amasyali...................................32 B5
Annibal.....................................33 C6
Boghjalian.................................34 B6

Halvah Shop..............................35 C6
Konak.......................................36 C6
Moyra.......................................37 A4
Özerlat......................................38 C6
Pasta Villa.................................39 A4
Pavement Cafés.........................40 B5
Pronto Bistro.............................41 A5
Sabor..42 C6
Saray Roof Restaurant...........(see 31)
Sedirhan Café.......................(see 20)
Umutlar Restaurant....................43 B5

SHOPPING
Koza.....................................(see 20)
Moniat Macun......................(see 20)

TRANSPORT
Budget Car Rental......................44 B6
Cyprus Turkish Airlines................45 A3
Itimat Bus Station.......................46 C5
Long-Distance Bus Station..........47 C3
Sun Rent-A-Car.........................48 B4
Taxi Stand.................................49 B5
Turkish Airlines..........................50 A4

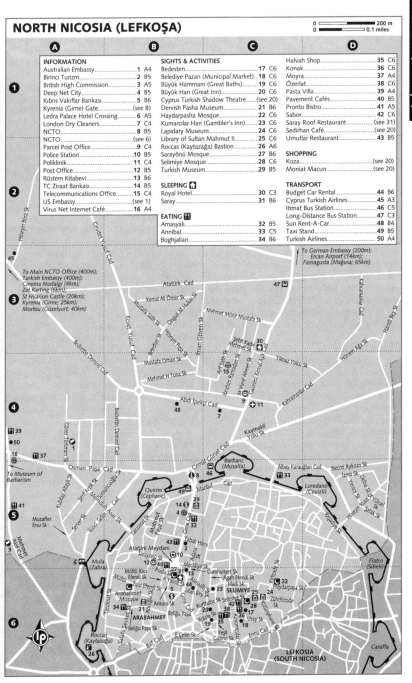

HISTORY

Up until 1963, North Nicosia, not surprisingly, shared much of the same history as its dismembered southern sector. For details of this period, see p57.

The capital was effectively divided into Greek and Turkish sectors in 1963, when violence against Turkish Cypriots by Ethniki Organosi tou Kypriakou Agona (EOKA; National Organisation for the Cypriot Struggle) insurgents forced them to retreat into safe enclaves or ghettos. The Green Line, as it has become known, was established when a British military commander divided up the city on a map with a green pen. The name has remained ever since. The Turkish military invasion of 1974, which most Turkish Cypriots saw as a rescue operation, formalised the division between the two halves of the city. A wary truce was brokered by the blue-bereted members of the UN peacekeeping forces, who had been guarding the Green Line since sectarian troubles broke out in 1963. It is now easy for visitors (and Cypriots) to cross over the border, but despite this, the city is still divided and its reunification looks far off.

ORIENTATION

The Old City is easy to navigate. If you get lost, head for the Venetian walls, which you can easily follow in order to reach the main point of reference, the Kyrenia Gate (Girne Kapısı in Turkish). Running south from the Kyrenia Gate is Girne Caddesi, which leads onto Atatürk Meydanı, the main square, identifiable by a large portrait of Kemal Atatürk. Around here you will find banks, shops and hotels. To the east of the square are the Korkut Effendi and Selimiye districts where most of North Nicosia's sights are found. To the immediate south, near the Green Line, is a small pedestrianised area with shops and restaurants. In the west of the Old City are the Karamanzade and Arabahmet districts.

The New City spreads some distance north from Kyrenia Gate, with Bedrettin Demirel Caddesi leading northwest to Kyrenia, and Gazeteci Kemal Aşik Caddesi leading northeast to Famagusta (Mağusa).

Visitors to North Nicosia will arrive to the west of the Old City via the Ledra Palace Hotel, at the UN-controlled checkpoint between Northern Cyprus and the Republic. From here it is a 10-minute walk to the Kyrenia Gate.

Maps

The North Cyprus Tourism Organisation (NCTO) produces a reasonably useful *City Plan of Lefkoşa* in both English and Turkish. These should be available at the Ledra Palace Hotel NCTO office. Otherwise you will have to ask at one of the NCTO offices in North Nicosia. Commercially produced maps of Cyprus available in your local bookshop at home sometimes have city maps that include North Nicosia. Maps of Lefkosia published by the Cyprus Tourism Organisation (CTO) in the South do not show street details for North Nicosia.

INFORMATION

Bookshops

Rüstem Kitabevi (☎ 228 3506; Girne Caddesi 22) Once almost legendary for its organised chaos, this place has taken control of its stock and all is now neatly arranged on shelves. It is still, however, a well-supplied store, with old and new books, and many English-language reads, plus a rack of all kinds of magazines.

Emergency

For emergencies, call ☎ 155.
Police station (☎ 228 3311; Atatürk Meydanı)

Internet Access

Deep Net City (☎ 227 9669; Girne Caddesi 73; per hr 1YTL; ☷ 24hr) This is a central, busy Internet outlet.
Virus Net Internet Café (☎ 0533 868 8086; Osman Paşa Caddesi C35; per hr 1YTL; ☷ 24hr) A little less busy than Deep Net, this is a good alternative.

Laundry

London Dry Cleaners (☎ 227 8232; Abdi Ipekçi Caddesi 30) Located in the New City, the London will do a service wash as well as dry-clean your clothes.

Medical Services

Burhan Nalbatanoğlu Devlet Hastahanesi (☎ 228 5441) North Nicosia's main hospital.
Poliklinik (☎ 227 3996; Gazeteci Kemal Aşik Caddesi) Where foreigners can seek medical treatment.

WHO WANTS TO BE A MILLIONAIRE?

The former millions of Turkish lira have had their zeroes knocked off, so now it's easier to count your dosh. Although some people may still quote prices in millions, the new currency is in daily use and the old notes are almost completely extinct.

THE ELUSIVE INSURANCE

Following the 2003 border-crossing changes, there has been a lot of talk of the North's car insurance, issued upon entry from the Republic. And after all this talk, things are clear as mud. If you ask about the insurance, you are likely to get numerous reactions and conflicting information. This is because the insurance 'law' concerning vehicles and drivers from the South is full of holes and open to interpretation (mainly by the North's police force).

When you enter the North by car (privately owned or rented) at any checkpoint, your own car insurance will no longer be valid, and you will have to purchase Turkish car insurance. It is third-party cover insurance, meaning that it covers anything up to CY£3000 worth of damage not caused by you. If *you* crash into someone or something, you will have to pay for the entire damage amount, and until you've coughed up the cash, you won't be able to leave the North.

If you're driving a rented car, keep in mind that, while the Republic's car-rental agencies have no objections against your taking rented cars to the North, it's up to you to decide whether this risk is worth taking, since establishing who is at fault in case of an accident can sometimes take a lot longer than one may think and be subject to many twists and turns.

The insurance prices are: CY£10 for one to three days for; CY£15 for one month; CY£20 for three months; CY£30 for six months; and CY£45 for one year.

Turkish-owned cars crossing into the South have to get the standard insurance, similar to that in other EU countries. The North's car-rental agencies did not allow taking rented cars into the Republic at the time of research.

Money

You can change your money into new Turkish lira (YTL) at any of the money-changing facilities just past the Ledra Palace Hotel passport-control booth. ATMs can be found at the **TC Ziraat Bankası** (Girne Caddesi) at the northern end of Girne Caddesi, or at the **Kıbrıs Vakıflar Bankası** (Atatürk Meydanı). Both change foreign currency, as do private-exchange offices nearby.

Post

Post office (Sarayönü Sokak) Just west of Atatürk Meydanı.

Telephone

There are public telephone booths scattered throughout the Old City, all of which use prepaid phonecards.

You can purchase phonecards from post offices.

Telecommunications office (Arif Salih Sokak; 8am-midnight) Situated in the New Town, west of the telecom tower.

Tourist Information

North Cyprus Tourism Organisation (NCTO; ☎ 227 9112; fax 228 5625; www.tourism.trnc.net) Kyrenia Gate (9am-5pm Mon-Fri, 9am-2pm Sat); Ledra Palace Hotel crossing (9am-5pm Mon-Sat, 9am-2pm Sun); main office (Bedrettin Demirel Caddesi; 9am-5pm Mon-Fri, 9am-2pm Sat) The NCTO has two convenient offices in the

city centre with maps and brochures on Northern Cyprus. If you don't find the information you want here, you can always make the 2km trek out to the main office. It's a long walk, so take a taxi from Kyrenia Gate (2YTL).

Travel Agencies

Birinci Turizm (☎ 228 3200; Girne Caddesi 158a) Issues ferry tickets to Turkey and airline tickets, and offers a range of other travel-related services.

DANGERS & ANNOYANCES

North Nicosia is a safe city at any time of the day, and you should feel no concern about walking the streets.

At night, the Old City can become rather quiet, and visitors may feel intimidated walking alone along dimly lit and sometimes narrow streets. It's best to avoid them if you feel uncomfortable. The areas abutting the Green Line look threatening, with large black-and-red signs that clearly forbid photography or trespassing in the buffer zone.

Do not take photographs on the Roccas (Kaytazağa) Bastion, at the western end of the Old City limits, where you can still look over into Greek Lefkosia. Despite the loosening of the border-crossing laws, the buffer zone is still a military area. Watchful soldiers stationed not so obviously on the bastion may accost you and even confiscate your camera.

SIGHTS & ACTIVITIES
Büyük Han & Kumarcılar Han
The **Büyük Han** (Great Inn; Arasta Sokak) is a wonderful example of Ottoman architecture and it's a rare surviving example of a medieval caravanserai. In the Ottoman world during the Middle Ages, travellers and traders could find accommodation at these *hans* (inns), as well as a place to stable their horses, trade their goods and socialise with fellow travellers.

The Büyük Han was built in 1572 by the first Ottoman governor of Cyprus, Musafer Pasha. Renovated in the recent years, it has once again become the centre of the Old City's bustle, with cafés, shops and traditional craft workshops housed in the 67 small cells that originally served as the inn's sleeping area. The central courtyard has in its middle a *mescit* (Islamic 'chapel'), and it is balanced on six pillars, over a *şadrvan* (ablutions fountain). This design is unique to this inn and only two others in Turkey.

Just to the north, on Agah Efendi Sokak, is the **Kumarcılar Han** (Gambler's Inn), a late-17th-century caravanserai, which worked in a similar way to the Büyük Han. It was closed for reconstruction at the time of research. Rumour has it that once it's been renovated, the building might once again become a place for gamblers. This would be no surprise considering the casino epidemic currently sweeping the North.

Belediye Pazarı (Municipal Market)
A fantastic place to check out local produce and local characters, the **market** (Belediye Pazarı; ⏱ 6am-3pm Mon-Sat) bustles with action: bargaining is rife, sellers either shout out their offers to shoppers, or sleep on the counters amid piles of vegetables and fruit. There is also an area with souvenirs where you can find something to take home.

Büyük Hammam
The **Büyük Hammam** (Tarihi Büyük Hamam, Great Baths; ☎ 228 4462; Irfan Bey Sokak 9; ⏱ 7.30am-10.30pm), in the process of being refurbished during this book's research, is a world-famous Turkish bath normally frequented by locals and tourists, both male and female. Stories of improper conduct on the part of the male-only masseurs made the news when two American tourists were allegedly molested in 2005, and soon after the hammam was closed for renovation. The refurbishment makes many hope that this bath will follow in the steps of the Omeriye Hammam in Lefkosia (p65), which would make it a safer and more appealing option.

The entrance is via an ornate low door, sunk six feet below street level. The door was originally part of the 14th-century Church of St George of the Latins. Inside you are able to see a nail that marks the point where the waters of the Pedieos River (Kanlı Dere) rose and drowned about 3000 Lefkosians in 1330.

It was not possible to have a bath in the hammam during research time, but visitors were allowed in to have a look from 9am to 5pm; pay CY£1 or €1 to the burly builder by the door.

Bedesten
Another building being renovated as part of the 'Nicosia Master Plan', the ruined and usually locked **Bedesten** (St Nicholas of the English) was originally a small Byzantine church built in the 6th century and augmented in the 14th century by the Catholic church.

During the 82 years of Venetian rule it became the Church of the Orthodox Metropolitan. After the Ottomans took Lefkosia in 1570, the church was used as a grain store and as a general market, but was basically left to disintegrate.

Today you can peer through the fencing and still make out the layout of the original churches. Medieval tombstones from various parts of Cyprus are currently kept in a section of the Bedesten. The north doorway has some splendid-looking **coats of arms** originally belonging to noble Venetian families.

These families may have been supporters of the Orthodox Church, which was nonetheless allowed to continue about its business despite the Catholic dominance of religious life in Cyprus.

The complex, on Selimiye Meydanı, was up for restoration during our research, so access to the site was not possible.

Selimiye Mosque
North Nicosia's most prominent landmark, which is also clearly visible from the southern half of the city, is the **Selimiye Mosque** (Selimiye Camii; Selimiye Meydanı; admission free). This

strange-looking building, a cross between a French Gothic church and a mosque, has an interesting history. Work started on the church in 1209 and progressed slowly. Louis IX of France, on his way to the Crusades, stopped by in 1248 and gave the building process a much needed shot in the arm by offering the services of his retinue of artisans and builders. However, the church took another 78 years to complete and was finally consecrated in 1326 as the **Church of Agia Sofia**.

Up until 1570 the church suffered depredation at the hands of the Genoese and the Mamelukes, and severe shakings from two earthquakes in 1491 and 1547. When the Ottomans arrived in 1570, they stripped the building of its Christian contents and added two minarets between which the Turkish Cypriot and Turkish flags now flutter.

The Gothic structure of the interior is still apparent despite Islamic overlays such as the whitewashed walls and columns, and the reorientation of the layout to align it with Mecca. Note the ornate west front with the three decorated doorways, each in a different style. Also look out for four **marble columns** relocated from Ancient Salamis and now placed in the apse off the main aisles.

Today the Selimiye Mosque is a working place of worship and you are able to go inside. Follow the usual etiquette when visiting a mosque: dress conservatively, take your shoes off, observe silence and don't take photos if prayers are in progress. The mosque has no set opening hours, but it's usually open during the day in the summer. Try to time your visit either just before or just after one of the five Muslim prayer sessions.

Library of Sultan Mahmut II

The **Library of Sultan Mahmut II** (Sultan II Mahmut Kütüpanesi; Selimiye Meydanı; 9am-2pm Jun–mid-Sep, 9am-1pm & 2-4.45pm mid-Sep–May) is housed in an octagonal building erected in 1829. It contains some 1700 books, and the interior is decorated with a calligraphic frieze in blue and gold. Some of the books are up to 700 years old and the more valuable tomes are displayed in special cases. The books were on loan to the National Archive Library of Cyprus during the time of research.

The same ticket also gives you access to the Bedesten and the Lapidary Museum.

Lapidary Museum

A visit to the **Lapidary Museum** (Taş Eserler Müzesi; Kirlizade Sokak; 9am-2pm Jun–mid-Sep, 9am-1pm & 2-4.45pm mid-Sep–May) is usually included in a visit to the Library of Sultan Mahmut II. This 15th-century building contains a varied collection of sarcophagi, shields, steles, columns, and a Gothic window rescued from a Lusignan palace that once stood near Atatürk Meydanı.

Haydarpasha Mosque

The **mosque** (Camii Haydarpaşa; Kirlizade Sokak; admission free; 9am-1pm & 2.30-5pm Mon-Fri, 9am-1pm Sat) was originally built as the 14th-century Church of St Catherine, but now functions as an art gallery. It is the second most important Gothic structure in North Nicosia after the Selimiye Mosque. The sculptures, both inside and out, are quite ornate, sprouting gargoyles, dragons, shields and human heads.

Dervish Pasha Museum

This small **ethnographic museum** (Derviş Paşa Konaği; Beliğ Paşa Sokak; admission 4.50YTL; 7.30am-2pm Jun–mid-Sep, 7.30am-1pm & 2-4.45pm mid-Sep–May) is housed in a 19th-century mansion. Built in 1807, it belonged to a wealthy Turkish Cypriot, Derviş Paşa, who published Cyprus' first Turkish-language newspaper. The house became an ethnographic museum in 1988. Household goods, including an old loom, glassware and ceramics, are displayed in former servants' quarters on the ground floor. Upstairs is a rich display of embroidered Turkish costumes and, in the far corner, a sumptuous *selamlık* (a retiring room for the owner of the mansion and his guests), replete with sofas and nargileh (Middle Eastern water pipes), and even some guests, in the form of eerie mannequins dressed up in suits.

Turkish Museum

The **Turkish Museum** (Mevlevi Tekke Müzesi; Girne Caddesi; admission 4.50YTL; 9am-5pm Mon-Fri May-Oct, 9am-1pm & 2-4.45pm Mon-Fri Nov-Apr) is a former 17th-century *tekke* (monastery) of the mystic Islamic sect known as the Mevlevi Order, or more familiarly, the Whirling Dervishes. Their spiritual philosophy, started in the Turkish town Konya, is based on the mystical branch of Islam called Sufism. Among the displays of the Dervishes are interesting

---

THE WHIRLING DERVISHES OF THE MEVLEVI ORDER

The founder of the Mevlevi Order was the poet Jelaluddin Mevlana, known in the West as Rumi, who was born in the 13th century. His most famous work is *Mathnawi*, a long poem that details Mevlana's teachings and understanding of the world, and emphasises the belief that an individual's soul is separated from the divine during one's earthly life; only God's love has the power to draw it back to its source. Rumi's teachings were also based on the belief that everything was created by God, so every creature was to be loved and respected. The order paid special attention to patience, modesty, unlimited tolerance, charity and positive reasoning. It forbade any expression or nurturing of anger, hierocracy and lies.

But most importantly, and shockingly to orthodox Muslims at that time, Rumi claimed that music was the way to transcend the mundane worries of life, and that one could connect with the divine through dancing, or indeed, whirling.

The slow, whirling trancelike dance of the Dervishes is called *sema*, and it is accompanied by the sound of the *ney* (reed flute), an instrument central to Rumi's idea of yearning for the divine. The sound of the *ney*, whose tonal range is equal to that of a human voice, is supposed to symbolise the soul's cry for God. The *oud* (Levantine lute) and *kudum* (paired drums) are the other instruments that accompany *sema*. During their dance, the Dervishes hold one palm upwards and the other downwards to symbolise humanity's position as a bridge between Heaven and Earth. The *sema* was performed exclusively as a spiritual exercise, and it was considered blasphemy to perform for money or show.

The Mevlevi Order flourished for 700 years in Turkish life and spread from Konya in Turkey to the Balkans and southeastern Europe, until they were banned in Turkey by Atatürk in 1925. Today the Dervishes perform in theatres all over the world, and it's possible to see their beautiful dance in most Western countries.

---

photographs of their dances in Nicosia in 1954. The most fascinating part of the museum is the former kitchen of the *tekke*, the centre of the hierarchical order in which the Dervishes lived and moved from 'interns' to achieving Dervish status. Each new intern would have to prove himself worthy by taking on the role of a kitchen servant for several years; at meal times, he would stand in the corner silently, watching out for subtle signals indicating the Dervishes' needs. Lifting a piece of bread indicated that the Dervish was thirsty and more water was needed.

The Turkish Museum also houses a room with the coffins of the 16 Mevlevi sheiks, and outside in the courtyard is a collection of Muslim tombstones.

Museum of Barbarism

Although the Turkish Cypriots may have removed the gruesome posters and photographs that used to greet arrivals at the Ledra Palace Hotel crossing, they have not forgotten the atrocities committed by Greek Cypriots and in particular EOKA thugs against the Turkish Cypriot community. The **Museum of Barbarism** (Barbarlık Müzesi; Irhan Sokak 2; admission 4.50YTL; ☼ 8am-2pm) is in a

quiet suburb to the west of the Old City and takes a bit of seeking out. On 24 December 1963, a mother and her children, along with a neighbour, were shot dead in their bath by EOKA gunmen. The bloodstained bath is retained as one of the exhibits in this rather macabre museum. There are other photo-documentary displays, particularly of Turkish Cypriots murdered in the villages of Agios Sozomenos and Agios Vasilios.

WALKING TOUR

Allow a leisurely two hours for this walk and extra time to see the sights.

Our self-paced walking tour is most conveniently started and finished at the **Ledra Palace Hotel crossing** (**1**; p63), especially if you are visiting North Nicosia on a day trip from the South. From the checkpoint, walk 100m and turn right onto Memduh Asar Sokak, and you will almost immediately cross into the Old City. Turn right along Zahra Sokak and walk past a line of old houses now undergoing renovation. These are the same houses that you can see from the Greek Cypriot side of the Ledra Palace Hotel crossing. Note the rusting oil barrels and gun placements on the Greek Cypriot side. Further along to your right, enter the small Yiğitler Park that sits atop the **Roccas Bastion** (**2**; p63) and stare out through the fence down into Greek Cypriot Lefkosia. This is the only point along the whole of the Attila and Green Lines where Turkish and Greek Cypriots can eyeball each other at such close quarters.

From the Roccas Bastion, head eastwards into the Old City along the narrow streets with tastefully restored houses of the Arabahmet neighbourhood. Make a left turn along Salahi Sevket Sokak, and then right into Beliğ Paşa Sokak to visit the **Dervish Pasha Museum** (**3**; p177), a small ethnographical collection housed in an old Turkish mansion. Follow Beliğ Paşa Sokak until it leads you into the pedestrianised zone in the centre of the city. Note the restaurants and cafés for lunch later. Follow Araşta

WALK FACTS

Start & Finish Ledra Palace Hotel crossing
Distance 4km

Sokak past the **Büyük Hammam** (**4**; p176) and detour to see the magnificent Turkish caravanserai, the **Büyük Han** (**5**; p176) and the nearby **Kumarcılar Han** (**6**; p176), under reconstruction. Continue a further 100m along Arasta Sokak until you arrive at the locked Ottoman bazaar called the **Bedesten** (**7**; p176), across the street from which is the municipal market, the **Belediye Pazarı** (**8**; p176). Hard to miss is the uncompleted former Lusignan cathedral of Agia Sofia, now the **Selimiye Mosque** (**9**; p176), incongruous with its soaring minarets added after the Ottoman conquest.

If you have time, seek out the **Library of Sultan Mahmut II** (**10**; p177) close by. Further east are the **Lapidary Museum** (**11**; p177) and **Haydarpasha Mosque** (**12**; p177), which was originally the 14th-century church of St Catherine. Head westwards along Idadi and Mecidiye Sokak, and make for the main square of **Atatürk Meydanı** (**13**), from where it's a short stroll north along Girne Caddesi to the Mevlevi Tekke, originally home of the Whirling Dervishes (see opposite), but now the **Turkish Museum** (**14**; p177).

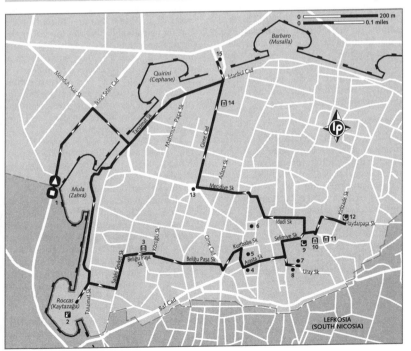

At the northern end of Girne Caddesi, you'll see **Kyrenia Gate (15)**, which was cut off from its protective walls when the British created a thoroughfare for traffic.

From Kyrenia Gate, it's a brisk 10-minute stroll inside the Venetian walls back to the Ledra Palace Hotel crossing, or to the pedestrian zone for lunch.

NORTH NICOSIA FOR CHILDREN

Considering the illustrious place of shadow theatre in the history of Cyprus, it's a surprise that the **Cyprus Turkish Shadow Theatre** (☎ 0542 850 3514; Büyük Han, Arasta Sokak) is the only place of its kind on the entire island. Shadow-puppet plays take place in the Büyük Han, but you will have to go there or call and inquire about details with Mehmet Ertuğ, the puppeteer.

If you fancy yourself as a bit of a Formula 1 whiz, go and pretend you are Michael Schumacher at **Zet Karting** (☎ 0533 866 6173; www .zetkarting.com; Lefkoşa–Güzelyurt Anayolu; 10-30YTL; ☺ 4pm-midnight Jun–mid-Sep, noon-8pm mid-Sep–Jun, closed Mon). Zet Karting has a large and very professional-looking series of circuits. You can rent carts from 10YTL for 10 minutes for the junior 300m course, 15YTL for the medium 900m course, or 30YTL for 10 minutes on the 1200m professional circuit. Unwind in the Z1 Bar or Z1 Cafeteria.

Zet Karting is just off the main roundabout on the road going out of North Nicosia. At the roundabout, take the turning to Güzelyurt (Morfou); it's on the left, after the Alaykoy turning.

SLEEPING

North Nicosia is terribly short of places to lay your head. The budget 'hotels' are around the Selimiye Mosque area and in the streets east of Girne Caddesi. They all have dorm-style rooms where a bed costs around UK£4 to UK£6, but they are pretty dire places with a bad reputation. We don't recommend any of them. Apart from that, there are only two hotels:

Saray (☎ 228 3115; saray@northcyprus.net; Atatürk Meydanı; s/d UK£27/41; ☒) The Saray, once a star on the Nicosia hotel scene, has a sense of faded glory about it. The rooms are spacious and resemble a '70s interiors ad, and the beds are soft and pretty uncomfortable for a price so high. It is right in the centre of the Old City, on Atatürk Meydanı, and is the city's best hotel and an unmissable landmark.

Royal Hotel (☎ 228 7621; ichangar@kktc.net; Gazeteci Kemal Aşik Caddesi; s/d UK£30/44; ☒ ☒) A much more upmarket place, it's popular with travellers on business. All rooms are fully serviced and have minibar, phone, satellite TV, and even a phone in the bathroom. There is also a swimming pool and a gym.

EATING

It's time to try those lovely kebabs. North Nicosia's eating scene is varied, with small kebab houses, *meyhane* (taverns), traditional restaurants, and chic, modern eateries. At the moment lunchtime eating is better than dinner, since there are more small kebab houses open offering a choice. At dinnertime the Old City gets very quiet and a little dark; so, apart from the two places we recommend, there are not that many options. There is a scattering of restaurants to the northwest of the Old City, usually hard to find and best reached by taxi; they are open evenings.

Old City

Boghjalian (☎ 228 0700; Salahi Şevket Sokak; meze around 10YTL; ☺ lunch & dinner) Housed in the former mansion of a wealthy Armenian, the Boghjalian is a quality restaurant and very popular in town. The set menu consists of either meze or mixed kebab. Food is served in a leafy courtyard. This place is almost always full for dinner and particularly for lunch, when visitors cross over from the South, especially as it's close to the Ledra Palace Hotel crossing point.

Sabor (☎ 228 8322; Selimiye Meydanı 29; mains 5YTL; ☺ lunch & dinner) Right next to Selimiye Mosque, this is decidedly North Nicosia's trendiest restaurant. Stylish wooden tables inside are surrounded by leather sofas in the lounge area; colourful lamps swing low; fashion photos adorn the walls. The large terrace is on the square, and on Wednesdays and Fridays there is live jazz piano music. Its excellent Italian and Spanish food is especially good for those days when you can't take another kebab, although there are oriental-style noodles too, and the prices are surprisingly low. The espresso and cappuccino are just right.

Konak (☎ 229 1210; Selimiye Meydanı 28; mains 10YTL; ☺ lunch & dinner) This traditional restaurant sits next to Sabor and is decorated in the

Ottoman style. It has a large garden, full of plants and flowers, and upstairs there is a wooden veranda and small coves for romantic dining. The food is eclectic: there is pasta, pizza, salads and kebabs, just take your pick.

Sedirhan Café (Büyük Han; mains 7YTL; 9am-5pm Mon, Wed, Fri, 9am-1am Tue & Thu, 9am-1pm Sat, closed Sun) This café is the best place to eat Turkish ravioli, while you admire the beauty of the Büyük Han (the Sedirhan is in its courtyard). You can also have a coffee or a beer, and eat some *börek* (meat or cheese rolled in thin pastry). On Tuesdays and Thursdays, the inn is a concert venue for (usually free) live music and the café stays open late.

Saray Roof (☎ 227 3115; Atatürk Meydanı; fixed-menu meals 12YTL; lunch & dinner) On the top of the Saray hotel, and commanding the best views of the city, this place is great for an evening cocktail. Unfortunately, the Turkish and 'European' food is unremarkable. The view is what you pay for, and you get to watch the city lights twinkle in the night.

For cheap kebabs on Girne Caddesi, the **Amasyali** (☎ 228 3294; Girne Caddesi 186; doner 1.50YTL; 9am-11pm) is open all day and does simple, tasty doner kebabs to eat in or take away. On the same street, the **Umutlar Restaurant** (☎ 227 3236; Girne Caddesi 51; kebabs 1.50YTL; 9am-11pm) is another kebab house for good food on the go.

In Araşta Sokak, opposite the Bedesten, is a shop that makes delicious halvah on the premises. Nearby is the **Belediye Pazarı** (6am-3pm Mon-Sat), a large, covered market selling fresh produce.

For coffee fetishists, the **Özerlat** (☎ 227 2351; Araşta Sokak 73; coffee 2.50YTL; 9am-6pm) has any kind of tea or coffee you can think of. A perfect place to take a break from a hard day's sightseeing.

New City

Unless you are staying in North Nicosia for a long time, or you decide to live here, you will rarely venture out into the frankly not very exciting eating scene in the New City. But if you do decide to go and boldly seek out where most tourists do not eat, try these places (all open for lunch and dinner):

Pasta Villa (☎ 228 4878; Mehmet Akif Caddesi 56; pasta dishes 7-10YTL) A self-service pasta restaurant that also does some OK pizza.

Pronto Bistro (☎ 228 6542; Mehmet Akif Caddesi; large pizza 8YTL) An eclectic option, located about 100m north of the British High Commission, where you can eat pizza, Tex-Mex and even a few Chinese and Indian dishes.

Moyra (☎ 228 6800; Osman Paşa Caddesi 32; meals 14YTL) For some Cypriot steaks and kebabs.

Annibal (☎ 227 1835; Saraçoğlu Meydanı; kebabs 9-11YTL) Another kebab house that has good, simple food, just outside the walls on the northern side of the Old City.

ENTERTAINMENT

Turkish Cypriots will themselves admit that nightlife in their capital is not all that hot, at least in the Old City. The Mehmet Akif Caddesi is quite animated, although if you're looking for a bit more noise and fun, most people go to Kyrenia, 25km away. Many North Nicosians go out to restaurants or have fun at home, which is not much use for travellers. But all is not lost, with a few OK spots where the young while away their time.

A popular drinking area in the Old City is behind the Belediye Pazarı inside the restored old market building. Resembling a kind of warehouse, with tall ceilings and low-hanging lamps, the space has a pretty, modern look. There are several bars inside, and the rather young clientele is keen on the nargileh-sucking. It's lively and fun for a drink in the Old City.

The Büyük Han has live music on Tuesday and Thursday evenings, in its central court.

Cinema Nostalgi Bar (☎ 227 7901; Kurtuluş Meydanı) On the northern side of town, this is perhaps the most popular of bars on North Nicosia's rock scene. Live music is on most evenings, but there is no cinema here – it's all in the name. The son of the North's Prime Minister, Mehmet Ali Talat, has been playing gigs here (he's a singer in a local rock band), so a bit of local celebrity spotting can be done too.

SHOPPING

The Büyük Han is the best place for a tourist to do some good shopping. Two places in particular are recommended:

Moniat Macun (☎ 229 0891; 9am-6pm) *Macun* is the art of fruit-preserving, and the lady who owns this shop has perfected that art. She preserves almost anything she comes across (so watch out), from exquisite green walnuts pickled while still raw, with a pungent, almost bitter taste; to the soft texture of melon and watermelon that melts in

NORTH NICOSIA (LEFKOŞA)

SHOPPERS BEWARE

A word of warning: if you're visiting from the South and decide to go on a shopping spree in the North or vice versa, beware the Greek Cypriot customs regulations. You can't take more than 200 cigarettes and 1L of alcohol or wine, plus CY£80 worth of other goods across the North–South border. So don't go carpet-buying!

---

the mouth. You can try the preserves before you commit, but a lovely jar will be a tasty reminder of summer fruits during the cold days of winter. Moniat is on the ground floor, opposite the Sedirhan café.

Koza (9am-6pm) Cyprus' heritage of producing silk from silk worms and the once ubiquitous mulberry trees comes alive in this shop, where the owner, Munise, together with her elderly mother, hand-weaves the silk patterns. The patterns were traditionally used for picture frames, or simply as framed wall decorations themselves. Koza is on the 1st floor, above Moniat Macun.

GETTING THERE & AWAY
Air
Ercan airport is about 14km east of North Nicosia and is linked to the city by an expressway. Many visitors to the North now fly to Larnaka airport, as the flights are direct and less subject to delays at Larnaka. There are scheduled flights to London and several destinations in Turkey. All charter flights operate from **Ercan** (Tymvou; 231 4703), although occasional flights are diverted to the military airport at **Geçitkale** (Lefkoniko; 227 9420), nearer to Famagusta, when Ercan is being serviced.

The two airlines serving Northern Cyprus are based in North Nicosia.

Cyprus Turkish Airlines (Kıbrıs Türk Hava Yolları, KTHY; 227 3820; www.kthy.net/kthyen/html; Bedrettin Demirel Caddesi)

Turkish Airlines (Türk Hava Yolları, THY; 227 1061; www.turkishairlines.com; Mehmet Akif Caddesi 32)

Bus
The long-distance bus station is on the corner of Atatürk Caddesi and Gazeteci Kemal Aşik Caddesi in the New Town. Buses to major towns leave from here. You may prefer the bus to the sometimes hair-raising rides in service taxis or *dolmuş* (minibuses).

Car & Motorcycle
Drivers and riders will enter North Nicosia via one of two main roads that lead directly to the Old City. If you come from Famagusta or Ercan airport, you will enter North Nicosia via Mustafa Ahmet Ruso Caddesi and then Gazeteci Kemal Aşik Caddesi. This road leads directly to Kyrenia Gate. Arriving from Kyrenia, you will enter North Nicosia via Tekin Yurdabay Caddesi and eventually Bedrettin Demirel Caddesi, which also leads towards Kyrenia Gate.

If you are entering North Nicosia from the Republic of Cyprus, the car crossing point is at Agios Dometios, west of the city. The easiest way into the Old City is to turn immediately right after passing the Ledra Palace Hotel crossing and enter via Memdah Asar Sokak. Turn left onto Tanzimat Sokak as soon as you cross the moat and you will reach Kyrenia Gate after about 200m.

Parking is usually not a problem, though finding a place in the Old City may get tricky if you arrive late in the morning on a working day. If you arrive early, you can easily park on Girne Caddesi.

Service Taxi & Minibus
Minibuses to local destinations and further afield start from various stations outside the Venetian walls, and also from the Itimat bus station, located just outside Kyrenia Gate. City destinations include Famagusta (1.50YTL, one hour) and Kyrenia (2.50YTL, 30 minutes). Service taxis also leave from the Itimat bus station.

GETTING AROUND
To/From the Airport
Buses to Ercan airport leave from the office of **Cyprus Turkish Airlines** (227 1240; Bedrettin Demirel Caddesi). They depart two hours before any flight and cost 2YTL. A taxi from Kyrenia Gate to the airport will cost 16YTL.

Bus
While there are public buses in North Nicosia, they tend to mainly service the suburbs outside the Old City. They are only really useful if you need to get to the Cyprus Turkish Airlines office or the main NCTO office (both on Bedrettin Demirel Caddesi), or a hitching spot, on a shoestring traveller's budget. Buses leave from near Kyrenia Gate.

Car

For car hire, try **Budget Car Rental** (☎ 228 2711; www.budgetcyprus.com; Irfan Bey Sokak) or **Sun Rent-A-Car** (☎ 227 2303; fax 228 3700; www.sunrentacar.com; Abdi Ipekçi Caddesi 10). If you are coming from the South, call ahead (see the boxed text, p231, for tips) and see if the company will meet you at the Ledra Palace Hotel crossing. Rates start at around UK£25 per day.

Taxi

There are plenty of taxi ranks in North Nicosia, though the most convenient and easiest to find is at Kyrenia Gate. A ride to anywhere in town should cost no more than 2YTL, though as a tourist you may be asked for more, say 2.50YTL. Above that, you are probably being ripped off. Ask the driver for the rate before getting into the taxi.

Among the more reliable taxi companies in North Nicosia are **Ankara Taxi** (☎ 227 1788), **Özner Taxi** (☎ 227 4012), **Terminal Taxi** (☎ 228 4909) and **Yılmaz Taxi** (☎ 227 3036).

When you cross into North Nicosia from the South, you will almost certainly be approached by tourist cab drivers offering to take you on tours of the North. They would prefer to give you the full treatment for around CY£30 (although Cyprus pounds are not generally used in the North, Turkish taxis at crossing points will always quote prices in Cyprus pounds), but in practice you can ask to be taken to wherever you like, such as Kyrenia for the day, and pay less accordingly.

These drivers are not rapacious – though they are keen for your custom – and they will often act as unofficial and at times informative guides.

This is the best solution if you want a taste of the North without the hassles of driving yourself.

Kyrenia (Girne) & the North Coast

As Northern Cyprus is being touted as 'pure Mediterranean' in tourist brochures, images of Kyrenia (Girne) harbour and castle are flooding the advertising spaces on Europe's urban buses and billboards. So potent is the romantic appeal of Kyrenia's harbour that it ranks as Cyprus' most beautiful vista. And although it's now commercialised and in reality not so romantic, the harbour is the centre of most tourist activity in the North, and the Gothic Kyrenia mountain range and the north coast have a strangely bewitching effect on the visitor.

The area was long ago 'discovered' by retired British civil servants, many of whom settled here after years of service in scattered lands throughout the former British Empire, to enjoy the region's mild climate. Kyrenia became a literary starlet in *Bitter Lemons of Cyprus,* written by Britain's most famous colonial son, Lawrence Durrell, who lived in Bellapais (Beylerbeyi), where he wrote his slow-paced nostalgic novel.

Bellapais, one of the island's most mesmerising villages, features the fascinating ruins of Bellapais Abbey, built in the 12th century by exiled Augustinian monks. Along the Kyrenia (Girne) Range, a displaced French dynasty left behind three Gothic castles, so dreamlike in appearance that one apparently inspired a fairytale production. The strategic position of the castles on the vertebra of the mountain range was carefully arranged, so that the three forts could communicate and warn each other of dangers by lighting torches.

Driving along the north coast from Kyrenia to Kaplıca (Davlos), you can catch the last of 'how Cyprus used to be': green, empty fields and a few village houses; unpicked olives soaking up the sun; the space and solitude of a rural Mediterranean landscape that has ceased to exist on much of the island. Unfortunately, the hollow skeletons of luxury villas are starting to flesh out here too. So hurry, before it's all over.

HIGHLIGHTS

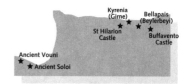

- Explore the nooks and cells of **Kyrenia Castle** and see one of the oldest shipwrecks ever recovered off the coast of Cyprus at the **Shipwreck Museum** (p187)

- Soak up the beauties of **Bellapais** (Beylerbeyi; p193): the abbey, the home of Lawrence Durrell, and the breathtaking views

- Get breathless climbing the many steps of the fairytale ruins of **St Hilarion Castle** (p196); then scale the wind-buffeted heights of **Buffavento Castle** (p196) and see Cyprus at your feet

- Drive east along the north coast from **Kyrenia to Kaplıca** (p197) and soak up the beauty and silence of the landscape

- Explore the sites of **Ancient Vouni** (p202) and **Ancient Soloi** (p202) on the northwest coast

KYRENIA (GIRNE)
KEPYNEIA

pop 22,000

Backed by its wide-bellied sand-coloured castle, Kyrenia's crescent-shaped harbour is like a sacred image among Cypriots. Promoted and praised by the Turkish Cypriots, and remembered in wistful songs and poems by Greek Cypriots, this small town is the centre of the North's tourism and home to the biggest British expat settlement on the island, with its own church and community centre. Perhaps Kyrenia is 'sold' too well to tourists. They are led to believe that the place will look the same as it did on the black-and-white photographs from the '50s, where a barefoot boy helps his fisherman father pull the nets out onto a small, wooden boat, surrounded by a sandy cove, with the burly castle brooding in the background.

Arriving at Kyrenia at midday, one discovers the small harbour that's jam-packed with bars, restaurants, cafés, boat-excursion touters, and waiters beckoning the passers-by in broken English. And not only that. This small town, no more than a 30-minute drive from the centre of the island's capital, is the place where North Nicosians come for the nightlife and good restaurants. Kyrenia (and its coastal surroundings) is lively and busy, with more hotels, restaurants and bars per square kilometre than anywhere else in the North. A picture-postcard, quaint seaside town it's not, but hey, you might have some fun.

HISTORY

Kyrenia's history is closely linked to the fortunes of its castle. Before the building of the castle, little is known about the town. It's thought that it was settled by mainland Greeks around 1000 BC. Kyrenia was certainly one of the city kingdoms of ancient Cyprus, but there is little left to document the town's earlier history. Arab raids of the 7th and 8th centuries AD levelled what there was of the settlement. It was only in the late 12th century, when the Byzantines built the castle, possibly over the remains of an earlier Roman fort, that Kyrenia's fortunes took an upward turn.

The Lusignans had a hand in the development of the castle, and it was used by them both as a residence and as a prison. During the course of their 82-year tenure, the Venetians extended the castle and built the bulbous seaward bulwark that can be seen today. During Ottoman rule, Kyrenia functioned primarily as a port – effectively the only port on the north coast. The harbour has long since ceded its role as the main port of the town; it's now far too small to service any craft other than the tourist boats and small yachts that crowd its cluttered quays. Two kilometres to the east, a large purpose-built harbour now receives commercial and passenger shipping, mainly from Turkey.

During British rule, the town became a favourite place for retiring ex-colonial British civil servants. Almost all Greeks and many British retirees fled in 1974 following the Turkish invasion, when the beaches to the west of Kyrenia were used as the prime beachhead for the landing of Turkish forces.

More than 25 years later, Kyrenia has recovered from the turbulence, and supports a growing tourist influx mainly from Britain, Germany and Turkey.

ORIENTATION

Kyrenia is spread out over a wide area, but the central Old Town – the tourist area – is fairly compact. Taxis and minibuses arrive at and depart from along Ecevit Caddesi and stop near the main square (Belediye Meydanı), which is about 200m immediately south of the Old Harbour. To the west of Belediye Meydanı runs Ziya Rızkı Caddesi, where you'll find shops and money-exchange offices. To the southeast runs Mustafa Çağatay Caddesi, which takes you to the New Harbour and the ferry to and from Turkey.

Long-distance buses arrive at the station on Bedrettin Demirel Caddesi at the junction with İnönü Caddesi, 1km south of the centre. If you arrive by car, there's a handy free car park immediately east of Belediye Meydanı.

Maps

The North Cyprus Tourism Organisation (NCTO) issues a free city map in English and Turkish. While it is lacking in detail

KYRENIA (GIRNE) & THE NORTH COAST

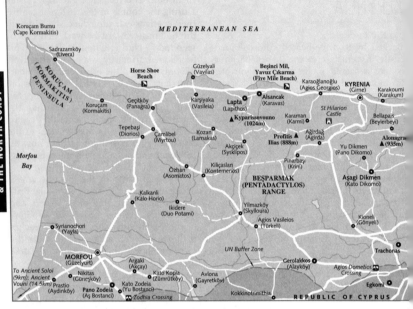

for the streets of the Old Town, it does give a good overall view of Kyrenia and most of the main regional destinations on a smaller inset.

INFORMATION

Bookshops

Green Jacket Bookshop (☎ /fax 815 7130; Temmuz Caddesi 20) West of the centre near the Astro supermarket, this is the place to go for foreign-language books. There's a varied range of travel and Cyprus-specific books, and a decent selection of LP guides to the region.

Internet Access

Kyrenia has at least two Internet cafés, including the following:

Bati Net Cafe (☎ 0542 873 1047; Ziya Rızkı Caddesi; per hr 1.50YTL; ☾ 10am-11pm) West of Belediye Meydanı; this modern centre has 14 terminals.

Cafe Net (☎ 815 9259; Efeler Sokak; per hr 1.50YTL; ☾ 10am-midnight) This is the best place for checking your mail, with 12 terminals. English-speaking owner Mehmet Çavuş serves up hot and cold drinks and jacket potatoes, and runs a small book exchange. Mehmet can also arrange for you to take out an Internet account in Northern Cyprus if you plan to stay any length of time.

Medical Services

Akçiçek Hastanesi (☎ 815 2254; Mustafa Çağatay Caddesi) Kyrenia's local hospital is about 500m southeast of the post office.

Money

There are a number of ATMs spread along the Ziya Rızkı Caddesi, including an HSBC. The **Türk Bankası** (Ziya Rızkı Caddesi) is located near Belediye Meydanı, and further west is the **İş Bankası** (cnr Ziya Rızkı Caddesi & Atatürk Caddesi).

You will also find a couple of efficient money-exchange offices along Ziya Rızkı Caddesi, including **Yazgın Döviz** (☎ 228 6673; Ziya Rızkı Caddesi), and **Gesfi Exchange** (Kordon Boyu 40), which is situated opposite the Dome Hotel.

Post

Post office (Mustafa Çağatay Caddesi) About 150m southeast of Belediye Meydanı.

Telephone

The telecommunications office is directly opposite the post office.

Toilets

There are public toilets on the breakwater, on the western side of the Old Harbour.

Tourist Information

Kyrenia Society (Mersin Caddesi; 🕙 10am-noon) A good place to drop by to see if there are any worthwhile events taking place. It is behind the post office. If no-one is there, the notice board will display details of upcoming events or excursions.

North Cyprus Tourism Organisation (NCTO; www .tourism.trnc.net; Girne Limanı; 🕙 8am-6pm) At the western end of the Old Harbour.

Travel Agencies

Tickets for ferries to Turkey are issued by two agencies, and also at the New Harbour.

Ertürk Turizm (☎ 815 2308; fax 815 1808; İskenderum Caddesi) Towards the New Harbour.

Ergün Denizcilik Şirketi (☎ 815 3866; Mustafa Çağatay Caddesi 6/2c)

SIGHTS

Kyrenia Castle & Shipwreck Museum

The wide, protective **Kyrenia Castle** (Girne Kalesi; admission 9YTL; 🕙 9am-6.45pm) is a powerful

backdrop to the dainty harbour. It is one of the town's only sights, and inside is an interesting mishmash of various bits of the area's history. The castle was built by the Byzantines and, while it might have staved off the Ottoman invasion of 1570, the Venetians quickly surrendered it when they saw how quickly Lefkosia had been overrun.

The large rectangular structure is guarded by four fortified bastions, one at each corner. You enter the castle via a stone bridge over a moat, which leads you to the small 12th-century **Byzantine Chapel of St George**, to the left of the entrance. The chapel, with its Corinthian columns, stood outside the walls until the Venetians incorporated it into the structure. Parts of its mosaics have survived.

In the northeast bastion, a Venetian tower has a display of eerie reconstructions of various military scenes. Dressed up in military armour and uniforms, the reconstructions (or rather, costumed mannequins) represent aspects of life in the castle's history and cover vast time periods, from the Byzantines to the British. One particularly gruesome reconstruction is in the north room, an infamous torture chamber. This is where King Peter I's mistress, Joanna L'Aleman, was thrown to be tortured by the king's jealous wife, Queen Eleanor, while Joanna was eight months pregnant with the king's child. The 'pregnant' mannequin gawping up at you from the dungeon below is sure to give you the creeps.

BUYER BEWARE

An estimated 4000 Britons live in Northern Cyprus. Low property and land prices in the North are drawing in buyers from abroad, and while this is a beautiful area for a summer home, beware of legal twists. Turkish land-holders have been known to sell Greek-owned land belonging to those displaced after the 1974 partition. There have been cases of buyers having to demolish the houses they built on such land, after the European Court of Human Rights ruled in the favour of the legal owners. So, if you're tempted to buy in the North, check if all the papers are valid and legal, or your foot might get knocked off the property ladder.

KYRENIA (GIRNE) & THE NORTH COAST

KYRENIA (GIRNE)

MEDITERRANEAN SEA

0 — 300 m
0 — 0.2 miles

KYRENIA (GIRNE) & THE NORTH COAST

To Green Jacket Bookshop (200m);
Scuba Cyprus (2km); Address
Restaurant & Brasserie (5km);
Beşinci Mil, Yavuz Çıkartma
(Five Mile Beach; 8km);
Alsancak (Karavas; 8km);
Alsancak (10km)

To Long-Distance Bus
Station (900m)

To Bellapais
(Beylerbeyi; 5km);
North Nicosia
(Lefkoşa; 29km)

To Ertürk Turizm (200m);
New Harbour (1km); Erol's Bar &
Restaurant (4km); Ozanköy (4km);
Anı (7km); Octopus Aqua
Park (7km); Çatalköy (7km)

Up along the ramparts, you can move between the four towers via routes marked by handrails. You are advised to stick to the marked routes since some sections are rather precipitous. The views of the harbour are fantastic from here. If you want to take good photographs of the town, climb up here in the early morning for guaranteed good light.

The highlight of the castle is the chamber containing the **Kyrenia Shipwreck**, the oldest shipwreck ever recovered from the waters around Cyprus.

This wooden-hulled cargo boat sank just off Kyrenia around 300 BC and was discovered in 1967 by a local diver. Based on its freight, which consisted mainly of almonds,

grain, wine and millstones from the Greek island of Kos, the crew most likely traded along the coast of Anatolia as far as the islands of the Dodecanese in Greece.

Antechambers display samples of the boat's cargo and photographs detailing the delicate salvage operation that was carried out to prevent the disintegration of the Aleppo pine from which the boat was constructed.

The boat is displayed in a dim chamber where you can examine the structure and layout of this remarkable marine archaeological find in considerable detail. A good reconstruction of the ship sits in Agia Napa's Thalassa Municipal Museum of the Sea (p162).

Folk Art Museum

This small **collection** (Halk Sanatları Müzesi; Girne Limanı; admission 2YTL; ☼ 9am-5pm Jun–mid-Sep), located along the harbourfront, contains a predictable but interesting collection of old household utensils, furniture and fabrics. Look out for the impressive wooden wine press on the ground floor.

ACTIVITIES
Diving

Scuba diving is well organised in Kyrenia. **Scuba Cyprus** (☎ 822 3430; fax 822 3429; Karaoğlanoğlu; ☼ 9am-5pm) runs PADI and BSAC diving courses. It is based at Santoria Holiday Village, about 2km west of Kyrenia. **Blue Dolphin Scuba Diving** (☎ 0542 851 5113; www .bluedolphin.4mg.com; ☼ 9am-5pm) is based in the Jasmine Court Hotel on Naci Talat Caddesi, but has a contact stand on the Old Harbour. Try-dives (in a pool) cost UK£20 while two regular dives cost UK£35. The prices also go up and down depending on the size of the group, so check before you go for it.

For information about the best dive spots in the South, see the boxed text Going Under, p86.

Boat Cruises

Kyrenia harbour's boat-cruise scene is like a market where everyone is selling the same thing, but with a detail here and there that differentiates one from the other. The basic formula is that for UK£20 you get cranked-up disco music to cruise by, swimming and snorkelling, followed by an on-board barbecue lunch (drinks extra). Most leave at 10.30am and return at 4.30pm, and take up to 28 passengers.

Aphrodite Boat Tours & Fishing (☎ 0533 868 0943; fantasia@superonline.com; Girne Limanı; UK£25) This outfit gives the passenger a little more intimacy by taking no more than 14 passengers at a time. The fishing trips, where you grill what you catch (but you don't go hungry if you catch nothing), are very successful. There is an option of deep-sea diving and scuba-diving excursions, arranged in advance, and at an extra charge. The friendly owner, Musa Aksoy, speaks four languages and is always around for a chat about his boat.

Hiking

British expat Barry Hurst runs a series of half- and full-day excursions to the Kyrenia (Girne) Range through **Cyprus Mountaineering Kyrenia** (☎ 0542 859 4542). For UK£25, you can walk, scramble and climb the rocky peaks and crags of the rugged Kyrenia Range. A restaurant lunch is included. Look for him in or near the Boaters Café on the harbour.

Another British expat, Tony Hutchinson, along with a group of other trekking enthusiasts, has pioneered a mountain-trekking trail from Koruçam Burnu (Cape Kormakitis) in the west to Zafer Burnu (Cape Apostolos Andreas) in the far east of Northern Cyprus. This long and challenging trek can be completed in about 10 days, walking around 22km a day. See the website of **Kyrenia Range Walks** (www.kyrenia-range-walks.com) for details.

Flower Walks

Tony & Maureen Hutchinson (☎ 0542 854 4329; www.walksnorchidsnorthcyprus.com; Hisarköy), long-term residents of Northern Cyprus, organise orchid and wild-flower walks during March and April on Tuesdays, Thursdays and Saturdays. The cost is UK£13 and includes lunch.

KYRENIA FOR CHILDREN

It's no wonder that water parks are all the rage in Cyprus, when the junior travellers love them so. **Octopus Aqua Park** (☎ 853 9674; Beşparmak Caddesi, Çatalköy; ☼ 8am-5pm), 8km east of Kyrenia, is a haven of water, where the little ones can climb, swing, slide and bounce on watery and dry spaces while the parents can relax at the pool bar or restaurant.

SLEEPING

The town centre has small guesthouses and little hotels, while the outskirts boast star-spangled giants. The following options are central.

Nostalgia Hotel (☎ 815 3079; fax 815 1376; Cafer Paşa Sokak 7; s/d UK£25/40; ⊠) A charming and nostalgic clutter of vintage radios, books, typewriters and large iron keys decorates the reception of this lovely hotel, set in an old townhouse. The rooms are decorated in an old-fashioned style, and have individual names. If you are after some luxury, the Venus room, with its four-poster bed, is on the ground floor. All rooms have TV, phone and air-con.

White Pearl Hotel (☎ 815 4677; www.whitepearl hotel.com; Girne Limanı; s/d UK£32/42; ⊠) The former Ergenekon Hotel has had a mighty face-lift.

The nine rooms in this boutique hotel have been renovated and decorated in an individual way, and bear the names of Northern Cyprus' towns with a cultural and historical heritage, like Salamis or Bellapais. The décor exudes cleanliness and understated style, and there are lovely views of the harbour. The roof terrace bar is good for late-night cocktails and drinks, even if you're not staying in the hotel.

Dome Hotel (☎ 815 2453; www.domehotelcyprus .com; Kordon Boyu Sokak; s/d UK£69/88; ☒) Mentioned in Durrell's *Bitter Lemons*, this dinosaur of Kyrenia's hotel scene is still considered the town's best hotel. The comfortable rooms have modern facilities, and there is a large seawater swimming pool to relax in. The Dome is on the seafront.

New Bristol Hotel (☎ 815 6570; fax 815 7365; Ziya Rızkı Caddesi 114; s/d UK£21/29; ☒) The New Bristol is like a faded star, with '70s décor that must have been attractive once upon a time. Now it's reminiscent of a socialist hotel, with slightly worn but tidy rooms, which all have mini bars and TVs.

Sidelya Hotel (☎ 815 6051; fax 815 6052; Nasır Güneş Sokak 7; s/d UK£8.50/17) This is a good budget option, with some spacious basic rooms, with views of the sea and the lighthouse on the pier. The owner, Yusuf Atman, speaks good English and offers endless supplies of black tea, but no breakfast.

Girne Harbour Lodge Motel (☎ 815 7392; fax 815 3744; Canbulat Sokak 46; s/d UK£16/29) Large rooms look onto the harbour, the ceilings are high, you're close to the restaurants and bars, but the unfortunate choice of neon striplighting ruins any prospects of cosiness. Only one room has a balcony, but all come with bathrooms.

Bingöl Guest House (☎ 815 2749; Efeler Sokak; r per person UK£10) A pretty dingy place, with a bar in the front and not a very jolly owner. Its saving grace is that it's cheap and on the main roundabout, so it's central. The rooms all have bathrooms.

EATING

Kyrenia's multitude of restaurants on the harbour are best avoided, with the exception of Set Fish Restaurant (right). This area is best for an evening drink, since the food is mainly aimed at the tourists, with a uniform menu of steak, burgers and chips. In any case, don't expect too many locals in any of the restaurants; they mainly eat simple kebab meals in Turkish-food joints. There are a couple of good restaurants in town, but serious diners tend to head out west towards Karaoğlanoğlu (Agios Georgios), or east to Çatalköy. Most places open for dinner only, unless otherwise indicated.

If you're planning a picnic or a mountain walk, grab the necessities at **Öz-Vip Supermarket** (☎ 815 3972; Efeler Sokak). It's well-stocked with all your favourites, including baked beans and Spam.

In Town

Brasserie (☎ 815 9481; Doğan Türk; mains 22-25YTL; ☷ dinner) A classy restaurant in an old colonial building, with a matching interior: a smoking room with dark wood-panelled walls, Hellenic statues, and a lot of warm brandy swigging. If you like good Italian food, this is the place for you, since it's run by an Italian. The menu has dishes like *risotto al tartufo* (risotto with truffles) and *penne alla vodka* (pasta with vodka; always gets the punters in), as well as meaty delicacies.

Padişah (☎ 815 9763; Ecevit Caddesi; kleftiko 7YTL; ☷ lunch & dinner) Run by a London-Cypriot returnee, this place is all about traditional food like *kleftiko* (oven-baked lamb) and meze. The décor is simple and stylish, and there is a nice garden for alfresco eating. It's in a nook, opposite the Colonial Hotel and the petrol station.

Idris ustanın yeri (Ecevit Caddesi; kebab 6YTL; ☷ lunch & dinner) This is a workers' eatery, with chicken, lamb, doner and shish kebabs, and massive salads and pickles on the side. Delicious, simple, and highly recommended.

Niazi's Restaurant & Bar (☎ 815 2160; Kordon Boyu Sokak; full kebab 10YTL; ☷ 11am-midnight) This place is renowned among kebab munchers, but its reputation seems to have compromised its quality. The jolly waiters will 'jokingly' bring you a large beer even if you've asked for a small one, then seriously charge you for it. The kebabs are plentiful, but the meat is pretty dry and uneventful. Niazi's is very popular with the locals, who flock here in their dozens, so booking is a good idea.

Set Fish Restaurant (☎ 815 2336; Girne Limanı; fish 20-45YTL; ☷ dinner) Fish, sweet fish. Straight from the sea, and onto your plate, and all while you're watching the boats bobbing in the harbour. This is the one exception among the harbour restaurants. The atmosphere is good, the fish delicious, and a frosty bottle of white wine will make the evening perfect. There's even lobster, in season.

Set Italian Restaurant (☎ 815 6008; Girne Limanı; pasta & pizzas 8-10YTL; 🕒 lunch & dinner) Sister of Set Fish Restaurant, but with an Italian twist. It features Turkish as well as European dishes, and the food is served in a pleasant, shaded courtyard.

Out of Town

Five Mile Restaurant (☎ 821 8330; www.escapebeach club.com/5Mile.html; mains 10-30YTL; 🕒 dinner) A modernist cube of a building with a wooden deck terrace and tables just above the sea, each lit by a hanging iron candle lamp. There's an outside bar with a lounge area, and inside are circular leather sofas for winter drinking. The menu encompasses just about everything: fresh fish, seafood, grilled tarragon chicken, Peking duck, noodles and pasta. The bar and club here are popular with nightbirds (right). Five Mile is on the western coastal road out of town, with a visible yellow sign, by Yavuz Çıkarma (Five Mile) Beach.

Address Restaurant & Brasserie (☎ 822 3537; Ali Aktaş Sokak 13; mains 11-16YTL; 🕒 dinner) If you decide to head out towards Karaoğlanoğlu, this is the restaurant to look out for, situated on the main road west. It's considered one of Northern Cyprus' best and is situated on a little point overlooking the sea. The menu is European-based and includes mostly fish, pasta and meat. The orange and tarragon chicken (13.50YTL) is a good dish to try.

Altınkaya I (☎ 821 8341; Yavuz Çıkarma Plaj; mains 10YTL; 🕒 dinner) Named after the nearby beach, this place is further west on the way to Lapta (Lapithos), around 10km west of town. The food is great value, with good meze and fresh fish main courses.

Erol's Bar & Restaurant (☎ 815 3657; Ozanköy; kleftiko 10YTL; 🕒 dinner) One of two good restaurants to the east, on the way to Bellapais (the other is Anı). Renowned for its good quality meat and meze, Erol's also serves homemade soup, garnish and pickles, and some good fish dishes. There are great views over the village of Ozanköy. Wednesday is *kleftiko* night.

Anı (☎ 824 4355; Zeka Adil Caddesi, Çatalköy; fish dishes 10-20YTL; 🕒 dinner) A lovely and affordable fish tavern, with fresh home-grown vegetables, and tasty meze. It is about 2.5km further east of Erol's. Many consider it the best fish restaurant in Cyprus.

DRINKING & ENTERTAINMENT

The bars and cafés on the waterfront are all much of a muchness when it comes to variety, but the following are good fun. All open after 8pm, except where noted.

Cyprian Bar (☎ 0533 863 6899; Cafer Paşa Sokak; 🕒 9pm-2am) A shady, leafy, cool garden bar, opposite the Nostalgia Hotel, popular with youngsters for drinks and rock music.

Ego Bar (☎ 0533 842 9999; Doğan Türk; 🕒 9pm-2am) Another open-air drinking space with a lounge atmosphere, Ego is decked out with hammocks and cow-print tablecloths. Just below the Brasserie (opposite).

Café 34 (☎ 815 3056; Girne Limanı; 🕒 4pm-2am) A bar on the harbour, good for a quiet drink during the day or a busy mishmash of tourists and local youngsters in the evening.

White Pearl Hotel Bar (☎ 815 4677; www.white pearlhotel.com; Girne Limanı) Great views of the harbour and elaborate cocktails (8YTL to 10YTL), on the roof terrace of the White Pearl Hotel (p189). Drinkers of all ages gather here, but a young crowd lingers after 11pm. Delicious non-alcoholic fruit cocktails are 3.50YTL.

Escape Beach Club (☎ 821 8330; www.escapebeach club.com) A massive open-air all-night club, with theme parties almost every week, DJs from London, Turkey and Cyprus, and lots and lots of people having fun. The club is just by Yavuz Çıkarma (Five Mile) Beach, overlooking the sea.

Five Mile Bar (☎ 821 8330; www.escapebeachclub .com/5Mile.html) Part of the restaurant of the same name (left), the food ceases around 10pm when the partying starts, and goes on until late. Similar to Escape, and run by the same people, it's also open-air, with a drinking, dancing and relaxing area.

If you really want to dispose of your surplus cash, there's an oversupply of casinos in Kyrenia. They're not necessarily the black-tie-and-tux establishments you might imagine, but glorified gaming-machine, get-rich-quick dens of iniquity for gambling-deprived Turkish mainlanders. Still, if you want to try your luck at blackjack, chemin de fer or roulette, or simply to exercise your fingers on the gaming machines, try **Dome Casino** (☎ 815 9283; www.domehotelcyprus.com; Kordon Boyu Sokak) for starters, or if that doesn't pull you a pile, move on to the **Casino Rocks** (☎ 815 9333; Kordon Boyu Sokak), where a tie and tux are not out of place.

SHOPPING

There is a small shopping mall with boutiques and brand-name imported goods off Ziya Rızkı Caddesi, as well as a wide range of tourist shops that sell everything from snorkelling gear to leather goods.

Round Tower (☎ 815 6377; Ziya Rızkı Caddesi; ❂ 10am-5.30pm) A small art and crafts shop with a selection of tasteful goods such as pottery, rugs and paintings in the restored Lusignan-era Round Tower in the central area of Kyrenia.

GETTING THERE & AWAY

The long-distance bus station is on Bedrettin Demirel, in the south of the New Town. *Dolmuş* (minibuses) to Famagusta (Mağusa; 2.50YTL, 1¼ hours) and North Nicosia (Lefkoşa; 2.50YTL, 20 minutes), as well as service taxis to North Nicosia (1.50YTL, 20 minutes). All depart from Belediye Meydanı.

There are express boats to Taşucu in Turkey at 9.30am daily (41.50YTL, three hours) from the New Harbour, east of town. There's also a slower daily ferry that takes about seven hours (33.50YTL). Tickets can be bought from the passenger lounge at the port or from **Fergün Denizcilik Şirketi** (☎ 815 2344; Mustafa Çağatay Caddesi 6/2c). During peak season, there is also a twice-weekly express ferry to Alanya in Turkey (UK£20, 4½ hours).

Cyprus Turkish Airlines (Kıbrıs Türk Hava Yolları, KTHY; ☎ 815 2513; www.kthy.net/kthyen/html; Philecia Ct, Suite 3, Kordon Boyu Sokak) has an office just west of the Old Harbour.

GETTING AROUND

Kyrenia is small enough for visitors to get around on foot. Should you need to travel further afield, there is a large number of car-hire outlets.

Generally, you will find that the prices are the same all over the island, with UK£25 per day being an average price. In Kyrenia, try **Oscar Car Rentals** (☎ 815 2272; Kordon Boyu), a large office based opposite the Dome Hotel. The price per day goes down the longer you have the car.

You can take a service taxis from Kyrenia to various destinations including Ercan airport (20YTL, one hour), Bellapais (7YTL, 20 minutes) and St Hilarion (2.50YTL, 25 minutes).

THE NORTH COAST

Kyrenia is in an ideal position for excursions to other parts of the island, with possibilities for days in the sun lounging on a beach, trekking, visiting castles on mountain tops, and bonding with nature in the region's wonderfully unspoilt northwestern corner. The distances are generally pretty short, so driving is the best option. Most roads have been resurfaced and can be covered easily in a conventional vehicle.

Hiking

The NCTO produces a small *Mountain Trails* brochure, available free from NCTO offices. It describes at least two walks in the Kyrenia Range that you may want to investigate. However, the brochure is not detailed enough for serious hikers, so you are advised to use a good map and join one of the organised local tours (see p189) and let others do the hard work of map reading.

For keen walkers, there is a trek from Ağirdağ (Agirda) to Geçitköy (Panagra). This is a fairly long hike that would need to be done in sections and perhaps broken over a few days. The hike runs west along the southern flank of the Kyrenia Range, beginning from the village of Ağirdağ on the Kyrenia–North Nicosia road and ending up at Geçitköy on the Kyrenia–Morfou (Güzelyurt) road. The trail can be broken or joined at Lapta. Most sections take two to three hours.

The hiking trail from Kantara to Alevkaya is fairly long (more than 40km), connecting Kantara Castle and the Alevkaya Herbarium and forest station (p197). The hike mainly follows forest trails along the spine of the Beşparmak (Pentadaktylos) Range. It passes through or near a number of villages along the way, and can be walked in sections.

Contact the **Association of Mountaineering** (☎ 0542 851 1800; mustafacemal@hotmail.com) for full details.

Beaches

Kyrenia's top swimming beach is west of the town and is known as **Yavuz Çıkarma (Five Mile) Beach**, which is overlooked by the restaurant of the same name (p191). This sandy cove has three names in Turkish. Altınkaya, after the rock next to it, is also the name of the recommended restaurant that overlooks the beach (p191). Its two other names are Beşinci Mil (Five Mile), and Yavuz Çıkarma (Resolute Outbreak). This beach was used by the Turkish Army to launch their invasion/rescue operation in 1974. The rather phallic-looking structure on the road overlooking the beach, known locally as 'the Turkish erection', is a monument to this event.

The beach is such a popular spot that on most days there's no room to swing a cat. It is protected from the open sea by a rocky islet, easily reached by paddling. Watch out for tricky currents on the open-water side: a few bathers have been caught out and swept away. There are water sports available, and umbrellas and sun loungers for hire, though there is not much natural shade.

If you fancy quieter and less developed beaches, go east of Kyrenia. With one notable exception, these are better loved by seekers of solitude. The first worth a mention is **Çatalköy Beach**, 7km from Kyrenia. It is reached via a signposted road off the main road. Look for Seamus O'Flynn's pub, turn here and continue for 1.5km; turn right at the junction. The beach is a narrow smile of sand in a pretty little protected bay. There are beach loungers to rent and a diving platform. The beach restaurant, **Körfez** (☎ 824 4354), serves juicy kebabs.

Next along is the private **Vrysi (Acapulco) Beach**, now looked after by the large three-star **Acapulco Holiday Village** (☎ 824 4110; fax 824 4455), which caters for package tourists, but takes in casual guests as well. Admission to the complex is 2.50YTL, and the beach offers many facilities. It's OK if you don't mind paying to park and swim. Popular with expats is **Lara (Vakıflar) Beach**, 3km further along and signposted just before the large power station. There is no charge to park and swim. The somewhat scruffy dark sand beach is nonetheless generally clean, and there are spotless toilets and changing rooms. A small **snack bar** serves beach goers.

Finally, about 19km from Kyrenia is **Turtle (Alagadı) Beach**, where the Society for the Protection of Turtles (SPOT) has a small monitoring station, affectionately called the 'Goat Shed'. The twin sandy beaches here

are generally undeveloped and are strictly speaking total turtle territory. Swim elsewhere if you can. The beach is closed from 8pm to 8am from May to October. For more about Cyprus' turtles, see the boxed text, p216. Have a meal at **St Kathleen's Restaurant** (☎ 0533 861 7640) nearby on the main road, where the meze, grills and fish dishes, such as *tsipura* (bream), are excellent and good value for money.

Getting Around

No public transport serves the area around Kyrenia, so it will have to be service or private taxis, a hire car or pedal power. The area does provide for some of the best cycling in Northern Cyprus. Other than some gradients in the Kyrenia Range escarpment, the east-west routes are generally flat and well serviced by facilities such as places to eat and beaches to swim at. There's a fine place to stay in the village of Kaplıca (Davlos), 63km east of Kyrenia. There are more options available if riding to the west.

BELLAPAIS (BEYLERBEYI)

The vertical road up to the gorgeous Bellapais village will keep you concentrating on the driving, so that when you finally park, inevitably by Bellapais Abbey, you will be stunned by two things: the endless views from the mountain village, and the abbey, which is always more spectacular than expected. Bellapais is the perfect day trip from Kyrenia, but it is even more perfect as a base for exploring the region, if you don't mind the drive to the village.

The village was made famous by the British writer Lawrence Durrell, who lived here before and during the Ethniki Organosi tou Kypriakou Agona (EOKA; National Organisation for the Cypriot Struggle) uprising against British rule in Cyprus. His immediate and lasting love for the village (and the island) is often hilariously described in *Bitter Lemons of Cyprus*.

Drivers should note that there is a large car park just past the monastery, on the left. Try to avoid parking in the already cluttered main street.

Sights
BELLAPAIS ABBEY
This lovely Augustinian **monastery** (admission 6YTL; ⏰ 9am-7pm Jun–mid-Sep, 9am-5pm mid-Sep–May)

A TALE OF TWO TREES

When writer Lawrence Durrell took up residence in Bellapais (Beylerbeyi) between 1953 and 1956, he little realised the minor controversy he would leave behind almost 50 years after he first described life in the then blissfully bucolic mixed community. His famous book *Bitter Lemons of Cyprus* describes the trials and tribulations of purchasing and renovating a house in the village, as well as the intrigues and gossip of village life in general. On a more sombre note, he sounded the alarm bell for the troubles that were to ultimately befall Cyprus not too many years later.

Among the villagers' favourite activities was to spend many an hour in idle conversation under the so-called 'Tree of Idleness', which dominated the main square. Throughout the whole book, Durrell never once mentions what kind of tree it was. A plane tree? A mulberry tree? An oak tree?

Today there are two trees that vie for the title of Tree of Idleness. One is a leafy mulberry tree overshadowing the coffee shop next to the monastery ticket office. The other contender, not 20m away, is a Japanese pagoda tree casting shade over the eponymous Huzur Ağaç (Tree of Idleness) Restaurant. In fairness, both trees could qualify for the role pretty well: both have their ardent supporters and draw an idle crowd of onlookers who like to sit and drink coffee or a cold beer, just as the villagers would have done in Durrell's day. So, pick your tree, order a coffee and engage in idle chatter. It's all the same in the end.

is reason enough to drive up to Bellapais. Near the end of the 12th century the Augustinian monks, who had fled Palestine following the fall of Jerusalem to the Saracen Saladin (Selahaddin Eyyubi) in 1187, came here. They established a monastery by the name of Abbaye de la Paix (Abbey of Peace), from which the corrupted version of the name Bellapais evolved. The original structure was built between 1198 and 1205, yet most of what we see today was constructed between 1267 and 1284 during the reign of Hugh III. The cloisters and the large refectory were added during the reign of Hugh IV (1324–59).

When Cyprus was taken by the Ottomans, the monastery was put under the protection of the Orthodox Church. This apparently wasn't enough to prevent villagers and later the British overlords from using the stone from the building for other purposes.

What is left today is a mixture of completion and destruction, with some parts of the monastery in an excellent state of preserve. The **refectory** to the north side of the cloister is frequently used for gatherings and events. From here, there are splendid views across to the sea and the plains below. Less well-preserved is the **kitchen court** on the west side, where all that remains are a few walls; the more daring can scramble onto a rather precarious section of wall for a better view. The now dim and dank church is in gener-

ally good condition, and remains much as it was in 1976 when the last of the Greek Orthodox faithful were obliged to leave.

The cypress-lined 14th-century **cloister** is the monastery's most poignant section, and is almost complete, apart from the western side, where it has fallen down or been pulled apart. This now looks out onto a restaurant (see opposite), where diners can gaze onto the open cloister courtyard over their meze.

Get your entry ticket from the not-so-obvious ticket booth set back a little to the left as you enter. You can exit the way you came in, or directly into the restaurant forecourt.

HOME OF LAWRENCE DURRELL

The second reason to visit Bellapais, but only if you know his work, is to visit the **home of Lawrence Durrell**. The village's only literary son, Durrell lived here in the early 1950s; although the near-idyllic, mixed-community days described in his book *Bitter Lemons of Cyprus* have long since gone, the novel remains compulsory reading for visitors to Cyprus. The **Tree of Idleness** (see the boxed text, above) under which Durrell's characters spent many an indolent hour still remains, these days more likely shading tourists clutching cold beers. Durrell's house is still a private residence, but a yellow plaque over the main door marks the spot where he spent his bohemian days.

To reach the house, head inland along the street to the right of the Huzur Ağaç Restaurant and walk about 200m more or less straight and upwards. You will come across the house on your left. Ask if you lose your way – not difficult in the winding, narrow alleyways.

Festivals & Events

Every year during May and June, the **Bellapais Music Festival** (☎ 0542 854 6417; www .cypnet.co.uk/ncyprus/culture/music/agenda/bellapais festival) takes place in and around the abbey. The festival consists of concerts, recitals and even brass-band performances in the refectory. Prominent posters advertising the events are on display around town, in Kyrenia and elsewhere.

Sleeping & Eating

Bellapais has some excellent places to stay. It's close enough to Kyrenia to be easily accessible, but far enough away to feel like somewhere different.

Residence (☎ 815 9296; www.cyprusparadise.com; r per person UK£40; 🗙 🖾) This hotel is a unique slice of style and comfort pretty much unmatched on the island (among the more affordable choices). The Residence has a colonial décor, with nine rooms named after the various empires that have left their mark on Cyprus, and each is individually and accordingly decorated. The rooms surround a small swimming pool, so silence is almost guaranteed. There is a 'secret garden' where you can chill out among cushions and candles. The power showers are heavenly. If you want to feel a bit pampered, this place breathes quality and care.

Hotel Bellapais Gardens (☎ 815 6066; www.bella paisgardens.com; s/d UK£30-45/60-90; 🗙 🖾) This luxurious resort has self-contained studios and one- and two-bedroom apartments, all with expansive sea views. A lush, almost tropical garden is at the centre, with a swimming pool and a bar to relax in. The abbey is just above you, so you can admire its curves from the pool. Breakfast is UK£4.50.

Abbey Inn (☎ 815 9444; fax 815 9446; r per person UK£30; 🖾) Just off the main street, the Abbey Inn is a small hotel with 10 doubles looking out onto a small swimming pool. The neat rooms are decorated with local antiques, wrought-iron beds and grand wooden wardrobes. It's run by the same owners as the Huzur Ağaç (Tree of Idleness) Restaurant.

Guthrie's Bistro Bar (☎ 815 2820; per person UK£16; 🕑 dinner, drinks all day) Deirdre Guthrie, the owner of Gardens of Irini (see the boxed text, below), runs a small restaurant in her gorgeous garden, serving freshly prepared food. And she cooks up a storm for dinner. The menu is normally a starter of gazpacho (cold tomato soup), or haloumi and tomatoes; the main is a choice of *kleftiko*, garlic and lemon chicken or sweet and sour pork; and for dessert you get ice cream or a fruit compote. Deirdre also serves Italian red and white wine, and makes a great brandy sour (see the boxed text, p105). Always book one day ahead.

Kybele (☎ 815 7531; meals 20YTL; 🕑 dinner) Surrounded by verdant foliage, this place has the best views of the abbey in the village: it's right next door to it. While the food is good and service very attentive, you can also just have a drink in the cool, welcoming gardens and enjoy the soothing music.

THE AUTHOR'S CHOICE

Gardens of Irini (☎ 815 2820; www.gardensofirini.com; per person UK£20) Right up at the top of the village, among green shrubbery and close to Lawrence Durrell's house, the Gardens of Irini is a real little paradise. There is one studio and a one-bedroom apartment (Lilly Cottage), both self-catering and adjacent to a traditional village house. Each has a little private courtyard, a kitchen decorated with lovely rustic cupboards and cookers, the main room has a fireplace, lovely rugs and Oriental rice-paper blinds; the beds are comfortable, and the bathrooms have a shower and bath – what more could you want? Food? Worry not. The charming owner Deirdre Guthrie cooks up a kicking breakfast, and for dinner (an extra charge), she prepares scrumptious food (see above). All meals are served in the cool, leafy garden. And if you're really lucky, Deirdre might tell you some great stories from her days as a professional flamenco dancer in Spain. Booking in advance is advisable.

Paşa (☎ 815 7586; meals 10YTL; ☺ lunch & dinner) A basic eatery at the end of the main village street, excellent for some *lahmacun* (Turkish pizza) and Turkish ravioli, which comes with a good portion of salad. Most tourists avoid this place for its lack of luxury, but for some homemade, tasty carbohydrates and meat, this is a treat.

Huzur Ağaç (Tree of Idleness) Restaurant (☎ 815 3380; fixed menu 15YTL; ☺ lunch & dinner) This is Durrell's famed Tree of Idleness. An atmospheric place where you can have a drink, but you're advised to avoid the tourist-oriented food.

ST HILARION CASTLE ΑΓΙΟΣ ΙΛΑΡΙΟΝ

The outline of the almost magical, fairytale remains of **St Hilarion Castle** (☎ 0533 161 276; admission 6YTL; ☺ 9am-4.45pm) will not become apparent until you are directly beneath it, so blended is the structure with the cliffside. The castle *(kalesi* in Turkish) has just enough hidden rooms, tunnels, overgrown gardens and steep staircases and paths to leave parents gasping for breath and the children asking for more.

Rumour has it that Walt Disney drew inspiration from the jagged contours of St Hilarion when he made *Snow White*. Local legend tells that the castle once had 101 rooms, the last of which was a secret garden belonging to a fairy 'queen'. She apparently used to enchant shepherds and hunters and rob them of their catch, as well as a few years of their lives, which they spent in a deep slumber.

The castle's real history is a bit more based on Planet Earth. This lofty fort is named after a monk called Hilarion, who fled persecution in the Holy Land. He lived and died in a cave on the mountain that overlooks the plain of Kyrenia and protects the pass between Kyrenia and North Nicosia. During the 10th century, the Byzantines built a church and monastery over the tomb of Hilarion. Earlier, the site's strategic position had been used mainly as a watchtower and beacon during the Arab raids of the 7th and 8th centuries. This was an important link in the communication chain between Buffavento and Kantara castles further east. In 1191, Guy de Lusignan decided to take control of St Hilarion by besieging and dislodging the self-styled Byzantine emperor of Cyprus, Isaak Komninos. St Hilarion was then extensively expanded and used both as a military outpost and a summer residence for the Lusignan court until the arrival of the Venetians.

The Venetians neglected the castle and it fell into disrepair. It only saw practical use again in 1964 when Turkish Cypriot activists from Turk Müdafaa Teskilati (TMT) were able to take control of the castle and fend off EOKA-inspired attacks. It has been in Turkish Cypriot hands ever since; a covetously protected Turkish military base on the ridge below the castle is testament to its ongoing status as a strategic location.

The site consists of three main parts, but this is not immediately obvious to the visitor as the stones and ruined buildings blend so seamlessly into the rocky landscape. Visitors enter by the **barbican** and the main gate into the **lower enceinte**, which was used as the main **garrison** and **stabling area**. A meandering path leads you up to the **middle enceinte**, which was originally protected and sealed off by a drawbridge. Here are the remains of a **church**, more **barrack rooms** and a four-storey **royal apartment**. There is also a large **cistern** for the storage of vital water.

Access to the **upper enceinte** is via a windy and steep track, thankfully paved and renovated in more recent years. You enter the upper castle via a **Lusignan gate** guarded by a **Byzantine tower** and reach an overgrown central courtyard. Around the courtyard are more **royal apartments**, **kitchens** and **ancillary chambers**. A final breath-sapping climb takes you to **Prince John's tower** where, as legend has it, Prince John of Antioch, convinced that his two Bulgarian bodyguards were planning to kill him, had them thrown over the steep cliff to their death.

The view from the top is stunning, and on a clear day you can see the **Taurus Mountains** in Turkey, more than 100km away. To the west, you can look down on the village of Karaman (Karmi). Kyrenia to the north, around 730m lower in elevation and several kilometres away, looks very small and insignificant.

Come early if you can; the climb to the top is tiring and can be quite difficult on a hot day. There is a small snack bar in the car park.

BUFFAVENTO CASTLE

The three castles of the Kyrenia Range are like three beautiful sisters in a folk tale. Each is in competition with the other, trying to be different in order to draw attention to themselves. Like some sisters, Kantara Castle (p216) is considered the most romantic of the trio and St Hilarion (opposite) the most interesting; but the lofty fortress of **Buffavento Castle** (Buffavento Kalesi; admission free; ☉ dawn-dusk) is the one that plays hard-to-get.

This majestic castle, whose name means 'buffeted by the winds', perches precariously 940m above the sea, overlooking the plain of the Mesarya (from the Greek word *mesaoria*, meaning 'between the mountains') to the south. In medieval times, it was called the Castle of the Lion, but little is known about its early history. It dates back at least to 1191 when Richard the Lionheart took it over from the daughter of the Byzantine emperor Isaak Komninos. The Lusignans used it as a prison and beacon tower, as it was in line of sight with both Kantara to the east and St Hilarion to the west.

The attraction of the castle is its remoteness and the views from the ruins, especially on a clear day when the winds aren't buffeting it. While it isn't in the best condition, there are still a couple of covered chambers in the lower castle, and a renovated stairway now allows access to the upper parts. The walkways are well protected and the views from the very top are truly magnificent.

The castle is divided into two main sections, the **lower enceinte** and the **upper enceinte**, which occupy a relatively small area on the rocky peak where it was constructed. The castle was built in such a way that no further fortifications were needed other than the outer walls of the main buildings, since there is no way in other than through the main entrance.

Getting there is half the fun. It is prominently signposted off the Beşparmak (Pentadaktylos) Pass as Buffavento Kalesi. From here, it is a 5km, 15-minute drive along a dirt track to the small parking area below the fortress. The walk up, which is fairly steep but gradual, should take between 30 and 40 minutes. Good footwear is necessary, and a walking stick or trekking poles are useful.

KYRENIA TO KAPLICA (DAVLOS)
ΔΑΥΛΟΝ

This is a wonderful area of Cyprus and most interesting for those who want to see the last untouched parts of the island that has changed so much over the last thirty

years. The meandering, narrow coastal road from Kyrenia to Kaplıca and on towards Kantara Castle runs eastward along plantations of olives and carobs, small village houses, and space and silence that you won't find elsewhere, apart from the Karpas (Kırpaşa) Peninsula. This road can either be a day's excursion on your way to Kantara Castle (see p216), or a long way around to the Karpas Peninsula.

The route passes some beaches (p192) and continues on for some 60km before the turning to Kantara Castle at the village of **Kaplıca**. On the way, you can stop for a swim, check out the deserted ruins of various churches, and closely examine the sand cliffs that look like something out of a lava lamp.

The further you go, the drier and more barren the land becomes. The road passes within metres of the sea for long stretches at a time. Look out for the long-abandoned **carob warehouses**, still standing sentinel from a time when this natural commodity, fairly unknown in the West, was a source of great wealth to Cyprus.

You will see the first sign to Kantara Castle (Kantara Kalesi) about 7km before Kaplıca. Ignore it: it is a longer route, and besides, you will miss out on the opportunity for a pre-castle swim at **Kaplıca Beach** shortly before the junction to Kaplıca village, which lies a kilometre or so up the hillside. The wonderfully sandy strand is the only decent place to swim along this long lonely stretch. The beachside **Kaplıca Beach Restaurant & Hotel** (Kaplıca Plaj; ☎ 387 2032; fax 387 2031; r UK£20) will feed you and give you a place to stay should you wish to break your journey, in simple rooms, but away from the crowds.

Turn right at the signposted junction for Kaplıca village and eventually you will see Kantara Castle perched precipitously high up above the coastline on a rocky spur.

ALEVKAYA HERBARIUM
A worthwhile visit can be made along the back road of the Beşparmak (Pentadaktylos) spur of the Kyrenia Range to see the **Alevkaya Herbarium** (admission free; ☉ 8am-4pm), a forest station on the mountain ridge between Esentepe (Agios Amvrosios) and Değirmenlik (Kythrea). The herbarium is home to samples of most of the endemic

Cypriot flora and it includes some 1250 native-plant species. On display are many dried and preserved specimens, as well as the fresh variety. The display developed out of a collection made by English botanist Deryck Viney, whose book *Illustrated Flora of North Cyprus* documented the country's varied botanical treasure-trove.

If ever you arrive outside opening hours, someone will usually let you in. To get to the herbarium, take a signposted forest road off the southern side of Pentadaktylos Pass, or from the northern coastal road signposted via Karaağaç (Harkia) or Esentepe.

LAPTA (LAPITHOS) ΛΑΠΗΘΟΣ

The village of Lapta is popular as a day trip for its proximity to Kyrenia as well as for its views and cool, leafy atmosphere. Forest fires devastated much of the Kyrenia Range escarpment in the mid-1990s, but fortunately Lapta managed to escape most of the ruination and still retains its old-world charm.

Lapta was one of the original city kingdoms of Cyprus and was a regional capital under Roman rule. Its abundant water and protected position have made it a favourite choice for foreign residents over many years. Greeks and Turks lived here in harmony until 1974. Today it is home to a scattering of expats, mainland Turks and original Turkish Cypriot villagers. The spread-out village is best visited on foot, particularly its leafy lanes.

The splendid former monastery, now the **Ayia Anastasia Resort** (☎ 821 8961; Maresal Fevzi Cakmak Caddesi; r per person UK£21) ripples out around a disused Orthodox church on top of a mountain overlooking Lapta. It caters very much for the rich mainland Turks, who stay here while they gamble down the hill at the casino, managed by the resort's owners. The atmosphere can be a little strange, with men in sharp suits drinking at the bar, and large BMWs parked in the middle of the courtyard as if on display. All rooms are spacious and have great views, telephones and satellite TV, and you can lounge around the two swimming pools, and dine in the two in-house restaurants.

The one other restaurant in the village, the **Hill Top** (☎ 821 8889; mains 15YTL), is open for lunch and serves OK food, although sometimes the chefs can go wild on the oil

in their dishes. The menu has *kleftiko*, liver and onions and (an oily) moussaka on offer. Follow the signs from the village centre.

The better restaurant, Başpınar, was closed at the time of research, but check out whether it has reopened. It's at the top of the village.

KORUÇAM (KORMAKITIS) PENINSULA
ΑΚΡΟΤΗΡΙ ΚΟΡΜΑΚΙΤΗ

The bare northwestern tip of Northern Cyprus is known as the Koruçam Burnu (Cape Kormakitis) and, apart from being yet another 'land's end' in the same sense as Cape Greco and Cape Arnaoutis in the South, or Zafer Burnu (Cape Apostolos Andreas) in the east, it is also home to one of Cyprus' least-known religious communities (see the boxed text, opposite).

A trip to the cape makes for a pleasant excursion from Lapta. There is at least one decent beach on the way with a popular grill and fish restaurant. Or you can take a picnic and enjoy your solitude at the cape itself.

A decent road now runs almost all the way to the cape. It is best tackled as a loop starting from the northern end of the Kyrenia–Morfou road at the junction just after the village of Karşıyaka (Vasileia). Look for the sign to Sadrazamköy (Livera).

Shortly after the turn-off is the neat little **Horse Shoe Beach**, with its eponymous **Horseshoe Beach Restaurant** (☎ 851 6664; grills 8YTL), which gets very busy at weekends with locals on a day out for a snorkel or swim followed by a lazy lunch of grilled fish or meats.

The coastal road towards the cape is winding but well maintained. You'll reach the rather scruffy settlement of Sadrazamköy after about 11km. Here, a rather curious boxlike resort in typical mainland-Turkish style has sprung up on the western edge of the village.

The road from here to the cape is a 3.5km dirt track – lumpy in parts, but driveable in a conventional vehicle. There is nothing at the end but bare rocks, a couple of abandoned buildings and a solar-powered shipping beacon. A small rocky islet lies offshore. This is also Cyprus' closest point to Turkey, which lies 60km across the sea.

Head back via the picturesque inland loop road through Koruçam village and

THE LANGUAGE OF JESUS: THE MARONITES OF KORUÇAM (KORMAKITIS)

To make his controversial religious blood'n'gore film *The Passion of the Christ* (2004), Mel Gibson probably took Aramaic language classes from the Maronites, an ancient Christian sect from the Middle East who still speak the language of Jesus. Along with Latin, Aramaic is the tongue painstakingly used throughout Gibson's film. And here, in the small village of Koruçam (Kormakitis) in Northern Cyprus, a unique dialect of this long-forgotten language is still spoken by 130 wrinkly Maronite Catholics.

Originally, the Maronites split from the prevailing Orthodox theory of Christianity that God was both man and god. In contrast, they followed the Monophysite religious line that states that God could only be viewed as one spiritual persona. Persecuted by Orthodox Christians, they first sought refuge in Lebanon and Syria, and came to Cyprus in the 12th century in the wake of the crusaders, whom they had helped as auxiliaries in the Holy Land campaign.

Aramaic is a Semitic language related to Hebrew and used as the main tongue for commercial dealings in the Middle East during Christ's time. Until the 1950s, it was believed that Aramaic was only spoken in Maaloula and two nearby villages in Syria, north of Damascus. But Koruçam's Maronites kept their Aramaic dialect going over hundreds of years, weaving into it words from Greek, Turkish, French and Italian, thus developing a strand of their own, which some experts have called 'Cypriot Maronite Arabic'. If Christ happened to visit Koruçam today – a village seemingly forgotten by everyone else – he would still be able to get by; the language of the Cypriot Maronites is to Christ's Aramaic what modern Italian is to Latin. The Aramaic verbs have been kept by the Maronites, but many nouns have been replaced by Turkish.

But if Christ decided to visit Koruçam in twenty or thirty years' time, it's likely he would get funny looks from the village's remaining inhabitants, who are predicted to lose the language if no youngsters decide to learn it. Post-1974, the Cypriot Maronites have clung to a tenuous existence in the village, where they still maintain a church. Over the years, the once-vigorous congregation has gradually left, and now barely one hundred remain to keep the old traditions and religion alive. The Maronites, like the Armenians and Latin religious communities, had to choose allegiance with either the Greek or Turkish communities in the 1960s. They chose the Greeks, and since '74 the youth from the village has gradually all but disappeared, crossing over into the South to study in Greek schools. Those who remained in the North have managed to tread the fine line between political and religious allegiances with some degree of success and, pre-2003, their relatives from the South were able to visit them on weekends.

However, there is still hope for Aramaic and its Cypriot speakers. Now that the borders have opened, the South's Maronites can visit for longer periods, although they are still not allowed to live in the North. With a bit of luck, some of them will have been inspired by Mel's passion and learn their ancient language.

take note of the huge Maronite **Church of Agios Georgios**, built in 1940 from funds raised by the villagers.

There's a small **coffee shop** in the village; if you speak Greek, you may get into conversation with the Greek- (and Aramaic-) speaking Maronites here.

The last leg back to the Kyrenia–Morfou road is along a rather poorly maintained road through a military area. There are a couple of prominent checkpoints, and you may be stopped.

Join the main highway at Çamlibel (Myrtou), from where you can loop back to Kyrenia, cut south to Morfou or veer southeast to North Nicosia.

THE NORTHWEST

The flat and parched landscape stretching east and west of North Nicosia is called the Mesarya, derived from the Greek word *mesaoria,* meaning 'between the mountains'. In its summer guise, it's less than inviting with the shimmer of the roasting soil radiating from the ground, but in winter the area metamorphoses when it comes alive with greenery and wildflowers. It is easy to navigate in a car, since it's quite flat, and the area's western side is more interesting than the east. If you want to get away from the coast and look for something a bit more alternative, the Mesarya can entertain you for a day or two.

The northwestern quadrant of Northern Cyprus loosely covers the territory south of the Kyrenia Range and westwards to the agricultural town of Morfou, Morfou Bay (Güzelyurt Körfezi), the one-time mining port of Gemikonağı (Karavostasi), the pretty hill village of Lefke (Lefka) and the two obscure but worthwhile archaeological sites of Ancient Soloi and Ancient Vouni in the far west.

Distances are relatively short and the whole excursion can be made into a loop, returning to North Nicosia via the Koruçam Peninsula and Kyrenia, or vice versa. You can now also cross into the South at the Zodhia crossing, near Morfou.

Beaches

A 12km stretch west of Gemikonağı has sandy and pebbly beaches, ending at the border with the Republic. First up is the prominently signposted **Zafer Gazinosu Beach**. It's mainly a pebble beach with some imported sand for those who prefer it. There is a wooden diving and swimming pier, changing rooms and toilets, as well as an attendant bar and restaurant.

From here, you are better advised to ignore the subsequent, rather scrappy beaches to the west and head for **Asmalı Beach**, fronting the border village of Yeşilırmak (Limnitis). This is a clean pebble beach with four restaurants catering to those who make it this far out. Of curious interest is a huge grapevine. Planted in 1947, the enormous vine completely covers the outside dining area of the Asmalı Beach Restaurant at the western end.

Towards the eastern end is **Green River Bar** (☎ 0533 855 8331; meals 8YTL), run by Turkish, Cockney-speaking Erdal (Eddie). Apart from dishing up large meals of kebabs, fish or *kleftiko*, he also offers a small, shaded area with seats and tables (5YTL entry) for independent picnickers.

Getting Around

There are regular daily buses to Morfou from North Nicosia (1YTL, every 30 minutes) and onward bus transport to Gemikonağı and Lefke (5YTL) every 30 minutes from Morfou. You may be able to charter a taxi from North Nicosia or Kyrenia for a round trip,

and this may work out more economical if there are at least two of you. Overall though, getting around is better conducted under your own steam, especially if you want to see Ancient Soloi and Ancient Vouni.

MORFOU (GÜZELYURT) ΜΟΡΦΟΥ
pop 15,000

The quiet and generally uneventful town of Morfou (known as Güzelyurt by Turkish Cypriots) was once the centre for Cyprus' lucrative citrus industry. Sunzest, the company owned by renegade and runaway Cypriot businessman, Asil Nadir, used to produce vast quantities of orange juice for the export market. The factory now languishes in receivership, and the potentially lucrative citrus industry has taken a severe downturn.

This is bittersweet news to the Greek Cypriots, who were particularly aggrieved when the citrus groves were lost to Turkish forces in 1974. Most were proudly owned by Greek Cypriots who, when meeting someone who has been to the North, invariably ask after the health of their beloved groves.

You can hardly miss the citrus groves – they start shortly before the village of Şahinler (Masari) and stretch all the way to the sea. The groves are watered by a series of underground aquifers. However, because of a drop in the level of the aquifer reserves and a rise in the salinity of the underground water, as well as a sometimes less-than-loving approach to cultivation and maintenance, the groves are beginning to feel the pinch. In fairness, this visible degradation is no doubt due, to some degree, to the disruption brought about by Sunzest's demise.

In better days, in the early half of the 20th century, oranges were shipped by train from Morfou to Famagusta for export overseas. It seems odd that facilities were never developed for orange export at the nearer port of Gemikonağı. Incidentally, the train route from Morfou to North Nicosia ceased passenger services in 1932, though it continued to transport freight until 1951. The line has long since fallen into disrepair.

Morfou today is really of no interest to the tourist, apart from a glimpse of a run-down, cluttered agricultural town with a few narrow, winding streets and small

shops, where life is totally unfazed by tourism and independent of it. The bus station
is on the south side of town. Follow Ecevit
Caddesi from the bus station for 800m to
reach the town centre.

By the large roundabout in the town
centre, you'll see the Orthodox church of
Cyprus' most beloved saint, tax-collector-
repelling **Agios Mamas**, which was once the
site of a pagan temple. The faithful used to
visit this place before 1974 to see the ancient
marble tomb of the patron saint, said to have
oozed a mysterious liquid when pierced by
the Ottomans who were looking for treasure. The liquid, which was supposed to have
curing effects on earaches, flowed freely at
irregular intervals; this is why ear-shaped
offerings surround the tomb. The church,
which is normally closed, vies for attention
with a splendid-looking new mosque that
has been built across the square.

Morfou does however have one of the
best meze houses in the North, according
to some. The **Şah** (☎ 714 3064; meze 8YTL), south
of the north-end roundabout, has quail and
lamb sausages included in the meze.

If you choose to stay here, the 13-room
Güzelyurt Otel (☎ 714 3412; guzelyurt@northcyprus
.net; Bahçelievler Bulvarı; s/d UK£33/51; ✸ ☾) is just
a little out of town. This basic hotel will
only be any good if you're totally stuck for
a place to stay, since it's quite overpriced
for the run-down look it sports. The rooms
have air-con, a phone and TV, and there's a
swimming pool, bar and laundry service.

GEMIKONAĞI (KARAVOSTASI)
ΚΑΡΑΒΟΣΤΑΣΗ
More citrus groves stretch westwards from
Morfou, towards Morfou Bay. The thin
strips of beach are not so great: there's no
shade, the pebbles are uncomfortable, and
it's all a bit narrow. But there aren't many
people about and the sea is pretty calm.
The villagers from the Troödos foothills in
the South used to make the short trip to
Morfou Bay to swim before 1974, but due
to the border, they now have to trek over
100km away to Larnaka.

The once-flourishing port of Gemikonağı
dominates the bay, and you will spot the
long-abandoned and slowly disintegrating
jetty before you actually catch sight of the
port itself. The town was once home to a
large American-run mining enterprise that

for many years mined the now scarred hinterland immediately south and east of town.
That industry ceased after 1974, and the
place has taken on a backwater appearance,
not unlike the town of Kato Pyrgos further
along the coast in Tylliria in the Republic.

Nonetheless, the town continues to support a small local tourist industry and a few
restaurants. Small beaches to the west of
Gemikonağı testify to the area's pull on the
few visitors who prefer alternative dining
and bathing options to the often crowded
and more expensive spots elsewhere in the
North. Gemikonağı is one place in the region to base yourself for a day or two.

A former caravanserai, the **Soli Inn Hotel**
(☎ 727 7575; soliinn@northcyprus.net; s/d UK£31/41;
☾) is a comfortable one-star hotel, sitting
by the sea on the west side of the town.
There are simple doubles and more elaborate suites, which have bathtubs and showers. All have a TV and a fridge, and there's a
pool for guests; rates include breakfast.

The nearby **Mardin Restaurant** (☎ 727 7527;
mains 5-6YTL; ☾ lunch & dinner) has excellent fish
and meze, but the *Adana* kebabs are also
pretty yummy. There is an artificial beach
next door, and the restaurant terrace overlooks the sea.

LEFKE (LEFKA) ΛΕΥΚΑ
From Gemikonağı, a road runs off at right
angles to the hillside village of Lefke. The
turn-off is not well signposted, but nonetheless it's hard to miss. The village, which is an
easy 10-minute drive along a fast, straight
road, is bizarrely the home of a hardy bunch
of British expats. The village derives its name
from the Greek word *lefka* (meaning 'pop-
lar'). There are seemingly more palm trees
than poplars these days, and Lefke's position
amid riotous greenery and rolling hills gives
the place a pleasant, fresh feel.

The years of Lefke's isolation on the country's western corner are almost over, with a
new border crossing at Zodhia, which can be
reached by the road going to Morfou. The
vast hinterland of Tylliria and Pafos Forest, which is in reality no more than 2km
away, can now be reached faster from here,
although the roads are quite windy going
through the mountains. There has been
some debate about opening a border crossing near Ancient Vouni in the future, which
would open up this region even more.

ANCIENT SOLOI

A good reason for venturing further west is to visit two archaeological sites. The first, **Ancient Soloi** (Soli Harabeleri; admission 6YTL; ☉ 9am-7pm), one of the ancient city kingdoms of Cyprus. Soloi traces its origin back to an Assyrian tribute list (700 BC) where the original city was referred to as Si-il-lu. In 580 BC, King Philokyprios moved his capital from Aepia to Si-il-lu on the advice of his mentor, the Athenian philosopher Solon. Philokyprios promptly renamed the citadel Soloi in honour of Solon. In 498 BC, Soloi, along with most of the other city kingdoms of Cyprus (Amathous being the exception), rose up against the Persians but was ultimately defeated. It languished until Roman times, when it flourished once again, thanks to the rich copper mines nearby. As happened in other parts of Cyprus, Soloi suffered looting and sacking at the hands of Arab raiders in the 7th century AD.

The site consists of two main parts: the basilica nearest the entrance to the site, and the theatre along a short path up a hill south of the basilica. The remains of a royal palace can also be found on the acropolis next to the theatre, though it is believed that this dates from a later period.

The **basilica** is now covered with a large, open-walled, tin-roofed structure that protects the remains and the archaeologists who are still working sporadically on the excavations. St Mark was baptised here by St Auxibius, and the first church is thought to have been built in the second half of the 4th century. As is the case with most archaeological remains, it is difficult to imagine the size and extent of the church, which by all accounts was an impressive structure. The remains of the **decorated floors**, on the other hand, are immediately obvious. Notable among them is a mosaic of a swan surrounded by floral patterns, and four small dolphins nearby. The heavy roof over the

sanctuary has spoiled the view of the mosaics as the light has been reduced.

The **Roman theatre** has been restored considerably. As much of its original stonework was carted away by the British to rebuild the dockside of Port Said in the late 19th century, the restoration does little for the imagination, but in its time the theatre could accommodate up to 4000 spectators. The famous Roman statuette of **Aphrodite of Soli** was discovered nearby. This is now in the Cyprus Museum in Lefkosia (p63).

ANCIENT VOUNI

Viewed in the early morning or late afternoon, this rather surreal and 'what's-it-doing-here?' site is a bit of a mystery. The hilltop location of **Ancient Vouni** (Vouni Sarayı Kalıntıları; admission 6YTL; ☉ 10am-4.30pm) is simply superb, and is reached along a narrow road off the main highway. Look for the black-and-yellow Vouni Sarayı sign pointing north and up the hill. Go up to the car park and the ticket office at the very top.

The site, which originally housed a palace or large complex of buildings, dates back to the 5th century BC. The palace was built by the leaders of the pro-Persian city of Marion (today's Polis) following the failed revolt by the Ionian Greeks against the Persians. The details of this incident were described by Herodotus in Book V of his *Histories*. Built to keep watch over the activities of nearby pro-Greek Soloi, the palace consisted of a discernible megaron (a three-part rectangular room with a central hearth and throne), private rooms and steps leading down to a courtyard under which is a cistern. A curious guitar-shaped stone seen there probably supported a windlass (a machine for raising weights). The palace was burned down in 380 BC and never re-established. Today the site stands forlornly on its magnificent hilltop, commanding some of the best views of the region.

Famagusta (Mağusa)
& the Karpas (Kırpaşa) Peninsula

The area around Famagusta (Mağusa) is shrouded in history. The wide sweep of Famagusta Bay and the sprawling flat Mesarya (Mesaoria) was home to three major settlements: the Bronze Age city of Ancient Enkomi (Alasia), which existed during the 17th century BC; the Mycenaean tombs from the 9th century BC, which support the description of a flourishing culture detailed in Homer's *Iliad*; and the illustrious kingdom of Salamis, which prospered in the 6th century BC. In Venetian times Famagusta was the wealthiest city in the eastern Mediterranean, with numerous opulent churches. After Cyprus' independence, it became the centre of all tourist activity, thanks to its golden, sandy beaches and the tourist resort town of Maraş (Varosia). Famagusta suffered the consequences of the '74 division, like all of Cyprus, but while other towns managed to either carry on with their business or invent a new 'identity' for themselves, Famagusta's former glory faded and it became a quiet, student town. Varosia was famously cut off and deserted, and its ghostly, gaping tower blocks still represent what is perhaps the deepest scar of the '74 division in many Cypriots' minds.

The Karpas (Kırpaşa) Peninsula stretches above Famagusta like a long finger pointing to the Asian mainland. It is the quietest, wildest and least developed part of the country, with the island's most fantastic beaches. Travellers seeking something truly different in Cyprus will love the Karpas. There is no electricity beyond the scattered village of Dipkarpaz (Rizokarpaso), the accommodation is mainly in simple wooden huts reminiscent of Thailand, wild donkeys roam the fields, endangered species of turtles lay their eggs in the beaches' warm sand, and the package tours are far, far away. At the tip of the peninsula is an Orthodox monastery that is dear to the Greek Cypriot population. Many make the twice-yearly pilgrimage from the Republic to the monastery; despite the politics of division on the island, this pilgrimage has allowed Cypriots from both sides of the Attila Line to mingle for a few hours every year.

FAMAGUSTA (MAĞUSA) & THE KARPAS (KIRPAŞA) PENINSULA

HIGHLIGHTS

- Gaze at the Gothic arches of **Lala Mustafa Paşa Mosque** (p207) in Famagusta (Mağusa)
- Walk and admire the historical grounds of the kingdom of **Ancient Salamis** (p211)
- Drive the length of the isolated **Karpas (Kırpaşa) Peninsula** (p214) and reach the land's end
- Swim on **Golden Beach** (Nangomi Bay; p215), the island's most stunning beach
- Walk up to **Kantara Castle** (p216) and admire the view from the heights of the Kyrenia (Girne) Range

FAMAGUSTA (MAĞUSA)
ΑΜΜΟΧΩΣΤΟΣ

pop 30,000

The walled city of Famagusta (Gazimağusa or Mağusa in Turkish; Ammohostos in Greek) has the melancholy air of a once-glamorous queen who has been forgotten by her courtiers. The city's roller-coaster history could warrant such a description. In the late 13th century, Famagusta became the main trans-shipment point in the region, and the city gained immense wealth almost overnight. A lavish and decadent lifestyle bloomed; more jewels sparkled in Famagusta than in all of Europe's royal courts, provoking scorn from angry and pious (or perhaps envious) foreigners who criticised the loose morals of Famagusta's citizens. This criticism was answered with a stampede towards spirituality, and the building of a great number of churches in the city.

The great city declined sooner than you could say 'Famagusta'. Following a bad turn in which the Genoese took over the city in the 14th century, utter decay set in with a siege that is said to have had the Ottomans firing more than 100,000 cannonballs in order to defeat and conquer the shattered city. Under the Ottomans, Famagusta rotted like a tooth. The ruined buildings have never been repaired, and walking around the city today feels like being in a strange, post-war, Gothic time warp.

But Famagusta peaked once more. It became Cyprus' top tourist destination in the 1960s and '70s; the resort town of Varosia (Maraş in Turkish), next to Famagusta in the south, pulled thousands of sun-seeking tourists every year. But, with the island's division in 1974, the town turned into a 'border zone', and took on its current guise of a quiet, student province. Varosia, deserted by its Greek population in anticipation of Turkish Army troops, became a large 'buffer zone', harrowing and hollow, with gaping, dark windows on its many tower blocks.

Present-day Famagusta presents a sombre cityscape. From the top of the Venetian walls, it looks bombed out or unfinished. A day trip to Famagusta is not to be missed: its crumbling beauty will remain in your memory. But, try basing yourself elsewhere, or else the city's crumbling hotel scene will remain in your memory too.

HISTORY

The current image of Famagusta is deeply connected to its past. The city was founded by Ptolemy Philadelphus of Egypt in the 3rd century BC. Its original Greek name was Ammohostos, which means 'buried in the sand'. The ramparts and harbour protect the town from indeed being buried in the sand, but the volatile landscape that surrounds the city, combined with Famagusta's current dilapidation, brings home the true origins of its name.

For a long time, Famagusta played second fiddle to the illustrious city kingdom of Salamis, standing just to the north. Despite an increase in population after the abandonment of Salamis in AD 648, Famagusta remained obscure and unimportant until the fall of Acre in 1291. At this point, the Christians fleeing the Holy Land took refuge in the city. From this sudden demographic boost, Famagusta grew exponentially and became one of the richest and most lavish cities in the eastern Mediterranean.

The fortunes of Famagusta took a tumble in 1372 when the Venetians and the Genoese had a dispute that resulted in the seizure of the town by the Genoese. This provoked an exodus of the city's wealthy and more illustrious citizens. Fortunes were never regained, even after the town was recaptured by the Venetians 117 years later. It was after this time that the huge walls and bastions were constructed, but even this belated measure did not prevent the capture of Famagusta by the Ottomans in 1571 following a bloody 10-month siege. Much of the damage caused during that siege is what you see today. The Turks have remained in residence in the Old Town – known as the Kaleici in Turkish – ever since.

ORIENTATION

Famagusta is not a difficult town to navigate, as the majority of your movements will be within or near the Old Town. Long-distance buses arrive at the Otobüs Terminali on Gazi Mustafa Kemal Bulvarı, on the west side of the Old Town. Minibuses and service taxis arrive at İtimat bus station, a

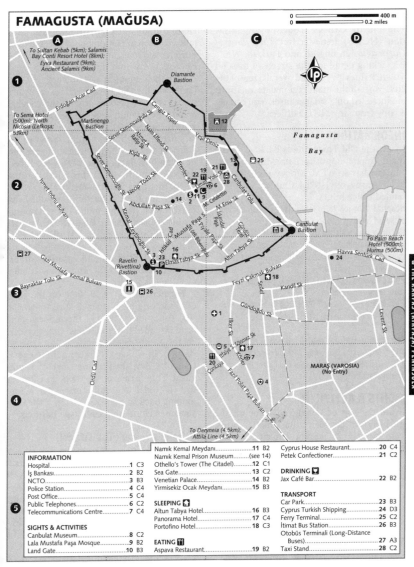

FAMAGUSTA (MAĞUSA)

small parking lot 400m further southeast, just off Yirmisekiz Ocak Meydanı. This large square, capped by an enormous black statue of Atatürk, is the major landmark in the New Town and impossible to miss.

Across from Yirmisekiz Ocak Meydanı is the Land Gate, the easiest way into the Old Town. There is a handy car park just

to the right as you enter the Old Town via the Gate. İstiklal Caddesi is a pedestrian street and the main thoroughfare running through the Old Town to Namık Kemal Meydanı, the square in front of Lala Mustafa Paşa Mosque.

Arrivals by ferry from Turkey will dock at the port to the east of the Old Town.

Maps

The North Cyprus Tourism Organisation (NCTO) issues a free *City Plan of Gazimağusa* in English and Turkish. While it's lacking detail for the streets of the Old Town, it does give a good overall view of the city. Most of the main regional destinations are included on a smaller inset. You can get a copy from any NCTO office.

INFORMATION

Inside the Old Town, the İş Bankası on the main square opposite Lala Mustafa Paşa Mosque has an ATM. Money-exchange offices nearby on İstiklal Caddesi keep extended office hours.

Hospital (☎ 366 2876; Fazıl Polat Paşa Bulvarı) South of the Old Town.

North Cyprus Tourism Organisation (NCTO; ☎ 366 2864; İstiklal Caddesi; ☷ 8am-5pm Mon-Sat) Recently moved from the New Town to the White Tower within the city walls, at the Land Gate.

Police station (☎ 366 5310; İlker Körler Caddesi) Also south of the Old Town.

Post office (☎ 366 2250; Fazıl Polat Paşa Bulvarı) Not far from the telecommunications centre, south of the Old Town.

Telecommunications centre (☎ 366 5332; İlker S Körler) South of the Old Town. There is a clutch of phonecard telephones on Liman Yolu Sokak adjacent to the Lala Mustafa Paşa Mosque.

SIGHTS & ACTIVITIES

From the top of Othello's Tower on the northeastern corner of the Venetian walls, Famagusta looks like a broken city. Its shattered churches and Gothic buildings punctuate the skyline, while low houses and winding streets make up the rest of this laid-back and crumbling sector of what was once Cyprus' most lavish and important city. A full day is recommended to take in the city leisurely on foot.

Venetian Walls

These impressive, sprawling defences define the extent of the Old Town. Colin Thubron, author of the last travelogue of the unified island, *Journey Into Cyprus,* mused over these walls, comparing them to Jerusalem's or Istanbul's. The walls' proportions (15m high and up to 8m thick in parts) are most certainly impressive. The walls hug the entire city protectively, and they were built to their present size by the Venetians in

the early 16th century for defence purposes. Despite their burly appearance, the walls failed to keep the Ottomans at bay, but they did manage to escape the havoc and damage wreaked within the city.

Like their counterparts in North Nicosia (Lefkoşa), the Old Town's walls were punctuated with 14 **bastions** around the roughly rectangular layout. While it is impossible to walk the length of the walls due to the military presence at various points, you can get a decent feel for them at the southern end near the **Land Gate** on the **Ravelin** (or Rivettina) Bastion. It was at this point that the Turks first breached the fortifications.

From the Ravelin Bastion the walls head northwards, passing four minor bastions, the **Diocare**, **Moratto** and **Pulacazara**, culminating in the steeply pitched **Martinengo** Bastion. This in turn leads seawards, passing the **Del Mezzo**, **Diamante** and **Signoria** Bastions, where it cedes into the impressive citadel, or Othello's Tower.

Further along, the **Sea Gate** on the eastern side originally opened directly to the sea. Today the wharfs of the modern port have extended the land bridge considerably. At the southeast extremity is the **Canbulat** Bastion, in which a Turkish hero, General Canbulat Bey, died in the siege of Famagusta. This corner of the walls now houses the Canbulat Museum (opposite) before looping back to the Land Gate via the **Composanto**, **Andruzzi** and **Santa Napa** Bastions.

Othello's Tower (The Citadel)

This **citadel** (Othello Kalesi; admission 6YTL; ☷ 9am-4.45pm) was built as an extension to the main walls of the Old Town on the northeast seaward side. Its name stems from a tenuous link with Shakespeare's *Othello,* which some think was set in Famagusta based on a stage instruction from the play: 'a seaport in Cyprus'. The Moor link may be a misunderstanding of the name of Cyprus' Venetian governor, Cristoforo Moro (r 1506–08), whose name means 'Moor'. In any case, the tower was constructed in the 12th century during Lusignan rule in order to protect the harbour and the Sea Gate entrance further south. In 1492, during the time of Venetian rule, the citadel was further reinforced by its transformation into an artillery stronghold in much the same way Kyrenia Castle was fortified.

Above the impressive entrance to the citadel you can spot the **Venetian Lion** inscribed with the name of the architect, Nicolò Foscarini. Yet another great name appears on Famagusta's 'celebrity list': it is said that Leonardo da Vinci gave advice on the refurbishment of the tower when he visited Cyprus in 1481.

The citadel consists of various towers and corridors leading to the artillery chambers, a large courtyard bordered on one side by a refectory and, above that, living quarters; both the refectory and the living quarters date back to the Lusignans. The courtyard has a stage for folkloric performances; on its far side is the Great Hall with beautiful vaults, whose sandstone walls are corroded by the salty sea air. There are ventilation shafts that look out onto the border ramparts, which lead to Lusignan corridors and sealed chambers. It's said that fortunes still lie hidden, buried forever by Venetian merchants in the face of the advancing Ottomans.

Other than wandering around the dusty corridors and the corroded sandstone walls, the main attraction is climbing up to the ramparts and enjoying the good views over the town, which are best sampled in the early morning or evening.

Lala Mustafa Paşa Mosque

This is the finest example of Lusignan Gothic architecture in all of Cyprus. It was built between 1298 and 1326, modelled on the Cathedral of Rheims in France, and it outshines its sister church in North Nicosia, the Church of Agia Sophia (now Selimiye Mosque, p176). It has been a **mosque** (Erenler Sokak; admission 4YTL; ☺ outside prayer times), or *camii* in Turkish, since the Ottoman invasion in 1571, and it dominates the skyline of the Old Town.

The Cathedral of Agios Nikolaos, as it was originally called, was the centrepiece of Famagusta's Lusignan heyday, and the last Lusignan king, Jacques II, and his infant son, Jacques III, were buried here. The church was damaged considerably during the Ottoman siege of Famagusta, when the twin towers of the church were destroyed. Afterwards, the Ottomans added a rather incongruous minaret, emptied the floor tombs, stripped the innards of all Christian accoutrements, and turned it into the Lala Mustafa Paşa mosque.

The west-facing façade is particularly impressive and easier to admire in totality now that the area in front of the mosque is a pedestrian zone. Three gracious portals point towards a six-paned window, which is decorated with a circular **rose**. The inside has been whitewashed in typical Islamic fashion, but the soaring Gothic architectural lines are easy to follow. Visits are allowed when prayers are not being conducted.

Venetian Palace & Namık Kemal Prison Museum

There is very little left of what was once a Venetian Palace in the area immediately to the west of Namık Kemal Meydanı. Known originally as the Palazzo del Provveditore, the palace now consists of some desultory cannon balls and a few arches supported by columns removed from Salamis. The one structure still standing is the former **prison** (admission 2YTL; ☺ 7.30am-2pm, also 3.30-6pm Mon) of Namık Kemal (1840–88) who was one of Turkey's best-known poets and playwrights. He was imprisoned here for six years after writing a play that was considered offensive to the sultan of the time. The square between the prison and the Lala Mustafa Paşa Mosque is named in his honour.

Canbulat Museum

The tomb of Canbulat Bey, who was an Ottoman hero, contains a small **museum** (Canbulat Yolu; admission 4YTL; ☺ 9am-5pm Mon-Sat) at the southeastern corner of the Venetian walls. During the siege of Famagusta, he ran his horse and himself into a gruesome protective device consisting of a wheel with spikes. He destroyed the device, himself and his horse in the process, thus precipitating the downfall of the then Venetian-held city.

The museum is a rather tired collection of cultural and historical artefacts, and a display detailing the 1974 campaign to liberate the Turkish enclave of the Old Town.

Maraş (Varosia) Βαρόσια

The ghostly sight of the barricaded Maraş district (known as Varosia in Greek) in southern Famagusta is one of this city's more haunting legacies, and is a lingering reminder of the dark days of 1974. Only a small part of the town is still inhabited, and the lights that still flicker do so alongside dark, deserted tower blocks. At some of the windows of these buildings, you can catch a glimpse of the wind playing with a curtain – a remainder of what was once a residential town. Reports by UN forces and journalists who have been allowed in on occasion tell of light bulbs burning for years and uncleared breakfast dishes, signs of a sudden departure from the apartment blocks.

Before '74, Maraş was a thriving community of Greeks, who also owned and ran most of the hotels in what was Famagusta's Riviera, overlooking some of the island's best resort beaches. Panic-stricken by Turkish advances into the North in July and August 1974, Maraş' residents fled in fear, taking with them little more than the clothes they wore. Most of them believed they would be returning within a few days when the emergency was over. As it happened, the Turkish army just walked in unimpeded and took an abandoned city. To this day, Maraş has remained empty.

Visitors cannot enter the area. Barbed wire fences and metal drums block the streets and prevent the passage of curious investigators. Rats, cats, snakes and weeds run the show now. Inside the town, hotels, shops and houses have remained untouched for 30 years. There are stories of a Toyota car dealership (or Alf Romeo, according to some reports) that apparently still has 1974 models, frozen in time, locked in the showroom windows. Nobody knows what has happened with the contents of Famagusta's Archaeological Museum, or whether the museum's collection is still on the premises.

Visitors with their own vehicles can drive down the western side of Maraş, alongside the fence, and peer in. Photography is forbidden. The perimeter road takes you almost as far as the Deryneia checkpoint, which, according to speculation, might open in the next few years.

Beaches

The best and most convenient beach in Famagusta is in front of Palm Beach Hotel (right), which nonguests can use as well. Look for the little 'To the Beach Club' sign south of the hotel, hard up against the Maraş barricades.

FESTIVALS & EVENTS

The **International Famagusta Culture & Art Festival** (www.magusa.org/festival) takes place between 21 June and 12 July every year. The festival has a wide range of music (classical, jazz, world, hip-hop and reggae) by international and local artists, theatre, and something called 'the plastic arts'. Performances are staged at Namık Kemal Meydanı, Othello Tower and the Ancient Salamis amphitheatre.

SLEEPING

Famagusta's hotels are as dilapidated as its Gothic ruins. The following are some options, and aside from the ultra-swanky hotels (most of which are said to have been built for the purposes of money laundering), the level of comfort is low, and some of the prices too high.

Altun Tabya Hotel (☎ 366 5363; Altun Tabya Sokak; s/d UK£13/16; ⊠) Probably your best option (if you're on a budget) in terms of location and price, adding the fact that it has air-conditioning. It is on a noisy street, and the rooms are run-down, but each has its own bathroom, and breakfast is included in the price. It's inside the city walls: follow the signs from the Land Gate.

Palm Beach Hotel (☎ 366 2000; bilfer@management.emu.edu.tr; Deve Limanı; s/d UK£51/64; ☒) If you want a good view of the Maraş closed zone, stay here. This was one of the few hotels to escape the sealing off of the ghost city immediately to the south, and is considered to be the best hotel in town. It has five stars, and decent, although by no means luxurious, rooms, as well as a hotel swimming pool. Its best feature is the sandy beach it is built on, which is just under your window. However, there have been reports from some travellers telling of shabbiness and things not working properly.

Portofino Hotel (☎ 366 4392; www.portofinohotel-cyprus.com; Fevzi Çakmak Bulvarı 9; r UK£35) The Italian song 'I found my love in Portofino' oozes out of the speakers when you look up this hotel on the Internet. But don't be fooled. You ain't gonna find your love in this Portofino. To the south of the Old Town, the only good thing about this place is the location. The rooms are spacious but very run-down, the bed sheets feel like plastic, the bathrooms are literally falling to pieces, and the breakfast is hurled at your table by a half-asleep waiter. It is also extremely overpriced, to say the least. Nevertheless, accommodation in Famagusta is scarce, and if you need a place to stay and the rest is all full, well… it'll do.

Sema Hotel (☎ 366 1222/1010; fax 366 1032; Gazi Mustafa Kemal Bulvarı; s/d UK£17/25; 🎫) A three-star modern block on the west side of the city, on the road out to North Nicosia. It has decent but unexceptional rooms with TVs and fridges, and there are two restaurants within the hotel. It's a fair distance from Famagusta's Old City and from any beach, so it's best if you have your own car.

Salamis Bay Conti Resort Hotel (☎ 378 8201; salamisbay@northcyprus.net; s/d UK£51/64; 🏊) Located 8km north of Famagusta, Salamis Bay is a luxurious five-star hotel with a large outdoor and indoor pool, an expansive sandy beach, bedrooms that you can swing several cats in, massage parlours, twinkling casinos and a Turkish bath. It's perfect if you're looking to stay in one place for a while and just relax in the sun. Rooms without a sea view are slightly cheaper.

Panorama Hotel (☎ 366 5880; fax 366 5990; İlker S Körler; s/d UK£13/18) Another hotel that's only recommended as an emergency option. It is in a dark, run-down section of the New Town, close to the buffer zone, and is best reached by car. The owner is friendly, the 'reception' seems like a gathering place for men with moustaches watching the telly, and the rooms are pretty basic. Breakfast is not included in the room rate.

EATING

Eyva Restaurant (☎ 378 8235; Salamis Yolu; mains 12-15YTL; ☾ dinner) Perfect for an evening-long dinner and music affair, traditional Cypriot style. It's best on weekends when live Greek and Turkish music gets going, and undoubtedly, a bit of dancing too. This is also a brilliant place to eat *kleftiko* (oven-baked lamb), freshly cooked and made to order, so you must order it a day in advance. The food and music spectacle costs 20YTL. To get here, take the road to Ancient Salamis; it's on your left at the Salamis junction.

Cyprus House Restaurant (☎ 366 4845; Fazıl Polat Paşa Bulvarı; mains 8 YTL; ☾ dinner) An old mansion in the New Town, with a cool, shady dining area. The kebab dishes are highly recommended, and you might get a belly dancer thrown in for good measure. It's about 400m southeast of Yirmisekiz Ocak Meydanı.

Hurma (☎ 366 4624; Kemal Server Sokak 17; mains 12-16YTL; ☾ dinner) A stylish restaurant in a hacienda-style house, with tall palm trees guarding the front, and a tranquil terrace at

the back where you eat and watch the sea – pure romance. The food is rather more *haute* than in most places, with things like *escargots* (snails), and fresh fish (25YTL to 30YTL) on the menu. This place is almost next door to the Palm Beach Hotel, which explains the prices.

Aspava Restaurant (☎ 366 6037; Liman Yolu Sokak 19; kebabs 10YTL; ☾ lunch & dinner) Succulent shish kebabs wait to be grilled under the glass counter, but you can also opt for mixed grills (15YTL) or meze, of course. Food is served in a vine-covered garden, looking onto the square, and the service is friendly and attentive.

Petek Confectioner (☎ 366 7104; Yeşil Deniz Sokak 1; 'Petekburger' & Coke 5YTL; ☾ 10am-11pm) A temple to all things saccharine. Turkish Delight is stacked up in multicoloured spirals and circles, geometrical rows and columns. There are honey cakes, nut cakes, chocolate cakes and all sorts of cakes for you to dip into and try a piece. Petek also serves burgers, and has foreign papers (not daily). It's at the eastern end of Liman Yolu Sokak.

Sultan Kebab (☎ 365 1961; kebabs 7YTL; ☾ 24hrs) About 5km from Famagusta, on the road to Ancient Salamis, this place is nothing to look at, but the kebabs are a killer. It's open 24 hours and there are customers eating kebabs here around the clock. Try the *Adana* kebab (spiced lamb) and a pot of *ayran*, the local yoghurt drink.

DRINKING

Famagusta is pretty dead when it comes to drinking or entertainment. The road going past the university and towards Salamis is packed with bars and cafés that all look like each other.

For a drink amid the ruins, try is **Jax Café Bar** (☎ 0533 864 6724; 6 Erenler Sokak), a bar in an old vault, with a back garden and a relaxed atmosphere, in the Old City.

GETTING THERE & AWAY
Boat

The ferries to Mersin in Turkey leave from the port east of the Old Town on Tuesdays, Thursdays and Sundays at 9pm; the trip takes about 10 hours. One-way tickets cost 50YTL (students 37.5YTL) per person and 65YTL per car, including departure tax. The ticket agents is **Cyprus Turkish Shipping** (☎ 366 5786; cypship@superonline.com; Bulent Ecevit Bulvarı).

Bus

The city's main bus station is **Otobüs Terminali** (Gazi Mustafa Kemal Bulvarı); services go to North Nicosia, Kyrenia (Girne) and Yenierenköy (Yiallousa) via Boğaz (Bogazi).

Minibuses for North Nicosia (2YTL, 45 minutes) depart frequently from the İtimat bus station on the south side of Yirmisekiz Ocak.

Also from here, minibuses for Kyrenia leave every half hour or so (2.50YTL, one hour).

GETTING AROUND

There are a couple of private taxi companies that operateing in and around Famagusta. **Bariş Taxis** (☎ 366 2349) operates a fleet of modern air-conditioned Mercedes taxis around the city and further afield.

Tariffs are generally fixed, but make sure you know the fare before accepting a ride. There's a taxi stand in the Old Town, near the Sea Gate.

There are no public buses within the city, but all the major sights and services are within walking distance anyway.

AROUND FAMAGUSTA

The sites around Famagusta are all around 9km to 10km north of the town. If you have a car, though, you can strike out further afield to the rarely visited northern Mesarya (Mesaoria) villages of Geçitkale (Lefkoniko) and İskele (Trikomo). You can also base yourself at any one of a scattering of hotels north of Famagusta, or at the little low-key resort of Boğaz.

Beaches

A lovely beach stretches all the way along the Ancient Salamis site north of Famagusta, but the sea is frustratingly knee-deep for a rather long time. From Salamis onwards are some excellent beaches all the way to Boğaz.

Getting Around

The best thing to do, if you want to have some freedom and time to explore the sites around Famagusta (unless you have your own car, of course) is hire a taxi. All of the sites are close enough for taxi rides to be

AROUND FAMAGUSTA (MAĞUSA)

0 ——— 10 km
0 ——— 6 miles

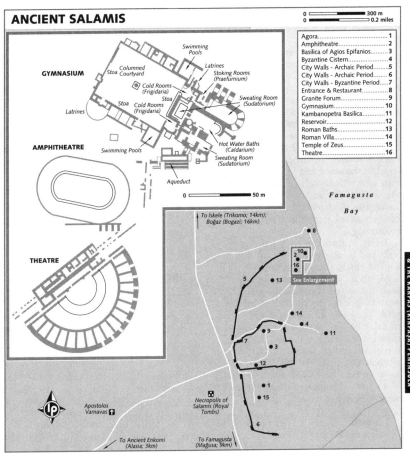

ANCIENT SALAMIS

Agora.............................	1
Amphitheatre......................	2
Basilica of Agios Epifanios......	3
Byzantine Cistern.................	4
City Walls - Archaic Period.......	5
City Walls - Archaic Period.......	6
City Walls - Byzantine Period.....	7
Entrance & Restaurant.............	8
Granite Forum.....................	9
Gymnasium.........................	10
Kambanopetra Basilica.............	11
Reservoir.........................	12
Roman Baths.......................	13
Roman Villa.......................	14
Temple of Zeus....................	15
Theatre...........................	16

FAMAGUSTA (MAĞUSA)
& THE KARPAS (KIRPAŞA) PENINSULA

affordable. A return taxi from Famagusta to Ancient Salamis will cost about UK£8 (prices will be quoted in British pounds).

There are buses between Famagusta and Yenierenköy that stop at Boğaz and pass near Salamis, but taking them would limit your options a lot, especially because they stop running at 5pm. It is also quite inconvenient to be waiting for them in the evening on the busy Salamis road.

Cycling is also a good way to see the sites mentioned here. However, there is nowhere to rent cycles in Famagusta.

ANCIENT SALAMIS

One the island's prime archaeological sites, **Ancient Salamis** (Salamis Harabeleri; admission 6YTL; 8am-7pm Jun–mid-Sep, 9am-1pm & 2-4.45pm mid-Sep–May) is not to be missed. It's extensive, and a minimum of half a day should be allowed for a visit. Take hats and bottles of water with you, as there's no shade within the site and the days can get very hot. Salamis is 9km north of Famagusta and is signposted (not very prominently) to the seaward side of the Famagusta–Boğaz highway.

Ancient Salamis was one of the city kingdoms of Cyprus. It was first mentioned on an Assyrian stele in 709 BC, where it was listed as paying a tribute to the Assyrian ruler Sargon II. Its period of major importance came during the 6th century BC under kings Evalthon and Evagoras when Salamis issued its own money and nurtured a thriving philosophical and literary scene, with Greek poets as regular visitors to the royal court.

The Persians destroyed Salamis in 306 BC, and it was placed under Ptolemaic rule from 294 BC to 58 BC, when the Romans took control and the city flourished once again. For three centuries its fortunes waxed and waned, and in AD 350 the city was renamed Constantia and declared an episcopal see. Constantia suffered the same depredation of 7th- and 8th-century Arab raids as the rest of Cyprus, and remained largely abandoned and forgotten from that time onwards. Much of the stone from the ancient city was carted away to build Famagusta. Archaeological explorations of the ancient site started in 1880 and are still continuing.

Today, visitors can see a fair number of walls and columns, although you will need a map to make sense of the jumbled layout. Look out for the **gymnasium**, **portico** and the **pools** that served as an exercise ground, and were built close by the columned courtyard. They give an idea of the glory days of Salamis. The northerly portico is surrounded by headless statues, beheaded by Christian zealots who considered them symbols of pagan idolatry. The ones still standing here have survived various raids. Many have 'disappeared' since 1974, while some were taken as exhibits to Lefkosia's Cyprus Museum (p63).

The **baths**, a Byzantine renovation of Hellenistic and Roman predecessors east of the portico, have an interesting exposed underfloor heating system, and a fascinating **fresco** fragment of two faces, painted over the south entry. Two of the site's best **mosaics** can be seen in the south hall of the baths, one showing part of the story of Leda and the swan, and the other what appears to be a scene of Apollo and Artemis fighting the Niobids. Some think this may in fact be a battle scene between men and Amazons. Both date back to late 3rd or early 4th century AD.

The **theatre**, dating from the time of Augustus (31 BC–AD 14), held 15,000 spectators in its day. Earthquakes in the 4th century destroyed much of the theatre and its stone was removed for building projects elsewhere. Today it has been restored to some degree, and occasionally hosts summer events. The **Roman Villa**, originally a

two-storey structure south of the theatre, was made up of a reception hall and central inner courtyard with columned portico. The nearby **Kambanopetra Basilica** was built in the 4th century and consisted of a columned courtyard. An intricate **mosaic floor** is visible inside. The **Basilica of Agios Epifanios** was once the largest basilica in Cyprus and was built during the episcopacy of Epifanios (AD 386–403).

Do look out for snakes when you are walking around, particularly in the hot summer days. Since the site is rather deserted most of the time, and in parts quite wild, they tend to relax and sunbathe, frightening the walking visitor.

A sandy beach stretches along the site, and it is perfect for a dip after a hot day's exploring. There is also a handy restaurant for lunch. For accommodation, the Salamis Bay Conti Resort Hotel (p209) is nearby.

CHURCH OF APOSTOLOS VARNAVAS

This important Orthodox **church** (☎ 378 8331; church & museum admission 6YTL; ⏲ 9am-7pm Jun–mid-Sep; 9am-1pm & 2-4.45pm mid-Sep–May) has had a privileged status in the hands of the Turks, who have kept an air of solemnity around it (and didn't destroy it). The Turks have been accused of a fair amount of desecration of Orthodox religious sites – and justifiably so in many cases – and many Greek Cypriots object to this church being turned into a museum. This bitterness is partly reinforced by the story of the three monks (and brothers), Barnabas, Stefanos and Khariton, who had lived in and governed the monastery from 1917. They tried to remain in the monastery after 1974, but left in 1976, unable to withstand alleged harassment by the Turkish authorities. They spent the rest of their days in the Stavrovouni Monastery (p151).

The church is dedicated to one of St Paul's good friends. Despite his name, Varnavas (Barnabas) was never an official apostle, but he is mentioned for his missionary work in the Acts of the Apostles in the Bible. He was born in Cyprus and carried out his missionary work here. The original church was built over the site of his tomb, which was discovered by Anthemios, the bishop of Constantia (Salamis), following a revelation in a dream. The current structure dates from the 18th century, though it does incorporate parts of the 5th-century original church.

The church today houses an **icon museum** and has a wide selection of well-preserved Orthodox icons, although none of them are particularly old. The oldest is called 'Herod's Banquet' and dates back to 1858.

There's also a small **archaeological museum** in the courtyard buildings, which contains an extensive selection of finds from Salamis and nearby Enkomi. It is also speculated that some of the contents from the Famagusta Archaeological Museum can be found in this collection, although this is, like many things in Cyprus, based on gossip and loose facts. The artefacts and the rooms are badly marked; clockwise from the entrance, the first room houses Bronze Age objects, the next has exhibits from the Venetian period, and there's a mixture of Ottoman and Classical periods in the final room. The most interesting exhibit is a statue of a woman holding a poppy, assumed to be the goddess Demeter.

The church is in the Mesarya hinterland, 9km northwest of Famagusta and close to Salamis. The church is well signposted off the Salamis road, and the turning is almost opposite the turning for Ancient Salamis.

NECROPOLIS OF SALAMIS

Commonly known as the **Royal Tombs** (Salamis Mezarlık Alanı; ☎ 378 8331; admission 5YTL; ☼ 9am-7pm), these are a scattering of 150 graves spread out over a wide area. This historic cemetery, dating back to the 7th and 8th centuries BC, confirms the account of Mycenaean tombs described by Homer in *The Iliad*. Kings and various other nobles were buried with all their favourite worldly goods, food and drink, even their favourite slaves, in order to make their afterlife a little easier. In one particularly gruesome reminder of this practice, two hapless horses were sacrificed after transporting a king to his tomb (No 79), where their agonised skeletons have been exposed to the public gaze. Most tombs have been looted over the years by unknown grave robbers, though at least three yielded enough treasure to make it to the Cyprus Museum in Lefkosia.

Further to the south and marked by a lone eucalyptus tree are the **Cellarka tombs**, also included in the admission price. These are smaller rock-cut tombs that were used for less noble members of the royal community. Each tomb has a flight of steps

leading down to the burial area in which the remains of the deceased were placed in stone urns pending their decomposition. After this, the bones were removed and the chambers reused.

The tombs are south of Salamis on the road to the Monastery of Apostolos Varnavas, and are prominently signposted.

ANCIENT ENKOMI (ALASIA)
ΕΓΚΩΜΗ (ΑΛΑΣΙΑ)

Heading further west from the Necropolis of Salamis, you will come across the Bronze Age city of **Ancient Enkomi** (Enkomi Ören Yeni; admission 5YTL; ☼ 9am-5pm), which dates back as far as 1800 BC. Most activity at the site, however, seems to have taken place during the Late Bronze Age period (1650–1050 BC) when Enkomi was a large copper-producing centre.

The name Alasia derives from Akkadian cuneiform slabs found in Tel el-Amarna in Egypt, in which the Pharaoh of the time received promises from the king of Alasia of copper in return for silver and other luxury items. Other textual evidence and a careful juxtaposition of data suggest that Alasia referred to either Cyprus as a whole or possibly just Enkomi itself.

The remains of the present site date from around 1200 BC and possibly beyond, when a rectangular grid layout was established and fine public buildings were erected. The arrival of the Mycenaeans on the island at this time ensured the ultimate demise of Enkomi. Its inland harbour silted up, and it is thought that the last residents moved to the coast, where they founded Salamis.

The site is fairly extensive and requires a bit of walking to get around, but there is a helpful leaflet handed out at the ticket office with a map of the site and a compact review of its history.

ICON MUSEUM OF İSKELE

If you're heading up to Kantara Castle or cutting across the northern Mesarya plain back to North Nicosia from Boğaz, you can easily make a brief stop at the little crossroads village of İskele (Trikomo), birthplace of Greek EOKA leader Georgos Grivas. Here is the Panagia Theotokou, which has been converted into an **icon museum** (İskele İkon Müzesi; admission 4YTL; ☼ 9am-7pm) with a small collection of 12th-century to 15th-century wall paintings and more recent icons from the 1950s and 1960s.

The building is a 12th-century single-sided domed church with arched recesses in the side walls. In the recesses you can see paintings of the **Virgin Mary of the Annunciation** as well as the **Prayer of Joachim & Anna**, who embrace each other as a girl peers curiously from behind a curtained window.

In the belfry outside the church, you can spot a marble inlay taken from the original iconostasis of the church.

The church is on the western edge of the village and is easy to spot.

BOĞAZ (BOGAZI) ΜΠΟΓΑΖΙ

Boğaz is a small fishing village about 24km north of Famagusta. It's the last beach halt before an excellent sealed road takes you inland to the Karpas (Kırpaşa) Peninsula proper. There is a little harbour, south of which is a stretch of developed beach with straw beach umbrellas and sun loungers for those few tourists on package holidays who base themselves in the low-key hotels in the village. For some reason, Russians seem to have taken a shine to Boğaz, and you are just as likely to hear Russian spoken in any of the beachside tavernas as you will hear German, as Germans make up the bulk of the remaining clientele.

Most of the hotels in Boğaz sit by the roadside, which makes them a little noisy, but the facilities are usually good.

Boğaz Hotel (☎ 371 2559; www.bogazhotel.com; r per person Jun–mid-Sep UK£21, mid-Sep–May UK£15; ✷ ☑) A comfortable three-star hotel with cream- and coffee-coloured rooms, a good-looking lounge with sofas, a small indoor pool that's good for children, and a Jacuzzi. At the time of research, an outdoor pool was being built by Boğaz Fish Restaurant, across the road. Rates include breakfast.

Exotic Hotel (☎ 371 2885; exoticmirillo@super online.net; s/d UK£25/36; ✷ ☑) Entertainment is a top priority here, with a pool for adults and for kids, both equipped with water-splashed slides, and colourful playthings. There is live music in the evening, and table tennis, so you will never be bored here, that's for sure. It doesn't have the same beachside location as the Boğaz Hotel, but it is more modern and the rooms have satellite TV, minibar, phone and safe, and prices include breakfast.

Boğaz Fish Restaurant (☎ 371 2559 ext 103; fish dishes 20-25YTL) Part of the Boğaz Hotel, and about 200m down the road, this restaurant is popular with the tourists, so the food and the evening entertainment is mainly aimed at them. Fresh fish are caught daily, so try a fish shish or a nice portion of sea bass.

KARPAS (KIRPAŞA) PENINSULA

For travellers wanting to experience a different Cyprus, the uniqueness and beauty of the Karpas (also known as Karpasia and the Turkish version, Kırpaşa) Peninsula cannot be overrated. The 'end' of Cyprus really feels like the world's end, far from the urban and tourist bustle. Miles of rolling fields, endless beaches, wildlife, fantastic swimming, and accommodation that's as wonderful as it is basic: wooden huts on stilts facing the sea, with the sound of the waves lulling you to sleep. The sea seems bluer and clearer than anywhere else in Cyprus, and the curves of the coast lure you seductively. This is heaven for cyclists and ramblers. The wildflowers that burst into colour in the spring are mesmerising (see the boxed text, p45).

Hopefully, developers will not get their hands on this wild and scarcely populated region, a prospect wonderfully deterred by the lack of electricity anywhere past the small village of Dipkarpaz (Rizokarpaso). Travellers who stay in the Karpas often make do with oil lamps or lighting powered by generators. The government has turned the area into a vast nature reserve, which is the only way of preserving the colonies of turtles that nest on the broad expanse of its southern beaches.

Virtually untouched by the traumatic events of 1974, the Karpas remains unique in that it is one of the few places on the island where Turks and Greeks have continued to live alongside each other, particularly in the village of Dipkarpaz, although this is now home to only a score of elderly Greeks. The only other village of any size is Yenierenköy, with a small centre and a good tourist office, which was set up in the hope of generating a greater number of travellers to the region.

Twice a year, Greek Cypriot pilgrims from the South make the long trip to the tip of the 'panhandle' to visit the Monastery of Apostolos Andreas (p218); in return, Turkish Cypriots visit the Hala Sultan Tekkesi (p150).

Beaches

Golden Beach (Nangomi Bay) can be the sole purpose of a trip to the Karpas, it is so enchanting. The white sand dunes, the gentle curves of the beach, the sea so calm and clear, you may never want to leave, and who could blame you? There is no development, a wild donkey grazes here and there on the hills, and everyone who comes is after the same thing: peace. It is unlikely that Golden Beach is going to see any development in the future, since it is considered to be a nature reserve. This is good news for the turtles that nest here and on other beaches on the north side of the panhandle, and for fans of nature who like it just the way it is.

About 5km short of Zafer Burnu (Cape Apostolos Andreas), the beach sits on either side of a scrubby headland, and stretches for several kilometres. Reached by quite passable sand and dirt roads, there is a trio of beach restaurants with basic but comfortable huts for accommodation (see p218).

Another fantastic beach is the **Agios Filon Beach**, near the church and Oasis hotel and restaurant (see p218). This is a great place to catch the sunset, having seen the sunrise at Golden Beach, and is another turtle-hatching area.

Getting Around

The only public transport in the area is the bus from Famagusta to Yenierenköy. Your own transport is necessary to get around this region, unless you are prepared to pay for taxis. The main road into the peninsula is excellent, though signs to some of the sites are lacking in clarity and prominence. It is really worth spending a few days on the peninsula; the distances are quite long, and you will need to plan your time carefully if you want to visit all the sights, as well as get some swimming in.

There are a couple of hikes in the area; see p192 for more information.

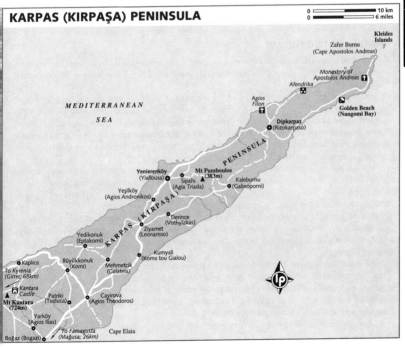

KARPAS (KIRPAŞA) PENINSULA

KANTARA CASTLE

The best vantage point on the Karpas is from this Lusignan Gothic castle, one of three in Cyprus. **Kantara Castle** (Kantara Kalesi; admission 5YTL; ☉ 9am-7pm), is the furthest east, the lowest in elevation and the best preserved. You can see the sea on both sides of the peninsula and, on a clear day, the coast of Turkey or even Syria.

The castle's documented history dates back to 1191 when Richard the Lionheart seized it from Isaak Komninos, the Byzantine emperor of Cyprus. Kantara was used as a beacon station to communicate with Buffavento Castle to the east. Its significance faded in the 16th century when Venetian military strategists began to depend more on firepower than elevation for protection, and the ports of Famagusta, Larnaka and Kyrenia gained importance at the expense of the once-crucial mountain fortresses.

Today, you can see the quite well preserved northern section of the castle with towers and walls still resolutely standing. You enter the fortress by the outer entrance, which leads into a now rather overgrown **barbican**. Two squat towers, the **north tower** and the **south tower**, guard the inner

entrance where you enter the castle proper. Inside the castle you can make out the **garrison**, **latrines**, and a **cistern**.

The highest point of the castle complex is the **lookout tower**, from which flares would be lit to alert residents of castles to the west of any impending danger. At the southwestern end, you can find more garrisons and the **postern gate**, used to catch would-be attackers by surprise.

You'll receive a useful map and potted history with your ticket, and you should allow an hour or so to make a relaxed tour and enjoy the views. Parents should keep small children under tight rein as there are some pretty serious unfenced drops, rough scrambling and uncapped holes to contend with. The view from the roof of the eastern tongue of the north tower is stupendous, but not for those suffering from vertigo – it is narrow and completely unfenced.

Kantara is best reached from Boğaz, and is at least a 45-minute drive. From Kaplıca on the coast, the ascent route is narrow but quite driveable, and there are regular passing places along the way. If coming from Kyrenia, allow at least 1½ hours for a comfortable drive. There is no public transport to the castle.

THE TALE OF TWO TURTLES

Turtles have been around on our planet for perhaps 200 million years, far longer than humans. There are eight species of turtles in the world, and two of these species live in the eastern Mediterranean.

The green turtle (Chelonia mydas) and the loggerhead turtle (Caretta caretta) have long lived in the Mediterranean basin and in particular on the island of Cyprus. It is estimated that the biggest population of the endangered green turtle lives in Cyprus, on both sides of the island, with a disproportionate number making the beaches of the north coast and the Karpas (Kırpaşa) Peninsula their favoured nesting grounds. The loggerhead turtle, classified 'vulnerable' by conservationists, also nests on these often pristine coastlines.

Gradual human encroachment into the turtles' territory means that the chances of survival of these lumbering marine animals has decreased over the years. Visitors to Cyprus' beaches should be aware that their presence at the wrong time (at night) disrupts the breeding cycle and contributes to the species' gradual disappearance.

In Northern Cyprus, Alagadı Beach 19km east of Kyrenia (Girne) is one of the turtles' prime breeding grounds. Golden Beach on the Karpas Peninsula and large sections of the vast Famagusta Bay are also popular breeding grounds, as is the largely untouched northern tract of the Karpas Peninsula.

When visiting a turtle beach, do so with caution and care. Some beaches such as Alagadı Beach are closed between dusk and dawn, and have the breeding areas staked out with protective cages. Place beach umbrellas as near to the water as possible to avoid crushing unhatched eggs. Do not use torches at night when hatchlings are emerging, and take only official 'turtle tours' if you are really keen to observe them.

Enjoy the turtles, but remember, they were here long before you.

YENIERENKÖY (YIALLOUSA) ΓΙΑΛΛΟΥΣΑ

This is another village once populated by Greeks and now resettled with the former residents of Erenköy (Kokkina; p136) in the South's Tylliria region.

The local **tourist information office** (☎ 374 4984; ☉ 10am–6pm Jun–mid-Sep, 9am–1pm & 2-5pm mid-Sep–May) is run by an enthusiastic English-speaking host, who is happy to share his knowledge about the peninsula with the scarce visitors. A large wall map of the Karpas Peninsula shows the better-known sites, as well as a few that he has discovered himself. Ask about the large 'undiscovered' **cave tombs** between Avtepe (Elisi) and Kuruova (Koroveia), and the **sandstone caves** near Kaleburnu (Galinoporni).

The **Theresa Hotel** (☎ 374 4266; www.theresa hotel.com; s/d UK£10/15) is a small seaside place with simple, neat rooms, all with balconies overlooking the sea, and spacious bathrooms. There is a sandy beach with parasols and loungers outside the hotel. It's 7km east of Yenierenköy, on the northern side of the Karpas. The hotel also has an in-house restaurant.

SIPAHI (AGIA TRIADA) ΑΓΙΑ ΤΡΙΑΔΑ

The small and rather strung-out village of Sipahi (Agia Triada) is home to a tiny community of some 134 Karpas Greeks who, like their brethren in Dipkarpaz, cling tenuously to life on the peninsula despite the political odds. The village is also home to a rather well preserved set of mosaics in the now-ruined **Basilica of Agia Triada** (☉ 9am-5pm) dating from around the 5th century. Bizarrely, it is a bunch of small children who 'look after' the place now, and run after you with a bottle of water, which they pour over the mosaics to expose their colour. There is no entrance fee, but the little ones may still try to charge you, shouting the only thing they know in English: 'Tickets! Tickets!', until their older sister comes to shoo them away.

While little is left of the main structure, the basilica has extensive flooring, intricately patterned with abstract mosaics. Greek inscriptions at both the northern and southern ends of what was once the nave reveal that the church was financed partially by a certain deacon Iraklios and three other men, who did so in response to a personal vow.

The site is at the eastern end of the village and is best approached from the Dipkarpaz end of Sipahi.

DIPKARPAZ (RIZOKARPASO)

The remotest and largest village on the peninsula, Dipkarpaz is where the electricity fizzles out and the generators kick in. Here, a mosque and an Orthodox church sit side by side, although the church is a mute companion whose bell cannot be sounded. A Greek and a Turkish coffee shop ogle each other from across the street, and there are around 350 Greek Cypriots who still live in the village. A small shop and petrol station are the only real facilities. Dipkarpaz is now mainly populated by mainland Turks who work the land and live in poor conditions.

Despite, or perhaps because of its isolation, Dipkarpaz has two wonderful hotels: the Oasis at Ayfilon (see the boxed text, p218); and **Karpaz Arch Houses** (☎ 372 2009; www.archouses .com; r UK£30). About 500m from the centre of the village, the Arch Houses is in fact one large arch-house with 11 units, all with self-catering facilities, surrounding a green garden and a courtyard. The house is almost like a small community, with guests barbecuing outside their rooms, and the generally friendly atmosphere of a shared space. The beach is a few minutes' drive away.

AGIOS FILON & AFENDRIKA

Standing in silent sentinel on a rather deserted coastline, some 5km north of Dipkarpaz and right next to the Oasis hotel, is the well-preserved shell of **Agios Filon** (admission free; ☉ no set opening hours), a 12th-century church built over an earlier 5th-century Christian basilica. Abstract mosaics from the earlier basilica can be viewed outside the standing walls of the later church.

The site is that of **Carpasia**, an ancient place of some importance during the Hellenistic period and the Middle Ages. A **Roman harbour** was also situated here and the remains of the breakwater can be seen out to sea.

A further 7km eastwards will bring you to **Afendrika** (admission free; ☉ no set opening hours), a rather desultory site that was one of the six major cities of Cyprus in the 2nd century BC. What's left is a set of contiguous ruins comprising three churches – **Agios Georgios** from the 6th century, and **Panagia Hrysiotissa** and **Panagia Asomatos** from around the 10th century. Nearby are a **necropolis** and the remains of a **citadel**.

MONASTERY OF APOSTOLOS ANDREAS

Twice a year, on 15 August and 30 November, coachloads of Greek Cypriots make the long trek to this **monastery** (admission free but donations accepted; ☺ no set opening hours), near the tip of the Karpas Peninsula.

Over the last 30 years, these were the only times when the Turkish Cypriot authorities allowed large numbers of Greeks to their side of the island, but nowadays, with eased border crossings, visiting is fairly straightforward. Nevertheless, the visit is undertaken with great fanfare and seriousness. The object of their pilgrimage is to visit this site where miracles reputedly take place.

The current main church dates from 1740, though additions were made in later years to the whole monastery complex. The monastery gained a reputation for miracles as far back as the time of St Andrew (the patron saint of sailors) who reputedly restored the sight of a ship's captain after arriving in Cyprus from Palestine. Attested miracles range from curing blindness, lameness and epilepsy to granting personal wishes. Before 1974, the monastery made a good living out of the pilgrims' votive offerings.

Today, with mass visits only twice a year, revenue is down and the monastery's fortunes look ever bleaker. It operates under the watchful eye of the Turkish Cypriot administration, with only a couple of Greek caretakers to look after the place, including a very old lady who cares for about fifty cats, all lounging outside the monastery.

In between pilgrimages, visitors may still come to the monastery during the day to be guided by one of the caretakers. Your contribution to the upkeep of the church will always be appreciated. There's a small market outside, selling cheap souvenirs.

ZAFER BURNU (CAPE APOSTOLOS ANDREAS)

A further 5km from the monastery, along a reasonable dirt road to the easternmost tip of Cyprus, the island ends (or begins) and drops off into (or rises from) the sea. You can gaze at the cluster of little rocky islets known collectively as the **Kleides** (Keys). If you have a 4WD, you can take a rough northern track from here back to Dipkarpaz, though the going can get rough in wet weather.

Most sleeping and eating places are on the expanse of Golden Beach (p215), ranging from basic to quite comfortable.

Blue Sea Hotel (☎ 372 2393; fax 372 2255; Dipkarpaz; s/d UK£10/15) Decorated like someone's house (it's actually the hotel owners' home), this is a nice place to stay, as an alternative to the more basic options. It's near Alagadı (Turtle) Beach, on the peninsula's south side, and is built on a rocky spur with ample shade from its shoreline trees. The hotel restaurant serves fresh fish caught by the hotel owner.

Seabird (☎ 372 2012; Apostolos Andreas; s/d UK£8/13) A kilometre or so past the Monastery of Apostolos Andreas is this get-away-from-it-all place, which is really more of a seasonal restaurant with a few basic rooms to rent.

THE AUTHOR'S CHOICE

Oasis at Ayfilon (☎ 0533 840 5082; www.oasishotelkarpas.com; s/d UK£18/24) As you're driving towards Dipkarpaz (Rizokarpaso), curious signs appear along the road, citron yellow and lime green in colour, with odd, poetic sentences like: 'Dine in the shadows of the whispering palms of ruined Carpasia', or 'Dawn zephyrs softly stroke the embers of the meltdown that was yesterday's sunset'. If you follow the world's only advert-by-poetry, taking the road going up on the left, past the mosque in Dipkarpaz, you'll get to Oasis. It's right next to the ruined church of Agios Filon (p217). Five luminous rooms overlook the sea. There's barely any decoration to speak of apart from a comfortable double bed, a mosquito net, and a small chest with an oil-lamp. The rooms are clean and minimalist, and look onto a small beach, and the bathrooms are shared, except for one room with an en suite. Perhaps the most memorable thing about Oasis, apart from the peaceful setting and the idyllic Agios Filon beach, is the Oasis restaurant. The fish in this place (15YTL per person), marinated in olive oil and grilled, is the best on the peninsula. The breakfast (included in the room price) is enormous, with toasted bread and haloumi (helimi), olives, tomatoes, cereals, jam, teas of all kinds, and so on. And at night, when the generators are switched off and the lights go out, the stars in the black sky shine like countless diamonds.

ORTHODOXY & ISLAM

While Turkish and Greek Cypriots may be separated by physical, human-induced barriers, they at least share the same God – even if they worship him via two different religions.

Cyprus is home to two major religious faiths: Eastern Orthodoxy and Sunni Islam. Much smaller religious communities such as the Maronites and the Jews also practise their faith on the island. Orthodoxy came to Cyprus with St Barnabas, companion and co-traveller of the apostle Paul in AD 45, while Islam arrived with the Ottoman conquerors in 1570.

Eastern Orthodoxy is a community of Christian churches that arose when the Greek-speaking Eastern section of the Latin-speaking Church split from Rome in what was known as the Great Schism in 1054. Orthodoxy means 'the right belief', and its adherents do not recognise the jurisdiction of the Catholic Pope. Instead, they recognise only the Patriarch of Constantinople as their leader. Other than dogmatic differences and an entrenched sense of separateness from Rome, the Eastern Orthodox Church is in many ways similar to the Catholic Church, and the two share some commonalities.

However, much of the Orthodox Church liturgy is steeped in tradition and conservatism, and little has changed since the schism. Church services are redolent with formality and ceremony, and often last up to three hours. Yet, at the same time, they are informal family affairs, with participants wandering in and out of the service at will, often exchanging small talk and gossip with other churchgoers. This is in stark contrast to the strict observances of behaviour in the Catholic Church, yet Catholicism has a more liberal approach to liturgy.

Islam is a monotheistic religion that came out of what is now Saudi Arabia in the early 7th century. The Arabic word 'Islam' means 'submission to God', and Muslims strive to submit their individual wills to the will of God alone. The religion of Islam was named in honour of its final prophet, Mohammed, after he was witness to a series of revelations about the one true God, Allah. These revelations are written up in the Islamic holy book, the Quran, and the dictates of the Quran constitute the basis for Islamic beliefs today.

Turkish Cypriots and mainland Turkish settlers in Northern Cyprus follow the Sunni branch of Islam, the traditional 'Orthodox' Islam that constitutes the majority in the Islamic world. However, Islamic life in Cyprus is far from the veiled world of Saudi Arabia or the strictures of Afghan Taliban Islam. Most Turkish Cypriots, while taking their religion seriously enough, are fairly liberal in the implementation of Islamic laws. Women dress much more freely than their Islamic sisters elsewhere, and alcohol is commonly available. Mosques can be seen in both Northern Cyprus and the Republic, while previously Christian churches have been recycled into mosques, a solution that is practical yet occasionally bizarre.

Clustered close to one another on Golden Beach are three low-key sets of wooden huts, where you can also set up your tent if you're camping. Inside the huts, you'll find double beds, mosquito nets and bathrooms. All have a laid-back cafeteria and restaurant, trees for shade, and the wonderful Golden Beach stretching for kilometres. Prices are the same for all three.

Hasan's Turtle Café & Restaurant (☎ 0533 864 1063; fax 372 2290; cabin s/d UK£6/12) is probably the best known and most remote of the cape's accommodation options. You'll find it signposted off the main road and located down a spiralling sandy track amid shady trees and sand dunes. Here, English-speaking Hasan Korkmaz, known in some quarters as the turtle man of Nangomi, runs seven small huts and a generator-powered restaurant. Bring a torch and lots of books, and prepare to seriously chill out. Rates include breakfast.

Next to Hasan's are the other two of the trio. **Burhan's** (☎ 0533 864 1051; cabin s/d UK£6/12) has wooden bungalows with bathrooms, and **Golden Beach Bar & Restaurant** (☎ 372 2146; cabin s/d UK£6/12) is a kilometre or so further west, with similar services. Both are prominently signposted from the main road.

For a meal with a golden view, the Big Sand Restaurant camping and picnic corner, just before the Monastery of Apostolos Andreas, offers good views from high up overlooking the magnificent beach scene. Expect no more than reasonably priced meat and fish grills.

Directory

CONTENTS

ACCOMMODATION

Accommodation in Cyprus ranges from huts on a beach to superluxurious five-star hotels on a beach. Prices vary between the South and the North, the latter mostly offering cheaper accommodation across all budgets. Note that the prices quoted in CY£ are for the Republic of Cyprus, and those quoted in UK£ are for Northern Cyprus. In this book, accommodation is categorised as budget (up to CY£30 and up to UK£20, for a double room), midrange (CY£30 to CY£100, and UK£20 to UK£70) and top end (CY£100 and up, and UK£70 and up). En-suite bathrooms and breakfast are included in the price, unless otherwise stated.

Budget places are usually small hotels. Unfortunately, with only a couple of exceptions, there is almost no culture of private room renting. It's often a gamble whether you get air-conditioning or not in the budget options. In the Republic you can sometimes stay overnight in a monastery, ostensibly for free, but a donation is expected. Sleeping rough is not recommended and is frowned upon, but you might get away with sleeping on a deserted beach as a one-off solution.

Midrange places almost always have a swimming pool, and this price range has the most versatile and interesting choice of accommodation.

Top-end places range from five-star hotels of international fame, such as the Intercontinentals or Holiday Inns of the world, to Cypriot-run temples to luxury and style.

August is the most expensive time of the year since it's Cyprus' holiday month; rates go down significantly before and after. The rates listed in the *Cyprus Hotel Guide*, issued free by the Cyprus Tourism Organisation (CTO), are maximum allowable prices, and will normally only be applicable in high season (July to August). Winter months offer a 20% to 30% discount, especially if you book online.

The prices quoted in this book are for the high season, unless otherwise stated.

B&Bs & Pensions

In the Republic, the B&B system is generally known as agrotourism. This is a superb and often very economical way for independent travellers to see the country. Guests stay in renovated village houses or purpose-built pensions. Most of them are self-contained and fully equipped. Rates range from CY£12 for a single room to CY£65 for a luxury studio.

BOOK ACCOMMODATION ONLINE

For more accommodation reviews and recommendations by Lonely Planet authors, check out the online booking service at www.lonelyplanet.com. You'll find the true, insider lowdown on the best places to stay. Reviews are thorough and independent. Best of all, you can book online.

PRACTICALITIES

■ The Republic of Cyprus' English-language newspapers are the *Cyprus Mail* and the *Cyprus Weekly*. In Northern Cyprus, look for the *Turkish Daily News* and *Cyprus Today*.

■ UK dailies, and German and French newspapers are widely available in the South and North.

■ Cyprus Broadcasting Corporation (CyBC) has programmes and news bulletins in English on Radio 2 (91.1FM) at 10am, 2pm and 8pm. British Forces Broadcasting Services (BFBS) 1 broadcasts 24 hours a day in English on 89.7FM (Lefkosia), 92.1FM (west Cyprus) and 99.6FM (east Cyprus). BFBS 2 broadcasts on 89.9FM (Lefkosia), 91.7FM (Lemesos) and 95.3FM (Larnaka). BBC World Service is picked up 24 hours a day on 1323AM.

■ Bayrak International is the voice of the North and has a lively English-language programme on 87.8FM and 105FM.

■ CyBC TV has news in English at 8pm on Channel 2. Many hotels have CNN, BBC, Sky or NBC.

■ The electricity current is 240V, 50Hz. Plugs are the large type with three square pins as in the UK. Multiplug adaptors are widely available.

■ Cyprus uses the metric system. A standard conversion table can be found on the inside front cover of this book.

However, the vast majority of agrotourism houses and pensions are away from major centres, so you will either need your own transport to get around, or have to rely on sometimes-sketchy public transport.

For an excellent colour brochure listing places to stay, contact **Cyprus Agrotourism Company** (☎ 2233 7715; www.agrotourism.net; PO Box 4535, CY-1390 Lefkosia) or check its listings online.

Camping
The South has seven licensed camping grounds, most with limited opening times. All are equipped with hot showers, a minimarket and a snack bar, and charge about CY£1.50 per day for a tent site, plus CY£1 per person per day. In the North, there are six camping grounds, but facilities are not as good or well developed as in the South. Costs are similar to those in the South.

Guesthouses
Domatia (rooms for rent), advertised by the word *camere*, are not common in Cyprus; in fact, the practice is officially discouraged. However, in Agia Napa you will see signs advertising rooms, and occasionally come across them in some of the more popular mountain resorts such as the Troödos Massif in the South.

Hostels
There are four Hostelling International (HI) hostels in the Republic of Cyprus. Try

contacting the **Cyprus Youth Hostel Association** (☎ 2267 0027; montis@logos.cy.net; PO Box 21328, CY-1506 Lefkosia). There are no HI hostels in Northern Cyprus.

HI cards are not mandatory for a stay in any of Cyprus' youth hostels, though an HI card may get you a 10% discount.

Hotels
In the South, hotels are classified from one to five stars; prices for a double room range from CY£30 to more than CY£200. While most hotels deal primarily with package-tour groups paying cheaper bulk rates, individual travellers can usually find a room even in ostensibly marketed 'resort' hotels. Quality varies markedly, though prices are strictly controlled by the CTO.

The quality of hotels in the North is generally good to excellent at the top end of the scale, though the supply is necessarily smaller. Package-tour visitors constitute the bulk of guests. The same principle applies to individual travellers as in the South: there will usually be a room available for walk-ins. The *North Cyprus Hotel Guide* is available from the North Cyprus Tourism Organisation (NCTO), if you ask specifically for it.

ACTIVITIES
There are outdoor activities to suit most tastes in Cyprus. Some activities, including cycling, skiing and hiking, are better

suited to the cooler months. Organised water-based activities in general run from mid-March to late October, though if you want to be active independently at any time of the year, all you need is your own equipment. The CTO produces a handy pocket-sized 150-page booklet called *Cyprus Travellers Handbook*. This alphabetically organised, free publication contains a wide range of data and information on the Republic of Cyprus, and is available from any CTO office.

Boating

Boats of all kinds can be hired at the major beaches in both Northern Cyprus and the Republic of Cyprus. Popular spots for boating include Geroskipou Beach and Coral Bay near Pafos, Polis and Latsi to the north of Pafos, Larnaka Public Beach, Dasoudi Beach near Lemesos and, in Northern Cyprus, Kyrenia (Girne). Costs range from CY£10 for 30 minutes in a 49HP speedboat to CY£30 for 30 minutes in a 150HP speedboat. Prices for hiring a craft in the North are somewhat cheaper.

Yachties might like to get a copy of Rod Heikell's *Turkish Waters & Cyprus Pilot*. The 6th edition has been extensively revised. It covers the coasts and islands from Istanbul, through the Sea of Marmara, the Dardanelles, the Aegean and Mediterranean coasts to the Syrian border, and includes Cyprus.

Cycling

The CTO produces a helpful brochure called *Cycling in Cyprus,* which lists a number of recommended mountain-bike trails using both surfaced and unsurfaced roads and off-road trails. This should be available from most CTO offices; if not, you can obtain a copy from the CTO head office in Lefkosia (South Nicosia; p61). The NCTO does not yet produce a similar cycling guide.

Overall, cycling in Cyprus is quite easy and not yet overrun by long-haul cyclists, due to the island's geographic isolation. The distances are relatively short, and quieter roads run parallel to the busy motorways that connect Lefkosia, Larnaka, Lemesos and eventually Pafos. Cyclists may use the wide, hard shoulder of the two-lane motorways, but the scenery of passing vehicles is

less enticing than that found on the less-busy roads.

Cyclists in the Troödos Massif in the South will find some of the island's most scenic areas, but bicycles with a good range of gears are necessary to cope with the long, though not necessarily steep, gradients that lead up and down the mountains. Mountain bikes can be hired in Troödos (p102) should you not relish the idea of riding your own bike uphill to the town.

In the North, cyclists will find the relatively trafficless roads of the Karpas (Kırpaşa) Peninsula the most rewarding. Only the narrow and quickly conquered Kyrenia (Girne) Range will provide any real obstacle to movement between the north coast and the interior plains. There are no places to rent bicycles in the North.

Diving

Diving is very popular in Cyprus as the island is free from seriously dangerous currents and other underwater perils. Organised subaqua clubs can be found at major tourist centres in both the North and the South, and most of them run one- to three-day training courses for novices. Dive responsibly: do not remove antiquities or sponges from the sea bottom.

For further information, contact the **Cyprus Federation of Underwater Activities** (CFUA; ☎ 2275 1757; fax 2275 5246; PO Box 21503, CY-1510 Lefkosia). For the lowdown on the island's best dive spots, see the boxed text, p86.

Hiking

Hiking in Cyprus is a major activity, except during July and August when the weather can get too hot. In the South, well-marked trails have been set up and maintained by the CTO. The most popular trails are in the Troödos Massif (p101), which sports at least four excellent, relatively easy trails around and close to Mt Olympus.

Other trails include a series of overland hikes in the Pitsylia region (p114) immediately east of Mt Olympus. These normally require a drop-off and pick-up arrangement for hikers. The trails of the Akamas Peninsula (p132) in the far northwest are circular, as are a couple of trails in the Stavros tis Psokas park immediately south of the Tyllirian wilderness in the northwest of the country (p137). Get a copy of the CTO brochure *Cyprus: Nature Trails* for details on the organised trails in the South.

The North has some excellent hiking opportunities as well, particularly in the Kyrenia Range (p189). Local hiking operators take people on guided walks around the mountains, but armed with a walking guide you can do it easily yourself. *Walks in North Cyprus*, by Christina Hessenberg, Alison Dowey and Derek Dowey, is a handy guide to walking in the North. This spiral-bound booklet describes 30 walks and lists a number of good bird-watching areas. The maps are hand drawn and lack a scale bar, but the fairly detailed descriptions should suffice. It's available locally in bookshops in Northern Cyprus or by email (adowey@iecnc.org).

Horse Riding
In the South there is a surprisingly well-developed and organised network of horse-riding facilities, with at least nine major centres to choose from. Rates run from CY£10 to CY£12 for either an hour's unsupervised riding or an hour's instruction. The CTO puts out a detailed flyer called *Horse Riding in Cyprus*, but for further details contact the **Cyprus Equestrian Federation** (☎ 2277 2515; fax 2235 7002; PO Box 14043, Aglantzia, CY-2153 Lefkosia).

Skiing
The Troödos Massif enjoys a brief, but often vigorous, skiing season; the sport is fairly popular for those who have the equipment and energy to get up to the slopes of Mt Olympus from early January to mid-March. There are four ski runs close to Troödos, which are operated and maintained by the **Cyprus Ski Club** (☎ 2236 5340; PO Box 22185, CY-1518 Lefkosia). There are also two runs on the north face of Mt Olympus; one is 350m long and the other 500m long. There are two more 150m runs in 'Sun Valley' on the southern side of Mt Olympus. For further information contact the Cyprus Ski Club or get the CTO leaflet, *Skiing in Cyprus*. There is no skiing in Northern Cyprus.

Snorkelling
Snorkelling is as popular as organised diving in Cyprus. Masks, snorkels and flippers can all be bought or hired if you haven't brought along your own, and no special permission is required. Possibly the best area for snorkelling is in the less-exposed coves of eastern Cyprus, especially around Protaras (p169). In the North, the beaches to the west of Kyrenia (p192) are probably the best bet.

Windsurfing
Windsurfing is a widespread activity in both halves of Cyprus, though the area around Protaras (p169) in the South is particularly popular. Windsurfing equipment can be hired for around CY£5 per hour for solo surfing, or for CY£5 with 30 minutes of instruction.

BUSINESS HOURS
Throughout Cyprus, restaurants are open from 11am to 2pm and from 7.30pm to 11pm daily. Public-service hours are 7.30am to 3.30pm weekdays and also 3pm to 6pm Thursday (September to June), or 7.30am to 2.30pm weekdays (July to August).

Republic of Cyprus
Shopping hours vary by season. In summer (June to mid-September), shops open at around 8.30am and close at around 7.30pm weekdays. In the major cities there is an afternoon break from 1pm to 4pm. In spring and autumn (April to May and mid-September to October), shops close at 7pm, and in the winter period (November to March) at 6pm. On Wednesday and Saturday early closing is at 2pm, and shops do not open on Sunday.

Banks maintain somewhat shorter hours: 8.30am to 12.30pm weekdays as well as 3.15pm to 4.45pm on Monday. In July and August banks open 15 minutes earlier. Centrally positioned banks also offer afternoon tourist services; you'll see notices posted on their doors. Currency-exchange bureaus operate over more extended hours and are often open until late in the evening.

Northern Cyprus
Banks are open 8am to noon, and 2pm to 5pm weekdays from September to March, and from 8am to 1.30pm, and 2.30pm to 5pm the rest of the year. Shops are open 7.30am to 2pm weekdays from May to August, and 8am to 1pm, and 2pm to 5pm the rest of the year. There is also late opening on Monday from 3.30pm to 6pm.

DIRECTORY

CHILDREN

Visiting Cyprus with junior travellers is very easy. Children are the focal point of family life for all Cypriots and will always be received very warmly. Children are welcome in restaurants and bars; they can be seen running around way past midnight at the many weddings that take place around the country during the summer.

Restaurants will often have highchairs for children, and hotels should be able to supply cots if requested in advance. Hotels also often provide child-minding facilities; check before you book your accommodation. Hire cars will not normally supply child safety seats, so check with the company beforehand if you need one.

While large, grassy playgrounds are few and far between in the main towns, there are several water theme parks around the country to keep kids occupied for the best part of a day, and there are usually video games and rides available at most tourist centres.

And there are always the beaches – most of them very safe with shallow water – and associated water activities to keep the little ones entertained all day.

For a rundown on how to amuse children on holiday, read Lonely Planet's *Travel With Children*.

CLIMATE CHARTS

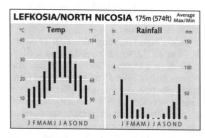

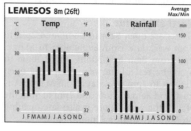

CUSTOMS

General EU customs rules apply to the Republic of Cyprus, since it entered the EU. This means that between EU countries, you are allowed to bring in or out an unrestricted amount of (legal) goods, as long as they are for your own consumption.

Entering or leaving Northern Cyprus, the limit is 200 cigarettes and 1L of spirits or wine. The importation of agricultural products, including dried nuts, seeds, bulbs and cuttings, fruit, vegetables, cut flowers and so on, are subject to strict quarantine control, and requires prior approval by the Ministry of Agriculture & Natural Resources.

DANGERS & ANNOYANCES

In general, Cyprus is a very safe place to travel, both for locals and for tourists, and personal safety is pretty well guaranteed. The crime rate is minimal and muggings are almost unknown, although petty theft and crime may be on the increase in urban centres – this applies equally to both the Republic and the North.

As a traveller, you run few risks of personal loss or harm in Cyprus, though you're advised to lock hotel rooms and keep personal belongings secure. The greatest risk will often come from fellow travellers in resorts with a high concentration of tourists, where petty theft and drunkenness are the most likely annoyances to be encountered.

Care must be exercised when travelling in the area of the Attila Line (known as the Green Line in the capital) that divides the North from the South. Be sure to only cross at designated checkpoints and nowhere else. The dividing line is normally clearly visible and identifiable by barbed wire, sentry boxes and UN watchtowers. Despite this, there have been cases of people inadvertently straying across the line towards the North, whereupon they have been arrested. The delineation between North and South is less clearly marked within the Dekelia Sovereign Base Area in the east, where there is no UN buffer zone as such. Extra care must be exercised here.

There are still occasional demonstrations and gatherings by Greek Cypriots at various points along the Attila Line, and tensions can run very high. In August 1996 two Greek Cypriots were murdered by Northern Cypriot counter-demonstrators

NORTH TO SOUTH CUSTOMS REGULATIONS

When crossing from the North into the South, you are allowed to bring in up to CY£80 of goods, 200 cigarettes and 1L of spirits or wine. Be aware that you will be subject to both British and the Republic's customs regulations when crossing at Pergamos (Larnaka District) and Agios Nikolaos (Famagusta District), as those two checkpoints are in the Dekelia Sovereign Base Area (Great Britain). The regulations are the same, but it might take a bit more of your time.

at Deryneia, close to Famagusta (Mağusa). At the same time, some Greek demonstrators and several foreigners were also injured by gunshots. See the boxed text, p167, for further details.

To avoid possible problems, travellers should not linger near military bases in the North or the South, and should obey prominent signs prohibiting photography.

DISABLED TRAVELLERS

Any CTO can send you the *What the Disabled Visitor Needs to Know about Cyprus* factsheet, which lists some useful organisations. The Republic's airports have truck lifts to assist disabled travellers. Some hotels have facilities for the disabled, but there's little help at historical sites and museums.

Wheelchair travellers might like to check out **GC Paraquip** (☎ 2694 9758; www.paraquip.com.cy; Ahepans 1, Pafos CY-8026). It offers a wide range of services and information on hotels, wheelchair hire and airport transfers.

In Northern Cyprus there are few facilities for the disabled visitor.

DISCOUNT CARDS

The most well-known and easily obtainable student ID card is the **International Student Identity Card** (ISIC; www.isic.org). This is available from your home educational institution before you depart. Its only real advantage in Cyprus is to obtain student discounts for admission to museums and archaeological sites.

There is no substantial student discount-travel scene, and no special student concessions on bus travel within Cyprus.

EMBASSIES & CONSULATES

It's important to realise what your own embassy – the embassy of the country of which you are a citizen – can and can't do to help you if you get into trouble.

In general, it won't be much help in emergencies if the trouble is remotely your own fault. Remember that you are bound by the laws of the country you are visiting. Your embassy will not be sympathetic if you end up in jail after committing a crime locally, even if such actions are legal in your own country.

In genuine emergencies you might get some assistance from the embassy, but only if other channels have been exhausted. For example, if you need to get home urgently, a free ticket is exceedingly unlikely – the embassy would expect you to have insurance. If you have all your money and documents stolen, it might assist with getting a new passport, but a loan for onward travel is out of the question.

Some embassies used to keep letters for travellers or have a small reading room with newspapers from home, but these days the mail-holding service is not common, and any newspapers tend to be out of date.

Cypriot Embassies & Consulates

The Republic of Cyprus has diplomatic representation in 26 countries, including the following:

Australia (☎ 02-6281 0832; fax 02-6281 0860; 30 Beale Cres, Deakin, ACT 2600)

Canada (☎ 416-944 0998; fax 416-944 9149; 365 Bloor Street East, Suite 1010, Toronto, Ontario, M4W 3L4)

France (☎ 01 47 20 86 28; fax 01 40 70 13 44; 23 Rue Galillée, F-75116 Paris)

Germany (☎ 030-308 68 30; fax 030-275 91 454; Wallstrasse 27, D-10179 Berlin)

Greece (☎ 21-0723 2727; fax 21-0723 1927; Irodotou 16, GR-106 75, Athens)

Ireland (☎ 01-676 3060; fax 01-676 3099; 71 Lower Leeson St, Dublin 2)

Israel (☎ 03-525 0212; fax 03-629 0535; 50 Dizengoff St, 14th fl, Top Tower, Dizengoff Centre, 64322 Tel Aviv)

Netherlands (☎ 070-346 6499; fax 070-392 4024; Surinamestraat 15, NL-2585 GG, Den Haag)

UK (☎ 020-7499 8272; fax 020-7491 0691; 93 Park St, London W1Y 4ET)

USA (☎ 202-462 5227; fax 202-483 6710; 2211 R St North West, Washington, DC 20008)

DIRECTORY

The Northern Cyprus administration has representative offices in countries including the following:

Canada (☎ 905-731-4000; 328 Highway 7 East, Suite 308, Richmond Hill, Ontario L4B 3P7)

France (☎ 01 40 50 01 77; fax 01 46 47 68 68; 4 Rue André Colledebousuf, F-75016 Paris)

Germany (☎ 0268-33 27 48; fax 0268-33 17 23; Auf Dem Platz 3, D-53577 Neustadt Wied-Neschen)

Turkey (☎ 0312-437 6031; fax 0312-446 5238; Rabat Sokak 20, Gaziosmanpaşa 06700, Ankara)

UAR (☎ 2627 2977; fax 2627 0844; Khalifa Bin Zayad St, Blue Tower, Suite 704-A, Abu Dhabi)

UK (☎ 020-7631 1920; fax 020-7631 1948; 26 Bedford Sq, London WC1B 3EG)

USA (☎ 212-687 2350; fax 212-949 6872; 821 United Nations Plaza, 6th fl, New York, NY 10017)

Embassies & Consulates in Cyprus

Countries with diplomatic representation in the Republic of Cyprus include the following, all in Lefkosia:

Australia (Map p60; ☎ 2275 3001; fax 2276 6486; cnr Leoforos Stasinou & Annis Komninis 4)

Canada (Map p58; ☎ 2277 5508; fax 2277 9905; Lambousa 1)

France (Map p58; ☎ 2277 9910; fax 2278 1052; Ploutarhou 12, Engomi)

Germany (Map p58; ☎ 2245 1145; fax 2266 5694; Nikitara 10)

Greece (Map p58; ☎ 2268 0645; fax 2268 0649; Leoforos Lordou Vyronos 8-10)

Ireland (Map p58; ☎ 2281 8183; fax 2266 0050; 7 Aiantas)

Israel (Map p58; ☎ 2266 4195; fax 2266 3486; Grypari 4)

Netherlands (Map p58; ☎ 2265 3451; fax 2237 7956; Hilton Hotel, Leoforos Arhiepiskopou Makariou III)

UK (Map p58; British High Commission; ☎ 2286 1100; fax 2286 1125; Alexandrou Palli)

USA (Map p58; ☎ 2277 6400; fax 2278 0944; cnr Metohiou & Agiou Ploutarhou, Engomi)

Countries with diplomatic representation in Northern Cyprus include the following, all in North Nicosia:

Australia (Map p173; ☎ 227 7332; Güner Türkmen Sokak 20, Köşklüçiftlik)

Germany (☎ 227 5161; Kasım 15)

Turkey (☎ 227 2314; fax 228 2209; Bedrettin Demirel Caddesi)

UK (Map p173; ☎ 228 3861; Mehmet Akif Caddesi 29, Köşklüçiftlik)

USA (Map p173; ☎ 227 8295; Güner Türkmen Sokak 20, Köşklüçiftlik)

If you're sending mail to any of these addresses in Northern Cyprus, ensure that you use the suffix 'Mersin 10, Turkey', not 'Northern Cyprus'.

FESTIVALS & EVENTS
Republic of Cyprus

In the South, Easter is the most important religious festival, and just about everything stops. Carnival celebrations begin around fifty days before Easter.

The diary of events, available from any CTO, is a useful publication for finding out about festivals in the South.

February
Lemesos Carnival This 11-day party starts 50 days before Easter, with the 'King of the Carnival', who leads the parade. See p87 for more.

March
Cyprus International Film Festival (www.ciff2006 .com) Events take place in Lefkosia, Larnaka and Lemesos. See p68 for more.

May
EU Accession Day The most important day in modern Cypriot history is celebrated on 1 May with a party in all of the island's towns.

July & August
Ancient Greek Drama Festival A fantastic opportunity to see some ancient Greek plays under the stars in Kourion's amphitheatre and other venues in Pafos, from 1 July to 3 August.

September & October
Pafos Aphrodite Festival Opera performances are staged at Pafos Fort from 2 to 4 September.
Lemesos Wine Festival From 30 August to 11 September, locals and tourists take to the streets of Lemesos and celebrate (lots of) wine.

December
New Year's Eve Fireworks and music into the night on Lefkosia's Plateia Eleftherias and in other towns on 31 December.

Northern Cyprus
May & June
Bellapais Music Festival (www.cypnet.co.uk /ncyprus/culture/music/agenda/bellapaisfestival) Taking place in and around Bellapais Abbey, the festival consists of concerts, recitals and even brass-band performances within the refectory of the abbey.

June & July
International Famagusta Culture & Art Festival
(www.magusa.org/festival) The North's biggest festival, with music, theatre and arts taking place in Famagusta's Othello Tower and town square, and in Ancient Salamis, from 21 June to 12 July.

FOOD

We have ordered our food choices primarily by author preference. The prices indicated are for a main course for one person, or in the case of meze, per person.

GAY & LESBIAN TRAVELLERS

Homosexuality is legal in the Republic; contact the **Gay Liberation Movement** (☎ 2244 3346; PO Box 1947, Lefkosia) for more information. You will find a useful link to gay activities in Cyprus on the website of **Gayscape** (www .gayscape.com).

In the North, homosexuality is technically illegal but in practice police maintain a generally liberal attitude, particularly to foreigners who won't be arrested unless caught in flagrante delicto. There are no organised support groups in Northern Cyprus.

HOLIDAYS
Republic of Cyprus

Holidays in the Republic of Cyprus are the same as in Greece, with the addition of Greek Cypriot Day (1 April) and Cyprus Independence Day (1 October). Kids are on holiday in August and over the New Year. Greek public holidays:
New Year's Day 1 January
Epiphany 6 January
First Sunday in Lent February
Greek Independence Day 25 March
(Orthodox) Good Friday March/April
(Orthodox) Easter Sunday March/April
Spring Festival/Labour Day 1 May
Kataklysmos (Deluge) June
Feast of the Assumption 15 August
Ohi Day 28 October
Christmas Day 25 December
St Stephen's Day 26 December

Northern Cyprus

Northern Cyprus observes Muslim religious holidays. Like Easter, these holidays change each year, since they are calculated by the lunar system. The two major holidays are Kurban Bayramı and Şeker Bayramı, both coming at the end of the month-long

Ramadan (Ramazan in Turkish) fast. The fast itself is not strictly observed in the North, and restaurants and cafés are open as normal. As in the South, kids are on holiday in August and over the New Year. Other holidays:
New Year's Day 1 January
Peace & Freedom Day 20 July
Victory Day 30 August
Turkish National Day 29 October
Proclamation of the TRNC 15 November

INSURANCE

Don't leave home without it! Choose a policy that covers theft, loss and medical expenses. Some policies offer a range of options for medical expenses; the more expensive ones are chiefly for countries such as the USA, which has extremely high medical costs. There is a wide variety of policies available, so check the small print to find one that suits you. Cyprus will normally be covered under 'European Countries' provisions.

Some policies specifically exclude 'dangerous activities', which can include scuba diving, motorcycling and even hiking. A locally acquired motorcycle licence is not valid under some policies.

You may prefer a policy that pays doctors or hospitals directly rather than requiring you to pay on the spot and claim later. If you have to claim later, make sure you keep all documentation. Some policies ask you to call (reverse charges) a centre in your home country where an immediate assessment of your problem is made.

Check that the policy covers ambulances or an emergency flight home.

Worldwide cover to travellers from more than 44 countries is available online at www .lonelyplanet.com/travel_services.

INTERNET ACCESS

Cyprus is well connected to the Internet for both private and public users, and Internet cafés abound in the North and the South. If you plan to bring your own laptop, note that the phone plugs are of the flat modular kind such as those used in the UK. Adaptors are easy to find in major towns. For more information on travelling with a portable computer, see the website www .teleadapt.com.

Your local Internet Service Provider (ISP) may well have Internet roaming agreements with Cyprus; check with your ISP for local dial-up numbers before you leave home. In the South, an easy way to connect without having to take out a local account is to use the Cytanet For All service. You only pay for time connected (CY£0.20 per 10-minute block). Dial ☎ 0992 6262 from anywhere in the South; enter 'cytanetforall' as the user-id and leave the password entry blank.

If you plan to spend any time in Cyprus, you can get a temporary account with one of the country's ISPs. **SpiderNet** (☎ 2284 4844; www.spidernet.net; 4th fl, Iasonos 1, CY-1082, Lefkosia), in the South, can provide a temporary 'Click & Connect' account for CY£20. With this you get three months of Internet access. Buy the CD package from any authorised dealer, or order it from the website.

In Northern Cyprus, Comtech is the main ISP. You can take out a temporary account for one month (UK£9.80), three months (UK£22.80) or one year (UK£75). Dial-up rates are cheap at only UK£0.13 per hour. Accounts can be opened at Kyrenia's Cafe Net Internet café (p186).

Most travellers use Internet cafés and free web-based email such as **Yahoo** (www.yahoo.com) or **Hotmail** (www.hotmail.com).

If you're travelling with a notebook or hand-held computer, be aware that your modem may not work once you leave your home country. The safest option is to buy a reputable 'global' modem before you leave home, or buy a local PC card modem if you're spending an extended time in any one country. For more information on travelling with a portable computer, see www.teleadapt.com.

LEGAL MATTERS

The importation of drugs or any psycho-tropic substances is strictly forbidden. Also, the police are very vigilant on speeding and drink-driving in both the South and North.

Read the boxed text Buyer Beware (p187) on the legal implications of buying property in Northern Cyprus.

MAPS

The free country and city maps available from the CTO (p232) for the Republic of Cyprus are adequate for getting around, but check the publication date (in the lower right-hand corner). These maps are not available commercially outside Cyprus, other than from CTO offices overseas.

The NCTO (p232) also produces a few free maps – a regional map and city maps of North Nicosia (Lefkoşa), Famagusta and Kyrenia. While they are fairly skimpy and cheaply produced, these maps cover a wider urban area than the equivalent city maps in this book. Similarly, these maps are only available in Northern Cyprus, or from NCTO outlets overseas.

Possibly the best map to cover Cyprus in general is the 1:200,000 *Cyprus Travel Map* by Insight. It's quite up to date and accurate and, most importantly, has both Turkish and Greek place names for Northern Cyprus – essential if you're touring the North by car, where road signs list only the Turkish names of the towns and villages. The nifty, pocket-sized and laminated *Cyprus Insight Flexi Map* is handy for quick references and folds very easily (a boon when you are on a bus or in a taxi), but does not have Turkish place names for the North.

You might also want to look at Kyriakou Travel Maps' *Cyprus Road & Town Maps,* which may be available in overseas book-shops. Collins' *Cyprus Holiday Map* offers less overall detail but good local maps, while the Kümmerly & Frey *Cyprus Traveller's Map* is similar to the Collins product. All of them are available internationally.

MONEY

The unit of currency in Northern Cyprus is the new Turkish lira (Yeni Turkye Lira; YTL). Exchange rates for the new Turkish lira are subject to fluctuations due to a high inflation rate (80% in 2002), and will most likely have changed by the time you read this. All prices in this book for Northern Cyprus are either in UK pounds for accom-modation and excursions, or new Turkish lira for restaurants, museum admissions and other sundry fees.

The Republic's unit of currency is the Cy-prus pound (CY£), divided into 100 cents. There are coins of one, two, five, 10, 20 and 50 cents and notes of one, five, 10 and 20 pounds. There is no limit on the amount of Cyprus pounds you can bring into the country, but foreign currency equivalent to US$1000 or above must be declared. You can leave Cyprus with CY£100 or the amount that you brought in, but exchang-ing Cyprus pounds outside Cyprus may be difficult, except in Greece and perhaps in

Egypt, Israel, Jordan, Lebanon and Syria, all of which have close commercial and tourist ties with Cyprus.

Banks in Cyprus exchange all major currencies in either cash or travellers cheques. Most shops and hotels in Northern Cyprus accept Cyprus pounds, and hard currencies such as UK pounds, US dollars and euros.

Note that Cyprus is expected to enter the euro zone by 2008.

See the inside front cover of this book for exchange rates for the Cyprus pound and new Turkish lira; see p14 for costs in the North and South.

ATMs

ATMs are as popular among Cypriots as they are among international visitors. ATMs are generally a convenient way to get cash at any time of the day, and the safest way to store your hard-earned dollars, pounds or euros until you need them.

Most banks now allow you to access your regular bank account directly from an overseas ATM, although in some cases you may have to use your credit card to access cash. It is a good idea to transfer some money to your credit card before you leave home. Be aware that your bank may levy a hefty charge each time you withdraw money from an overseas ATM.

You will find ATMs in most towns and in most larger villages throughout the Republic of Cyprus. In Northern Cyprus, ATMs are currently limited to North Nicosia, Famagusta and Kyrenia.

Cash

In the Republic, you can get a cash advance on Visa, MasterCard, Diners Club, Eurocard and American Express at a number of banks, and there are plenty of ATMs. In the North, cash advances are given on Visa cards at the Vakıflar and Kooperatif banks in North Nicosia and Kyrenia; major banks (such as İş Bankası) in large towns will have ATMs.

Having cash is a fail-safe way to carry money around from one country to another. It is also the least secure method. Once you lose it, it's gone. It's a good idea to only carry as much cash as you need for three days or so. However, a safety stash of about €100 sewn into your backpack or suitcase will see you through a temporary cash-flow problem.

Foreign-currency notes may be OK to use in major tourist centres in Cyprus, but are not much use in Troödos Massif villages. In the North, foreign currency is more likely to be widely accepted in lieu of new Turkish lira.

Currency-exchange bureaus in tourist centres operate over extended hours and most weekends.

Credit Cards

Just as popular as ATMs, credit cards can be used in stores, restaurants, supermarkets and petrol stations. In the latter, you can even buy petrol after hours with your credit card from automatic dispensers.

The Republic of Cyprus is more credit-card friendly than Northern Cyprus, though the main restaurants, hotels and car-hire companies in the North will happily take plastic.

International Transfers

If you need to access your funds, international transfers are possible from your home bank to any of Cyprus' major banks. While this method is reliable, it is usually slow – taking a week or more – and not helpful if you need a cash infusion quickly. Telegraphic transfers are nominally quicker (and cost more) but can still take up to three working days to come through.

Private financial agencies such as Western Union are usually the best bet, as you can often obtain your transferred money the same day.

Tipping

In both parts of the island, a 10% service charge is sometimes added to a restaurant bill; if not, then a tip of a similar percentage is expected. Taxi drivers and hotel porters always appreciate a small tip. Bargaining is not normally part of the shopping scene in Cyprus, neither in the North nor the South.

Travellers Cheques

These are not as popular as they used to be, but are a good stand-by in an emergency. Restrictions on their use are naturally greater, though many hotels and larger establishments accept them readily. Always keep the receipts listing the cheque numbers separate from the cheques themselves, and keep a list of the numbers of those you have already cashed. This will reduce problems in the event of loss or theft.

PHOTOGRAPHY & VIDEO

Digital photography has taken over in a big way in Cyprus, and you can buy a range of memory cards from camera stores. Film is still widely available, but it can be expensive in smaller towns. You'll find all the gear you need in the photography shops of Lefkosia/North Nicosia and major towns.

It's possible to obtain video cartridges easily in larger towns and cities, but be sure to buy the correct format. It is usually worth buying at least a few cartridges duty-free to start off your trip.

For tips on taking great travel photos, take a look at Lonely Planet's *Travel Photography*.

Film & Equipment

All makes of cameras and film are catered for in Cyprus, though technical services may be more limited in the North. Same-day or even one-hour film development and printing is available in both the North and the South; slide development will take up to three days.

The cost of a 36-exposure print film is CY£2.50 in the South and UK£2 in the North. To develop a 36-exposure print film will cost you CY£5 and UK£3.90, respectively. A better idea is to bring your own film and video tapes with you, especially if you can buy them duty free.

Cyprus uses the PAL video system.

Photographing People

When handled correctly, Cypriots make engaging and often very willing subjects for photos. However, it is bad form simply to point a camera at someone without at least acknowledging your subject. A simple greeting of 'kalimera' (in the South) or 'merhaba' (in the North) or a just a smile may be all that is required to break the ice and set up a potential portrait scene.

It is not culturally appropriate to take photographs in mosques when people are praying or when a service is in progress. However, outside of these restrictions, it is usually OK to take a photograph. It is less intrusive without a flash (and draws less attention to yourself).

Restrictions

In general, you can photograph anywhere in Cyprus, with some fairly obvious exceptions. You cannot normally photograph anywhere near the Attila Line (the Green Line, in the capital). In practice, this is rarely monitored other than on both sides of the Green Line in Lefkosia/North Nicosia, where sensitivities run high. Warning signs, usually a camera with a line through it, are normally displayed prominently, so heed them.

Military camps are another no-go area and, while there are military installations in both parts of Cyprus, you will be more aware of them in the North. Do not even get a camera out if you see a warning sign.

Airports, ports and other government installations are normally touchy photo subjects, so you are advised to keep your camera out of sight near these places too.

Museums do not normally allow you to photograph exhibits unless you have written permission.

Churches with icons do not allow the use of a flash, and, depending on the commercial value of the pictures you take, may not allow photos at all.

POST

Postal services on both sides of the island are generally very efficient. Post offices are located in all major towns and villages. Services are normally only related to selling stamps and some packing materials. Stamps can also be bought at newsagents and street kiosks. Post boxes are everywhere (in the South, they are yellow, and in the North, red).

In the Republic of Cyprus, postal rates for cards and letters are between CY£0.31 and CY£0.41. There are poste-restante services in Lefkosia, Larnaka, Lemesos and Pafos. Post office opening times (except Wednesday) are normally 7.30am to 1.30pm, and 3pm to 6pm.

In Northern Cyprus, postal rates are between UK£0.26 and UK£0.32. There are poste-restante services in North Nicosia, Kyrenia and Famagusta.

Opening times are normally 7.30am to 2pm, and 4pm to 6pm. Note that all mail addresses in Northern Cyprus must be followed by 'Mersin 10, Turkey', rather than 'Northern Cyprus'.

SHOPPING

Cyprus is well equipped with stores catering for all tastes and requirements. Lefkosia in particular has smart, fashionable boutiques, as well as British chain stores such as Marks & Spencer and Woolworths. The North is not as well provided for when it comes to major department stores, but there is, nonetheless, a wide range of goods on display. Hypermarket-style shopping malls are beginning to take off in the South, and the major cities will have at least one of these shopping centres in the suburbs somewhere.

While there are not all that many hi-tech consumer items that are cheap in Cyprus, many people purchase high-grade optics such as spectacles, which are probably considerably cheaper than back home. Other good buys include leather goods, woven goods, ceramics, copperware, silverware, baskets and Lefkara lace.

Local spirits such as *zivania* (*rakı* in the North), brandy, Commandaria liqueur wine and other better-quality Cypriot wines are also good purchases.

Shoes, shirts and imported textiles are of high quality and most likely much cheaper than back home.

SOLO TRAVELLERS

Solo travellers will not come across many difficulties in Cyprus. Hotels are more keen to rent rooms to more than one person, as single-bed rooms are uncommon here, but that is only in the high season.

If you're eating alone in Cyprus, you'll probably end up chatting to the restaurant owner or anyone else working there, as Cypriots are friendly people.

As everywhere else, look after your luggage, and don't leave it unattended, although theft is rare in Cyprus. Also, when going to the beach by yourself, take as little of value with you as possible; but again, keep in mind that this is a safe country.

TELEPHONE

For information on ringing the North from the South, or vice versa, see the boxed text, below.

There are no area codes as such in Cyprus; they are an integral part of the telephone number.

In both the North and the South, mobile phones are popular. If you have an international GSM-equipped phone, check with your local service provider if global roaming is available.

You can make overseas calls from any public telephone box.

Republic of Cyprus

In the South, there are two types of public phones: those that accept prepaid phonecards and those that accept coins. Phonecard-operated phones have explanations in English and Greek. Cards to the value of CY£3, CY£5 and CY£10 can be purchased from banks, post offices, souvenir shops and street kiosks, and from Cyprus Telecommunications Authority (CYTA) offices in all towns.

At peak times, a three-minute call to the USA or the UK will cost CY£1.75, and CY£0.88 during off-peak periods (10pm to

---

NORTH–SOUTH DIALOGUE

Despite the easing of crossing the border from the South to the North and vice versa, telephoning the other side of the island is still done via half of Europe and Asia.

Phone calls to Northern Cyprus are usually routed through Turkey. That means you first dial Turkey (international access code ☎ 90), then the regional code for Northern Cyprus (☎ 392), and finally the local number. This can be difficult, as the lines are few and far between. However, there is fortunately a back-door route via a special line through which you can talk to the North quite easily from the South. Dial ☎ 0139, wait for the dial tone and then dial the local North number. To call from North to South, dial ☎ 0123 and follow the same procedure.

If you have a mobile phone from outside Cyprus with global roaming activated, it's possible to tune into the GSM networks of either side. If you have bought a pay-as-you-go Cypriot card from either side, note that it will only pick up its own network in Lefkosia/North Nicosia. Go any further away from the Green Line, and you will have to revert to your international card, as roaming is not supported between the two local mobile networks.

8am Monday to Saturday and all day Sunday). Rates to Australia are approximately double.

In the South, mobile-phone numbers begin with ☎ 99, and the only network is CYTA. If you plan to spend any time in the South, you may want to rent a mobile phone. CYTA's SoEasy pay-as-you-go mobile-phone plan is the only option. For around CY£28, you get a start-up kit consisting of a SIM card with a new number, full connection instructions in both English and Greek, and a CY£5 recharge card to get you started. Visit www.soeasy.cyta.com.cy for details.

Northern Cyprus

In Northern Cyprus, public telephone boxes take phonecards (5YTL/UK£1.90 for a 100-unit card) bought at a Turkish Telecom administration office or at a post office. A peak three-minute call to the UK will set you back UK£1.15, and off-peak UK£0.95.

In the North, mobile-phone numbers commence with either ☎ 0542 (Telsim) or ☎ 0533 (Turkcell). To call a local number, you'll need to dial the full 11-digit number, ie including the Northern Cyprus code of ☎ 0392.

TIME

Cyprus is normally two hours ahead of GMT/UTC, but has daylight-saving time during the summer months. Clocks go forward one hour on the last weekend in March and back one hour on the last weekend in October.

Also see the World Time Zones map (p270).

TOURIST INFORMATION
Republic of Cyprus

The main tourist organisation in the south of the island is the **Cyprus Tourism Organisation** (CTO; ☎ 2233 7715; www.visitcyprus.org.cy; Leoforos Lemesou 19, Lefkosia), known in Greek as Kypriakos Organismos Tourismou (KOT). Its leaflets and free maps are excellent. The CTO's headquarters are in Lefkosia's New City, on the road to Larnaka and Lemesos. However, it should only be approached for written inquiries, as it's not really geared to handling over-the-counter queries from the public. The CTO has branch offices in

the major towns in Cyprus (Agia Napa, Lefkosia, Lemesos, Larnaka, Pafos, Polis and Platres), where brochures and assistance can be found easily. Contact details for CTO branches are given in the regional chapters.

The CTO has branches in most European countries. Apart from those listed below, there are branches in the Czech Republic, Hungary, Poland and Russia.

Contact details for CTO offices include the following:

Austria (☎ 01-513 1870; zyperntourism@aon.at; Parkring 20, A-1010 Vienna)

Belgium (☎ 02-735 0621; cyprus@skynet.be; Rue De Crayer 2, B-1050 Brussels)

France (☎ 01 42 61 42 49; cto.chypre.paris@wanadoo.fr; 15 Rue de la Paix, F-75002 Paris)

Germany (☎ 069-251 919; cto_fra@t-online.de; An der Hautwache 7, D-60313 Frankfurt am Main)

Greece (☎ 21 0361 0178; cto-athens@ath.forthnet.gr; Voukourestiou 38, GR-106 73 Athens)

Israel (☎ 03-525 7442; cto@netvision.net.il; Top Tower, Dizengoff Centre, 14th fl, 50 Dizengoff St, Tel Aviv 64332)

Italy (☎ 02 58 31 98 35; info@turismocipro.it; Via Santa Sofia 6, I-20122 Milan)

Japan (☎ 03-3497 9329; Palais France Bldg, 729, 1-6-1 Jingumae Shibuya-Ku, Tokyo 150-0001)

Netherlands (☎ 020-624 4358; cyprus.sun@wxs.nl; Prinsengracht 600, NL-1017 KS, Amsterdam)

Sweden (☎ 08-10 50 25; cypern@telia.com; Norrlandsgatan 20, S-111 43 Stockholm)

Switzerland (☎ 01-262 3303; ctozurich@bluewin.ch; Gottfried Keller Strasse 7, CH-8001 Zürich)

UK (☎ 020-7569 8800; ctolon@ctolon.demon.co.uk; 17 Hanover St, London W1S 1YP)

USA (☎ 212-683 5280; gocyprus@aol.com; 13 East 40th St, New York, NY 10016)

Northern Cyprus

The main office of the **North Cyprus Tourism Organisation** (NCTO; ☎ 228 1057; www.tourism.trnc .net; Bedrettin Demirel Caddesi) is located in North Nicosia. There are also branch offices in North Nicosia at Kyrenia (Girne) Gate and at the Ledra Palace Hotel crossing point. It also maintains tourist offices in Famagusta, Kyrenia and Yenierenköy (Yiallousa), which have free country and town maps, plus an increasing number of brochures.

The NCTO can be found in the UK, Belgium, the USA, Pakistan and Turkey; otherwise inquiries are handled by Turkish tourist offices. The following two offices may provide useful information:

UK (☎ 020-7631 1930; fax 020-7631 1873; 29 Bedford Sq, London, WC1B 3EG)
USA (☎ 212-687 2350; 821 United Nations Plaza, 6th fl, New York, NY 10017)

VISAS

In both the Republic of Cyprus and Northern Cyprus, nationals of the USA, Canada, Australia, New Zealand and Singapore can enter and stay for up to three months without a visa. Citizens of South Africa may enter for up to 30 days without a visa. EU citizens have no work or stay restrictions in the South, but can stay in the North for up to three months.

When you are crossing from the South into the North, you must fill in a visa paper, which requires your personal details, such as name and date of birth, and your passport number.

You can use the same visa paper for several entries and exits, and it gets stamped each time you cross. You must have your passport to cross from one side to the other.

The same border-crossing rules apply for Greek and Turkish travellers as for everyone else.

For more details on travelling across the border, see the boxed text, p235.

WOMEN TRAVELLERS

Women travellers will encounter little sexual harassment, although you'll get more or less constant verbal 'approaches' from Cypriot men. This is common for both foreign and Cypriot women, but foreign women merit particular attention from these verbal Romeos. This can get rather tiresome, if not outright offensive. It is best to remain polite and try to ignore the advances.

Solo women travellers should take reasonable care at rowdy nightclub resorts, such as in Agia Napa, where inebriated foreign males may be a nuisance.

Transport

THINGS CHANGE

The information in this chapter is particularly vulnerable to change. Check directly with the airline or a travel agent to make sure you understand how a fare (and ticket you may buy) works, and be aware of the security requirements for international travel. Shop carefully. The details given in this chapter should be regarded as pointers and are not a substitute for your own careful, up-to-date research.

GETTING THERE & AWAY

Most visitors to Cyprus arrive by air and many of them come on charter flights. Tickets on scheduled flights to Cyprus tend to be expensive, but Europe-based travellers may be able to pick up cheap last-minute tickets with charter companies if they shop around. This applies in practice only to travellers to the Republic of Cyprus, as charter tickets to Northern Cyprus are rarely available. If you're already in Greece, you can pick up reasonably priced one-way or return tickets to the South from travel agents in Athens, Thessaloniki or Iraklio. The only way to arrive in the South by sea is by a cruise boat; there are no longer any passenger ferries, but vehicles may travel unaccompanied. However, there are fast and slower passenger ferries and car-ferry

services linking the Turkish mainland with Northern Cyprus.

Travelling between the South and North is easy nowadays, since the restrictions on crossing the border have been eased. However, you are only allowed to cross at designated checkpoints, so read the boxed text, opposite, for full information.

Flights, tours and rail tickets can be booked online at www.lonelyplanet.com /travel_services.

ENTERING THE COUNTRY

Entering Cyprus is a smooth process, providing your papers are in order of course. The immigration officers are pretty relaxed, and will usually give you only a cursory glance.

Passport

You will need a valid passport to enter Cyprus (North or South), and you will need one to cross between the North and South. You'll need to produce your passport or ID card every time you check into a hotel in Cyprus, and when you conduct banking transactions. For visa requirements, see p233.

As a foreigner, it's best to carry your passport or ID card with you at all times, in case you are stopped by the police or the military for routine checks.

AIR

There are scheduled flights and a limited amount of charter-only flights to Cyprus from most European cities and the Middle East, with discounts for students. Flights are heavily booked in the high season.

Airports & Airlines

The Republic's airports are at **Larnaka airport** (LCA; ☎ 2481 6130) and **Pafos airport** (PFO/LCPH; ☎ 2624 0506), while the North is served by **Ercan airport** (ECN; ☎ 231 4806).

Note that on most airline schedules Larnaka is listed as 'Larnaca' and Pafos as 'Paphos'. This is particularly important to know when making online bookings.

Ercan airport, 14km east of North Nicosia (Lefkoşa) in Northern Cyprus, is not recognised by the international airline authorities, so you can't fly there direct. Airlines

CROSSING THE THIN GREEN LINE

Once only a distant memory, crossing freely between the North and the South has become pretty straightforward since the easing of border restrictions in 2003. It is now possible to cross at five points on the island, and there are ongoing negotiations between the two sides about opening more. At the time of going to print, you could cross at: Ledra Palace Hotel (pedestrians only), Agios Dometios, Pergamos, Agios Nikolaos, and Zodhia (vehicles). If you don't have your own transport, a taxi will take you across the border and onto anywhere you want to go.

When you cross from the South into the North, you will have to fill in a visa paper, giving your name, date of birth and passport number. You will then be issued with a 'visa' (the small piece of paper will be stamped) and you'll be allowed to stay for up to three months in Northern Cyprus. It is important to look after this piece of paper, since you will be required to show it when you leave. There are no restrictions on how many times you can cross backwards and forwards. The visa paper is enforced only in the North.

You are now also allowed to cross into the Republic of Cyprus if your point of entry into the country is in the North. The border is open 24 hours a day, and many cross in the middle of the night, after a night's clubbing or gambling at the casinos in the North. There are no requirements for crossing from the North into the South, apart from a valid passport (see p233).

must touch down first in Turkey and then fly on to Northern Cyprus. Ercan is smaller than Pafos airport and not particularly well-equipped with arrival facilities such as baggage carts and other conveniences. Car hire must be arranged beforehand. Taxis are your only choice to and from the airport.

Cyprus Airways is the national carrier of the Republic of Cyprus, and Northern Cyprus is served primarily by Turkish Airlines (Türk Hava Yolları; THY).

Airlines flying to & from Cyprus

Aegean Airlines (A3; ☎ 22 71 65 00; www.aegeanair .com; hub Athens International Airport, Athens)

Air Malta (AMC; ☎ 2266 1666; www.airmalta.com; hub Malta Airport, Valetta)

Alitalia (AZA; ☎ 2267 8000; www.alitalia.com; hub Rome Fiumicino Airport, Rome)

Austrian Airlines (AUA; ☎ 2288 1222; www.aua.com; hub Vienna International Airport, Vienna)

British Airways (BAW; ☎ 2276 1166; www.britishair ways.com; hub Heathrow Airport, London)

Cyprus Airways (CYP; ☎ 2266 3054; www.cyprusair ways.com; hub Larnaka Airport, Larnaka)

Cyprus Turkish Airlines (KTHY; ☎ 231 4142; www .kthy.net; hub Ercan Airport, Famagusta)

First Choice Airways (FCA; ☎ 2258 8000; www .firstchoice.co.uk; hub Gatwick Airport, London)

GB Airways (BA; ☎ 2276 1166; www.gbairways.com; hub Gatwick Airport, London)

Helios Airways (ZU; ☎ 2481 5700; www.flyhelios.com; hub Larnaka Airport, Larnaka)

Lufthansa (DLH; ☎ 2287 3330; www.lufthansa.com; hub Frankfurt Airport, Frankfurt)

Malev (MAH; ☎ 2268 0980; www.malev.hu; hub Budapest Ferihegy Airport, Budapest)

Turkish Airlines (TK; ☎ 228 3901; www.turkishair lines.com; hub Istanbul Ataturk Airport, Istanbul)

Tickets

Tickets to Cyprus are at their most expensive in August. It's a good idea to try picking up flight-only deals with package-holiday companies during this time. Prices depend to a large degree on the season, and to a lesser degree on the day of the week or even the time you fly.

CHARTER FLIGHTS

Vacant seats on charter flights block-booked to Cyprus by package-tour companies are cheap, but conditions apply. First, you can rarely get more than two weeks for your itinerary and, second, the departure and arrival times are quite inflexible once booked. That said, a percentage of all package-tour seats is given over to flight-only travellers, so give it a go. More information on charter flights is given later in this book under specific point-of-origin headings.

INTERCONTINENTAL (RTW) TICKETS

Neither Cyprus Airways, Olympic Airways nor Turkish Airlines are signatories to any round-the-world (RTW) ticket agreement, but Olympic Airways often has very reasonable add-on deals to its intercontinental flights to Athens. Check with your local travel agent for prices.

> **DEPARTURE TAX**
> Departure tax in Cyprus is normally included in the cost of your air fare. For the record, you are paying CY£19.50 for the privilege in the Republic. Leaving from the North, the equivalent fee is UK£3.50.

Africa

Travellers in Africa can get to Cyprus most easily via Johannesburg and Nairobi on one of Olympic Airways regular flights through Athens. An alternative route into Cyprus is from Cairo to Larnaka direct with either Egypt Air or Cyprus Airways. Both airlines fly twice a week for US$150/200 one way/return. Tickets are available from **Egypt Panorama Tours** (☎ 359 0200; ept@link.net; 4 Rd 79, Maadi, Cairo). Cash payment is advisable in preference to credit cards, which may incur a 10% surcharge.

Asia

STA Travel, which is reliable throughout Asia, has branches in Hong Kong, Tokyo, Singapore, Bangkok and Kuala Lumpur. The Singapore office of **STA Travel** (☎ 6737 7188; retail@statravel.com.sg; 33A Cuppage Rd, Cuppage Tce, Singapore) is a good one-stop shop. Flights from Singapore to Larnaka cost from S$770/950 one way/return to around S$1000/1400 one way/return.

Australia & New Zealand

There are no direct services from Australia to Cyprus, but Emirates flies more or less directly from Melbourne or Perth via Singapore, with a change of aircraft in Dubai. Olympic Airways flies to Athens from Melbourne and Sydney, and can usually offer good value add-on Cyprus legs. Singapore Airlines flies into Athens three times a week, and there are daily connections with Cyprus Airways and Olympic Airways. You can also fly Malaysia Airlines from Melbourne to Beirut via Kuala Lumpur, and pick up a Royal Jordanian connection in Beirut to Larnaka.

Cyprus Airways is represented in Australia by **Cyprus Tourist Agency** (☎ 03-9663 3711; 237 Lonsdale St, Melbourne).

STA Travel (☎ 1300 733 035; www.statravel.com.au) and **Flight Centre** (☎ 133 133; www.flightcentre.com.au) are major dealers in cheap air fares. Fares

are some 10% cheaper if booked online. Another good website to check fares from Australia is www.travel.com.au.

Axis Travel Centre (☎ 08-8331 3222; www.axistravel.com.au; 176 Glynburn Rd, Tranmere, SA 5073) specialises in travel to and from the Middle East, Greece and Cyprus.

Return ticket prices from Australia to Cyprus cost around A$2200/2835 in low/high season. Discounted fares of around A$1555 can also be found, but these have restricted conditions.

In New Zealand, as in Australia, **STA Travel** (☎ 0508 782 872; www.statravel.co.nz) and **Flight Centre** (☎ 0800 243 544; www.flightcentre.co.nz) are popular travel agents. Connections to Cyprus are as for Australia, with the additional cost of flying to and from Australia.

Sample fares from the above websites for return flights to Larnaka from Auckland range from around NZ$2535 with Emirates to NZ$3950 with Qantas and British Airways.

Canada

The *Vancouver Sun* and *Toronto Globe & Mail* carry ads from travel agents. The magazine *Great Expeditions* is useful; it's available at newspaper and magazine stores.

Travel CUTS (☎ 1-866-246-9762; www.travelcuts.com) has offices in all major cities. Its Montreal office, **Voyages Campus Travel CUTS** (☎ 514-843-8511), is a good place to ask about cheap deals. You should be able to get to Larnaka and back from Toronto, Montreal or Vancouver for C$1500.

Olympic Airways (Montreal ☎ 514-878-3891; Toronto ☎ 905-676-484) has two flights a week from Toronto to Athens via Montreal. From Athens, you can connect with either an Olympic Airways or Cyprus Airways flight to Larnaka.

You can use the same online sites as for the USA to search and book return flights from Canada to Cyprus. Return ticket prices include C$1420 from Toronto to Larnaka with British Airways or Lufthansa, and from C$2800 flying from Vancouver to Larnaka with various combinations of Lufthansa, Air Canada and British Airways.

Continental Europe

Many European carriers fly into Larnaka airport, and some also stop in Pafos, though the bulk of the traffic is made up of charter flights.

FRANCE

There are regular services between France and the South with **KLM** (☎ 08 90 71 07 10) and **Cyprus Airways** (☎ 01 45 01 93 38). **Austrian Airlines** (☎ 08 20 81 68 16) also has daily flights to Larnaka via Vienna. **Turkish Airlines** (☎ 01 56 69 33 50) links Paris with Ercan airport in Northern Cyprus daily via Istanbul. Costs range from €339 to €485 return.

Reliable travel agents that you can check out include the following:

Héliades (☎ 01 42 60 87 81; 63 Rue Sainte-Anne, Paris)
Nouvelles Frontières (☎ 01 45 68 70 00; www
.nouvelles-frontieres.fr; 87 Blvd de Grenelle, Paris)
OTU Voyages (☎ 01 40 29 12 12; www.otu.fr; 39 Ave
Georges Bernanos, Paris)
Planète Havas (☎ 01 53 29 40 00; www.havasvoyages
.fr; 26 Ave de l'Opéra, Paris)

GERMANY

In Berlin, try **Alternativ Tours** (☎ 030-881 20 89; www.alternativ-tours.de; Wilmersdorfer Strasse 94), which has discounted fares to just about anywhere in the world.

STA Travel (SRS Studenten Reise Service; ☎ 030-285 82 64; www.statravel.de; Gleimstrasse 28) offers special student (aged 34 or under) and youth (aged 25 or under) fares.

Travel agents that offer cheap flights advertise in *Zitty*, Berlin's fortnightly entertainment magazine.

In Frankfurt, try **STA Travel** (☎ 069-904 36 970; frankfurt.berger118@statravel.de; Berger Strasse 118). There is also an office for **Cyprus Airways** (☎ 069-695 89 30; Hahnstrasse 68) in Frankfurt.

GREECE

Not surprisingly, Greece is well-connected to Cyprus, with up to seven flights daily to and from the South. **Olympic Airways** (reservations ☎ 0801 44444; www.olympic-airways.gr) flies up to four times weekly from Thessaloniki and twice daily from Athens to Larnaka, while **Cyprus Airways** (☎ 21-0372 2722) flies from Athens to Larnaka up to five times daily, and to Pafos twice weekly. There is an additional service from Iraklio in Crete to Larnaka three times a week. Ticket prices are reasonable but not overly cheap. Bank on around €220 to €250 for a return ticket from any of these destinations.

It's possible to fly to Northern Cyprus from Greece. Daily flights with Turkish Airlines from Athens to Istanbul connect with a daily evening flight to Ercan. Contact **Turkish Airlines** (☎ 21-0324 6024; Filellinon 19, Athens) for details.

Some reputable travel agents in Greece worth seeking out are **STA Travel** (Athens ☎ 21-0321 1188; statravel@robissa.gr; Voulis 31, Athens; Thessaloniki ☎ 231-022 1391; Tsimiski 130, Thessaloniki), **Aktina Travel Services** (☎ 21-0324 9925; syntagma@aktinatravel.gr; Nikodimou 3, Athens) and **Prince Travel** (☎ 281-028 2706; 25 Avgoustou 30, Iraklio).

NETHERLANDS

You can fly to Cyprus from the Netherlands daily. The cheapest return deal is with Austrian Airlines (via Vienna) for €330, followed by Alitalia via Rome (€350), Lufthansa via Frankfurt or Munich (€365), and KLM (€400) direct from Amsterdam.

Travel agents in Amsterdam include the following:

Kilroy Travels (☎ 020-524 51 00; www.kilroytravels
.com; Singel 413)
Malibu Travel (☎ 020-626 32 20; postbus@point
topoint.demon.nl; Prinsengracht 230)
MyTravel Reiswinkels (☎ 020-692 77 88;
postbus@pointtopoint.demon.nl; v Baerlestraat 82)

Middle East

With Cyprus so close to the Middle East, transport links between the countries of the Levant and Larnaka are good, but tickets are rarely discounted. Cyprus Airways is represented in Israel by **Open Sky** (☎ 03-795 1570; Ben Yehuda 23, Tel Aviv), in Jordan by **Petra Travel & Tourism** (☎ 06-562 0115; Abdulhamid Sharaf St, Amman), in Syria by **Al Patra Travel & Tourism** (☎ 011-232 4513; 29th May St, Alani Ave, Damascus) and in Lebanon by **Cyprus Airways** (☎ 01-371 136; Starco Center Block B, Beirut Central).

A good place in Israel to buy discounted tickets is **Israworld** (☎ 03-522 7099; www.israworld
.com; Ben Yehuda 66, Tel Aviv). It quoted US$110/150 for a one-way/return ticket to Larnaka with Cyprus Airways.

UK & Ireland

Trailfinders (☎ 020-7937 1234; www.trailfinder.co.uk; 215 Kensington High St, W8 6BD) produces a lavishly illustrated brochure that includes air-fare details. **STA Travel** (☎ 020-7361 6161; www.statravel
.co.uk; 86 Old Brompton Rd, SW7 3LQ) has branches in the UK. Look in the Sunday papers and *Exchange & Mart* for ads. Also look out for the free magazines and newspapers widely available in London. Those that are especially useful include *Footloose, Supertravel*

Magazine, *TNT* and *Trailfinder*. You can pick these up outside the main train and underground stations.

Most British travel agents are registered with the Association of British Travel Agents (ABTA). If you have paid for your flight at an ABTA-registered agent that goes out of business, ABTA will guarantee a refund or an alternative. Unregistered bucket shops are riskier but sometimes cheaper.

If you book directly with the airline companies, the best deals are with **British Airways** (☎ 0845 722 2111), which flies to Larnaka directly daily. A return ticket costs UK£150/215 in low/high season. **Olympic Airways** (☎ 0870 606 0460) flies twice daily (via Athens) for UK£200/250. **Lufthansa** (☎ 0845 773 7747) flies two to four times a week (via Frankfurt) for UK£200/300. There are some flights to Pafos, but they cost around UK£300 return.

Although there is a London office for **Cyprus Airways** (☎ 020-8359 1333; 5 The Exchange, Brent Cross Gardens, NW4 3RJ), it's cheaper to buy its tickets through a travel agent.

A good website for booking your own tickets is **Travelocity** (www.travelocity.co.uk). A quick search of the website brought up return fares ranging from UK£100 with Czech Airlines to UK£180 with Austrian Airlines. **Expedia** (www.expedia.co.uk) is another good online booking site, but a search for return tickets to Larnaka brought up return fares including UK£139 with British Airways and UK£240 with Cyprus Airways. Another UK website, **Cheaptickets** (www.cheaptickets.co.uk), brought up return fares ranging from UK£240 with Cyprus Airways to UK£560 with Lufthansa.

Return tickets to Ercan airport in Northern Cyprus range from UK£320 to UK£470 with **Turkish Airlines** (☎ 020-7766 9300).

Package holidays to the Republic of Cyprus come in all shapes and sizes, and range in price from UK£350 to UK£700 for one week's accommodation with breakfast in a decent-sized hotel in Pafos. See p243 for a selection of reputable package-holiday operators.

USA

You can fly to Cyprus from the USA with a number of airlines, but all involve a stop and possibly a change of airline in Europe. The *New York Times*, *LA Times*, *Chicago Tribune* and *San Francisco Examiner* all produce weekly travel sections in which you can find any number of travel agents' advertisements.

Council Travel (www.counciltravel.com) and **STA Travel** (www.sta-travel.com) have offices in major cities nationwide. The magazine *Travel Unlimited* publishes details of the cheapest air fares and courier possibilities for destinations all over the world from the USA.

Among the cheaper fares offered by travel agents are return tickets with United Airlines and American Airlines connecting with Cyprus Airways flights. Tickets start at US$1515. Other permutations with British Airways, Continental Airlines, Olympic Airways or KLM are a little more expensive at US$1580. Cyprus Airways in the US is represented by **Kinisis Travel & Tours** (☎ 718-267 6882; 34-09 Broadway, Astoria, New York).

You can often get cheaper deals by booking online. Check out the following for some good ticket deals:

- www.travel.com
- www.itn.net
- www.hotwire.com
- www.travelocity.com

Return tickets from these sites cost from US$1450 from New York to Larnaka and from US$1850 from Los Angeles or San Francisco.

SEA

There are currently only passenger ferry services from Turkey to Northern Cyprus. The Republic of Cyprus used to be connected to mainland Europe by a regular passenger- and car-ferry service between Lemesos and Piraeus, Greece, with stops in Patmos and Rhodes, or sometimes in Crete instead. Cyprus was also connected to the Middle East by an onward service to Haifa in Israel.

Unfortunately, in October 2001 the two shipping companies that held the monopoly on travel to the South suspended all passenger services until further notice. Check the website of **Salamis Lines** (www.viamare.com) for the latest information.

Lemesos is the South's main arrival and departure port, and the port is 3km southwest of the town centre. It's reasonably well-equipped for sea travellers but with the suspension of passenger ferries, facilities are now mainly used by cruise-ship passengers. The terminal building has banks, tourist information facilities and duty-free shops.

GETTING AROUND

Cyprus is small enough for you to get around easily. Roads are good and well signposted, and traffic moves smoothly and without the excesses and unpredictability sometimes found in other countries in the Middle East or Mediterranean Europe.

Public transport is limited to buses and service taxis (stretch taxis that run on predetermined routes). There is no train network and no domestic air services in either the North or the South. Four-lane motorways link Lefkosia with Lemesos and Larnaka, and this network has now been expanded west to Pafos and east to Agia Napa. In Northern Cyprus, there is only one motorway, which runs between North Nicosia and Famagusta.

It is feasible to ride around Cyprus by bicycle along ordinary roads, which generally parallel the motorways, where cycling is not allowed.

Distances overall are generally short, with the longest conceivable leg in the South (Polis to Paralimni) no more than 220km. The North is equally compact, but it is quite a drive out to Zafer Burnu (Cape Apostolos Andreas) at the tip of the Karpas (Kırpaşa) panhandle from North Nicosia or even from Famagusta (Mağusa). From Morfou (Güzelyurt) to Zafer Burnu is 210km.

BICYCLE

Cycling is a cheap, convenient, healthy, environmentally sound and, above all, fun way of travelling. However, it's advisable to limit long-distance cycling trips to winter, spring or autumn, as high summer temperatures will make the going tough.

It's best to stick to cycling on ordinary roads, many of which parallel motorways, where cycling is not allowed. The roads are generally good, but there is rarely extra roadside room for cyclists, so you will have to cycle with care. You will need a bicycle with good gears to negotiate the long hauls up and around the Troödos Massif and Kyrenia (Girne) Range.

Towns and cities in general are much more cyclist-friendly than their counterparts in other parts of the Mediterranean. In some tourist centres such as Protaras and Agia Napa there are urban bicycle paths.

In the Republic of Cyprus, the Cyprus Tourism Organisation (CTO) produces a very helpful brochure entitled *Cyprus for Cycling,* which lists 19 recommended mountain-bike rides around the South. These range from 2.5km to 19km from the Akamas Peninsula in the west to Cape Greco in the east.

Bicycles can be brought over to Cyprus by plane. You can take them to pieces and put them in a bike bag or box, but it's much easier simply to wheel your bike to the check-in desk, where it should be treated as a piece of baggage. You may have to remove the pedals and turn the handlebars sideways so that it takes up less space in the hold; check all this with the airline before you make a booking.

You cannot, however, take bicycles on all buses.

Hire

Bicycles can be hired in most areas, but particularly in the Troödos Jubilee Hotel (p102), where you can hire multigeared mountain bikes. Rates start from around CY£10 a day and CY£5 for a half-day. Cycle hire is also very popular in the Agia Napa resort area.

Purchase

If you are really keen on cycling, you can purchase a decent bicycle in the Republic of Cyprus. You could try one of the specialist shops in Lefkosia, such as **Zanetos Bicycles** (☎ 2259 0945; 34 Agiou Dometieu, Strovolos). Northern Cyprus offers less of a choice when it comes to purchasing a bicycle; it's better not count on it.

BUS

Buses in the South are frequent, although some of the rural buses look like relics from 1950s England. However, bus travel is comfortable, cheap, and other than services to rural areas, offers reasonably well-timed services. Some buses, usually those running on the main intercity routes, can transport bicycles.

Buses run from Monday to Saturday, and there are no services on Sunday. Urban and long-distance buses are operated by about six private companies. The major bus companies and destinations in the South include the following:

TRANSPORT

BUS FARES

Republic of Cyprus

Lefkosia (South Nicosia): Lemesos (CY£1.50 to CY£2, one hour); Pafos (CY£3 to CY£5, 1¾ hours); Larnaka (CY£1.50, 45 minutes); Troödos (CY£1.50, one hour); Agia Napa (CY£2, one hour); Paralimni (CY£2.50, 1¼ hours); Polis (CY£5, 2½ hours)

Lemesos: Pafos (CY£2, 45 minutes); Larnaka (CY£1.70, 45 minutes); Platres (CY£2.50, one hour).

Larnaka: Lefkosia (South Nicosia; CY£2.50, one hour); Lemesos (CY£1.70, one hour); Agia Napa (CY£2 to CY£2.50, 50 minutes); Paralimni (CY£3, 1¼ hours)

Northern Cyprus

North Nicosia (Lekfoşa): Kyrenia (Girne; 1.50YTL, 20 minutes); Famagusta (Mağusa; 2YTL, 45 minutes)

Kyrenia (Girne): Famagusta (Mağusa; 2.50YTL, 1¼ hours)

Alepa Ltd (☎ 9962 5027; Plateia Solomou, Lefkosia) Lefkosia to Lemesos & Pafos.

Clarios Bus Co (☎ 2275 3234; Constanza Bastion, Lefkosia) Lefkosia to Troödos & Kakopetria.

Eman Buses (☎ 2372 1321; Constanza Bastion, Lefkosia) Lefkosia to Agia Napa.

Intercity Buses (☎ 2266 5814; Plateia Solomou, Lefkosia) Lefkosia to Larnaka & Lemesos.

Nea Amoroza Transport Co Ltd (☎ 2693 6822, 2693 6740; Plateia Solomou, Lefkosia) Lefkosia to Pafos.

PEAL Bus Co (☎ 2382 1318; Stasinou 27, Lefkosia) Lefkosia to Paralimni & Deryneia.

Buses in the North are a varied mix of old and newer privately owned buses too numerous to list here. See the regional chapters for more details.

Costs

Bus ticket prices in the South are regulated by the government. Tickets range in price between CY£1 and CY£5 for long-distance buses, while urban buses charge between CY£0.40 and CY£0.80. Bus prices in the North generally cost 1.50YTL or 2YTL for longer distances.

See the Bus Fares box (above) for an idea of the ticket prices between major towns in Cyprus. Also read the individual city and town entries for bus frequency and departure times.

Reservations

Bus reservations are not normally required in either the South or the North. The one exception to this is the service to some of the Troödos Massif resorts, where phone reservations are required if you want to be picked up from either Platres or Troödos in order to return to Lefkosia.

CAR & MOTORCYCLE

Driving or riding your way around Cyprus is the only really effective way to get around the country properly. Having your own vehicle is essential if you want to see some of the out-of-the-way places in the Troödos Massif or the Tyllirian wilderness, where bus transport is more or less nonexistent. The scenery throughout the country is varied, petrol stations are everywhere (although there are less in remoter areas like the Troödos Massif or the Karpas Peninsula), and facilities for bikers and motorists are very good. Picnic areas in the Troödos are usually only accessible if you have your own transport. Traffic is lighter in the North, but the roads are not as good as in the South.

Parking in the South is quite cheap, with CY£0.30 buying you two hours in central Lefkosia. Parking is free in all towns in the North.

Automobile Associations

In the South, there is a **Cyprus Automobile Association** (☎ 2231 3233; www.cyprusaa.org; Hrysostomou Mylona 12, Lefkosia). The 24-hour emergency road assistance number is ☎ 2231 3131. There is no equivalent organisation in Northern Cyprus.

Bring Your Own Vehicle

For a stay of more than three weeks, the high cost of bringing your own vehicle to Cyprus will be outweighed by the cost of hiring a vehicle locally. You will need to send your car by ferry and take a plane for yourself, unless you are arriving in Kyrenia (p192) or Famagusta (p209) from Turkey.

Driving Licence

For citizens of the EU, your home driving licence is sufficient for use throughout Cyprus. As with your passport or ID card, keep a photocopy of the main details separate from the licence itself.

Citizens from outside the EU may not be expressly required to hold an International Driving Permit (IDP) in the North or the South, but it is a good idea to get one in any case. These permits are obtained easily and quickly from your home country's motoring association. You will normally need to provide only your regular driving licence and a photo in order to obtain an IDP.

Fuel & Spare Parts

Being a nation that loves its motors, Cyprus is well equipped for all driving needs, with an abundance of petrol stations, spare parts and repairs, and usually a friendly local happy to give you a hand if your car breaks down. Normally, if you've rented a car, the rental agency will be responsible for repairs.

Hire

Cars and 4WDs are widely available for hire, and cost between CY£15 and CY£50 a day in the South and around UK£25 per day in the North. In some towns, you can also rent motorcycles (from CY£12 to CY£20) or mopeds (CY£8). Rental cars are usually in good condition, but inspect your vehicle before you set off. Open-top 4WDs

are popular options (the Troödos Massif literally swarms with them on hot weekends). They offer the option of dirt-track driving, that adventure 'look', and natural air-con. If you hire a 2WD, make sure it has air-conditioning and enough power to get you up hills.

Rental cars in both the North and the South carry black on red 'Z' plates – so called because of the initial letter. Other road users normally accord a fraction more respect to 'Z' car drivers and the police are more likely to turn a blind eye for minor infractions, but don't count on it.

If you rent a car before going to Cyprus, you'll find that it is common practice for the rental agency to leave your vehicle at the airport, unlocked, with the key waiting for you under the floor mat. Don't be surprised: with the obvious red hire-car plates and a nonexistent car theft record, the car is as safe as can be.

Insurance

The Republic of Cyprus issues full car insurance when you rent a car. The North also issues full insurance to cars rented in the North, but has a special third-party insurance for cars coming in from the South. For more information, see the boxed text, p175.

Road Rules

Traffic travels on the left in Cyprus in both the North and the South, and locally registered cars are right-hand drive. Left-hand

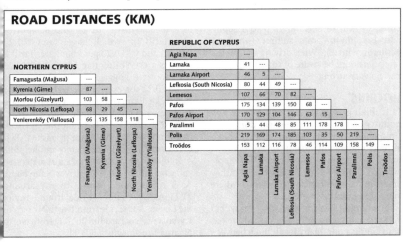

ROAD DISTANCES (KM)

NORTHERN CYPRUS

	Famagusta (Mağusa)	Kyrenia (Girne)	Morfou (Güzelyurt)	North Nicosia (Lefkoşa)	Yenierenköy (Yiallousa)
Famagusta (Mağusa)	---				
Kyrenia (Girne)	87	---			
Morfou (Güzelyurt)	103	58	---		
North Nicosia (Lefkoşa)	68	29	45	---	
Yenierenköy (Yiallousa)	66	135	158	118	---

REPUBLIC OF CYPRUS

	Agia Napa	Larnaka	Larnaka Airport	Lefkosia (South Nicosia)	Lemesos	Pafos	Pafos Airport	Paralimni	Polis	Troödos
Agia Napa	---									
Larnaka	41	---								
Larnaka Airport	46	5	---							
Lefkosia (South Nicosia)	80	44	49	---						
Lemesos	107	66	70	82	---					
Pafos	175	134	139	150	68	---				
Pafos Airport	170	129	104	146	63	15	---			
Paralimni	5	44	48	85	111	178	178	---		
Polis	219	169	174	185	103	35	50	219	---	
Troödos	153	112	116	78	46	114	109	158	149	---

TRANSPORT

drive cars circulating in Northern Cyprus have usually been brought over from Turkey. The speed limit on motorways in the South is 100km/h and is often rigidly enforced by speed-camera-wielding police officers. The speed limit on ordinary roads is 80km/h, and in built-up areas 50km/h, unless otherwise indicated. There is just one short stretch of motorway in the North linking North Nicosia with Famagusta. Speed limits in the North are 100km/h on open roads and 50km/h in towns.

Front seat belts are compulsory, and children under five years of age must not sit in the front seat. Driving a motorcycle, vehicle or even a bicycle with more than 0.009mg of alcohol per 100mL of blood is an offence.

In the Republic, car drivers must be 21 years and over, motorcycle riders 18 years and over to drive a motorcycle with an engine capacity over 50cc, or 17 years old to drive a motorcycle under 50cc. In the North, you must be 18 years or over to drive a car; for motorcycles, the same regulations as in the South.

Road distances across the country are posted in kilometres only. Road signs are in Greek and Latin script in the Republic; in the North, destinations are given in their Turkish version only. Destination road signs in the North are white on blue, and are often indistinct or small. International drivers need to be aware of the differences between their own domestic road signs and those used outside their home countries.

It's advisable to avoid rush hours in main cities, ie 7am to 8.30am, 1pm to 1.30pm, and also 6pm to 7pm in summer (one hour earlier in winter). When driving west in the late afternoon, be aware of sun glare, which can be very strong.

HITCHING

Hitchhiking is never entirely safe in any country in the world, and we don't recommend it. Travellers who decide to hitch should understand that they are taking a small but potentially serious risk. People who do choose to hitch will be safer if they travel in pairs and let someone know where they are planning to go.

Hitching in Cyprus is relatively easy, but not very common. In rural areas, where bus transport is poor, many locals hitch between their village and the city. If you do decide to hitch, stand in a prominent position with an obvious space for a ride-giver to pull in, keep your luggage to a minimum, look clean and smart, and, above all, happy. A smile goes a long way.

Hitching in the North is likely to be hampered by a lack of long-distance traffic, and, in any case, public transport costs are low enough to obviate the need to hitch.

LOCAL TRANSPORT
Bus
While urban bus services exist in Lefkosia, Lemesos, Larnaka and Famagusta, about the only two places where they are of any practical use are in Larnaka (to get to and from the airport) and Lemesos, where buses go to and from the port (where cruises depart and dock). Distances between sights in most towns and cities are fairly short, so negate the need to depend on the bus service. Buses also run to and from Kourion from Lemesos Fort, though these are tourist buses designed to get travellers from Lemesos out to the sights around Kourion rather than to move locals around.

Taxi
In the South, taxis are extensive and available on a 24-hour basis; they can be hailed from the street or taxi rank, or booked by phone. Taxis are generally modern, air-conditioned vehicles, usually comfortable Mercedes, and, apart from outside the major centres, are equipped with meters that drivers are obliged to use. The two tariff periods are: 6am to 8.30pm (tariff 1); and 8.30pm to 6am (tariff 2). Tariff 1 charges are CY£1.25 flag fall and CY£0.22 per kilometre. Tariff 2 charges are CY£1.65 flag fall and CY£0.26 per kilometre. Luggage is charged at the rate of CY£0.22 for every piece weighing more than 12kg. Extra charges of CY£0.60 per fare apply during most public holidays.

'Taxi sharing', which is common in Greek cities such as Athens, is not permitted. Taxi drivers are normally courteous and helpful.

In the North, taxis do not sport meters, so agree on the fare with the driver beforehand. As a rough guide, expect to pay around 2YTL to 2.50YTL for a ride around any of the towns. A taxi ride from North Nicosia to Kyrenia will cost around 20YTL; from North Nicosia to Famagusta 50YTL.

SERVICE TAXI

Taking up to eight people, service taxis are a useful transport option. They are run by an amalgamation of private companies called **Travel & Express** (☎ 07 77 477) with one national phone number. The individual offices can also be contacted directly: **Lefkosia** (☎ 2273 0888); **Lemesos** (☎ 2536 4114); **Larnaka** (☎ 2466 1010) and **Pafos** (☎ 2693 3181).

You can get to and from Lefkosia, Lemesos and Larnaka by service taxi, but usually not directly to or from Pafos; a change in Lemesos is often the case. The fixed fares are competitive with bus travel. Either go to the service taxi office or phone to be picked up at your hotel. Note that pick-ups can often be up to 30 minutes later than booked, so build this into your plans if time is tight. Similarly, if you're departing from a service-taxi depot, expect to spend up to 30 minutes picking up other passengers before you actually get under way.

The North has minibuses (sometimes referred to as *dolmuş*) between Kyrenia and North Nicosia only, which cost 2.50YTL per person.

TOURIST TAXIS

The 'tourist' taxis that await you near the Turkish Cypriot checkpoint at the Ledra Palace Hotel in North Nicosia will take you anywhere you want to go around Northern Cyprus. A round-trip day tour to Kyrenia, Famagusta, Bellapais (Beylerbeyi), Buffavento Castle and St Hilarion Castle costs around CY£30. (Although Cyprus pounds are not in general use in the North, most people will accept them if you have no other currency; Turkish taxis at crossing points will always quote their prices in Cyprus pounds.)

TOURS

Travel agencies around Cyprus offer a wide variety of prepackaged excursions. Some reputable tour agencies in the South include the following:

Amathus Tours (☎ 2536 9122; main@tourism.ama thus.com.cy; Plateia Syntagmatos, Lemesos)

National Tours (☎ 2236 6666; tourism@louisgroup .com; Leoforos Evagorou I 54-58, Lefkosia)

Salamis Tours Excursions (☎ 2535 5555; fax 2536 4410; Salamis House, 28 Oktovriou, Lemesos)

Land tours in the South usually run out of the main tourist centres. They range from full-day tours to Troödos and the Kykkos Monastery from Pafos for CY£15; day trips to Lefkosia from Agia Napa or Larnaka for CY£15; boat trips to Protaras from Agia Napa for CY£12; and half-day tours of Lemesos, a winery and Ancient Kourion for CY£11. These kinds of tours are not available in the North.

TRANSPORT

Health

BEFORE YOU GO

Prevention is the key to staying healthy while abroad. A little planning before departure, particularly for pre-existing illnesses, will save trouble later. Bring medications in their original, clearly labelled, containers. A signed and dated letter from your physician describing your medical conditions and medications, including any generic names, is also a good idea. If you're carrying syringes or needles, be sure to have a physician's letter documenting their medical necessity. If you are embarking on a long trip, make sure your teeth are OK and take your optical prescription with you.

INSURANCE

Citizens of EU countries are entitled to free or cheaper medical care in most European countries, but need to carry proof of their entitlement in the form of the European Health Insurance Card (EHIC), which replaced the E111 form at the end of 2005. In the UK, the card is available directly from the **Department of Health** (☎ 0845 606 2030; www.dh.gov .uk/travellers) or by using a form obtained from any post office. Note that this card might not cover all medical expenses while abroad (eg repatriation) and that some insurance policies aren't valid without an EHIC.

Citizens from other countries should find out if there is a reciprocal arrangement for free medical care between their country and Cyprus.

If you do need health insurance, make sure you get a policy that covers you for the worst possible scenario, such as an accident requiring an emergency flight home. Find out in advance if your insurance plan will make payments directly to providers or reimburse you later for overseas health expenditures.

RECOMMENDED VACCINATIONS

No jabs are required to travel to Cyprus, but a yellow-fever vaccination certificate is required if you are coming from an infected area. The WHO recommends that all travellers should be covered for diphtheria, measles, mumps, rubella and polio.

INTERNET RESOURCES

The World Health Organization's publication, *International Travel and Health*, is revised annually and is available online at www.who.int/ith/. Other useful websites include the following:

www.mdtravelhealth.com Travel health recommendations for every country; updated daily.

www.fitfortravel.scot.nhs.uk General travel advice for the layperson.

www.ageconcern.org.uk/AgeConcern/fs26.asp Advice on travel for the elderly.

www.mariestopes.org.uk Information on women's health and contraception.

IN TRANSIT

DEEP VEIN THROMBOSIS (DVT)

Blood clots may form in the legs during plane flights, chiefly because of prolonged immobility (the longer the flight, the greater the risk). The chief symptom of DVT is swelling or pain of the foot, ankle, or calf, usually but not always on just one side. When a blood clot travels to the lungs, it may cause chest pain and breathing difficulties. Travellers with any of these symptoms should immediately seek medical attention. To prevent the development of

DVT on long flights you should walk about the cabin, contract your leg muscles while sitting, drink plenty of fluids and avoid alcohol and tobacco.

JET LAG

To avoid jet lag, drink plenty of nonalcoholic fluids and eat light meals. Once you arrive, get exposure to natural sunlight and readjust your schedule (for meals, sleep and so on) as soon as possible.

IN CYPRUS

AVAILABILITY & COST OF HEALTH CARE

If you need an ambulance, call ☎ 119 in the Republic of Cyprus, or ☎ 112 in Northern Cyprus. Pharmacies can dispense medicines that are available only on prescription in most European countries, so you can consult a pharmacist for minor ailments. Emergency medical treatment and assistance is provided free of charge at government hospitals or medical institutions. However, payment of the prescribed fees is required for outpatient and inpatient treatment. Make sure your medical insurance covers any emergency.

Hospitals can be overcrowded and hygiene is not always what it should be. Conditions and treatment are better in private hospitals, but these are expensive. All this means that a good health-insurance policy is essential.

TRAVELLER'S DIARRHOEA

If you develop diarrhoea, be sure to drink plenty of fluids, preferably in the form of an oral rehydration solution such as Dioralyte. If diarrhoea is bloody, persists for more than 72 hours or is accompanied by fever, shaking, chills or severe abdominal pain, you should seek medical attention.

ENVIRONMENTAL HAZARDS
Heatstroke

Heatstroke occurs following excessive fluid loss with inadequate replacement of fluids and salt. Symptoms include headache, dizziness and tiredness. Dehydration is already happening by the time you feel thirsty; aim to drink sufficient water to produce pale, diluted urine. To treat heatstroke, drink water and/or fruit juice, and cool the body with cold water and fans.

Jellyfish, Sea Urchins & Weever Fish

Avoid contact with jellyfish, which have stinging tentacles. Stings from jellyfish in Cyprus can be very painful, but are not dangerous. Dousing in vinegar will deactivate any stingers that have not 'fired'. Calamine lotion, antihistamines and analgesics may reduce the reaction and relieve the pain.

Watch out for sea urchins around rocky beaches; if you get sea-urchin needles embedded in your skin, immersing the limb in hot water will relieve the pain (test the water temperature first!). You'll then need to get a doctor to remove the needles in order to prevent infection. If you try to remove them yourself, some travellers report that olive oil applied to the skin helps to loosen needles.

Watch out for weever fish, which bury themselves in the seabed with just their dorsal fin showing, as stepping on this dorsal fin is very painful. However, instances are very rare. The only treatment is to put the affected limb in water as hot as the victim can stand without causing scalding.

Parasites
LEISHMANIASIS

This is a group of parasitic diseases transmitted by infected sandflies, which are found in Cyprus and Turkey. Cutaneous leishmaniasis affects the skin tissue, causing ulceration and disfigurement; and visceral leishmaniasis affects internal organs. Seek medical advice, as laboratory testing is required for diagnosis and treatment. Avoiding sandfly bites is the best precaution. Bites are usually itchy and yet another reason to cover up and apply repellent.

TICK-BORNE DISEASES

Lyme disease, tick-borne encephalitis and typhus may be acquired in Cyprus. Seek immediate medical treatment if you believe you have any of these diseases.

Lyme disease usually begins with a spreading rash at the site of the tick bite, and is accompanied by fever, headache, extreme fatigue, aching joints and muscles, and mild neck stiffness.

Tick-borne encephalitis can occur in forest and rural areas. Symptoms include blotches around the bite, which is sometimes pale in the middle. Headache, stiffness and other flulike symptoms, as well as extreme tiredness, appearing a week or two after the bite, can progress to more serious problems.

Typhus is spread by ticks, mites or lice. It begins with fever, chills, headache and muscle pains, followed a few days later by a body rash. There is often a large, painful sore at the site of the bite, and nearby lymph nodes are swollen and painful.

Seek local advice on areas where ticks pose a danger, and always check your skin carefully for ticks. An insect repellent can help, and walkers in tick-infested areas should consider having their boots and trousers impregnated with benzyl benzoate and dibutyl phthalate.

Snakes

There are eight species of snakes in Cyprus, three of which are poisonous. They usually show up in spring and summer only. The most dangerous to humans is the (thankfully) rather rare blunt-nosed viper *(koufi),* recognised by its yellow, hornlike tail. The other two poisonous snakes are the cat snake and the Montpellier snake; although they can inflict a nasty bite, they're not as dangerous as the blunt-nosed viper.

To minimise your chances of being bitten, be sure to wear boots, socks and long trousers when walking through undergrowth where snakes may be present. Don't put your hands into holes and crevices, and be careful when collecting firewood.

Snakebites do not cause instantaneous death, and antivenins are usually available. If bitten by a snake that may be venomous, immediately wrap the bitten limb tightly, as you would for a sprained ankle, and then attach a splint to immobilise it. Keep the victim still and seek medical help. Take the dead snake with you for identification, but if it's still alive, don't attempt to catch it if there's a possibility of being bitten again. Tourniquets and sucking out the poison are now comprehensively discredited.

TRAVELLING WITH CHILDREN

Make sure children are up to date with routine vaccinations, and discuss possible travel vaccines with a health professional well before departure, as some vaccines are not suitable for children under one year old. Lonely Planet's *Travel with Children* includes travel health advice for younger children.

WOMEN'S HEALTH

Emotional stress, exhaustion and travelling through different time zones can all contribute to an upset in the menstrual pattern.

If using oral contraceptives, remember that some antibiotics, diarrhoea and vomiting can stop the pill from working. Time zones, gastrointestinal upsets and antibiotics do not affect injectable contraception.

Travelling during pregnancy is usually possible, but always consult your doctor before planning your trip. The most risky times for travel are during the first 12 weeks of pregnancy and after 30 weeks.

SEXUAL HEALTH

Condoms are readily available in Cyprus, but emergency contraception may not be, so take the necessary precautions.

Language

CONTENTS

Visitors to Cyprus are unlikely to encounter any serious language difficulties since many people in the North and the South speak English as a matter of course. However, if you have a smattering of Greek or Turkish and wish to fine tune your linguistic skills, there are a few pointers you should be aware of. Talking Cypriot is not as simple as it might seem.

In the South the Cypriots speak Greek, but it's not the same as what you'll hear in Greece. To an ear familiar with the standard language, Cypriot Greek sounds harsh and even incomprehensible. Consonants are palatalised so that the guttural 'ch' becomes 'sh', 'k' becomes 'tch' and the vocalised 'b' becomes 'p'. Many other phonetic variations distinguish Cypriot Greek. The vocabulary has its own set of words not heard outside Cyprus, though both standard Greek terms as well as Cypriot versions will be familiar to most Cypriots. Speakers

of Greek from the mainland are known as *kalamarades* or 'penpushers' – a hangover from the days when the only educated speakers of the language in Cyprus were from Greece.

Turkish Cypriots have their own dialect, which is distinguished from the Turkish spoken on the mainland by a number of peculiarities. These include a slurred, lazy mode of articulation, and the use of verb forms not used in standard Turkish, as well as a whole lexicon of Cyprus-specific words.

Neither Greek nor Turkish Cypriots will expect a visitor to be able to speak their respective languages – let alone the Cypriot variants. However, an hour's practice on the words and phrases in this chapter will go a long way to breaking the ice and to demonstrating to your new Cypriot friends your interest in their country. For a more in-depth guide to the languages of Cyprus, look for Lonely Planet's compact and comprehensive *Greek Phrasebook* and *Turkish Phrasebook*.

GREEK

Most Cypriots in the Republic speak English and nearly all road signs are in Greek and English. Since mid-1995 the Republic has converted all place names into Latin characters according to the official system of Greek transliteration, which has resulted in some place names being changed (see p33 for more information). Greek may still be spoken by some Turkish Cypriots who formerly lived in the South, though they may be understandably reluctant to speak it in public. Greek is also spoken by small numbers of Greeks enclaved in villages in the northeast on the Karpas (Kırpaşa) Peninsula, and in the northwest, by Maronites living on the Koruçam (Kormakitis) Peninsula (who also speak Aramaic – see p199 for more).

PRONUNCIATION

Cypriot Greek pronunciation treats some consonants differently with κ and χ being pronounced as 'tch' and 'sh' respectively.

THE GREEK ALPHABET

Greek	Pronunciation Guide	
Α α	a	as in 'father'
Β β	v	as in 'vine'
Γ γ	gh	like a rough, breathy 'g'
	y	as in 'yes'
Δ δ	dh	as in 'there'
Ε ε	e	as in 'egg'
Ζ ζ	z	as in 'zoo'
Η η	i	as in 'feet'
Θ θ	th	as in 'throw'
Ι ι	i	as in 'feet'
Κ κ	k	as in 'kite'
Λ λ	l	as in 'leg'
Μ μ	m	as in 'man'
Ν ν	n	as in 'net'
Ξ ξ	x	as in 'ox'
Ο ο	o	as in 'hot'
Π π	p	as in 'pup'
Ρ ρ	r	as in 'road'
		a slightly trilled 'r'
Σ σ, ς	s	as in 'sand'
Τ τ	t	as in 'tap'
Υ υ	i	as in 'feet'
Φ φ	f	as in 'find'
Χ χ	h	as the 'ch' in Scottish 'loch' (like a rough 'h')
Ψ ψ	ps	as in 'lapse'
Ω ω	o	as in 'hot'

Combinations of Letters

ει	i	as in 'feet'
οι	i	as in 'feet'
αι	e	as in 'bet'
ου	u	as in 'mood'
μπ	b	as in 'beer'
	mb	as in 'amber'
ντ	d	as in 'dot'
	nd	as in 'bend'
γκ	g	as in 'God'
γγ	ng	as in 'angle'
γξ	ks	as in 'minks'
τζ	dz	as in 'hands'

The Greek question mark is represented with the English equivalent of a semicolon ';'.

Greek Cypriots tend to talk more slowly than their mainland brethren, but speech modulation and word syncopation, especially in rural areas, may make understanding Cypriot Greek difficult. The Pafos region is well known for the difficulty of its local accent.

All Greek words of two or more syllables have an acute accent, which indicates where word stress falls. In the transliterations used in this language guide, italic letters indicate word stress. It's also worth noting that **dh** is pronounced as 'th' in 'then' and **gh** is a softer, slightly guttural version of 'g'.

ACCOMMODATION

I'm looking for ...
psa·hno yi·a ...   Ψάχνω για ...
a room
e·na dho·ma·ti·o   ένα δωμάτιο
a hotel
e·na kse·no·dho·chi·o   ένα ξενοδοχείο
a youth hostel
e·nan kse·no·na   έναν ξενώνα
ne·o·ti·tas   νεότητας

Where's a cheap hotel?
pou i·ne e·na fti·no xe·no·do·hi·o
Πού είναι ένα φτηνό ξενοδοχείο;
What's the address?
pya i·ne i dhi·ef·thin·si
Ποια είναι η διεύθυνση;
Could you write the address, please?
pa·ra·ka·lo bo·ri·te na ghra·pse·te ti· dhi·ef·thin·si
Παρακαλώ, μπορείτε να γράψετε τη διεύθυνση;
Are there any rooms available?
i·par·chun e·lef·the·ra dho·ma·ti·a
Υπάρχουν ελεύθερα δωμάτια;

I'd like to book ...
tha i·the·la na kli·so ...   Θα ήθελα να κλείσω ...
a bed
e·na kre·va·ti   ένα κρεββάτι
a single room
e·na mo·no·kli·o·no   ένα μονόκλινο
dho·ma·ti·o   δωμάτιο
a double room
e·na dhi·kli·no   ένα δίκλινο
dho·ma·ti·o   δωμάτιο
a double-bed room
e·na dho·ma·ti·o me   ένα δωμάτιο με
dhy·o kre·va·ti·a   δυό κρεββάτια
a room with a bathroom
e·na dho·ma·ti·o me   ένα δωμάτιο με
ba·ni·o   μπάνιο

How much is it per night?
po·so ka·ni ti vra·dhya   Πόσο κάνει τη βραδυά;
May I see it?
bo·ro na to dho   Μπορώ να το δω;

CONVERSATION & ESSENTIALS

Hello.
ya sas (pol)	Γεια σας.
ya su (inf)	Γεια σου.

Good morning.
ka-*li me*-ra	Καλή μέρα.

Good afternoon/evening.
ka-*li spe*-ra	Καλή σπέρα.

Good night.
ka-*li nikh*-ta	Καλή νύχτα.

Goodbye.
an-*di*-o	Αντίο.

Yes.
ne	Ναι.

No.
o-hi	Οχι.

Please.
pa-ra-ka-*lo*	Παρακαλώ.

Thank you.
ef-ha-ri-*sto*	Ευχαριστώ.

That's fine/You're welcome.
pa-ra-ka-*lo*	Παρακαλώ.

Sorry. (excuse me, forgive me)
sigh-*no*-mi	Συγγνώμη.

What's your name?
pos sas *le*-ne	Πώς σας λένε;

My name is ...
me *le*-ne ...	Με λένε ...

EMERGENCIES – GREEK

Help!
vo-*i*-thya	Βοήθεια!

There's been an accident.
ey-i-ne a-*ti*-hi-ma	Εγινε ατύχημα.

Go away!
fi-ye	Φύγε!

Call ...!
fo-*nak*-ste ...	Φωνάξτε ...!
a doctor e-na yi-a-*tro*	ένα γιατρό
the police tin a-sti-no-*mi*-a	την αστυνομία

HEALTH

I'm ill.
i-me *a*-ro-stos	Είμαι άρρωστος.

It hurts here.
po-*nai* e-*dho*	Πονάει εδώ.

I have ...
e-ho ...	Εχω ...
asthma *asth*-ma	άσθμα
diabetes	
za-ha-ro-dhi-a-*vi*-ti	ζαχαροδιαβήτη
diarrhoea	
dhi-*a*-ri-a	διάρροια

I'm allergic to ...
i-me a-ler-yi-*kos*/	Είμαι αλλεργικός/
a-ler-yi-*ki* ... (m/f)	αλλεργική ...
antibiotics	
sta an-di-vi-o-ti-*ka*	στα αντιβιωτικά
penicillin	
stin pe-ni-ki-*li*-ni	στην πενικιλλίνη
nuts	
sta fi-*sti*-ki-a	στα φυστίκια

condoms	pro-fi-la-kti-*ka*	προφυλακτικά
	(ka-*po*-tez)	(καπότες)
contraceptive	pro-fi-lak-ti-*ko*	προφυλακτικό
medicine	*farm*-a-ko	φάρμακο
sunblock cream	*kre*-ma i-*li*-u	κρέμα ηλίου
tampons	tam-*bon*	ταμπόν

LANGUAGE DIFFICULTIES

Do you speak English?
mi-*la*-te an-gli-*ka*	Μιλάτε αγγλικά;

Does anyone here speak English?
mi-*lai* ka-*nis* an-gli-*ka*	Μιλάει κανείς αγγλικά;

I don't understand.
dhen ka-ta-la-*ve*-no	Δεν καταλαβαίνω.

Please write it down.
ghrap-ste to pa-ra-ka-*lo*	Γράψτε το, παρακαλώ.

NUMBERS

0	mi-*dhen*	μηδέν
1	e-nas	ένας (m)
	mi-a	μία (f)
	e-na	ένα (n)
2	dhi-o	δύο
3	tris	τρεις (m&f)
	tri-a	τρία (n)
4	te-se-ris	τέσσερεις (m&f)
	te-se-ra	τέσσερα (n)
5	pen-de	πέντε
6	e-xi	έξη
7	ep-ta	επτά
8	oh-to	οχτώ
9	e-ne-a	εννέα
10	dhe-ka	δέκα
11	e-de-ka	έντεκα
12	dho-dhe-ka	δώδεκα
13	dhe-ka-tris	δεκατρείς (m&f)
	dhe-ka-tri-a	δεκατρία (n)
14	dhe-ka-te-se-ris	δεκατέσσερις (m&f)
	dhe-ka-te-se-ra	δεκατέσσερα (n)
15	dhe-ka-pe-de	δεκαπέντε
16	dhe-ka-ex-i	δεκαέξι
17	dhe-ka-ef-ta	δεκαεφτά
18	dhe-ka-oh-to	δεκαοχτώ
19	dhe-ka-e-ne-a	δεκαεννέα
20	i-ko-si	είκοσι

21	i-ko-si e-nas/mi-a	είκοσι ένας/μία (m/f)
	i-ko-si e-na	είκοσι ένα (n)
22	i-ko-si dhi-o	είκοσι δύο
30	tri-an-da	τριάντα
40	sa-ran-da	σαράντα
50	pe-nin-da	πενήντα
60	ex-in-da	εξήντα
70	ev-dho-min-da	εβδομήντα
80	ogh-dhon-da	ογδόντα
90	e-ne-nin-da	ενενήντα
100	e-ka-to	εκατό
1000	hi-li-i	χίλιοι (m)
	hi-li-ez	χίλιες (f)
	hi-li-a	χίλια (n)

SHOPPING, SERVICES & SIGHTS

I'd like to buy ...
the-lo n'a-gho-ra-so ...   Θέλω ν' αγοράσω ...
How much is it?
po-so ka-ni   Πόσο κάνει;

Do you accept ...?	dhe-che-ste ...	Δέχεστε ...;
credit cards	pi-sto-ti-ki kar-ta	πιστωτική κάρτα
travellers	tak-si-dhi-o-ti-kes	ταξιδιωτικές
cheques	e-pi-ta-ghes	επιταγές

more	pe-ri-so-te-ro	περισσότερο
less	li-gho-te-ro	λιγότερο
smaller	mi-kro-te-ro	μικρότερο
bigger	me-gha-li-te-ro	μεγαλύτερο

I'm looking for ...	psach-no ya ...	Ψάχνω για ...
a bank	mya tra-pe-za	μια τράπεζα
the ... embassy	tin ... pres-vi-a	την ... πρεσβεία
the market	ti lai-ki a-gho-ra	τη λαϊκή αγορά
the post office	to ta-hi-dhro-mi-o	το ταχυδρομείο
a public toilet	mya dhi-mo-sia	μια δημόσια
	tu-a-let-ta	τουαλέτα
the telephone	to ti-le-fo-n-i-ko	το τηλεφωνικό
centre	ken-dro	κέντρο
the tourist office	to tu-ri-sti-ko	το τουριστικό
	ghra-fi-o	γραφείο

beach	pa-ra-li-a	παραλία
bridge	ye-fira	γέφυρα
castle	ka-stro	κάστρο
hospital	no-so-ko-mi-o	νοσοκομείο
island	ni-si	νησί
market	a-gho-ra	αγορά
ruins	ar-he-a	αρχαία

TIME & DATES

What time is it?	ti o-ra i-ne	Τι ώρα είναι;
It's (2 o'clock).	i-ne (dhi-o i o-ra)	Είναι (δύο η ώρα).
in the morning	to pro-i	το πρωί

in the afternoon	to a-po-yev-ma	το απόγευμα
in the evening	to vra-dhi	το βράδυ
today	si-me-ra	σήμερα
tomorrow	av-ri-o	αύριο

Monday	dhef-te-ra	Δευτέρα
Tuesday	tri-ti	Τρίτη
Wednesday	te-tar-ti	Τετάρτη
Thursday	pemp-ti	Πέμπτη
Friday	pa-ras-ke-vi	Παρασκευή
Saturday	sa-va-to	Σάββατο
Sunday	kyri-a-ki	Κυριακή

January	ia-nou-ar-i-os	Ιανουάριος
February	fev-rou-ar-i-os	Φεβρουάριος
March	mar-ti-os	Μάρτιος
April	a-pri-li-os	Απρίλιος
May	mai-os	Μάιος
June	i-ou-ni-os	Ιούνιος
July	i-ou-li-os	Ιούλιος
August	av-ghous-tos	Αύγουστος
September	sep-tem-vri-os	Σεπτέμβριος
October	ok-to-vri-os	Οκτώβριος
November	no-em-vri-os	Νοέμβριος
December	dhe-kem-vri-os	Δεκέμβριος

TRANSPORT

What time does the ... leave/arrive?
ti o-ra fev-yi/fta-ni to ...   Τι ώρα φεύγει/φτάνει το ...;

boat	pli-o	πλοίο
(city) bus	a-sti-ko	αστικό
(intercity) bus	le-o-fo-ri-o	λεωφορείο
ferry	fe-ri-bot	φερρυμπώτ

I'd like (a) ...
tha i-the-la (e-na) ...   Θα ήθελα (ένα) ...
   one way ticket
   a-plo isi-ti-ri-o   απλό εισιτήριο
   return ticket
   i-si-ti-ri-o me e-pi-stro-fi   εισιτήριο με επιστροφή

I want to go to ...
the-lo na pao sto/sti...   Θέλω να πάω στο/στη ...

bus stop	sta-si le-o-fo-ri-u	στάση λεωφορείου
the first	to pro-to	το πρώτο
the last	to te-lef-te-o	το τελευταίο

Directions

Where is ...?
pou i-ne ...   Πού είναι...;
Can you show me on the map?
bo-ri-te na mo-u to   Μπορείτε να μου το
dhi-xe-te sto har-ti   δείξετε στο χάρτη;

SIGNS – GREEK	
ΕΙΣΟΔΟΣ	Entry
ΕΞΟΔΟΣ	Exit
ΓΥΝΑΙΚΩΝ	Women (toilets)
ΑΝΔΡΩΝ	Men (toilets)
ΑΣΤΥΝΟΜΙΑ	Police
ΤΡΟΧΑΙΑ	Traffic Police
ΑΠΑΓΟΡΕΥΕΤΑΙ	Prohibited
ΝΕΚΡΗ ΖΩΝΗ	Buffer Zone

Straight ahead.
  o·lo ef·*thi*·a   Ολο ευθεία.
Turn left.
  strips·te a·ri·ste·*ra*   Στρίψτε αριστερά.
Turn right.
  strips·te dhe·ksi·*a*   Στρίψτε δεξιά.
far
  ma·kri·*a*   μακριά
near (to)
  kon·*da*   κοντά

TURKISH

Ottoman Turkish was written in Arabic script, but this was phased out when Atatürk decreed the introduction of Latin script in 1928. The Turkish spoken in Cyprus differs somewhat from that spoken on the mainland, both in pronunciation and vocabulary. In big cities and tourist areas, many locals know at least some English and/or German. For a more in-depth look at Turkish, get a copy of Lonely Planet's compact and comprehensive *Turkish Phrasebook*.

PRONUNCIATION
Vowels
Be careful of the symbols ı and i – the ı is undotted in both lower and upper case (like Isparta), while the i has dots in both cases (like İzmir). It's easy to read both of these as an English 'i', but you can be misunderstood if you don't pronounce the two sounds distinctly – *sık* means 'dense', 'tight' or 'frequent' but *sik* is a certain 'f' word meaning 'to copulate'. Take the same care with **o/ö** and **u/ü**.

TURKISH	PRONUNCIATION GUIDE	
a	a	as in 'father'
ay	ai	as in 'aisle'
e	e	as in 'red'
ey	ay	as in 'say'
ı	uh	as the 'a' in 'ago'
i	ee	as in 'bee'
o	o	as in 'go'
ö	er	as in 'her' with no 'r' sound
u	oo	as in 'moon'
ü	ew	'ee' with rounded lips, like in 'few' or French *tu*

Consonants

TURKISH	PRONUNCIATION GUIDE	
c	j	as in 'jam'
ç	ch	as in 'church'
j	zh	as the 's' in 'pleasure'
ş	sh	as in 'ship'

Word Stress
Word stress is quite light in Turkish, and generally falls on the last syllable of the word. Most two-syllable place names are stressed on the first syllable, and in three-syllable names the stress is usually on the second syllable.

ACCOMMODATION
Where's a ...?
Nerede ... bulabilirim?   ne·re·de ... boo·*la*·bee·lee·reem
  guesthouse
  misafirhane   mee·*sa*·feer·ha·ne
  hotel
  otel   o·*tel*
  youth hostel
  gençlik hosteli   gench·*leek* hos·te·*lee*

Can you recommend somewhere cheap?
  Ucuz bir yer tavsiye edebilir misiniz?
  oo·*jooz* beer yer tav·see·*ye* e·*de*·bee·leer mee·see·*neez*
What's the address?
  Adresi nedir?
  ad·re·*see* ne·deer
Could you write it down, please?
  Lütfen yazar mısınız?
  lewt·fen ya·*zar* muh·suh·*nuhz*

Do you have a ... room?
  ... odanız var mı?
  ... o·da·*nuz* var muh
  single
  Tek kişilik   tek kee·shee·*leek*
  double-bed
  İki kişilik   ee·*kee* kee·shee·*leek*
  twin/two-bed
  Çift yataklı   cheeft ya·tak·*luh*

How much is it per night?
Geceliği başına   ge·je·lee·ee ba·shuh·na
ne kadar?   ne ka·dar

May I see it?
Görebilir miyim?   ger·re·bee·leer mee·yeem

bathroom
banyo   ban·yo

CONVERSATION & ESSENTIALS

Hello.
Merhaba.   mer·ha·ba

Goodbye.
Hoşçakal.   hosh·cha·kal (person leaving)
Güle güle.   gew·le gew·le (person staying)

Yes.
Evet.   e·vet

No.
Hayır.   ha·yuhr

Please.
Lütfen.   lewt·fen

Thank you.
Teşekkür ederim.   te·shek·kewr e·de·reem

You're welcome.
Birşey değil.   beer·shay de·eel

Excuse me.
Bakar mısınız.   ba·kar muh·suh·nuhz

Sorry.
Özür dilerim.   er·zewr dee·le·reem

What's your name?
Adınız nedir?   a·duh·nuhz ne·deer

My name is ...
Benim adım ...   be·neem a·duhm ...

HEALTH

I'm ill.
Hastayım.   has·ta·yuhm

It hurts here.
Burası ağrıyor.   boo·ra·suh a·ruh·yor

I'm ...
... var.   ... var
  asthmatic
  Astımım   as·tuh·muhm
  diabetic
  Şeker hastalığı   she·ker has·ta·luh·uhm

I'm allergic to ...
... alerjim var.   ... a·ler·zheem var
  antibiotics
  Antibiyotiklere   an·tee·bee·yo·teek·le·re
  penicillin
  Penisiline   pe·nee·see·lee·ne
  nuts
  Çerezlere   che·rez·le·re

EMERGENCIES – TURKISH

Help!
İmdat!   eem·dat

There's been an accident!
Bir kaza oldu!   beer ka·za ol·doo

Leave me alone!
Git başımdan!   geet ba·shuhm·dan

Call ...!   ... çağırın!   ... cha·uh·ruhn
  a doctor   Doktor   dok·tor
  the police   Polis   po·lees

---

condoms
kondom   kon·dom

contraceptives
doğum kontrol ilaçları   do·oom kon·trol ee·lach·la·ruh

diarrhoea
ishali   ees·ha·lee

medicine
ilaç   ee·lach

sunblock cream
güneş kremi   gew·nesh kre·mee

tampons
tampon   tam·pon

LANGUAGE DIFFICULTIES

Do you speak English?
İngilizce konuşuyor musunuz?
een·gee·leez·je ko·noo·shoo·yor moo·soo·nooz

Does anyone here speak English?
İngilizce bilen var mı?
een·gee·leez·je bee·len var muh

I don't understand.
Anlamıyorum.
an·la·muh·yo·room

Could you write it down, please?
Lütfen yazar mısınız?
lewt·fen ya·zar muh·suh·nuhz

NUMBERS

0	sıfır	suh·fuhr
1	bir	beer
2	iki	ee·kee
3	üç	ewch
4	dört	dert
5	beş	besh
6	altı	al·tuh
7	yedi	ye·dee
8	sekiz	se·keez
9	dokuz	do·kooz
10	on	on
11	on bir	on beer
12	on iki	on ee·kee

13	on üç	on ewch
14	on dört	on derrt
15	on beş	on besh
16	on altı	on al·tuh
17	on yedi	on ye·dee
18	on sekiz	on se·keez
19	on dokuz	on do·kooz
20	yirmi	yeer·mee
21	yirmi bir	yeer·mee beer
22	yirmi iki	yeer·mee ee·kee
30	otuz	o·tooz
40	kırk	kuhrk
50	elli	el·lee
60	altmış	alt·muhsh
70	yetmiş	yet·meesh
80	seksen	sek·sen
90	doksan	dok·san
100	yüz	yewz
1000	bin	been

SHOPPING, SERVICES & SIGHTS

I'd like to buy ...
... almak istiyorum.   al·mak ees·tee·yo·room
How much is it?
Ne kadar?   ne ka·dar

Do you accept ...?
... kabul ediyor musunuz?
... ka·bool e·dee·yor moo·soo·nooz
  credit cards
  Kredi kartı   kre·dee kar·tuh
  travellers cheques
  Seyahat çeki   se·ya·hat che·kee

more	daha fazla	da·ha faz·la
less	daha az	da·ha az
smaller	kü çük	kew·chewk
bigger	büyük	bew·yewk

Where's a/the ...?	... nerede?	... ne·re·de
bank	Banka	ban·ka
... embassy	... elçilik	... el·chee·leek
market	Pazar yeri	pa·zar ye·ree
post office	Postane	pos·ta·ne
public phone	Telefon kulübesi	te·le·fon koo·lew·be·see
public toilet	Umumi tuvalet	oo·moo·mee too·va·let
tourist office	Turizm bürosu	too·reezm bew·ro·soo

beach	plaj	plazh
bridge	köprü	ker·prew

castle	kale	ka·le
hospital	hastane	has·ta·ne
island	ada	a·da
market	pazar yeri	pa·zar ye·ree
ruins	harabe	ha·ra·be

TIME & DATES

What time is it? Saat kaç?   sa·at kach
It's (10) o'clock. Saat (on).   sa·at (on)

in the morning	öğleden evvel	er·le·den ev·vel
in the afternoon	öğleden sonra	er·le·den son·ra
today	bugün	boo·gewn
tomorrow	yarın	ya·ruhn

Monday	Pazartesi	pa·zar·te·see
Tuesday	Salı	sa·luh
Wednesday	Çarşamba	char·sham·ba
Thursday	Perşembe	per·shem·be
Friday	Cuma	joo·ma
Saturday	Cumartesi	joo·mar·te·see
Sunday	Pazar	pa·zar

January	Ocak	o·jak
February	Şubat	shoo·bat
March	Mart	mart
April	Nisan	nee·san
May	Mayıs	ma·yuhs
June	Haziran	ha·zee·ran
July	Temmuz	tem·mooz
August	Ağustos	a·oos·tos
September	Eylül	ay·lewl
October	Ekim	e·keem
November	Kasım	ka·suhm
December	Aralık	a·ra·luhk

TRANSPORT

The Turkish names for North Nicosia, Famagusta and Kyrenia are Lefkoşa, Mağusa and Girne respectively (see p33 for more information on place names).

bus stop	otobüs durağı	o·to·bews doo·ra·uh
the first/last	ilk/son	eelk/son

LANGUAGE

What time does the ... leave?
... ne zaman kalkacak?
... ne za·man kal·ka·*jak*
What time does the ... arrive?
... ne zaman varır?
... ne za·man va·*ruhr*

| boat | *Vapur* | va·*poor* |
| bus | *Otobüs* | o·to·*bews* |

I'd like a ... ticket.
... bir bilet lütfen. ... beer bee·*let lewt*·fen
  one-way
  Gidiş gee·*deesh*
  return
  Gidiş-dönüş gee·deesh·der·*newsh*

Directions

Where is ...?
... nerede? ... *ne*·re·de
Can you show me (on the map)?
  Bana (haritada) ba·*na* (ha·ree·ta·*da*)
  gösterebilir misin? gers·te·*re*·bee·leer mee·seen
It's straight ahead.
  Tam karşıda. tam kar·shuh·*da*
Turn left/right.
  Sola/Sağa dön. so·*la*/sa·*a* dern
far (from)
  uzak oo·*zak*
near (to)
  yakınında ya·kuh·nuhn·*da*

Also available from Lonely Planet:
Greek Phrasebook and *Turkish Phrasebook*

Glossary

For items dealing with Cypriot cuisine, see p51. Abbreviations: (Fr) = French; (Gr) = Greek; (Tr) = Turkish; (m) = masculine; (f) = feminine; (n) = neutral.

agios (m), **agia** (f; Gr) – saint
ano (Gr) – upper, eg Ano Pafos (Upper Pafos)
Attila Line – furthest point of advancement of the Turkish army following its 1974 invasion of Cyprus; it now separates Northern Cyprus from the Republic of Cyprus; see also *Green Line*

baglam (Tr), **baglamas** (Gr) – very small, bouzouki-like stringed instrument
barbican – gatehouse of castle
bedesten (Tr) – covered market
belediye (Tr) – town hall
bouzouki (Gr/Tr) – stringed lutelike instrument associated with *rembetika* music
bulvarı (Tr) – boulevard, avenue
burnu (Tr) – cape
Byzantine Empire – Hellenistic, Christian empire lasting from AD 395 to 1453, centred on Constantinople (Istanbul)

caddesi (Tr) – road
camii (Tr) – mosque
commandery – a district under the control of a commander of an order of knights
CTO – Cyprus Tourism Organisation, the Republic of Cyprus' official tourism promotion body
CTP (Tr) – Cumhuriyetçi Türk Partisi (Republican Turkish Party)
Cypriot syllabary – a writing system based on symbols representing syllables; used in Cyprus from the 6th to the 3rd centuries BC
CYTA – Cyprus Telecommunications Authority (Republic of Cyprus)

dolmuş (Tr) – minibus (literally 'stuffed')
dragoman – 'interpreter' (Turkish *tercüman*), or liaison officer between the Ottoman and Orthodox authorities

enceinte (Fr) – enclosed area within a castle
enosis (Gr) – union (with Greece); the frequent demand made by many Greek Cypriots before 1974
entrepôt (Fr) – commercial centre for import and export
EOKA – Ethniki Organosi tou Kypriakou Agona (National Organisation for the Cypriot Struggle), nationalist guerrilla movement that fought for independence from Britain

EOKA-B – post-independence reincarnation of EOKA, which mostly fought Turkish Cypriots
ethnarch (Gr) – leader of a nation

garigue (Fr) – low, open scrubland with evergreen shrubs, low trees, aromatic herbs and grasses, found in poor or dry soil in the Mediterranean region
Green Line – section of the Attila Line that divides Greek Cypriot Lefkosia (South Nicosia) from Turkish Cypriot North Nicosia (Lefkoşa); see also *Attila Line*

hammam (Tr) – public bathhouse
hastanesi (Tr) – hospital

kafeneio (Gr) – coffee shop
kalesi (Tr) – castle
kartzilamas (Gr), **karşılama** (Tr) – folk dance
kato (Gr) – lower, eg Kato Pafos (Lower Pafos)
KKTC (Tr) – Kuzey Kıbrıs Türk Cumhuriyeti (Turkish Republic of Northern Cyprus)
KOT – Kypriakos Organismos Tourismou; the official tourist organisation of the Republic of Cyprus; see *CTO*
körfezi (Tr) – bay
KTHY (Tr) – Kıbrıs Türk Hava Yolları (Cyprus Turkish Airlines)
Kypriako (Gr) – the Cyprus problem; politically sensitive and never forgotten by Greek Cypriots and Greeks alike

Laïki Yitonia – 'popular neighbourhood'; renovated old areas now designated as urban tourist centres
leoforos (Gr) – avenue
Lusignan – Cypriot dynasty founded by French nobleman Guy de Lusignan in 1187, which lasted until 1489

machiolation – an opening in the floor of a gallery or roof of a portal for discharging missiles upon assailants below
Mamelukes – slave soldiers who won political control of several Muslim states during the Middle Ages
maquis (Fr) – thick, scrubby underbrush of Mediterranean shores, particularly of the islands of Corsica and Cyprus
Maronites – ancient Christian sect from the Middle East
megaron – ancient Greek and Middle Eastern architectural form consisting of an open porch, a vestibule and a large hall with a central hearth and throne
Mesaoria (Gr), **Mesarya** (Tr)– the large plain between the Kyrenia (Girne) and the Troödos Massif
meydanı (Tr) – square
meze (s), **mezedes** (pl) – literally 'appetiser'; used in Cyprus to mean dining on lots of small plates of appetisers

mezedopolio (Gr) – small restaurant specialising in *mezedes*
moufflon (Fr) – endangered indigenous wild sheep of Cyprus

narthex (Gr) – railed-off western porch in early Christian churches used by women and penitents
neos (m), **nea** (f), **neo** (n; Gr) – new; common prefix to place names
NCTO – North Cyprus Tourism Organisation; Northern Cyprus' tourism-promotion body

odos (Gr) – street
Ottoman Empire – Turkish empire founded in the 11th century AD, which ruled Cyprus from 1570 to 1878; it was abolished in 1922

panagia (Gr) – church
panigyri (Gr) – feast or festival
Pantokrator (Gr) – the 'Almighty'; traditional fresco of Christ, painted in the dome of Orthodox churches
paşa (Tr) – Ottoman title roughly equivalent to 'lord'
periptero (Gr) – street kiosk selling newspapers, drinks and small items
pitta (Gr) – flat, unleavened bread
plateia (Gr) – square
Ptolemies – Graeco-Macedonian rulers of Egypt in the 4th century BC

rembetika (Gr) – Greek equivalent of American blues music, believed to have emerged from 'low-life' cafés in the 1870s

saz (Tr) – long-necked stringed instrument
sokak (Tr) – street
Sufi (Tr) – adherent of the Sufi variant of Islam

taksim (Tr) – partition (of Cyprus); demanded by Turkish Cypriots in response to Greek Cypriots' calls for enosis
taverna (Gr) – traditional restaurant that serves food and wine
tekkesi (Tr) – gathering place of the Sufi; mosque
tholos (Gr) – the dome of an Orthodox church
THY (Tr) – Türk Hava Yolları (Turkish Airlines)
TMT (Tr) – Turk Müdafaa Teskilati, Turkish (underground) defence organisation
TRNC (Tr) – Turkish Republic of Northern Cyprus (see *KKTC*)

UBP (Tr) – Ulusal Birlik Partisi (National Unity Party)
Unesco – United Nations Educational, Scientific & Cultural Organisation
UNFICYP – United Nations Forces in Cyprus; the UN body responsible for peacekeeping in Cyprus

yeni (Tr) – new; common prefix to place names

Behind the Scenes

THIS BOOK

This 3rd edition of Lonely Planet's *Cyprus* was written by Vesna Maric. The 1st and 2nd editions were written by Paul Hellander. This guidebook was commissioned in Lonely Planet's London office, and produced by the following:

Commissioning Editors Michala Green, Tasmin McNaughtan
Coordinating Editor Liz Heynes
Coordinating Cartographer Natasha Velleley
Coordinating Layout Designer Pablo Gastar
Managing Cartographers Shahara Ahmed, Mark Griffiths
Assisting Editors Roy Garner, Emma Gilmour, Laura Stansfeld,
Assisting Cartographers Tony Fankhauser, Jolyon Philcox
Cover Designer James Hardy
Project Manager Chris Love
Language Content Coordinator Quentin Frayne

Thanks to Gabbi Wilson, Carolyn Boicos, Gina Tsarouhas, Andrew Smith, Adriana Mammarella, Sally Darmody, Celia Wood, Wibowo Rusli and Indra Kilfoyle

THANKS
VESNA MARIC

I wish to thank all those who made my trip around Cyprus such a wonderful experience. Namely, *efharisto* to Maia Woodward-Dyason and Arto Malian for all their help, knowledge, kindness and laughs, I am forever grateful; Elena Savvides and Bassam Doghman for the fantastic time we spent together eating mangoes; Rafael Estefania for his support and help, always; Gabriel Gatehouse for braving the thousands of words I made him read; Buğu Gursesler for showing us North Nicosia; and Deirdre Guthrie for her help.

Thank you to Michala Green at Lonely Planet for giving me this opportunity, and to Tasmin McNaughtan who took over and answered all my questions. Thanks also to my editors.

OUR READERS

Many thanks to the travellers who used the last edition and wrote to us with helpful hints, useful advice and interesting anecdotes:

Antonio Asenjo, Harry Blackley, Penny Brownrigg, David Bruggen, Jose de Carvalho, Francis Celdart, Lynne Corcoran, Pauline Cuthell, John Douglas, Louise Dulson, Deborah First, Jenny Forbes, Clare Furneaux, Francis Geldart, Ian George, John Grant, John Heywood, Russell Huntington, Savvas Iacovides, June Johnson, Jude Jusayan, Gert Klingenberg, David Lash, Bill Maiert, Andoni Rodelgo, Franco Rossi, Elaine Rowley, Rudi Scobie, Tony & Jane Vollebregt, John Wallington, Sue Ward, Pat & Derek Westcott, Sarah Wong, Alison Woodcock, Tony Woods, Alan York

ACKNOWLEDGMENTS

Many thanks to the following for the use of their content:

Globe on back cover ©Mountain High Maps 1993 Digital Wisdom, Inc.

THE LONELY PLANET STORY

The story begins with a classic travel adventure: Tony and Maureen Wheeler's 1972 journey across Europe and Asia to Australia. There was no useful information about the overland trail then, so Tony and Maureen published the first Lonely Planet guidebook to meet a growing need.

From a kitchen table, Lonely Planet has grown to become the largest independent travel publisher in the world, with offices in Melbourne (Australia), Oakland (USA) and London (UK). Today Lonely Planet guidebooks cover the globe. There is an ever-growing list of books and information in a variety of media. Some things haven't changed. The main aim is still to make it possible for adventurous travellers to get out there – to explore and better understand the world.

At Lonely Planet we believe travellers can make a positive contribution to the countries they visit – if they respect their host communities and spend their money wisely. Every year 5% of company profit is donated to charities around the world.

SEND US YOUR FEEDBACK

We love to hear from travellers – your comments keep us on our toes and help make our books better. Our well-travelled team reads every word on what you loved or loathed about this book. Although we cannot reply individually to postal submissions, we always guarantee that your feedback goes straight to the appropriate authors, in time for the next edition. Each person who sends us information is thanked in the next edition – and the most useful submissions are rewarded with a free book.

To send us your updates – and find out about Lonely Planet events, newsletters and travel news – visit our award-winning website: **www.lonelyplanet.com/feedback**.

Note: We may edit, reproduce and incorporate your comments in Lonely Planet products such as guidebooks, websites and digital products, so please let us know if you don't want your comments reproduced or your name acknowledged. For a copy of our privacy policy visit www.lonelyplanet.com/privacy.

Index

INDEX

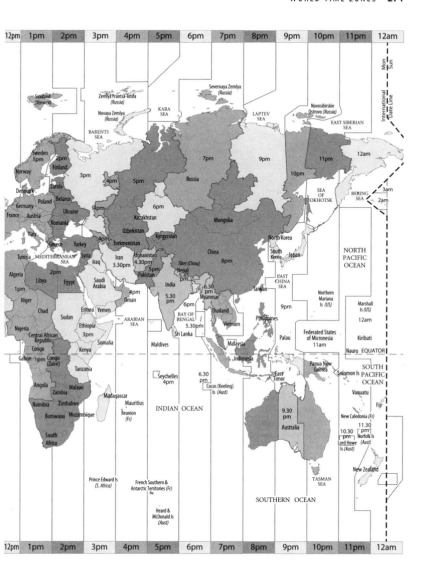

272

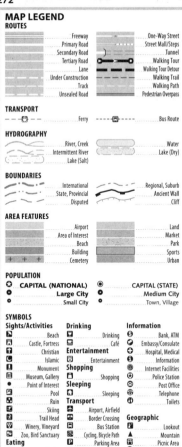

MAP LEGEND
ROUTES

Freeway
Primary Road
Secondary Road
Tertiary Road
Lane
Under Construction
Track
Unsealed Road

One-Way Street
Street Mall/Steps
Tunnel
Walking Tour
Walking Tour Detour
Walking Trail
Walking Path
Pedestrian Overpass

TRANSPORT
Ferry
Bus Route

HYDROGRAPHY
River, Creek
Intermittent River
Lake (Salt)
Water
Lake (Dry)

BOUNDARIES
International
State, Provincial
Disputed
Regional, Suburb
Ancient Wall
Cliff

AREA FEATURES
Airport
Area of Interest
Beach
Building
Cemetery
Land
Market
Park
Sports
Urban

POPULATION
CAPITAL (NATIONAL)
Large City
Small City
CAPITAL (STATE)
Medium City
Town, Village

SYMBOLS
Sights/Activities
Beach
Castle, Fortress
Christian
Islamic
Monument
Museum, Gallery
Point of Interest
Pool
Ruin
Skiing
Trail Head
Winery, Vineyard
Zoo, Bird Sanctuary
Eating
Eating

Drinking
Drinking
Café
Entertainment
Entertainment
Shopping
Shopping
Sleeping
Sleeping
Transport
Airport, Airfield
Border Crossing
Bus Station
Cycling, Bicycle Path
Parking Area
Taxi Rank

Information
Bank, ATM
Embassy/Consulate
Hospital, Medical
Information
Internet Facilities
Police Station
Post Office
Telephone
Toilets
Geographic
Lookout
Mountain
Picnic Area
Waterfall

LONELY PLANET OFFICES

Australia
Head Office
Locked Bag 1, Footscray, Victoria 3011
☎ 03 8379 8000, fax 03 8379 8111
talk2us@lonelyplanet.com.au

USA
150 Linden St, Oakland, CA 94607
☎ 510 893 8555, toll free 800 275 8555
fax 510 893 8572
info@lonelyplanet.com

UK
72–82 Rosebery Ave,
Clerkenwell, London EC1R 4RW
☎ 020 7841 9000, fax 020 7841 9001
go@lonelyplanet.co.uk

Published by Lonely Planet Publications Pty Ltd
ABN 36 005 607 983

© Lonely Planet Publications Pty Ltd 2006

© photographers as indicated 2006